YOUTH IN TRANSITION

This book is published in cooperation with the National Welfare Grants Program, Social Development and Education Group, Human Resources Development Canada.

YOUTH IN TRANSITION

Perspectives on Research and Policy

Edited by
Burt Galaway *(University of Manitoba)* and
Joe Hudson *(The University of Calgary)*

THOMPSON EDUCATIONAL PUBLISHING, INC.
Toronto

Requests for permission to make copies of any part of the work should be directed to the publisher.
14 Ripley Avenue, Suite 105
Toronto, Ontario
M6S 3N9
Tel (416) 766–2763 / Fax (416) 766–0398

Canadian Cataloguing in Publication Data

Main entry under title:

Youth in transition : perspectives on research and policy

Includes bibliographical references.
ISBN 1-55077-078-0

1. Youth - Canada. 2. Youth - Services for -
Canada. 3. Youth - Services for - Great Britain.
4. Youth - Services for - Australia. 5. Youth -
Services for - United States. I. Galaway, Burt,
1937 -   . II. Hudson, Joe.

HV1441.C2Y68   1996   305'.235'0971   C96-930093-X

Cover: **Trackwalker** painted by Horst Guilhauman,
1984, oil on canvas. © Horst Guilhauman.

Printed and bound in Canada.
1 2 3 4   99 98 97 96

Table of Contents

PART VI:
Research Agenda

Acknowledgements

Earlier versions of the papers presented in this volume were developed for a Research and Policy Symposium funded by National Welfare Grants, Human Resources Development Canada. The symposium was co-sponsored by The University of Calgary Faculty of Social Work and the University of Manitoba Faculty of Social Work. We extend our deepest appreciation to Maryanne Pentick, Sheryl Harris, and David Thornton of National Welfare Grants for their support, encouragement, and assistance in planning both the Symposium and this publication. The book is only possible because of the hard work of the authors whose papers are presented here. We thank them for their efforts and appreciate the spirit of cooperation as we worked under tight timelines. A special word of thanks is due to many people whose hard work was essential in the production of this volume. Diane Dennis, Research Associate, The University of Calgary, Faculty of Social Work (Edmonton Division), prepared volumes of correspondence and other materials in preparation for the Symposium. Claudette Cormier of the University of Manitoba Faculty of Social Work was responsible for manuscript production. Finally, we appreciate the assistance of Keith Thompson, Thompson Educational Publishing, who helped move this from manuscript to book form. This volume is a collaborative responsibility and would not have been possible without the assistance of many people. Ideas and points of view expressed in the chapters, however, are solely the responsibility of the various authors. Materials presented in this volume do not necessarily represent the policies or views of National Welfare Grants or the sponsoring organizations.

Foreword

Today's youth are facing challenges not seen by previous generations as they make the transition to adulthood. Communities, families, schools and other institutions which have traditionally provided support are now struggling to meet the changing needs of young people in innovative and more effective ways.

Youth in Transition to Adulthood was the subject of National Welfare Grants' fourth annual research and policy symposium, co-sponsored by The University of Calgary and the University of Manitoba, and held in Alberta, Canada, from April 25 to 29, 1995. Researchers and senior policy and program decision makers from Canada, the United States, Britain, Germany, and Australia came together to discuss four themes: supports, policies and programs facilitating the transition to responsible adulthood; preparation for the world of work, including job training and education; preparation for intimacy and family life; and preparation for responsible community living.

The objectives of the 1995 Symposium were to identify and critically assess current thinking on youth transitions, to identify the implications of current research for Canadian policy and programming, to develop a working agenda for future research efforts and—more importantly—to share information and promote dialogue among key Canadian and international researchers and decision makers. The symposium provided an opportunity to look across disciplines and sectors at the issues affecting youth today. This book is the result of the presentations and discussions that took place.

For thirty years, National Welfare Grants has been known as a national social research and development program, supporting and promoting knowledge and resources addressing significant social issues. Initially a program of Health and Welfare Canada, and more recently part of the Department of Human Resources Development, National Welfare Grants is now in the process of being integrated into a new Grants and Contributions Program with a broadened focus encompassing employment, child care, and services to persons with disabilities. It is my sincere wish that the new program will both reflect and build on the expertise developed at National Welfare Grants, and continue to produce timely and thoughtful information central to social and economic policy and social service delivery. This book is the fourth in a series—and I hope not the last.

I am indebted to the Symposium's organizing group which worked so hard both to organize the event, and to oversee publication of this book. Joe Hudson, of the Faculty of Social Work, The University of Calgary, and Burt Galaway, Faculty of Social Work, University of Manitoba, co-directed the Symposium. Sheryl Harris, Michael McKnight, and Maryanne Pentick of National Welfare Grants were responsible for identifying themes, reviewing submissions, and assisting with all of those myriad last-minute details which inevitably crop up. I commend them all, and am delighted to have been associated with this project.

David Thornton, Ph.D.,
Director, National Welfare Grants (1988-1995)

Contributors

Adams, Gerald R. Professor, Department of Family Studies, University of Guelph, Guelph, Ontario.

Anisef, Paul. Associate Professor, Department of Sociology, Arts, York University, North York, Ontario.

Armitage, Andrew. Associate Professor, School of Social Work, University of Victoria, Victoria, British Columbia.

Assogba, Yao. Professeur, Département de travail social, Université du Québec à Hull, Hull, Québec.

Axelrod, Paul. Professor, Division of Social Science, Arts, York University, North York, Ontario.

Bourassa, Bruno. Professeur, Département d'orientation, d'administration et d'évaluation en éducation, Faculté des sciences de l'éducation, Université Laval, Québec.

Butcher, Janice. Associate Professor, Faculty of Physical Education and Recreation Studies, University of Manitoba, Winnipeg, Manitoba.

Coles, Bob. Head of Social Policy, Department of Social Policy and Social Work, University of York, U.K.

Copeland, Brenda. Research Associate, Child, Family and Community Research Program, School of Social Work, University of Victoria, Victoria, British Columbia.

DeKeseredy, Walter S. Associate Professor, Department of Sociology and Anthropology, Carleton University, Ottawa, Ontario.

Donaldson, E.L. Associate Professor, Faculty of Education, University of Calgary, Calgary, Alberta.

Erickson, Patricia G. Senior Scientist, Addiction Research Foundation, and Professor, Department of Sociology, University of Toronto, Toronto, Ontario.

Erwin, Lorna. Assistant Professor, Department of Sociology, York University, North York, Ontario.

Gabor, Peter. Professor, Faculty of Social Work, The University of Calgary, Calgary, Alberta.

Galaway, Burt. Professor, Faculty of Social Work, University of Manitoba, Winnipeg, Manitoba.

Gee, Ellen M. Chair and Professor, Department of Sociology and Anthropology, Simon Fraser University, Burnaby, British Columbia.

Geller, Gloria. Associate Professor, Faculty of Social Work, University of Regina, Regina, Saskatchewan.

Griffiths, Curt T. Professor, School of Criminology, Simon Fraser University, Burnaby, British Columbia.

Grindstaff, Carl F. Professor, Department of Sociology, University of Western Ontario, London, Ontario.

Hagan, John. Dahlstrom Professor, Department of Sociology and Faculty of Law, University of North Carolina at Chapel Hill, Chapel Hill, North Carolina, U.S.A. and University of Toronto, Toronto, Ontario.

Hay, Deborah. Psychologist, Youth Services Program, Saskatoon District Health, and Adjunct Professor, University of Saskatchewan, Saskatoon, Saskatchewan.

Heinz, Walter R. Professor and Chair, Life Course Research Centre, University of Bremen, Germany, and Visiting Chair of German and European Studies, Centre for International Studies, University of Toronto, Toronto, Ontario.

Hiebert, Bryan. Professor, Department of Educational Psychology, University of Calgary, Calgary, Alberta.

Hill, Jennifer Leigh. Associate Professor, Faculty of Education, University of Victoria, Victoria, B.C.

Hudson, Joe. Professor, Faculty of Social Work, The University of Calgary, Calgary, Alberta.

Keating, Leo J. Data analyst, Department of Family Studies, University of Guelph, Guelph, Ontario.

Kennett, Deborah J. Associate Professor, Department of Psychology, Trent University, Peterborough, Ontario.

Kerr, Gretchen A. Assistant Professor, School of Physical and Health Education, University of Toronto, Toronto, Ontario.

Ketsetzis, Maria. Masters Student, Department of Family Studies, University of Guelph, Guelph, Ontario.

King, Alan J.C. Director, Social Program Evaluation Group, Duncan McArthur Hall, Queen's University, Kingston, Ontario.

Krysik, Judy. Assistant Professor, Faculty of Social Work, The University of Calgary, Calgary, Alberta.

Looker, E. Dianne. Professor, Department of Sociology, Acadia University, Wolfville, Nova Scotia.

Lowe, Graham S. Professor, Department of Sociology, University of Alberta, Edmonton, Alberta.

Manychief, Santanita. Coordinator, Out-Patient/Mental Health, Blood Tribe Department of Health, Standoff, Alberta.

Marshall, Sheila. Doctoral Student, Family Relations and Human Development, Department of Family Studies, University of Guelph, Guelph, Ontario.

Martin, Fay E. Toronto, Ontario; Doctoral candidate, University of Bristol.

McAlpine, Donna D. Research Associate, Centre for Health and Well-Being, University of Western Ontario, London, Ontario.

McCarthy, Bill. Associate Professor, Department of Sociology, University of Victoria, Victoria, British Columbia.

McGrath, Samuel J. Education Consultant, Newfoundland Department of Education and Training, St. John's, Newfoundland.

McKay, Stacey L. Research Associate, Faculty of Physical Education and Recreation, University of New Brunswick, Fredericton, New Brunswick.

Mitchell, Barbara A. Research Associate, Gerontology Research Centre, Simon Fraser University, Vancouver, British Columbia.

Mortimer, Jeylan T. Director, Life Course Center, and Professor of Sociology, Department of Sociology, University of Minnesota, Minneapolis, Minnesota.

Peart, Marjorie J. Research Associate, Social Program Evaluation Group, Duncan McArthur Hall, Queen's University, Kingston, Ontario.

Pelletier, René. Recreation Consultant, Department of Municipalities, Culture and Housing, Miramichi, New Brunswick.

Perron, Jacques. Professeur, Département de Psychologie, Université de Montréal, Montréal, Québec.

Reid, Ian S. Director of Undergraduate Studies, Faculty of Physical Education and Recreation, University of New Brunswick, Fredericton, New Brunswick.

Rutman, Deborah. Research Director, Child, Family and Community Research Program, School of Social Work, University of Victoria, Victoria, British Columbia.

Ryan, Bruce A. Associate Professor, Family Relations and Human Development, Department of Family Studies, University of Guelph, Guelph, Ontario.

Sharpe, Dennis B. Associate Professor, Faculty of Education, Memorial University of Newfoundland, St. John's, Newfoundland.

Sorenson, Ann Marie. Associate Professor, Department of Sociology, University of Toronto, Toronto, Ontario.

Tardif, Marc. Professeur, Centre de recherche sur l'éducation au travail, Faculté d'éducation, Université de Sherbrooke, Sherbrooke, Québec.

Thériault, Jocelyne. Professeure, Department of sexology, Université du Québec à Montréal, Montréal, Québec.

Thibodeau, Steven. Chief Therapist, Native Mental Health, Blood Tribe Department of Health, Standoff, Alberta.

Thomlison, Barbara. Associate Professor, Faculty of Social Work, The University of Calgary, Calgary, Alberta.

Tremblay, Mark S. Assistant Professor, Faculty of Physical Education and Recreation, University of New Brunswick, Fredericton, New Brunswick.

Turcotte, Daniel. Professeur, École de service social, Université Laval, Québec, Québec.

Unrau, Yvonne. Assistant Professor, Faculty of Social Work, The University of Calgary, Calgary, Alberta.

Varpalotai, Aniko. Associate Professor, Division of Educational Policy Studies, Faculty of Education, The University of Western Ontario, London, Ontario.

Venne, Rosemary A. Assistant Professor, Department of Industrial Relations and Organizational Behaviour, College of Commerce, University of Saskatchewan, Saskatoon, Saskatchewan.

Wood, Darryl. Assistant Professor, Justice Center, University of Alaska, Anchorage, Alaska, U.S.A.

Wyn, Johanna. Director and Associate Professor, Youth Research Centre, The University of Melbourne, Victoria, Australia.

Introduction

Burt Galaway and Joe Hudson

The series of international papers by Walter Heinz from Germany, Johanna Wyn from Australia, Bob Coles from the United Kingdom, and Jeylan Mortimer from the United States as well as the paper by Rosemary Venne presenting demographic changes in the Canadian population, provide background for four groups of papers reporting Canadian research on the process by which Canadian youth make the transition from adolescence to adulthood. Sub-themes examine services necessary to facilitate transitions, processes by which youth are prepared for the world of work, prepared for intimacy and family life, and prepared to be responsible contributing members of the community. The final chapter describes policy implications and an agenda for research.

Several themes emerge from this research. First, that transition is a process, not a single event. Second, being adult is more than a matter of self-support. Third, the process of transition is not the same for everyone; there may be important differences among various sub-groups in the population. Fourth, success in the transition process depends both on the skills and qualities of the individual as well as the opportunities available in the socioeconomic environment. What researchers choose to study is an important question often based on the ideological framework researchers bring to their work and therefore the final section of this introduction identifies several questions not included in the research reported in the chapters that follow.

TRANSITION AS A PROCESS

Based on research in their respective countries, Heinz, Wyn, Coles, and Mortimer all establish that the transition to adulthood is a process rather than an arbitrary event in one's life, such as graduation from high school or turning 18. The way in which the process is supported or not supported by social institutions may have a profound long-term effect on the adult life experiences of the individual. This theme is addressed by a number of the Canadian researchers. Barbara Mitchell and Ellen Gee examine the phenomena of young adults, some in their 30s, returning to the parental home. A few of these young adults return home to provide care to aging parents but more typically the return relates to economic and social support needs of the young adult. Fay Martin notes the absurdity of public policies that arbitrarily end public support for young adults who have been taken into public care at a predetermined age such as 18.

Much of the research focuses on the process of transitioning from secondary school to university and from school to work. Coles notes that this is a stage in the life course involving three main transitions—from full-time education to employment, attaining relative independence of family origins, and moving away from the family home. Venne notes that the school-to-work transition may be more prolonged and complex for youth today because they have received high aspirations from the baby boom generation that preceded them and that there are comparatively fewer job opportunities for the current generation than the previous one. Samuel McGrath examines correlates to post-secondary participation in a cohort of Newfoundland youth, finding that high-school academic achievement, barriers to university enrolment, value placed on education, advanced mathematics, academic attainment, and a sense of well being were consistently related to participation in post-secondary education. Bruno Bourassa and Mark Tardif suggest that a close partnership between education and business/industry is necessary if young people are to move from the academic world into the world of work; they believe that schools have dominated this process in the past and that industry needs to play a greater role with the partners agreeing on common goals, rules, and an outline of their respective roles. Alan King and Marjorie Peart found that secondary school programs tend to be driven by university preparation requirements as opposed to preparation for work and that students remain in university-oriented programs long after aspirations for university attendance are unlikely to be realized; the majority of secondary school dropouts and graduates will leave without work-related skills. Bill McCarthy and John Hagan found that the transition experience for adolescent street youth is particularly difficult; nevertheless some find stable employment or return to school which tends to encourage a withdrawal from street activities. An implicit assumption among these authors is that the work role is the most important indicator of adulthood.

ADULTHOOD IS MORE THAN SELF-SUPPORT

An important part of the transition to adulthood is to develop the ability to support one's self, usually through paid, legal employment, although Patricia Erickson suggests that the illicit drug market may also provide opportunities for inner city youth. But adulthood involves more than supporting oneself; there are a number of domains in which youth must be prepared to function if they are to successfully make the transition to adulthood. These include the ability to engage in intimate relationships, participate in family life, and participate in the life of the community. Lorna Erwin studied how a group of female college students balanced career aspirations and their interest in marriage and family; she found that they were realistic in their assessments of the difficulty of finding suitable marriage partners and they anticipate that their future partner's willingness to share household and child-rearing responsibilities would be limited. Gloria Geller studied how a group of Canadian university women balanced their aspirations for careers and family life and suggests that they may not be very realistic in terms of the demands family life will place upon their time. Geller found that women who had children experienced difficulties trying to deal with the double load of parenting and career.

Deborah Hay found that child sexual abuse poses a significant risk to healthy social emotional development and compromises an individual's ability to develop close relationships by distorting perceptions of self, others, and relationships. Walter DeKeseredy's work suggests that sexual abuse in dating relationships may begin in elementary school and be carried on in secondary school and university. Jocelyne Thériault found that sexual competence among adolescents, defined as the ability to postpone initiation of sexual activity, is associated with the development of family and social competence and may contribute to the development of latent parental competence in the adolescent. Donna McAlpine and her colleagues studied 213 women who had their first child during adolescence. They looked at characteristics of the family of origin and how these impacted on the mothers' levels of perceived competence during their adulthood; feelings of mastery and self-esteem were partially shaped by experiences in the family of origin and parental substance abuse, parental depression, lack of emotional support from families, abuse, and parental overprotectiveness, all contributed to low self esteem and lack of mastery. The influence of these family characteristics persist even when controlling for economic situation, education level, and marital status. Gerald Adams and his colleagues studied how the influences of family, faculty, advisors, classmates and peers impacted on the characteristics of decision-making, commitment, and emotional autonomy and how these in turn affected the nature of close relationships during the first year of university. Family, university and individual characteristics were predictive of the nature of intimacy and social relations. Family and peer relations contributed to the nature of intimacy among college students. Aspects of decision-making, commitment, and emotional autonomy predicted both intimacy in relations and importance of social relations.

Several authors also identify that living as a contributing adult member of the community involves living healthy lifestyles. This takes on particular urgency with rising health care costs and concerns about how government may be able to handle these costs. Janice Butcher reviews the research on associations between physical activity and health and concludes that there is a link. Gretchen Kerr found a number of psychosocial benefits to participating in physical activity; the academic standards of athletes were equal or greater to those of non-athletes and athletes are more likely than non-athletes to aspire to post-secondary education and less likely to leave school early. Disadvantaged youth seem to reap more academic benefits and athletes have an enhanced self-image, sense of mastery and control, greater popularity, and lower delinquency rates than non-athletic peers. Athletic participation may be an important mechanism to enhance the psychosocial development of youth. Stacey McKay and her colleagues found that youth participation in sport contributes to positive attributes such as increased self-esteem, confidence and mastery, and reduced delinquency; these studies suggest that sport participation in adolescence may help prepare youth for responsible community living. The studies, however, need to be taken with some caution given that there is no indication of how the researchers controlled for positive selection as well as the risks of drawing causal conclusions from correlational studies.

VARIATIONS IN THE PROCESS

A number of authors make the point that both the amount of time required as well as the nature of the transition process may vary across sub-groups in the population. Wyn suggests that transitions to adulthood have become increasingly fragmented and less certain primarily because the youth labour market has collapsed and is no longer viable. She finds that the diversity of experience and heterogeneity in the characteristics of young Australians stands in marked contrast to the prevailing policy emphasizing a mainstream of certain kinds of young people and a minority of young people who are at risk. E. Dianne Looker used data from a longitudinal study of youth in three areas of Canada and found gender and rural/urban differences in the transition to employment. Coles notes that the transition is particularly difficult for vulnerable youth and that studies of the experiences of these youth are particularly important. Martin suggests that youth in care are a severely disadvantaged group in comparison with their age cohort even though they aspire to a normal adult life. Dennis Sharpe and McGrath, from work in Newfoundland, suggest that the educational preparation for the transition to the world of work in that province is geared primarily to youth planning to pursue post-secondary education and is not addressing the transitional needs of youth moving into the work force. Paul Axelrod and Paul Anisef, from a longitudinal study of 2,555 Ontario graduates in 1973, found that generally class advantage, being male, and living in a city fostered greater social and economic advantage; the young adults, however, did not see their lives through sociological lenses but rather assumed personal responsibility for educational, occupational, and family related decisions. Peter Gabor, Steven Thibodeau, and Santanita Manychief note the challenges confronting Aboriginal youth as they make the transition especially as they move from the reserve to an urban center. Jennifer Hill indicates that the amount of education required to pursue many career opportunities has been steadily increasing and that persons with disabilities are severely handicapped because of barriers for their participation in post-secondary education. This research suggests that there is not one but many routes by which young people may make the transition from adolescence to adulthood and that there may be systematic variations in these routes based on ethnicity, social class, gender, rural/urban residence, as well as other variables.

INDIVIDUAL QUALITIES AND OPPORTUNITIES

The transition experience must be examined in relation to both the qualities and skills required by the individual to move into adulthood as well as the opportunities provided by the social and economic structures. The transition experience and adult functioning is influenced by both. This is a theme supported by a number of the authors. Deborah Kennett found that unemployed youth possessing general resourcefulness skills, having positive self-efficacy expectations about work, and who used specific job seeking and job keeping skills were more successful at attaining and maintaining employment than less resourceful youth; she found no significant differences between the employed and unemployed youths on education, vocational counselling, age, gender, or previous job experience. Daniel Turcotte and Yao Assogba question the appropriateness of employability programs for youth that may prepare young people for non-existent jobs. Aniko Varpalotai notes the importance of providing young women the opportunity to participate in single sex organizations as part of their preparation for adulthood. Darryl Wood and Curt T. Griffiths suggest that Inuit youth may be a lost generation because of rapid social change as their culture moved from a hunting and gathering society to settlement; these youth have been left without role models and socialization experiences to teach them how to function in a changed society. McCarthy and Hagan found that homeless youth can move into work and stable residence if opportunities are made available for them to do so, and Erickson suggests that youth may move into the illicit drug market because of lack of other opportunities.

Several papers examine barriers to preparation for work. King and Peart found that secondary school programs tend to be driven by university preparation requirements as opposed to preparation for work. Others look at barriers to pursuing post-secondary education. Looker found that school counsellors serve primarily the academically better students. Sharpe reports data from four comprehensive studies of a large cohort of Newfoundland youth—barriers to continuing education included funding, lack of courses close to home, entrance requirements, and time. Scarcity of jobs and lack of work experience were problems in the early transition years. Hill notes barriers to higher education for persons with disabilities that disadvantages them in the labour market. E.L. Donaldson found that changes in teaching style in college chemistry had increased participation and learning in the course even among students who were floundering at university. Jacques Perron found that ethnic identity, other group orientation, and personal and social identity significantly improved the predictions to post-secondary educational aspirations.

UNADDRESSED QUESTIONS

This book presents a rich array of research papers regarding the transition experiences of Canadian youth moving into adulthood. The authors draw out some of the policy implications from their work and the final chapter presents a proposed research agenda. But some interesting matters are ignored in both the research and the policy implications.

No explicit attention is given to the role of formal, governmental organizations in the preparation of young people for the transition to adulthood, compared to the role of families and informal social support systems. An underlying assumption seems to be that this is primarily a responsibility of government to be delivered through the formal, education system and that policies need to be directed towards changing and strengthening the ability of the educational system to adequately prepare youth for adulthood. Given the evidence in this book that the formal educational system, especially counselling and guidance, has not been very successful at preparing youth for the transition to either higher education or to the world of work, it is surprising that none of the researchers question whether alternative, informal social mechanisms need to be strengthened to perform this function. Gabor and his colleagues note that Aboriginal youth depend heavily on family support as they make the transition to adulthood and are reluctant to turn to formal agencies, even Aboriginal sponsored agencies, for assistance. Mitchell and Gee note the phenomena of young adults returning home for economic and social support. An area that is entirely unaddressed in this volume is the phenomena of home schooling; are young people who are home-schooled more or less likely to successfully make the transition to adulthood than those who are schooled in formal educational institutions? Are we placing too much faith in formal, governmental sponsored institutions? Or, conversely, do we need to pursue policies to strengthen families and informal networks of social support to help young people make the transition?

Most of the research and policy implications perceive adulthood in terms of independence, usually meaning self-support obtained through salaried employment. There is some limited attention given to maintaining intimate relations and a healthy lifestyle through exercise. But isn't adulthood more than this? Are we really seeking independence or is interdependence a more appropriate concept? Interdependence would imply the ability to function in a community—both to receive benefits and to contribute to the well-being of others. How are we preparing young people to give of themselves—to volunteer time? to help others? to be a good neighbour? Are we even creating the expectation that this is a part of adult functioning? And does living as an interdependent member of a community require us to rethink concepts of privacy and confidentiality? Does privacy, at least some of the more exaggerated forms, lead to isolation and interfere with interdependent community living? Do adults have the responsibility to establish and work at maintaining stable relationships? And is procreating children (either fathering or mothering) without the resources to provide a stable home acceptable adult behaviour? Research on how young people can be prepared for these responsibilities and how they can be prepared to be contributing members of society beyond employment has been largely ignored by these researchers.

The matter of economic independence is perceived largely in terms of income from salaried employment. Considerable attention was given to what jobs young people are being prepared to do and whether or not employment opportunities for these jobs exist in the labour market. No one, however, reports on research or considers the policy implications of preparing young people to start businesses. Why do we talk to young people in terms of what type of job they would like to have instead of what type of business they would like to start? Given the evidence that small businesses are likely to fuel the economy and to provide employment opportunities in the future, are we not failing to pursue policies that encourage and support young people to consider starting businesses? What type of research is needed to assess how to train young people as entrepreneurs and to establish small businesses? A demographic bulge involving a large number of people who will be retiring early next century suggests possible service areas for budding young entrepreneurs. These are likely to be missed, however, if the focus is solely on preparation for employment.

Finally, researchers have not adequately addressed the effects of simultaneously performing roles of income earner, parent, and home manager. The assumption is that the income earner role is the most important; there is some research looking at the difficulty young women may have as they simultaneously try to fulfil aspirations of being both income earner and parent. The underlying assumption in most of these papers is that self-worth and importance to the community is derived from one's job or business. Why should this be so? What are the effects of this relatively limited vision of adult functioning? Is it possible for one person to adequately perform the three roles of income earner, parent, and home manager? If not, are public policies either intentionally or inadvertently encouraging this? Should not adults, both men and women, derive an equal sense of satisfaction and importance from parenting and home management as from income producing? Is it possible to create conditions in which this is possible without replicating traditional sex role stereotyping? Can the roles be distributed, at least in an aggregated sense, in a gender neutral manner?

PART I

International Perspectives

1

Youth Transitions in Cross-Cultural Perspective: School-to-Work in Germany

Walter R. Heinz

The concept of transition (e.g., status passages, pathways, life stages) will be introduced in a life course framework to delineate a research approach that combines institutional and individual perspectives. Recent research on transitions to employment in England, Germany, France and Canada will be discussed. The discussion will focus on:

- The extent to which different transition systems institutionalize pathways to work and facilitate or restrict labour market integration (inequality dimension).
- The options and problems of using the German dual system as a model for reforming transitions to employment in other societies (policy dimension).
- Relationships between transition systems and the life plans of young people (biographical dimension).

TRANSITIONS IN THE LIFE COURSE PERSPECTIVE

Research on life transitions has its focus on the ways by which social and historical contexts shape the life course (Elder, 1985; Mayer, 1991; Heinz, 1991a; George, 1993). There are two research perspectives. The life course approach applies standardized research methods to discover how social-cultural circumstances interact with the timing and duration of life events and the social positions of different generations or cohorts. The biographical approach is mainly interested in the individual's experiences and decisions that are related to transitions. Both approaches have introduced the dimensions of personal and historical time and the interaction between social structure and individual mobility through time and space. They extend the models of socialization and of role theory about age-related status entry and exit processes by embedding them in a life course perspective on transitional pathways.

The principles of the life course perspective are (Elder 1985; Heinz 1991a; George 1993):

- It designates a social phenomenon which reflects the intersection of social and historical events and conditions with the personal biography.

- It focuses on socially recognized sequences of transitions. Transitions are status changes that occur in a certain time frame (usually related to age) and they are parts of long-term patterns of life course stability and change.

- Life course studies require a longitudinal design in order to uncover the dynamics of various transitions as they construct or feed into life trajectories.

Societal differences and thus, inter-cohort and intra-cohort variations in the timing of standard transitions—leaving school, first full-time job, first marriage, occupational career sequences, retirement—can be substantial. Therefore, social class, gender and ethnicity must be taken into account in order to understand the variability of biographies. Early adulthood has become a focus for life course research because transitions that are more extended and less predictable concentrate in the years after leaving school (Buchmann, 1989; Kerckhoff, 1990; Krahn, 1991; Evans & Heinz, 1994). Most life course studies are descriptive cohort studies in the sense of showing differences in the timing and duration of life events and transitions in different generations. These "population studies have been more successful in describing changes in transition patterns and life course events than in explaining them" (George, 1993, p. 361). Thus, studies about biographies in social contexts are needed to discover the micro processes or status passages that are particular to various transitions and the way they influence other concurrent or subsequent transitions like school-to-work or labour market entry and marriage.

Transitions are best conceptualized as co-products of individual biographies and decisions and available opportunities as well as imposed restrictions. For instance, timing and sequences of the transition from school to work not only have effects on labour market entry but also on long-term social placement. Deciding for an apprenticeship instead of continuing full-time education will have consequences on occupational career and income level. The life course framework suggests that transitions are shaped by cultural norms and societal opportunity structures, and that they are constructed by individuals who use various pathways to accomplish a continuous and meaningful biography. Chisholm (1994) has pointed out that the study of youth transitions permits charting continuities and discontinuities in the relationship between social and economic change and the social construction of the life course. This requires analysis of the ways social inequality is reproduced by different pathways to adulthood and to document the extent to which transitions from school to work are related to social class, gender, ethnicity, and region.

There are remarkable differences in the ways modern societies organize the transition from school to work (Rosenbaum et al., 1990). In Germany, school leavers are confronted with vocational and educational training institutions which guide and, to a certain degree, control, entry, duration, and exit of status passages to employment. Thus, institutions may contribute to a higher degree of standardization of life course transitions in Germany than in other industrialized service societies. Yet, there is little systematic life course research that deals with institutions and biographies in more than one societal context (for exceptions see Müller & Karle, 1993; Ashton & Lowe, 1991; Bynner & Roberts, 1992; Evans & Heinz, 1994). Such research requires that the dimensions for comparison are delineated in advance, and similar methods are being used.

This permits movement from comparative description to comparative statements; for instance, about the relationship between educational and training institutions, transition sequences, and the social placement of young men and women. Case studies can inspect one particular transition system in detail by applying quantitative and qualitative methods to discover the interrelationship between labour markets, social contexts, training sequences, and individual transition experiences and employment outcomes. They provide rich data for linking opportunity structures, institutional and/or market networks, and individual career experiences in different labour market or company settings. Comparative case studies can be used as building blocks for hypotheses about the way class, gender, and regional inequalities are reproduced or changed by the interaction of vocational and academic transition systems and by young people's achievements and failures in the labour market.

It is difficult to link survey and case study approaches in comparative transition research. But it is a challenge that could improve policy concerning the future of young people. The lagged effects of vocational and educational training (VET) pathways and informal training on sequences and turning points between education, training, and employment require longitudinal studies that follow young people's transitions from school at least to the first years in the labour market (Banks et al., 1992; Bynner & Roberts, 1992; Evans & Heinz, 1994). Most surveys focus on routes and outcomes within the education or the employment system, neglecting the various pathways between school and labour market entry.

It is more difficult for Canada and Britain than for Germany to define pathways through education and training independently of pathways through the labour market. Whereas British surveys investigate the relationships between the level of education and employment, German studies look at pathways that lead from school to VET and from VET to employment, returning to school, or to higher education. The apprenticeship is institutionalized in Germany as the dual system (vocational school and firm-based training) that structures the school-to-work transition as a two-step process.

There are three important aspects for comparative transition research.

First, sound conclusions about their transferability to other societies are impossible without analyzing the social context and institutional fabric of particular national school-to-work transition systems. Transition research should also cover issues of social policy, in the sense of demonstrating the long-term consequences of different transition regimes from school to work on the person's life chances and living arrangements. Thus, cross-cultural transition research should be contextual and study:

- The social and economic conditions that stabilize or change the institutional fabric of youth transitions (e.g., apprenticeship, youth training schemes, or work creation programs) and their consequences for individual's placement and opportunities in education, training and the labour market.
- The job structures (the mix of manufacturing, private and public services) that define the range of transition options for young women and men as well as the development of education, training and employment policy.

Cross-cultural research tends to assume nationally homogeneous transition regimes and outcomes. Case study material, however, sheds light on the interaction between regional employment opportunities and the efforts of parents, educators, and business to provide education, training and work experiences at community level.

Second, cross-cultural research should not only describe the modus operandi of different transition systems but also look at the linkages between years and quality of schooling and durations and sequences of training and employment to assess the effects of VET institutions, social networks, and market structures on successful transitions (Rosenbaum et al., 1990) and analyze the interrelationship between vocational and academic transition patterns, opportunity structures, class and gender inequalities.

Third, stability and change of young women and young men's occupational choices, educational, and work aspirations should be studied cross-culturally and related to the course and outcome of their school-to-work transitions. It is also relevant for policy making to know how changes in young people's life plans interact with their transition experiences.

LABOUR MARKET SEGMENTATION AND TRANSITION STRUCTURES

In contrast to most French and German studies, British and Canadian research conceptualizes the transition to work in a sociological framework by relating it to the labour market structure. VET systems are linked with labour market segments. Occupational markets operate on more formalized procedures of skill training that are more or less independent from any particular employer's needs; internal labour markets, in contrast, rely on more informal training which is required to serve specific job assignments. Occupational markets permit workers' mobility between companies because they recognize certified vocational skill profiles; internal markets tie employees to companies which provide on-the-job training and internal advancement. Finally, there is the casual labour market where skill requirements are low and job security is minimal (Ashton, 1993; Marsden & Ryan, 1991; Heinz, 1991b). The youth labour market in Canada and USA consists mainly of part-time work in this casual segment. In Germany, non-college-bound youth are integrated in a socially valued VET system that provides skill training, work experiences, and certification.

The examples of Canada and USA demonstrate that where internal markets dominate, preparation for work occurs at school and by on-the-job training. Where occupational markets are important, there is a specific institutional network of organized vocational socialization. In Germany, Austria, and Switzerland the organizational form of VET is the apprenticeship. In these countries the apprentice has a specific labour force status, distinguished from education and employment. Young persons are assigned to a mixed social role, not yet junior workers, but skilled workers in the making, who do not receive wages but a training allowance, and follow a standardized sequence of skill acquisition and general education under supervision of both master craftsmen and teachers. Curricula, instruction, and examinations are publicly regulated and supervised by the school administration as well as by the chambers of commerce, crafts, and industry. But, Germany still has a three-tier school system that is linked to different pathways into the labour market. The access to high-quality VET with prospects, provided by medium and large enterprises and public employers, tends to be restricted to the most qualified school leavers from Realschule (10 years) or Gymnasium (13 years). Less qualified young people coming from Hauptschule (9 years) are referred to small crafts and service firms which tend to use their apprentices as cheap workers and usually cannot offer job security and promotion. Since the 1980s, the traditional two-step flow from school to employment has been interrupted. Finding an apprenticeship (first threshold) and entering stable employment after 3 years of VET (second threshold) have become more difficult. The dramatic rise of university enrolment in the 1990s is partly a response to the declining exchange value of an apprenticeship for stable employment and career prospects.

Britain has dismantled its apprenticeship system in contrast to the transition policy of continuity and reform of the German dual system. Today, young people are treated as workers who are trained on the job and receive wages. According to Marsden and Ryan (1991), the UK has moved towards a high-pay, high-quality, low-volume VET, thereby almost abolishing the social role of the apprentice. The trend towards internal labour markets together with rising costs for training young people has caused companies to discontinue the broad occupational training. "The British labour market has been moving unevenly from occupational to industrial structures and from apprenticeship to job training, thereby eroding the institutions needed for government training policy to work" (Ryan, 1991, p. 12). In contrast to Germany, training in Britain is seen by many employers as a mere exposure to job specific skills and experiences rather than a process of socialization for work that includes work habits, life concepts, and social competence which are vital for participation in teamwork and organizational innovation. This approach to training resembles the transition policy in USA and Canada where high-schools offer vocational and academic courses in their curriculum. This creates a two-track structure: labour market-bound youth take vocational courses, college-bound youth academic subjects. The absence of an institutionalized transition structure that consists of a systematic combination of education and vocational training and recognized certification procedures shifts the responsibility for vocational education and training from industry to the education system and individual work experiences.

SCHOOL-TO-WORK TRANSITION AND THE DECLINING YOUTH LABOUR MARKET

A leitmotif of youth research in the 1980s was the growing discrepancy between the number of school leavers looking for jobs and the supply of unskilled or semi-skilled employment which used to be the pathway into the labour market for non-college-bound youth in Britain and North America. Ashton and Maguire (1986) investigated the structure of opportunities and experiences of young people in Britain by studying 18- to 24-year-olds in contrasting labour market regions. This study documents that gender, age, and skill level are indicators for segmented opportunities in the labour market. Youth and adult labour markets are separated; there is a group of young adults who have never had the opportunity to experience full-time employment but who move between governmental schemes, casual employment, and unemployment. Additional information was collected by intensive interviews with employers about the social types of applicants they tend to recruit. These case studies were related to labour force survey data. In the 1980s there was a reduction of unskilled and semi-skilled jobs, a decline of skilled jobs in manufacturing industries, a growth in the service sector with stable part-time work, and an increase of administrative and professional jobs. These processes contributed to a continuously shrinking labour market for early school leavers (16- to 18-year-olds) in all labour markets under review.

A German longitudinal study (Mönnich & Witzel, 1994) compares the transition from school to work in the Bremen and Munich urban labour market regions; they traditionally have had high and low rates of unemployment, respectively. There was substantial variation in transition outcomes, depending on occupation and region five years after graduation from apprenticeship. For example, 60% of the office clerks were still employed in their occupation compared to 38% of the car repair mechanics. Almost one third of the bank clerks had moved on to the university, but none of the hair dressers had. There were considerable variations between Bremen and Munich concerning the retention rates for office workers, sales persons, and hair dressers. In Bremen, 40% of the trained bank clerks go on to university but only 25% in Munich. Today, apprenticeship does not necessarily guarantee job continuity for all young people who have learned a trade. Various occupations offer different career opportunities and there are substantial regional variations in the proportion of young people who are employed, unemployed, in retraining, or on the academic route after having completed their VET. Thus, it is not surprising that recent data about occupational choice indicate that skilled blue-collar and crafts occupations have lost their attractiveness for school leavers in Germany. These jobs are not regarded as having much career prospect and social recognition. After five years only half of the apprenticeship cohort of blue-collar workers is still employed in their trained occupation. For a growing number of apprentices, VET has become a transition episode from which to embark to more advanced levels of education or technical training. This is caused by two mutually reinforcing developments. There is a growing demand for a general theoretical knowledge base and a wider scope of vocational competence instead of job-tailored skills and routines. Thus, the transition to employment becomes more demanding and requires at least an intermediate level of schooling.

TRANSITION STRUCTURES AND PRODUCTION CONCEPTS

Lutz (1976) compared the linkages between education and employment systems in Germany and France, and found that education was not subordinated to the employment system nor were these two systems decoupled. Rather, there were specific patterns of company organization and employment structure which correspond to the transition system and its certification procedures. Lutz argued that differences in the education to work pathways are crucial. VET precedes employment in Germany but in France vocational preparation is provided by the school in the framework of a highly stratified and selective educational system. In France, therefore, changing job demands require new learning processes at each level which have to be supervised by technicians and engineers. In Germany, however, companies can rely on a broader skill base that permits flexible adaptation and continuous training for the majority of the labour force who had completed an apprenticeship.

Drexel (1993) has compared the routes to middle-level technical and supervising positions in French and German factories. How are education requirements and career patterns related? Are skilled workers promoted to middle-level positions or are outsiders recruited from the external market for technical and supervisory jobs? In France, the training of technicians is mainly performed by college-type education; in Germany, there is promotion of senior skilled workers to the master's position. Drexel (1993) concludes that the transition and promotion patterns in France and Germany can be characterized by specific national developmental logics. These logics constitute a particular interdependence of education, training, employment, and careers. Interdependence tends to stabilize the transition patterns as long as both economic and technological developments and social class and gender specific pathways from education to employment maintain a certain balance. However, both transition systems recently have come under pressure. The French college-based technical education is criticized because it blocks the promotion of senior workers in the internal labour market of a company. Another more recent pressure stems from the increasing unemployment among school leavers. The German apprenticeship system is in trouble, too, because of the blocked career opportunities for skilled workers whose advancement to the master's position (Industriemeister) has become more difficult because the companies tend to recruit more and more technicians and engineers.

Drexel's study demonstrates a two-fold structural asymmetry. On the one hand, companies can establish training routes that improve, neutralize, or revise the influence of public education. On the other hand, companies can decide whether they recruit from the external labour market (Seiteneinsteiger) or to promote members of their labour force in order to fill vacancies at the level of middle management and shop floor supervision.

The hiring strategies of medium and large firms are directed by new production and service programs (Schumann et al., 1994) that require employees with technical, planning, and communication skills. Only about one tenth of the skilled blue-collar workers gain from these more qualified jobs in today's Germany; employers have started a major restructuring campaign to restrict the supply of apprenticeships and have become more selective in respect to applicants' educational accomplishments. Employers' recruiting and promotion practices send signals for educational and training decisions by parents and young people, and indirectly initiate or directly influence changes in transition behaviour. The apprenticeship is not a promising route to a career when college or university graduates are also hired for skilled blue- and white-collar jobs. This may devalue the VET certificate to such an extent that the dual system will only attract young people with low or intermediate education whose learning potentials are stimulated by the combination of on-the-job training and vocational schooling.

Figure 1-1: School-to-Work Transition Patterns in West Germany

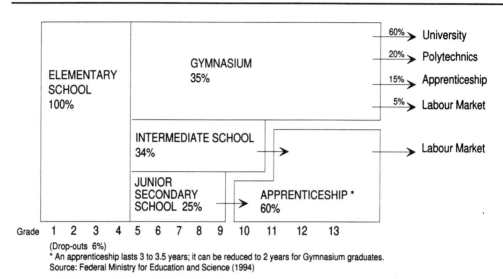

Grade 1 2 3 4 5 6 7 8 9 10 11 12 13
(Drop-outs 6%)
* An apprenticeship lasts 3 to 3.5 years; it can be reduced to 2 years for Gymnasium graduates.
Source: Federal Ministry for Education and Science (1994)

CHANGES IN GERMAN EDUCATION AND ITS CONSEQUENCES FOR TRANSITION SYSTEMS

In the last 20 years Germany has experienced a continuous upgrading of educational qualifications. The proportion of young people without any school-leaving certificate has dropped from 18% in 1970 to 6% in 1990. The percentage of school leavers from the lowest level (Hauptschule) has dropped from 45% to 25% and the proportion of those with university entrance qualification (Abitur) has increased from 12% to 35% (Federal Ministry for Education and Science, 1994). This dramatic growth of intermediate and higher qualifications extends the transition to employment; the enrolment at polytechnical colleges (Fachhochschulen) and universities is growing at a faster rate than all educational planners had predicted. The dual system is still the main route for most young men and fewer young women, but it is in competition with a more promising pathway—the academic route. In 1991, for the first time, there were as many students enroled in polytechnic colleges and universities as there were apprentices in training. However, the average duration of a university education has increased to about seven years while an apprenticeship lasts three years. Despite the popular dramatization of an over-academization of the German labour force, two thirds of the school leavers still enter an apprenticeship, about 8% enrol in polytechnical colleges (Fachhochschulen), and 20% in universities (Tessaring 1993).

The undisputed advantage of the apprenticeship pathway is that its graduates learn to combine theoretical knowledge and practical skills with responsible, flexible, and team-related work habits. They possess skill profiles with the potential to participate in innovations on the job and in the organization. This potential usually is not available from a labour force that consists of persons who have been trained on the job and therefore possess rather circumscribed workplace-specific skills (Hamilton, 1990; Lempert & Hamilton, 1993). By learning and participating in various divisions of a company, apprentices contribute to the firm's productivity and learn about its organization at the same time. They become employees who can be put to work immediately and in a flexible way. This helps to prevent misplacements. Responsibility and competence of skilled workers is still in demand because their practical and organizational experiences cannot be replaced by technical specialists who are recruited from college. However, the journey-man (Facharbeiter) qualification is changing from a life-long guarantee of employment to a solid base for job-flexibility, continuing education, and training. This development has also been recognized by the recent reform of VET curricula in the German dual system that combines general and basic qualifications with work-specific skills in 360 white- and blue-collar occupations. Pressures on the dual system call for a modernization of training procedures and content as well as more permeability between the vocational transition routes and the routes to higher education and employment in white-collar and professional jobs.

Germany, however, can still be characterized as a vocational transition culture. In contrast, young people in Canada are more committed to higher education and tend to stay in school instead of looking for vocational training before finishing high school or college. It is customary to perform part-time work and to move back and forth between education and paid work until full-time employment is attained (Krahn, 1991; Ashton & Lowe, 1991). There is not a clear, progressive transition pattern in Canada but, rather, a continuous and almost parallel process of movement through both the educational system and the labour market as young adults attempt to construct their pathway towards a career.

BIOGRAPHIES AND SEQUENCES OF TRANSITION

Any account of the structure of school-to-work transitions has to be related to the micro-social level, i.e., the socialization experiences. Does the general prolongation of the time needed for work integration constitute a socially recognized and stable pattern of progression or do young people have to individually discover their own routes into employment and to risk marginalization in this process? What are the consequences of different pathways, short cuts and detours on timing and continuity of labour market integration as compared to extended and certified VET passages? Are there institutionalized re-entry opportunities for drop-outs? Are interrupted education or training sequences recognized as an asset for embarking on the pathway to higher education?

Comparative studies have shown (Bynner & Roberts, 1992; Evans & Heinz, 1994; Roberts, Clark, & Wallace, 1994) that by age 18 young people in Great Britain could have experienced a youth training scheme, some post compulsory education, casual employment, and unemployment without gaining a single qualification in the process; no one among German respondents had a comparable transition biography. Respondents expressed their individual experiences that they had choices among various options between education, VET, and employment. English respondents had to make more decisions because they could not rely on an institutionalized transition model. They had to arrange themselves with short-time alternatives. Among the German respondents, most who did not continue to full-time schooling entered the apprenticeship route, albeit rarely obtaining their first choice occupation. There were differences within each English and German labour market in the extent to which respondents felt able to construct their transition according to their preferences. There were more choices connected to higher status passages through academic pathways and the VET systems than for young people who were on training schemes or in employment. The latter had to modify their goals according to the local opportunity structure. In Germany, however, those who did not manage to enter an apprenticeship or who had dropped it (approximately 20%) faced high risks of marginalization, and their transition results were rather restricted.

In each country, the routes young people were travelling toward the employment system mirrored the segmentation of occupational structures into which their specific route was leading. In both countries, transitional patterns could be used in a more or less flexible way by young people to decide about options that were defined by ranges of opportunity by gender, labour market region, social background, and educational achievement. "In both countries our samples' career examples were best understood in terms of structured individualization" (Roberts, Clark, & Wallace, 1994, p. 51). Even when young persons had moved consistently towards preformulated goals, these aims and the individuals' abilities to realize them were products of their structural locations and social contexts. Cross-cultural evidence shows that the various transition pathways mediate socialization experiences that contribute to the individuals' responses to blocked or open pathways and to their life goals (Baethge et al., 1988).

TRANSITIONS AND LIFE COURSE POLITICS

Comparative transition research cannot be a task for itself; it has to assess the adaptability of school-to-work pathways to social change and the modernization of the male and female life course. But there are a series of contradictions. In some European countries there is increasing educational potential for modernizing VET curricula and credentials in order to adapt to new skill requirements (Collins, 1993). However, transition systems have to adapt to different learning styles of school leavers with contrasting educational experiences. Transition systems should be able to integrate disadvantaged social groups and attract privileged social groups at the same time. They should open the gate to various occupational careers, and should not block access or return to school and higher education. They should provide a platform for launching self-determined life trajectories.

Policy responses differ. Britain does not have a coordinated policy-making mechanism that could address the consequences of social change on the transition of young people. British responses, in contrast to Germany, have been mainly ad hoc. The failure of youth training schemes in Britain shows that a partial transplant of firm-based training without the schooling part and without a standardized certification procedure is insufficient if it does not include the institutional and cultural features that make the dual system still work in Germany.

Changes in the transition system particular to a society have to be accompanied by efforts to restructure educational and labour market systems. Employers must be convinced that a stable transition system, which combines general education with work-related training, will pay in the long run, instead of following the routines of short-term profit which also means to reduce training costs. Furthermore, giving VET a good educational quality would improve its attractiveness for more qualified school leavers and provide a stock of skilled and responsible workers in the future.

There are very few real structural alternatives to a flexible combination of general education and work experience. The internal training and upgrading route, which is favoured in England and France, presupposes vocational enrichment of school curricula and a more general and longer government provided education; employers would only finance job-specific training. This alternative reduces the flexibility of the work force in coping with modern production and service organizations. Fostering a combination of vocational and further training by making the apprenticeship the standard transition sequence for non-academic occupations requires that government, industry, and unions share their responsibility for both young people's future and economic competitiveness of the country. Government and employers must provide clear and permeable routes for how to progress from one level of VET to another. This will support young people's decisions, give transparency to their movements from educational institutions onto the labour market, and provide options for revising earlier decisions. Transition decisions are crucial for life course politics and they should not be left to young people and their families alone. Government, employers, educators, and unions share responsibility to provide resources and regulations for school-to-work pathways with career prospects.

References

Ashton, D., & Maguire, M. (1986). *Young adults in the labour market* (Research paper No. 55). London: Department of Employment.

Ashton, D., & Lowe, G. (Eds.). (1991). *Making their way: Education, training and the labour market in Canada and Britain*. Milton Keynes: Open University Press.

Ashton, D. (1993). Understanding change in youth labour markets: A conceptual framework. *British Journal of Education and Work, 6*, 5–12.

Baethge, M., Hantsche, B., Pelull, W., & Voskamp, U. (1988). *Jugend: Arbeit und Identität*. Opladen: Leske and Budrich.

Banks, M., Bates, I., Breakwell, G., Bynner, J., Eissler, N., Jamieson, L., & Roberts, K. (1992). *Careers and identities*. Milton Keynes: Open University Press.

Buchmann, M. (1989). *The script of life: Entry into adulthood in a changing world*. Chicago: University of Chicago Press.

Bynner, J., & Roberts, K. (Eds.). (1992). *Youth and work: Transition to employment in England and Germany*. London: Anglo-German Foundation.

Chisholm, L. (1994). Is this a way of understanding education-work relations? Paper prepared for the Conference of the Centre National de Recherche Scientifique. Paris.

Collins, H. (1993). *European vocational education systems*. London and Philadelphia: Kogan Page.

Drexel, I. (1993). *Das Ende des Facharbeiteraufstiegs? Neue mittlere Bildungs- und Karrierewege in Deutschland und Frankreich*. Frankfurt and New York: Campus Verlag.

Elder, G., Jr. (Ed.). (1985). *Life course dynamics*. Ithaca, NY: Cornell University Press.

Evans, K., & Heinz, W. (Eds.). (1994). *Becoming adults in England and Germany*. London: Anglo-German Foundation.

Federal Minister for Education and Science. (1994). *Berufsbildungsbericht* 1994 (Report on Vocational Training). Bonn: Author.

George, L. (1993). Sociological perspectives on life transitions. *Annual Review of Sociology, 19*, 353–373.

Hamilton, S. (1990). *Apprenticeship for adulthood*. New York: Basic Books.

Heinz, W. (Ed.). (1991a). *Theoretical advances in life course research*. Weinheim: Deutscher Studien Verlag.

Heinz, W. (1991b). Youth and labour markets: Promises of comparative research on transition processes. In Ashton & Lowe (Eds.), *Making their way: Education, training and the labour market in Canada and Britain*. Milton Keynes: Open University Press.

Kerckhoff, A. (1990). *Getting started: Transition to adulthood in Great Britain*. Boulder, CO: Westview.

Krahn, H. (1991). The school-to-work transition in Canada: New risks and uncertainties. In Heinz, W. (Ed.), *The life course and social change: Comparative perspectives*. Weinheim: Deutscher Studien Verlag.

Lempert, W., & Hamilton, S. (1993). *The impact of apprenticeship on youth: A prospective analysis*. Ithaca, NY: Cornell Youth and Work Program.

Lutz, B. (1976). Bildungssystem und Beschäftigungsstruktur in Deutschland und Frankreich. In Institut für Sozialwissenschaftliche Forschung (ISF) (Ed.), *Betrieb, Arbeitsmarkt, Qualifikation*. Frankfurt: Campus Verlag.

Mayer, K.U. (Ed.). (1990). Lebensverläufe und sozialer Wandel. (*Kölner Zeitschrift für Soziologie und Sozialpsychologie*, Special Issue No. 31). Opladen: Westdeutscher Verlag.

Marsden, D., & Ryan, P. (1991). Initial training, labour market structure and public policy: Intermediate skills in British and German industry. In P. Ryan (Ed.), *International comparisons of vocational education and training for intermediate skills*. London: Falmer Press.

Mönnich, I., & Witzel, A. (1994). Arbeitsmarkt und Berufsverläufe junger Erwachsener; *Zeitschrift für Sozialisationsforschung und Erziehungssoziologie, 14*, 262–277.

Müller, W., & Karle, W. (1993). Social selection in educational systems in Europe. *European Sociological Review, 9*, 1–23.

Roberts, K., Clark, S., & Wallace, C. (1994). Flexibility and individualization: A comparison of transitions into employment in England and Germany. *Sociology 28*, 31–54.

Rosenbaum, J., Kariya, T., Settersten, R., & Maier, T. (1990). Market and network theories of the transition from high-school to work. *Annual Review of Sociology, 16*, 263–299.

Ryan, P. (Ed.). (1991). *International comparisons of vocational education and training for intermediate skills*. London: Falmer Press.

Schumann, M., Baethge-Kinsky, V., Kuhlmann, M., Kurz, C., & Neumann, U. (1994). *Trendreport Rationalisierung*. Berlin: Sigma Verlag.

Tessaring, M. (1993). Das duale System der Berufsbildung in Deutschland: Attraktivität und Beschäftigungsperspektiven. *Mitteilungen aus Arbeitsmarkt und Berufsforschung, 2*, 131–161.

2

Youth in Transition to Adulthood in Australia: Review of Research and Policy Issues

Johanna Wyn

Young people in Australia are all in transition to adulthood. However, the commonalities end here. Young people in Australia negotiate their transitions towards achieving legitimate adult status with very different perspectives and resources. Young Aboriginal men in the southwest of Western Australia, for example, have a very different experience of growing up from young women growing up in suburban Sydney (Palmer & Collard, 1993; Walker, 1993). These young people have more in common with the older people in their own communities than they do with each other as young people. The transition to adulthood for the vast majority involves engaging with the institutions of education or of welfare or the family, and negotiating the complexities of the labour market. The interaction of these processes of individual biography and institutions contributes to the construction of youth—the 1990s experience of the transitions towards adulthood. This chapter draws on current Australian research to provide an overview of the central issues facing different groups of young people in Australia and the impact of current policy developments on the nature of their transitions to adulthood.

During the last two decades there has been a dramatic change in the processes young people negotiate to achieve independent adult status. Foremost among these is the gradual but systematic failure of the labour market to provide a majority of young people with access to an adequate livelihood. Education has become one of the most significant institutions through which young people negotiate the points of transition into adulthood. Outcomes from compulsory schooling now constitute the most important gateway for access to further education and training and to jobs. Post-compulsory education and training has officially become the major point of access to jobs, and it is the goal of the Federal Government that 95% of 19-year-olds will be engaged in or have completed education or training by the year 2001 (Finn, 1991).

PREPARATION FOR THE WORLD OF WORK: EDUCATION AND TRAINING

Research on the relationship between youth and education reveals a gap between education and training policy in the 1990s and the experiences of young people. Focusing on key groups, such as early school leavers, has made an important contribution to understanding the role of education in the transition to adulthood for different groups of young people. There is strong evidence that the government's aim of having almost universal participation in post-compulsory education by the year 2001 is unrealistic (Dwyer, Wyn, Lamb & Holden, 1995). The extent and meaning of participation in post-compulsory education varies widely but, in attempting to make the completion of a certain level of education or training a precondition of adulthood, the government is creating the expectation that the normal experience of youth involves this single pathway through education and training.

Patterns of early school leaving in Australia reveal that young people from working-class backgrounds constitute the vast majority of those leaving school early. The absolute numbers of early school leavers have declined over the last decade, but they remain a distinctive group. Early school leavers are now more likely than ever to experience extended periods of unemployment, to take up short-term, unskilled work, to fail to obtain an immediate post-school qualification, to miss out in the competition for a base-level traineeship, and to remain dependent for long periods on government and other welfare assistance (Dwyer, Wyn, Lamb, & Holden, 1995). A comprehensive analysis of data from the Australian Longitudinal Survey (ALS) and the Australian Youth Survey (AYS) found little change in the social and class groupings of early school leavers since the initial rise in school retention rates (Lamb, 1994). Early school leavers still come from the same types of family and schooling background that characterised educational inequality before the changes in policy. In 1988, 77% of young women and 79% of young men who left school before completing year 12 were from families where the father's occupation was skilled or non-skilled manual work. Over three quarters of young men and young women came from families where the mother had no post-secondary education herself. Other patterns also persist. Among early school leavers in 1988, young women and young men took up different options, along traditional gender lines, with 53% of young women going into sales and related work compared to 9% of the boys; 43% of young men went into apprenticeships and 38% into labouring work.

Young people who leave school early are seriously disadvantaged for two reasons. First, the labour market in which they seek jobs is the secondary labour market of part-time, short-term, contract jobs with little continuity and poor conditions (Whyte & Probert, 1991; Wilson, 1992; Sweet, 1992). Second, pathways back into education and training are not easy for them to access. Early school leavers are displaced by young people who complete their secondary schooling in the technical and further education (TAFE) system that was once an option for early school leavers. Once young people have left school, many find it difficult to complete their secondary education, even if they do re-enter school (Holden, 1992). Early school leaving is a process that contributes to the structuring of social divisions among young people in Australia.

Some researchers, in view of the serious consequences of becoming alienated from education, have drawn attention to the nature of the curriculum and have sought to understand its impact on different groups of young people. Research on some groups of young women and young aboriginal people suggests that there are significant dimensions of the preparation for adult life that schooling continues to ignore. Research by Dave Palmer and Len Collard (1993) on young Nyungar Aboriginal people in Western Australia reveals that identity is connected with kin relations as well as with factors such as sex and age. Young Nyungar people grow up in a context where the transition to adulthood is intricately linked with family and community responsibilities and expectations. Both their commitment to school and to employment are undertaken in relation to their responsibilities and obligations to their kinship group. Relationships with family and the responsibilities that derive from placing a priority on connections with others are also a central issue for many young women. A recent report on girls and young women in Australian schools found that there are crucial aspects of their adult lives that education fails to address: the "prospects of childrearing and domestic responsibilities" were equally important with "getting a job in the paid work force"; despite the fact that girls were aware of equal opportunity policy, they were "uncertain about whether and how family and career are to be reconciled" (Australian Education Council, 1992, p. 86). Many girls and young women faced their transitions into adulthood on the basis of poor information about the often conflicting, contradictory, and complex issues of adult women's lives. Many educators have noted a bias in the curriculum (Anderson, 1983; Freeland, 1992; Poole, 1992; Wilson & Wyn, 1987; Yates, 1993) centering around the type of person seen as a worker. The type of worker envisaged is one whose responsibility for maintenance of the physical or personal aspects of a domestic unit is irrelevant. Their main location is in the paid work force. The Australian post-compulsory education person envisaged by educational policy fits the traditional masculine experience.

Research on these and other complexities of the transitions to adulthood for different groups of young Australians has lead to questions about the relevance of the school curriculum. The focus on the vocational aspects of education as a preparation for participation in the work force has tended to ignore dimensions such as the relationship between paid and unpaid labour and social relationships. Research into the experiences of young women (Carrington, 1993; Buchanan, 1993), the experiences of young people who are outside the mainstream (Holden, 1992; Beasley, 1991; Wilson & Wyn, 1987), historical studies (Johnson, 1993), and on young Aboriginal people (Palmer & Collard, 1993) reveals that the multiple transitions into adulthood are not easily located within universal age categories. The distinction between public and private aspects of work and life are not helpful in understanding young people's experience. It is important to focus on the interconnections between paid and unpaid labour and social identities across work and personal relationships.

INTIMACY AND FAMILY LIFE: YOUNG PEOPLE IN RELATION TO THE FAMILY

Australian research on the transitions towards adulthood has tended to ignore the significance of young people's relationships with their families. Approaches to the study of youth have placed an emphasis on transitions towards independence and on the changing power relationship between young people and their parents.

The overwhelming majority of young people grow up in families, and their lives and opportunities are shaped by their family resources and experiences to a significant degree. Overall, approximately 60% of 15–24 year-olds live with their parents. Even at what is now seen as the "top end" of the youth period (20–24 year-olds), an estimated 37% of males and 21% of females live with their parents. At the lower end of the range, the percentage of 15-year-olds living with parents could be as high as 97% (Hartley, 1994: 16).

These broad patterns however mask enormous diversity in the relationships between young people and their families. The notion that growing up involves a linear process from dependence on family to independence is too simplistic. The paths towards adulthood are diverse, involving complex relationships of interdependence between young people and their parents, siblings, and other family members such as grandparents.

One of the trends is the prolonged period of dependence of young people on their families. But even this broad trend has many variations and exceptions. For example, the economic relationship between parents and children is not necessarily one-way. In many families young people have responsibilities, as well as rights, well before they leave home. Payment of board, other financial contributions, and unpaid labour such as childcare, house maintenance, and domestic labour are an important part in some family economies. Young people in low income families are more likely to pay board than their counterparts in medium to high income families (Hartley, 1989); non-English speaking background parents were much less likely than Anglo-Australian parents to expect sons and daughters to pay board. In many cases, paying board was seen as part of establishing a sense of responsibility, rather than to cover the real costs of living (Hartley & Wolcott, 1994).

Subsuming youth policy under education and training has resulted in a focus on transitions to adulthood that tends to ignore young people's position in relation to families and their relationships with each other. The dramatic increase in the number of young people who are employed in part-time work while at secondary school (30%), for example, has been linked to schooling and work (Robinson & Long, 1992), but is seldom discussed in terms of young people's relationships with their families. Only recently has the nature of young people's relationships with each other, their understandings about sexuality, and the role of the family in this process been the subject of systematic research (Wyn 1991, 1994; Rosenthal, Moore, & Buzwell, 1944). Young people have multiple roles and social relations that have an impact on their experiences as workers and consumers. Getting a job is fundamental to the establishment of an adequate livelihood but it is not the only consideration. Establishing a livelihood means establishing oneself as a legitimate member of society (Wilson & Wyn, 1987; Connell, 1994). Paid work provides both a wage and opportunities to establish relationships with other people, to use skills, and to make a positive contribution. Establishment of a livelihood is one of the most important aspects of becoming adult—of belonging and engaging in the social practices of dependence, independence, responsibility and reciprocity.

RESPONSIBLE COMMUNITY LIVING: ESTABLISHING A LIVELIHOOD

The complex issue of establishing social relationships and developing social responsibility has added complexity because of the uncertainty now associated with establishing economic independence. Research on the perspectives that young people bring to their decisions about the transitions to adulthood reveals considerable continuity between this generation and the previous one in terms of their goals in life. A survey of disadvantaged young people in communities around Australia found that "their hopes and aspirations were almost identical to those of the baby-boomers a generation earlier" in terms of the jobs they wanted (Daniel & Cornwall, 1993, p. 9). Many of the young participants espoused a sense of responsibility for Australia's future but very few had a sense that they belonged to their communities. A sense of being outsiders has direct implications for young people's involvement in key aspects of community life, such as political decision-making.

In 1988 the Australian Electoral Commission reported that young Australians were disturbingly ignorant and apathetic about Australian political institutions (Standing Committee on Employment, Education and Training, 1988). A subsequent report concluded that young people did not register to vote because "they do not see any direct link between the government or government institutions and their own lives" (Australian Electoral Commission, 1989, p. 36). Many young people tend not to be involved in formal political processes and to have a low representation in trade unions which may be associated with their marginal status in the youth labour market. Some groups of young people, however, are committed to political involvement and action directly concerned with the environment (van der Veen, 1994). Although there is still relatively little research, it is evident that, for a majority of young people, the transitions towards adulthood do not appear to offer them full rights as citizens.

> It seems that an increasing number of young people find themselves in dire circumstances; it seems also that current government policies are based on the assumption that social and economic inequalities can be ameliorated through the wages system. The collapse of the youth labour market, in particular, and the failure of the labour market to provide full employment for adults has ensured that an increasing number of young people and families are denied the right to enjoy a certain minimum standard of life, economic welfare and security. Because of their marginal relationship to the job market, they "slip through" the welfare measures that are intended to ensure basic citizenship rights all too easily. In other words, citizenship rights associated with full participation as adult members of our society, in its political, social and cultural arenas, is dependent on economic status (Youth Research Centre, 1989).

This conclusion draws attention to the fundamental issue that social and economic circumstances have gradually undermined the juxtaposition of biological age with adult status. In a real sense, growing up for an increasing number of people has no finite end point, as many adults are now unable to achieve an adequate livelihood. The assumption that youth and adulthood are primarily age categories is historically and culturally inaccurate. Buchanan's research on young women illustrates the complexities they face in establishing adult identity and demonstrates the multidimensional nature of the transitions towards adulthood (Buchanan, 1993). She concludes that age is not the main issue for women in achieving full citizenship, and confirms Sylvia Walby's (1994) argument that citizenship, as a fundamental aspect of adulthood in developed societies, is a highly gendered and ethnically structured process. Walby argues that women's caring work in the family is a major barrier to their full citizenship. For Australian Aboriginal people coming of age no longer bestows rights to full participation in society, in terms of recognition of their land rights and other aspects of the political process. A substantial proportion of the Aboriginal population are young people; in 1991, 51% of the Aboriginal population and 47% of the Torres Straight Islander population were under 20 years (Hartley & Wolcott, 1994). The transitions into adult life for these youth are undertaken in circumstances where their opportunities to contribute to their communities are jeopardised. Their poor access to education, high rates of unemployment, poor health, poverty, and high rates of incarceration add urgency to addressing their specific circumstances as they move into adulthood (Brady, 1991).

RESEARCH PRIORITIES AND POLICY IMPLICATIONS

There are many transitions that young people make towards becoming legitimate adults in our society (Blakers, 1990). Over the last decade there has been a steady accumulation of research that documents the nature of becoming adult for different groups of young people including research on young people's health (Centre for Adolescent Health, 1993; Rosenthal, Moore, & Brumen, 1990), homelessness (MacKenzie & Chamberlain, 1995), young people in rural and isolated areas (Quixley, 1992) and unemployment (Beasley, 1991). The research offers insights into the complexity of the transitions towards establishing independence, and the need to take a holistic approach to the pathways to full participation in Australian society.

Australian Government policies have developed a narrow approach to the concept of pathways and transitions, viewing young people primarily in terms of their future role in Australia's restructured work force. "Australia's future depends upon the ideas, skills and knowledge of our work force. We need to link our education and training programs more closely to the current needs of the labour market and to future employment opportunities" (Commonwealth Department of Employment, Education, and Training, 1994, p. 89). This statement echoes the voice of economic rationalism and offers a simplistic approach to the issues facing young people in Australia. An alternative view on the preparation young people should receive suggests, "Our children's futures and that of Australia depend on a system of education that produces young people who are creative, critical, cultured, compassionate and coura- geous" (Deakin Centre for Education and Change, 1994).

Youth research has a significant role in offering an understanding of the full experience of the transitions to adult life. Buchanan (1993) suggests that we need to understand the multiple identities of young people and their simulta- neous involvement in a range of public and private domains. Research must offer a perspective on the multiple determinants of the life situation and life chances of young people, including an analysis of sexism, class relations, and racism. Research informing policy and programs aimed at assisting the transi- tions to adulthood needs to encompass both the concepts of diversity and continuity. The concept of youth can mask the vast differences among young people and the increasingly tenuous link between biological age and the achievement of adult status in Australian society. The concept of youth can also mask the important continuities that exist across generations, encouraging a superficial focus on sensational aspects of some young people's lives (Wilson & Wyn, 1993). Achieving adulthood involves getting a good job, as well as establishing intimate and social relationships and participating at a political level. The main issue for the transition process is to establish a livelihood.

Research on young people that sensationalises aspects of their lives (such as homelessness, youth gangs and drug abuse) contributes to the notion that there are identifiable at risk groups of young people, whom government policies should target. This legitimates a mainstreaming concept, increasingly apparent in youth and education policy, in which it is assumed that only a very small minority of young people face disadvantage. The evidence from research on the experiences and perspectives of young people suggests that their experiences of the transitions to adulthood remain those of the struggle against inequalities based on class, gender, ethnicity, and race. The very concept of a mainstream is flawed. The mainstreaming assumption has led to the rebirth of educational practices of the 1950s, such as standardised testing, the effects of which are to legitimate the marginalisation of large groups of young people from access to education and training pathways linked to the establishment of a livelihood (Connell, 1994; Marginson, 1994). The mainstreaming policy is apparent in the assumption that all families are able to give young people the support they need financially, emotionally, and in terms of housing. The range of services and programs available for young people who need support are offered on the basis of very stringent eligibility criteria, and only support a below-poverty-level existence (Hartley & Wolcott, 1994, p. 93). Furthermore, young unsupported people under the age of 16 tend to fall between Commonwealth and State responsibilities, contributing to the social injustices borne by young people. Many young people live in poverty (Bell, Rimmer, & Rimmer, 1992). Hartley (1989) points out that the levels of stringency regarding welfare measures for young people have been criticised for contravening the United Nations Convention on the Rights of the Child.

Finally, research on young people has identified a tension in government policy, in which youth has become a reference point for future lives, and the present of young people's lives is seen as insignificant in itself. Interest in the transition process tends to be presented in terms of concern about the role young people will play as adults, rather than an interest in the position of young people in the community per se. The positioning of youth in this way relegates them to a less significant realm than those who have reached adult life, with the result that young people's paid and unpaid work tends to be rendered invisible and their participation in decision making in the institutions in which they are most involved is a privilege not a right. Responsible community living for young people, involving the rights and responsibilities of adult citizenship and independence, also involves responsibilities on the part of the community for young people. This means that older young people should have access, in their own right, to allowances and services that will allow them to pursue education or training, acknowledging older young people as independent persons, acknowledging "the often considerable steps they have already taken towards autonomy, and of their actual and potential contributions to their family" (Hartley & Wolcott, 1994, p. 94) and to their communities.

CONCLUSION

This chapter has offered a perspective on young people in Australia which focuses on youth as a social process. Two main issues stand out. First, the universal term youth masks significant and enduring inequalities among groups of young people. Social divisions based on gender, class, ethnicity, and race continue to mark the experience young people have of growing up. What is different in the 1980s and 1990s is that the stakes are higher. The youth labour market now offers limited, seldom sustaining, employment for young people. The systematic failure of the adult labour market to provide full employment means that the transition to economic independence is not achievable for all. Second, subsuming youth policy under education and training policy means that complex issues about the nature and processes of the transitions to adulthood are dominated by a narrow, instrumental perspective. Central to this perspective is a mainstreaming approach to curriculum and to social justice. This approach creates the impression that only a minority of young people are a concern. These, the at risk, can be targeted by special initiatives and programs that are intended to bring them back in line with the mainstream experience. This approach hides the diversity and divisions among the different populations that make up the broad category of young people in Australia.

References

Anderson, D.S. (1983). Transition from school: A review of Australian research. In D.S. Anderson & C. Blakers (Ed.s), *Youth, transition and social research.* Canberra: Australian National University Press.

Australian Education Council. (1992). *Listening to girls.* Canberrra: Ashenden and Associates.

Australian Electoral Commission. (1989). *Sources of electoral information* (Research Report No. 1). Canberra: Author.

Beasley, B. (1991). Transitions to nowhere: The effects of government policies on young working-class people's access to employment/training. In R. White & B. Wilson (Eds.), *For your own good: Young people and state intervention in Australia* (pp. 65–77). Bundoora: La Trobe University Press.

Bell, D.N.F., Rimmer, R.J., & Rimmer, S. (1992). Poverty in Australia: A study of the implications of education, household formation and the labour market experience of the young. In R.G. Gregory & T. Karmel (Eds.), *Youth in the eighties: Papers from the Australian longitudinal survey research project.* Canberra: Centre for Economic Policy Research, Australian National University.

Blakers, C. (1990). *Youth and society: The two transitions* (Research Monograph No 38). Melbourne: Australian Council for Educational Research.

Brady, M. (1991). *The health of young Aborigines.* Canberra: National Youth Affairs Research Scheme.

Buchanan, J. (1993). Young women's complex lives and the idea of youth transitions. In R. White (Ed.), *Youth subcultures, theory, history and the Australian experience* (pp. 61–66). Tasmania: National Clearinghouse for Youth Studies.

Carrington, K. (1993). Cultural studies, youth culture and delinquency. In R. White (Ed.), *Youth subcultures, theory, history and the Australian experience* (pp. 27–34). Tasmania: National Clearinghouse for Youth Studies.

Centre for Adolescent Health. (1993). Adolescent health survey 1992, basic health characteristics. Melbourne: Centre for Adolescent Health.

Commonwealth Department of Employment, Education and Training (White paper). (1994). *Working nation: Policies and programs.* Canberra: Australian Government Publishing Service.

Connell, R.W. (1994). Poverty and education. *Harvard Educational Review, 64* (2), 125–149.

Daniel, A., & Cornwall, J. (1993). *A lost generation?* Sydney: The Australian Youth Foundation.

Deakin Centre for Education and Change. (1994). *Schooling, What Future?* Geelong: Deakin University.

Dwyer, P., Wyn, J., Lamb, S., & Holden, E. (1995). *Early school leavers and post-compulsory pathways.* Melbourne: Youth Research Centre.

Finn, T. (1991). *Young people's participation in post-compulsory education and training* (Report of the Australian Education Council Review Committee). Canberra: Australian Government Publishing Service.

Freeland, J. (1992). Education and training for the school-to-work transition. In T. Seddon & C.E. Deer (Eds.), *A curriculum for the senior secondary years.* Melbourne: Australian Council for Educational Research.

Hartley, R. (1989). *What price independence? A report of a study on young people's incomes and living costs.* Melbourne: Youth Affairs Council of Victoria, Australian Institute of Family Studies, and National Youth Affairs Research Scheme.

Hartley, R., & Wolcott, I. (1994). *The position of young people in relation to the family.* Hobart: National Clearinghouse for Youth Studies.

Holden, E. (1992). *Getting a life: Pathways and early school leavers* (Working Paper No. 9). Melbourne: Youth Research Centre.

Johnson, L. (1993). *The modern girl: Girlhood and growing up.* Sydney: Allen and Unwin.

Lamb, S. (1994). Dropping out of school in Australia. Recent Trends in Participation and Outcomes. *Youth and Society, 26* (2), 194–222.

MacKenzie, D., & Chamberlain, C. (1995). The national census on homeless school students. *Youth Studies Australia, 14* (1), 22–28.

Marginson, S. (1994). Emerging patterns of education in Victoria. In *Schooling, what future?* Melbourne: Deakin Centre for Education and Change.

Palmer, D., & Collard, L. (1993). Aboriginal young people and youth subcultures. In R. White (Ed.), *Youth subcultures: Theory, history and the Australian experience* (pp. 114–121). Hobart: National Clearinghouse for Youth Studies.

Poole, M. (Ed.). (1992). *Education and work.* Melbourne: Australian Council for Educational Research.

Quixley, S. (1992). *Living, learning and working: The experiences of young people in rural and remote communities in Australia.* Canberra: National Youth Coalition for Housing.

Robinson, L., & Long, M. (1992). Student workers. *Youth Studies Australia, 11* (3), 14–24.

Rosenthal, D., Moore, S., & Brumen, I. (1990). Ethnic group differences in adolescents' responses to AIDS. *Australian Journal of Social Issues, 25* (3), 220—239.

Rosenthal, D., Moore, S., & Buzwell, S. (1994). Homeless youths: Sexual and drug-related behaviour, sexual beliefs and HIV/AIDS risk. *AIDS Care, 6,* 83–94.

Standing Committee on Employment, Education and Training. (1988). *Education for Active Citizenship,* Australian Government Printing Service, Canberra.

Sweet, R. (1992). Can Finn deliver vocational competence? *Unicorn, 18* (1), 31–43.

Van der Veen, E.W. (1994). Young people and the environment. *Youth Studies Australia, 13* (4), 24–29.

Walby, S. (1994). Is citizenship gendered? *Sociology, 28* (2), 379–395.

Walker, L. (1993). Girls, schooling and subcultures of resistance. In R. White (Ed.), *Youth subcultures: Theory, history and the Australian experience* (pp. 144–150). Hobart: National Clearinghouse for Youth Studies.

Whyte, S., & Probert, B. (1991). *Young workers in technologically advanced industries.* Hobart: National Clearinghouse for Youth Studies.

Wilson, B. (1992). Full-time shifts: The effect of industry restructuring on young workers in full-time employment. *Youth Studies Australia, 11* (3), 34–39.

Wilson, B., & Wyn, J. (1993). Youth culture: Disturbing priorities? In R. White (Ed.), *Youth subcultures: Theory, history and the Australian experience* (pp. 35–40). Hobart: National Clearinghouse for Youth Studies.

Wilson, B., & Wyn, J. (1987). *Shaping futures: Youth action for livelihood.* Sydney: Allen and Unwin.

Wyn, J. (1991). Safe from attention: Young women, STDs and health policy. *Journal of Australian Studies, 31,* 94–107.

Wyn, J. (1994). Young women and sexually transmitted diseases: The issues for public health. *Australian Journal of Public Health, 18* (1) 32–39.

Yates, L. (1993). *The education of girls: Policy, research and the question of gender.* Melbourne: Australian Council for Educational Research.

Youth Research Centre. (1989). *Pathways, personal issues, public participation* (Research Report No. 1). Melbourne: Youth Research Centre.

3

Youth Transitions in the United Kingdom: A Review of Recent Research

Bob Coles

This chapter is based on a conceptualization of youth as a set of inter-related processes rather than a group of people sharing a common chronological age. Recent attempts in the UK have defined youth as the interstitial phase in the life course between childhood and adulthood (Coles, 1995; Jones & Wallace, 1992). Childhood is typified by dependency on adult society for nurturing, support, and protection from abuse, and a period during which considerable state investment is made in the preparation of young people for the fulfilment of adult roles. Adult citizenship is defined as a form of emancipation in which economic independence, through participation in the labour market, is key (Jones & Wallace, 1992; Lister, 1990). The school-to-work transition has received most attention. Yet, two other transitions are of considerable importance. The domestic transition involves attaining a relative independence from families of origin (including beginning family formation) and, second, the housing transition involves moving away from the parental home and may or may not be associated with the school-to-work and/or the domestic transition (Jones, 1995). All three transitions interact and occur in different ways for different groups of young people with different characteristics. We need to understand the relationship between all three as well as understand how the relationship has changed in response to rapid social, cultural, and economic transformations.

The age at which the transition to adulthood roles takes place has changed markedly over the last two decades. Thus youth must be defined as a series of processes (transitions) rather than by chronological age, something which policy makes and legislators have found difficult to do, with calamitous consequences. As late as the mid–1970s, most young people in the UK followed traditional transitions. Most left school at minimum school-leaving age (two thirds left school at 16) and immediately obtained employment (Roberts, 1984). They formed new partnerships as wage earners, became engaged, married and moved away from the parental home to set up new households and start families of their own (Jones & Wallace, 1992; Wallace, 1987). By the mid-1990s, however, fewer than 1 in 4 young people leave school at minimum school-leaving age and more than one third continue into higher education between the ages of 18–21 (Central Statistics Office, 1995). Thus the school-to-work transition is more protracted for the majority of young people (Coles, 1995).

This, in turn, has changed the patterns of the other two main transitions—leaving home and family formation (Jones, 1993; Jones, 1995). A young person's housing career is rarely a simple, one-step move. Rather, many young people leave home temporarily for education and training, only to return at a later stage (Jones, 1987; Jones, 1995). The average age at which men and women have their first child has also been rising from 24, for women in the 1970s, to 27.5 by the 1991 census. The average age of becoming a father has remained consistent—two years older than for women (Kiernan, 1995). Research on all three dimensions of youth transitions emphasises both growth in their complexity and in their extended forms (Coles, 1995; Jones & Wallace, 1992; Roberts, 1993).

One theme, that has been recognized in much youth research for the last half century, is that youth is the phase in the life course during which the social and material inequalities of the parent generation are translated into the socially unequal life chances of the next (Bourdieu & Passeron, 1977; Furlong, 1992; Griffin, 1985; Willis, 1977). Yet, there is a need to re-examine and re-think what this means and how it takes place. Opportunities to make traditional transitions have collapsed and dependency on families has extended to last for longer periods of time; as a result, a significant number of young people experience fractured or failed transitions as they experience long periods of unemployment, homelessness, social isolation, and unstable, insecure (and sometimes non-existent) family support (Coles, 1995; Jones, 1995). Families are expected to support young people for longer periods of time as extended transitions have become the norm. Continuing family support is assumed by UK government policy (Craig, 1991; Harris, 1989; Jones, 1993; Jones, 1995). Yet, for some young people, family support is tenuous, brittle, and based upon social, psychological, and economic conditions which are far from secure (Jones, 1995). Family research emphasises that support for young people from family members is far from contractual. Indeed it is something which is often controlled by the giver (it may be offered, but cannot be demanded) and may also have a price (the re-affirmation of the status of dependency) that a young person may not be willing to accept (Finch & Mason, 1993; Jones, 1995). A growing interest in Britain and throughout Europe has, therefore, turned to the nature, origins, and implications of social exclusion and the growing alienation of young people from traditional or legitimate opportunities of community involvement (Bagguley & Mann, 1992; Coles, 1995; Williamson, 1993).

MAJOR SOURCES OF DATA ON YOUTH TRANSITIONS IN THE UK

Research on youth transitions in the UK has taken several forms, differing in scope, perspective, and methodology. One set is based on the study of age cohorts: the ESRC 16–19 Initiative; the Youth Cohort Studies (YCS); and the National Child Development Studies (NCDS). In the 1980s, the Economic and Social Research Council (ESRC) commissioned a multi-disciplinary project, based on large questionnaire surveys of two main age cohorts in four different locations in the UK (Banks, et al., 1992). The study complemented questionnaire surveys with a series of semi-structured interviews with sub-samples identified in the initial survey as following the main school-to-work trajectories: academic education (A levels); vocational education (post–16 education not involving A levels); school to job; school to youth training to job; and school to youth training and unemployment. This interview-based research examined home life, sociability and leisure, and beliefs and attitudes including the responses of young people to politics and political parties. An important third strand to the project was a more intensive ethnographic study of the impact of various forms of education and training on identity formation, paying particular attention to gender and social class differences (Bates & Riseborough, 1993).

The ESRC studies produced a huge and rich array of quantitative and qualitative data. One of the central findings of the ESRC studies is that decisions about which career option to follow at the minimum school-leaving age of 16 serve to lock young people into a particular relationship with education and the labour market that it is difficult to reverse (Banks, et al., 1992). Second, the two most discriminating variables in determining post–16 career were the qualification level attained at the age of 16 and the locality in which a young person lived. This latter serves to emphasize the impact of local labour markets on levels of youth employment and unemployment (Ashton, et al., 1986; Coles, 1988). Qualifications gained at 16 and 18 are of critical significance in providing a passport for young people to migrate out of collapsed labour markets (MacDonald, 1988). Third, one of the senior researchers on the project is clear that youth transitions are best thought of as class trajectories (Roberts, 1993). His claim is that young people from middle-class families are twice as likely to be locked into successful trajectories than their working-class contemporaries, with two thirds of young people from working-class backgrounds unsuccessful in securing stable and secure routes to employment between the ages of 16 and 18. The major sub-divisions within this broad picture relate to gender and locality. In areas of low unemployment, young people were twice as likely to have continued with the traditional transition and to have obtained employment straight from school. In the cities experiencing high unemployment, however, young people were diverted from the traditional transition, being re-routed either through youth training or through short courses of vocational post–16 education. Early entrants to the labour market, whether undertaking training or not, became articulated to a tight range of gender stratified jobs. The ethnographic studies of particular groups describe in rich detail the micro-sociology of how the extended economic socialisation of young people takes place (Bates & Riseborough, 1993).

The ESRC studies collected data about young people's lives during the second half of the 1980s. Annual statistics from government departments and regular surveys of age cohorts help to correct and update this picture. Since 1985, the Youth Cohort Studies (YCS) have collected data, mainly about young people's educational qualifications, social background, and experience of youth training and the labour market, from large representative samples of young people between the ages of 16 and 19 (Courtney & McAlleese, 1993; Courtney & McAlleese, 1994). The YCS help to document major changes which occurred in the late 1980s and 1990s, unreported and unpredicted by the ESRC studies. In the mid–1980s only 4 in 10 young people stayed on in education at minimum school-leaving age but by the mid-1990s staying on rates had risen to 8 out of 10. Furthermore, the relationship between levels of unemployment and staying on rates has altered significantly since the late 1980s. In the early 1980s, rising unemployment rates resulted in a displacement of young people into youth training; as unemployment rates increased in the late 1980s more and more young people *chose* extended periods in education as a preferred route from school to work. Given this change in choice patterns, attention must be paid to more than mechanistic economic, geographic, and social class variables to understand what determines the school-to-work transition. Decisions made by policy makers, young people, and their parents have fundamentally changed the transition patterns. The changed relationship between unemployment and staying on rates in the UK highlights, in policy terms, the importance of recognising the potential of educational reform and investment in transforming levels of education and training attainment. Conceptually, it also helps to emphasize the vital importance of treating young people and their parents as active consumers of education and training, rather than regard them as insignificant pawns in a game driven only by macro-economic circumstance. The decline in popularity of youth training is, in part, a response by young people and their parents to the experience of poor quality programs designed for the least able, and resulting in unfulfilling jobs or poor long-term employment prospects (Coles, 1995). Furthermore, whilst those responsible for the organization and delivery of youth training are trying to reposition themselves in the education and training market place by promising vocational qualifications for those undertaking work-based training, there are increasing worries that the client group of early school leavers includes social casualties, requiring social support, as well as those deficient in vocational skills or qualifications who require post–16 vocational training.

Family Life and the Youth Transitions

One of the main limitations of both the YCS and the ESRC 16–19 initiative is the restricting research on youth transitions to the 16–19 age group. Many of the problems faced during youth transitions are set in train long before young people reach minimum school-leaving age and, for many, the transitions to adulthood are not accomplished until well into their third decade (Kiernan, 1992). The National Child Development Studies (NCDS) are a third major source of data that are currently reaping an important dividend although not initially conceived as a study of youth transitions. These studies are based on birth cohorts, the last of which was of a large sample of children born in the first week of March 1958. Members of the sample have been followed up at the ages of 7, 11, 16, 23, and 33. This long time perspective allows an examination of the relationship between the family experiences of children and young people, the impact of this upon their educational and occupational careers, and their later experiences of partnering and parenthood (Kiernan, 1992). The data are providing vital new evidence on the interrelationship between family background, educational, and occupational careers and later patterns of family life even though the 1958 birth cohort reached minimum school-leaving age before the large rises in youth unemployment.

At first glance, the picture appears to be one in which the traditional two-parent family is alive and well in the UK. By the age of 33, 76% of women and 65% of men had become parents and 85% had had children after marriage and within their first marriage or cohabiting union (Kiernan, 1995). On the other hand the UK does have a teenage fertility rate ten times that of

Switzerland, four times that of Italy, three times that of France and Sweden, and twice that of Germany; there is continuing concern about what this means for the quality of family life (Kiernan, 1995). These concerns are based on a recognition of the cost of bringing up children, a concern for how young parents cope if they are economically dependent upon only one youth wage, and what this might mean for the later careers of children brought up in these families (Bradshaw & Miller, 1991).

The analysis of NCDS data indicates a number of correlates of teenage parenting (Kiernan, 1995). Teenage mothers are likely to have been brought up in families which experienced financial problems throughout their schooling years—three times more likely than those who parent after their teens. Teenage mothers were more than twice as likely as mothers giving birth at a later age to have left school with no formal school qualifications (61% compared to 26%) and were twice as likely to have been ranked in the lowest quartile of educational attainment. They are also reported to have manifested much lower scores on emotional well-being. In short, teenage mothers are poorly educated, brought up in poverty, and vulnerable. It is tempting to leap to the conclusion that this early parenting was the result of poor sex education (including advice and support in contraception use), or inadequate preparation for the responsibilities and realities of family life. Yet many teenage mothers had wanted early marriage and pregnancy and had similar aspirations about the size of their families as their contemporaries who conceived at a later age (Kiernan, 1995). Some young people may deliberately choose to seek fulfilment in early domestic careers because of a realistic view of their career prospects in the labour market; early domestic transitions may be linked to poor prospects in the school-to-work transition.

Kiernan (1992) reports that young people who experienced marital breakdown were much more likely to leave school at the age of 16 than those who hadn't. Girls, especially, were more likely to leave home by the age of 18 if they had experienced any form of family disruption and, especially so, if they had experienced parental marital breakdown. Young women from families involving step parents, together with young men who had experienced family disruption (with the notable exception of those living with lone mothers), were much more likely to have left home under adverse circumstances, mainly because of family friction with parents or step-parents. Other, more recent, research has connected this with youth homelessness (Jones, 1993; Jones, 1995).

The evidence from government statistical sources suggests that the proportion of young people being brought up in non-traditional families in the UK is growing. Data from the Office of Population and Censuses (OPCS) indicate that the number of lone-parent families has more than doubled between 1971 and 1991 (Burghes, 1994). Since the 1960s there has been a four fold increase in the number of divorces and a three-fold increase in remarriages. In static, cross sectional terms, OPCS data also indicate that, whilst three quarters of children and young people are living with their biological parents, 17% are living in lone-parent families, and 8% are living in re-constituted families with a parent who has either re-married or is cohabiting (Haskey, 1994). Many families change during the period in which a child is growing up; thus, this static picture must be re-interpreted by projecting trends in family development.

Haskey concluded that, by age 16, nearly a quarter of young people will have experienced the divorce of their parents and many of these may live in reconstituted families (Haskey, 1994). More startlingly, Kiernan and Wicks have estimated that, given current trends in divorce and lone parenthood, the percentage of young people being brought up with both their married biological parents until they are grown up, will have fallen to as low as 50% by the end of the century (Kiernan & Wicks, 1990). The worry for the late 1990s is that, while most young people will follow extended transitions, an increasing number of young people will live in family circumstances that have adverse effects upon youth transitions and are less able to offer the extended patterns of support they need.

YOUNG PEOPLE BROUGHT UP IN, AND LEAVING, CARE

There are particular groups of young people for whom policy makers have particular reasons to be concerned—the unemployed, the homeless, those detached from families, and those rejecting conventional transitions, including those who choose careers involving crime rather than participation in the labour market (Craine & Coles, 1995). They have been referred to as vulnerable youth in that they are most likely to face the most acute problems in attempting the three main transitions (Coles, 1995). Four particular groups may be identified: young people in and leaving care, young people with disabilities and/or special educational needs, young people who are excluded from education (expelled from school), and young people who become involved in crime and/or subject to the penal system. These groups have all been the subject of specialised study although this chapter refers to only one. Young people brought up in the public care represent groups of young people who are most likely to have been brought up in adverse family circumstances. Young people admitted to care are eight times more likely to have been living with a single adult rather than in a two parent family, three times more likely to have a mother living on benefit, and twice as likely to have a mother under the age of 21 (Bebbington & Miles, 1989). Although, as the result of government policy, the numbers of children and young people formally in care have been reduced markedly during the 1980s, the circumstances in which young people are received into the public care, are precisely those which family research predict will increase in future years.

Much of the recent research on young people in, and leaving, care confirm that the latter is correlated with very poor educational performance which has serious and long-term implications for the school-to-work transition (Garnett, et al., 1992). There is some variation in educational success according to the type of care in which a young person is placed, with those in long-term foster care proving the most successful. Being taken into care, of course, may result from a whole series of reasons which may span a considerable time. Some young people are reported as truanting from school well before they are taken into care. Others report that Children's Homes were tolerant of them truanting and many social workers were ignorant about their educational record (Biehal, et al., 1992). Being brought up as a young person in care has been described in government reports as an education hazard (Social Service Committee, 1984).

Because of this, it is unsurprising to find that young people being discharged from care are likely to find themselves unemployed.

The domestic and housing transitions are also matters for concern. Most young people in care are discharged by the age of 18. Many are required to live independently, with very few supported foster placements available after formal discharge. Few are able to return to their families on leaving care. Biehal and colleagues (1995) report that a quarter of their sample had a poor or non-existent relationship with their parents, whilst a third had experienced rejection, with parents refusing to allow them to return home. As young care leavers move to independent living, following the implementation of the Children Act of 1989, they are increasingly given some training in practical skills, such as budgeting, shopping, cleaning and so forth, and some form of after care support. Some attempt is now being made to consult with, offer support, and provide forms of transitional housing and living arrangements for young people as they leave care. They may also be provided with leaving care grants, but these are given under permissive powers granted to local authorities that have a number of competing claims for help and very restricted budgets. A number of leaving care schemes have recently been reviewed, and whilst many appear to be appreciated by young people, some regarded them as a form of domestic combat course, divorced from the real world where budgeting was much harder and exploitation and abuse difficult to resist (Biehal, et al., 1995). Furthermore, for young people leaving care, moving to independent living is often accompanied by early family formation. In one survey, a quarter of young women in the sample were pregnant or already had a child by the time they were discharged from care at the age of 18.

The picture of young people attempting youth transitions after having been brought up in care raises a number of questions about the quality of care, and how care leavers could be better supported. One area of concern is the major educational disadvantage young people in care suffer. The ESRC and YCS studies indicate that qualifications at 16 are critical to the later life chances of all young people. Given this, there is a clear need for compensatory systems for young people in care who, often over a long period of their lives, experience a lack of interest and support for their educational development. How can young people in care realistically entertain the possibility of extended transitions from school to work if there are relatively few opportunities for extended support from surrogate families beyond the age of 16 or 17? Aftercare systems designed by the Department of Health are almost oblivious to changes in education and training promoted in other departments of State. These young people must be afforded the type of surrogate family support the state now expects of those in "normal" family systems if any genuine equality of opportunity is to be offered to those young people for whom the State acts in loci parentis. Compensatory education and training must be accompanied by other forms of extended social and financial support. Many young people who leave care are probably being realistic about their lack of opportunities for a successful career in the labour market and, in such circumstances, may actively seek early partnerships and patterns of family formation rather than stumble into them by accident. We know that early parenting, even for young people not brought up in care, is likely to lead to financial hardship and social deprivation. What is needed is a proper understanding of this complex issue and a far-sighted approach to systems of support rather than to stigmatize and scapegoat, teenage mothers (Coles, 1995).

CONCLUSIONS

There are likely to be huge and long-term costs, both to the public and the private purse, if government avoids confronting the importance of developing a coherent and coordinated youth policy. Academic and social researchers are now taking the lead in calling for youth research to be better coordinated and for that research to be more focused on a policy agenda (Coleman & Warren-Adamson, 1990; Coles, 1995; Jones & Wallace, 1992). Academics in the UK are calling on government departments to think about the inter-relationships between the various strands of youth transitions, how these occur differently for different groups, and how policy can be more co-ordinated so as to manage better the interventions in the economic and social contexts of young people's lives. The cost of youth policy failures are huge. There has been a doubling of male teenage suicides, a huge growth in homelessness amongst the young, and unprecedented rises in youth crime following the cuts in welfare programs which occurred in the UK in the 1980s (Anderson, et al., 1993; Coles, 1995; Craine & Coles, 1995; Woodroffe, et al., 1993). The annual cost of youth crime alone has been estimated to be at least £7 billion—a third of the size of the education budget (Coopers & Lybrand, 1994). The full- and long-term costs of welfare for young people who are marginalised in the community, or experience failed transitions, has yet to be calculated. We may think that we cannot afford the cost of a comprehensive and coherent approach to youth policy. But neither can we afford the huge and long-term cost of youth policy failures.

References

Anderson, I., Kemp, P., & Quilgars, D. (1993). *Single homeless people.* London: HMSO.

Ashton, D.N., & Maguire, M.J., with Bowden, D., Dellow, P., Kennedy, S., Stanley, G., Woodhead, G., Jennings, B. (1986). *Young adults in the labour market* (Research Paper No. 55). London: Department of Employment.

Bagguley, P., & Mann, K. (1992). Idle, thieving bastards? Scholarly representations of the underclass. *Work, Employment and Society, 6,* 113–26.

Banks, M., Bates, I., Breakwell, G., Byner, J., Emler, N., Jamieson, L., & Roberts, K. (1992). *Careers and identities.* Buckingham: Open University Press.

Bates, I., & Riseborough, G. (1993). *Youth and inequality.* Buckingham: Open University Press.

Bebbington, A., & Miles, J. (1989). The background of children who enter local authority care. *British Journal of Social Work, 19,* 349–68.

Biehal, N., Clayton, J., Stein, M.C., & Wade, J. (1992). *Prepared for living.* London: National Children's Bureau.

Biehal, N., Clayton, J., Stein, M.C., & Wade, J. (1995). *Moving on: Young people and leaving care schemes.* London: HMSO.

Bourdieu, P., & Passeron, J. (1977). *Reproduction in education, society and culture.* London: Sage.

Bradshaw, J.R., & Millar, J. (1991). *Lone-parent families* (Department of Social Security Research Report 6). London: hmso.

Burghes, L. (1994). *Lone parenthood and family disruption: The outcomes for children.* London: Family Policy Studies Centre.

Central Statistical Office. (1995). *Regional trends.* London: HMSO.

Coleman, J.C., & Warren-Adamson, C. (Eds). (1992). *Youth policy in the 1990s: The way forward.* London: Routledge.

Coles, B. (Ed.). *Young Carers.* Milton Keyner, England: Open University Press.

Coles, B. (1995). *Youth and Social Policy: Youth citizenship and young careers.* London: UCL Press.

Coopers & Lybrand—ITV Telethon/Princes Trust (1994). *Preventative Strategy for Young People in Trouble.* London: Coopers & Lybrand.

Courtnay, G., & McAleese, I. (1993). *England and Wales youth cohort study. Cohort 5: Aged 16–17 years old in 1991, report on sweep 1* (Youth Cohort Series No 22). Sheffield, England: Employment Department, Research and Development Series.

Courtnay, G., & McAleese, I. (1994). *England and Wales youth cohort study. Cohort 4: Aged 17–18 years old in 1990, report on sweep 2* (Youth Cohort Series No 27). Sheffield, England: Employment Department, Research and Development Series.

Craig, G. (1991). *Fit for nothing? Young people, benefits and youth training.* London: The Children's Society.

Craine, S., & Coles, B. (1995). Alternative careers: Youth transitions and young people's involvement with crime. *Youth and Policy, 48,* 6–26.

Finch, J., & Mason, J. (1993). *Negotiating family responsibilities.* London: Routledge.

Furlong, A. (1992). *Growing up in a classless society? School-to-work transitions.* Edinburgh, Scotland: University of Edinburgh Press.

Garnett, L. (1992). *Leaving care and after.* London: National Children's Bureau.

Griffin, C. (1985). *Typical girls: Young women from school to the job market.* London: Routledge and Kegan Paul.

Harris, N.S. (1989). *Social security for young people.* Aldershot, England: Avebury.

Haskey, J. (1994). Stepfamilies and stepchildren in Great Britain. *Population Trends, 76,* 17–28.

Jones, G. (1993). On the margins of the housing market: Housing and homelessness in youth. In *Young people in and out of the housing market* (Working Paper 3). Edinburgh, Scotland: Centre for Educational Sociology, University of Edinburgh.

Jones, G. (1995). *Family support for young people.* London: Family Policy Studies Centre.

Jones, G., & Wallace, C. (1992). *Youth family and citizenship.* Milton Keynes, England: Open University Press.

Kiernan, K. (1992). The impact of family disruption in childhood on transitions made in young adult life. *Population Studies, 46,* 213–34.

Kiernan, K. (1995). *Transitions to parenthood: Young mothers, young fathers—associated factors and later life experiences.* London, Suntory-Toyota International Centre London School of Economics, WSP/113.

Kiernan, K., & Wicks, M. (1990). *Family change and future policy.* York, England: Joseph Rowntree Memorial Trust, Family Policy Studies Centre.

Lister, R. (1990). Women, economic dependency and citizenship. *Journal of Social Policy, 19* (5), 445–67.

MacDonald, R. (1988). Out of town, out of work: Research on the post–16 experience in two rural areas. In B. Coles (Ed.), *Youth Careers.* Milton Keynes, England: Open University Press.

Roberts, K. (1984). *School Leavers and their prospects: Youth and the labour market in the 1980s.* Milton Keynes, England: Open University Press.

Roberts, K. (1993). Career trajectories and the mirage of increased social mobility. In I. Bates & G. Riseborough (Eds.), *Youth and Inequality.* Buckingham, England: Open University Press.

Social Services Committee (1984). *Children in care.* London: hmso.

Utting, W. (1991). *Children in the Public Care* (The Utting Report). London: Department of Health, Social Service Inspectorate.

Wallace, C. (1987). *For richer for poorer: Growing up in and out of work.* London: Tavistock Publications Limited.

Williamson, H. (1993). Youth policy in the United Kingdom and the marginalisation of young people. *Youth and Policy, 40,* 33–48.

Willis, P. (1977). *Learning to labour.* Farnborough: Saxon House.

Woodroffe, C., Glickman, M., Barker, M., & Power, C. (1993). *Children, teenagers and health: The key data.* Buckingham, England: Open University Press.

4

U.S. Research on the School-to-Work Transition

Jeylan T. Mortimer

Understanding the predictors of early achievement was a major preoccupation of U.S. research in the late sixties and seventies. Sociologists in the status attainment school examined the social and behavioral antecedents of educational and occupational aspirations, and the consequences of these attitudes for educational and early occupational attainments (Sewell, et al., 1969; Sewell, et al., 1970; Hauser, 1971; Gordon, 1972). They demonstrated links between educational and occupational origins (as indicated by fathers' achievements) and adolescents' own educational and occupational aspirations; parental encouragement and school performance largely mediated these effects (Kerckhoff, 1974; Hauser, 1971; Duncan, et al., 1972: Alexander, et al., 1975; Wilson & Portes, 1975). This body of work, focused on the transition to adulthood in the United States, laid the groundwork for subsequent elaborations of the status attainment model. A wide array of achievement-related attitudes and motivations, diverse attainment outcomes, socialization processes, and subgroup differences have been studied. At the same time, cross-national studies have alerted researchers to structural divergences in processes of achievement-relevant socialization and allocation, which contribute to our understanding of the problems of youth in American society.

EXPANSION OF THE PSYCHOLOGICAL PRECURSORS AND ATTAINMENT OUTCOMES

The early attainment researchers focused on aspirations and more realistic plans with respect to future education and occupation. But, as Spenner and Featherman's (1978) review of the literature on achievement ambitions showed, a much wider array of psychological dimensions are implicated in achievement. Economists speak of tastes for employment and the propensity to work or, conversely the propensity for unemployment, the taste for leisure (Corcoran & Hill, 1980), and the taste for vacation (Coe, 1978) as sources of occupational outcomes. Psychologists assess work motivation, the need for achievement, expectations about the consequences of achievement-related behaviours, and perceptions of the opportunity structure. Social psychologists (Spenner & Featherman, 1978; Schwalbe & Gecas, 1988) point to the self-concept as a source of achievement motivation. Investigators have noted positive relationships between self-esteem and educational plans (Kerckhoff, 1974), as well as occupational aspirations (Gordon, 1972). Spenner and Otto (1985) found that women with higher self-esteem, measured while still in high school, experienced fewer months of subsequent unemployment over a thirteen-year period.

Whereas self-esteem refers to the global sense of worth, another set of self-conceptions may be even more pertinent to early achievement. Internal control orientation, mastery, self-efficacy and the sense of competence all reflect expectations about the likelihood of successful goal attainment. Bandura (1988) summarizes a large body of research demonstrating the importance of self-efficacy for work-related behaviours. Our ongoing study of adolescents in St. Paul, Minnesota, the Youth Development Study (YDS), provides support for Bandura's formulation (Call, et al., 1993). We attempted to determine the social psychological antecedents of educational success among youth who come from poor families (those whose family incomes fall below the poverty line). Poor youth who appeared to be on a successful educational trajectory were compared to those who were not. The successful youth had not dropped out of school, had a B average or above, and had taken some action to prepare for college admission (e.g., taken the Scholastic Achievement Test, talked to a counsellor about college, sent for or submitted a college application, or engaged in other concrete activities). There were no significant differences between the two groups in aspirations or plans for educational attainment, nor were there differences in their occupational aspirations. However, the more successful poor adolescents had significantly higher economic self-efficacy. Further analyses, based on data collected from the panel during the first two years after leaving high school, show that students with higher economic efficacy were more successful in realizing their early educational goals (Pimentel, forthcoming).

Other social psychologists have focused on occupational reward values and occupational choices (Rosenberg, 1957; Davis, 1964; Mortimer & Kumka, 1982). Study (Mortimer, et al., 1986) of a panel of University of Michigan men showed that emphasis on extrinsic occupational values while still in college predicted employment stability and income attainment a decade following graduation. In addition to higher incomes, college seniors with higher extrinsic values—who emphasized money, advancement, prestige and security—had less unemployment, involuntary part-time employment and underemployment, as well as fewer changes in career direction during the ten years following college graduation. Earlier interest in the intrinsic rewards of work predicted autonomy on the job a decade later; people-oriented values—an interest in working with people and being of use to the society—fostered adult work that was high in social content. More recent research on the St. Paul high-school students (the YDS) shows that their occupational values increasingly predict the features of their part-time jobs as they move through high school (Mortimer, et al., 1994).

SOCIALIZATION OF ACHIEVEMENT ORIENTATIONS

What kinds of experiences favour the development of psychological orientations that promote early educational and occupational achievement? Gecas (1979) has documented linkages between social class and modes of parental control, family power, and communication which foster achievement-related psychological advantages or disadvantages in children. Kohn (1969, 1981) argues that class differences in parental values with respect to self-direction and conformity limit intergenerational mobility. That is, emphasis on conformity among blue-collar workers would promote values and behaviours in children that are adaptive for similar work, but would not equip them with the self-directed orientations and behaviours facilitative of success in managerial and professional roles. There is evidence that occupational values are transmitted intergenerationally through close and communicative parent child relations that promote identification and modelling. A study of University of Michigan men (Mortimer & Kumka, 1982) found that the closeness of the father-son bond fostered intrinsic values in professional families and extrinsic values in business families. Supportive relations with fathers also stimulated higher levels of anticipated work involvement (Mortimer, et al., 1986). Our current YDS research suggests that the link between socio-economic background and occupational reward values emerges during the high-school years. Work values become more strongly linked to socio-economic origins as students mature. Furthermore, close relations between the more self-directed fathers and adolescent sons fostered intrinsic occupational values.

Educational sociologists focus on school-related determinants (such as tracking, ability grouping, and external rewards) of intrinsic motivation and effort in school, which influence academic achievement and educational attainment (Hallinan, 1994). The influence of high-school track placement (e.g., academic, vocational, commercial, etc.) and ability grouping on achievement orientations is largely mediated by socialization processes, especially teacher-student and peer relationships. Students also learn of their likely occupational destinations through observation of their own tracks and the fates of similarly-situated predecessors; they form aspirations accordingly. Investigators have extensively examined the influence of significant others—including parents, teachers, and peers—on aspirations, but the ways in which the organization of adolescents' networks of associations influence orientations to achievement have been given little attention (Bidwell, et al., 1994).

There is substantial evidence that adolescents' own work experience is also implicated in the attainment process. Approximately 70% of 16-18-year-olds (Manning, 1990) are employed in the U.S. during high school. A growing literature on the benefits and costs of youth employment (Mortimer, 1991; Greenberger & Steinberg, 1986; Greenberger, 1988; Steinberg & Dornbusch, 1991; Steinberg, et al., 1993; Bachman & Schulenberg, 1993; Finch, et al., forthcoming) yields strong evidence that employment during high school has economic benefits for non-college youth in terms of subsequent employment stability and earnings, especially if the earlier employment involves more substantively complex tasks (Stern & Nakata, 1989; Steel, 1991). For this reason, the lower rates of employment among black youth (relative to those of Whites and Hispanics) prior to leaving high school is cause for concern (Ahituv, et al., 1994; Mortimer, et al., 1994).

Even the much-maligned naturally occurring youth jobs, while seemingly mundane from an adult standpoint, provide opportunities to acquire useful skills. What is learned at work, even in a so-called menial job, is not inconsequential: how to relate to supervisors, cooperate with coworkers, deal with customers and clients, manage money, be on time, take responsibility and even gain task-related skills that are transferable to other jobs (e.g., learning to use a cash register, a keyboard or computer, etc.). Whereas most prior studies have focused on the quantity of youthwork, that is, the number of hours worked per week, it is the quality of work that really matters for adolescents in the YDS (Mortimer, et al., 1994). For example, employed adolescents who have opportunities for advancement on their jobs, perceive little conflict between school and work, and who feel that they are paid well (and thus, appreciated by their employers) increase in self-efficacy over a one-year period (Finch, et al., 1991). Employed girls with opportunities to help others on the job manifest a stronger sense of self-efficacy over time. Moreover, chances to learn skills on the job heighten occupational value formation. Employed adolescents with such opportunities become more aware of the variety of rewards that work has to offer, affecting both intrinsic and extrinsic value dimensions. When boys have work that involves mastery of new skills, the quality of their relationships with their parents and their peers improves over time (Mortimer & Shanahan, 1991, 1994). However, when young people experience problems in the job setting—e.g., time pressure, overload, or conflicts between school and work—they express more depressive affect over time (Shanahan, et al., 1991).

If the quality of work is so important, we must consider whether adolescents actually have high or low-quality jobs. We find that naturally-occurring employment presents, for the most part, rather salutary experiences (Mortimer, et al., 1994). Most of the job quality indicators are positively skewed. For example, only a minority of employed students feel that their jobs do not provide them with "a chance to learn new things" (16%) or challenges (19%), put them under time pressure (31%), or subject them to role conflict (22%). On the other hand, 70% report that it is somewhat or very true that the job "gives me a chance to be helpful to others," and 65% say they are never or rarely held responsible for things that are really outside their control. Moreover, adolescents' jobs become increasingly complex, as indicated by U.S. Department of Labor Dictionary of Occupational Titles ratings, involve increasingly lengthy training, and more supervisory responsibility as they move through high school (Mortimer, et al., 1994). Nonetheless, reports of various kinds of conflict between school and work are rather frequent and they are a source of distress for adolescents. But still, the adolescent participants in the Youth Development Study do not express dissatisfaction with work nor do they indicate widespread exposure to stressful work environments. In fact, the young people, and their parents (Phillips & Sandstrom, 1990), are quite satisfied with their jobs. The positive association between adolescent part-time work and both employment and income in the years immediately following high school (Millham, et al., 1978; Freeman & Wise, 1979; Meyer & Wise, 1982: Mortimer & Finch, 1986; Steel, 1991; Stern & Nakata, 1989) may be at least partially attributable to the salutary psychological outcomes of positive work experiences, and the fact that most youth do not have developmentally deleterious (e.g., stressful) jobs. The current study of the St. Paul youth's transition to adulthood will provide direct evidence with respect to such processes of social psychological mediation.

SUBGROUP DIFFERENCES

Gender-specific attitudinal predictors of attainment are of growing interest. Employment is now common among adult women; adolescent girls, however, still encounter traditional values emphasizing the importance of appearance,

popularity, marriage and parenthood that may interfere with achievement-related effort and occupational advancement. Bidwell and colleagues (1994)
present evidence that cohesive peer networks strengthen boys' ambitions,
while reducing those of girls. Moreover, by observing the experiences of their
mothers and other adult women, girls may become increasingly aware of the
dilemmas and role conflicts involved in combining family life and work, as
well as the sex-typed job market and other obstacles to women's achievement.
High occupational attainments may come to be seen as incompatible with the
achievement of familial goals. Though there has been much controversy about
causal order, for women, a high level of anticipated family involvement and
plans for larger family size are associated with lower levels of socio-economic
achievement. Early studies—in the sixties and before—showed that boys have
higher achievement orientations than girls; studies in the seventies and eighties
indicated no consistent gender difference. More recent research shows that
adolescent girls' aspirations often surpass those of boys. In the Youth Development Study panel (Dennehy & Mortimer, 1993) girls have educational
aspirations and plans, as well as occupational aspirations, that exceed those of
boys. However, their sense of economic efficacy—their predictions about the
likelihood of their actually being able to achieve their economic goals, such as
owning their own home or having a job which pays well—is significantly lower
than that of boys (Dennehy & Mortimer, 1993).

Studies also demonstrate that girls have a weaker sense of self-efficacy than
boys in general (Maccoby & Jacklin, 1974; Simmons & Blyth, 1987; Gecas, 1989,
p. 305; Finch, et al., 1991). If, in fact, it is not so much aspirations that stimulate
persistence in achievement-related behaviour, but a real sense of efficacy and
confidence that one's efforts are likely to be successful, girls may still be
psychologically disadvantaged despite high aspirations. Furthermore, adolescent girls have been found to have lower self-esteem than boys (Simmons &
Blyth, 1987) and higher levels of depressive affect (Rutter, 1986), attributes which
could also impede success in the job market. Differences between young men
and women in planning strategies have also been revealed. Young women
tend to view their futures as contingent on future spouses, children, and others,
diminishing their propensity to make firm plans given unpredictability in the
needs and demands of others (Hagestad, 1992). In fact, despite large increases
in women's employment, for recent cohorts of young women (ages 18–24
between 1980 and 1986) marriage and parenthood increase the frequency of
job exits for reasons other than to return to school (Koenigsberg, et al., 1994).
Such employment interruptions have negative implications for women's future
socio-economic attainment. Consistent with the traditional male family bread-
winner role, however, marriage and parenthood had negative effects on men's
employment exits.

Racial and ethnic differences in the early achievement process are being
given increasing scrutiny. Ogbu (1989) finds that despite high aspirations, black
youth are easily discouraged in their attempts to achieve. Many black youth
believe that they will confront obstacles in their quest for occupational and
economic attainments even if they are successful in the educational system.
Instead of pressing forward in the face of difficulties, their "folk culture of
success" leads them to assume a somewhat fatalistic posture, "What's the use
of trying?" In this way, black youth are channelled away from schoolwork and

toward behaviours that diminish the likelihood of legitimate employment success. Wilson (1987) and Sullivan (1989) document the absence of employment opportunities for young people in the U.S. inner city, indicating the realism of these attitudes. Black youth continue to experience great difficulties in finding jobs despite decreasing rates of high-school dropout (from 27 to 15 percent from 1968 to 1988 for youth ages 16–24; at that time the white rate was 13 percent) (Ahituv, 1994). In a recent report based on the National Longitudinal Survey of Youth (persons aged 13 to 16 in 1978), Ahituv and colleagues (1994) report three ethnically differentiated patterns of transition to work in the U.S.: (1) overlap of school and work activities from ages 16–24, the characteristic pattern among white youth; (2) early school departure combined with early labor market entry, typical of Hispanic youth; and (3) prolonged schooling in the absence of work experience, common among black youth. For the latter, military service is most likely to provide pre-employment training experiences. The phenomenon of idleness—spells of time without schooling, military service, or work—is more characteristic of minority young adults, particularly in American inner cities (Wilson, 1987). In the NLSY data, by the age of 23, 12 percent of black men, 10 percent of Hispanic men, and 6 percent of white men were in this state (Ahituv, et al., 1994, p. 26).

There is need for careful monitoring of gender differences in achievement orientations and their consequences. What experiences determine whether girls will be oriented to careers or to more traditional gender roles? Moreover, little is known about the achievement orientations of minority groups other than Afro-Americans. Are the attitudes which predict attainments in the general population also characteristic of high-achieving Asian-Americans? And what about very recent newcomers to the United States, such as the Hmong, who exhibit high aspirations coupled with factors mitigating against their achievement—a background of familial poverty as well as early marriage and fertility in the adolescent generation (McNall, et al., 1994; Hutchison & McNall, 1994). We know very little about the patterns of transition to adulthood among the many recent Asian immigrants (Hotz & Tienda, 1992).

THE DYNAMICS OF ACHIEVEMENT

Early studies examined the socio-economic precursors of educational and occupational aspirations, assuming that the status of the family of origin was fixed. The faultiness of this assumption has become increasingly apparent given growing attention to intragenerational mobility. Parental socio-economic status may change during childhood and adolescence, a time when important vocational socialization is taking place (Featherman and Spenner, 1988). Family socio-economic mobility may foster redirection in children's trajectories of achievement. Kerckhoff's study (1974) suggested that adolescents form their educational and occupational aspirations during the high-school years, and that aspirations were not as stable as assumed in the status attainment literature. The Youth Development Study of adolescents in St. Paul found that both boys' and girls' educational aspirations and plans actually declined as they moved through high school (Dennehy & Mortimer, 1993). The same pattern was true of their occupational aspirations. These decreasing levels of aspiration may indicate growing realism as adolescents become more aware of labor market realities. Another study indicates instability in aspirations in the years after high school as well. Rindfuss and his colleagues (1990), using National Longitudinal Survey data from 1972, the respondents' last year of high school, and follow-ups in 1973, 1974, 1976, and 1979, found that less than one quarter of the youth had the same occupational expectation at all time periods.

Given these changes, it is especially important to investigate the manner in which psychological orientations influence attainments, and how success in work (or the lack thereof) affects work-related psychological orientations and behaviours. A teenager, upon leaving full-time schooling, might be motivated to find a job, at least in part, by a desire for independence and dissatisfaction with continued economic and other forms of dependency upon parents (Borman, 1991). In contrast, the older youth's job search and relocation attempts, and other achievement-related behaviours, may be more closely linked to economic needs, the position of work in the hierarchy of identities (Stryker, 1985) and the level of investment in, and commitment to, the work role. Once a person has entered the work force, employment and joblessness, as well as the quality of work (Mortimer et al., 1986; Kohn & Schooler, 1983), can influence diverse psychological attributes that influence subsequent occupational success. The early work career may be especially important in this regard, given that the work orientations of youth are in a particularly formative stage. If early jobs are unstable and unrewarding, young workers may become alienated, develop poor work habits, and become less attached to the work force (Corcoran & Hill, 1980: 40).

STRUCTURAL DETERMINANTS OF THE SCHOOL-TO-WORK TRANSITION

The status attainment model has come under increasing criticism given its lack of attention to structural barriers and segmentation in the labor market (Kerckhoff, 1995). There has been little attention to differences in culture, social structure, or the institutional linkages between school and work that could lead certain psychological dimensions to be more important for achievement in one context than another. For example, the level of institutional connection between school and work could moderate the effects of achievement orientations. The system of further education in Britain places much emphasis on the acquisition of credentials after leaving the general education system and entering the world of work (Kerckhoff, 1990). Highly focused, specialized programs after full-time labor force entry provide nationally recognized credentials and increase youth's economic productivity. Germany also has an elaborate system of nationally recognized credentials achieved through the apprentice system (Hamilton, 1990; Rosenbaum, et al., 1990). Because of clear institutionalized connections between particular schools and firms in Japan, the student's prior academic achievement and teacher recommendations are highly consequential for obtaining placement in high-quality jobs (Rosenbaum, et al., 1990). Such institutional linkages between school and work provide clear economic incentives for the acquisition of job-related knowledge and skills prior to and/or following the completion of secondary education even for those who are not college bound. In such circumstances, psychosocial variables that influence school achievement could have greater relevance for early attainment outcomes than in the United States.

Comparable structures promoting non-college youth's continuing motivation to learn and to enhance their human capital are generally lacking in the United States. The U.S. educational system produces "graduates" who are quite varied in their educational backgrounds (Kerckhoff, 1994). High schools are differentiated by tracks and the quality of their programs are quite variable (for example, between inner cities and suburbs). At the post-secondary level, there are technical institutes, community colleges, and both private and public colleges and universities. The students, however, are quite undifferentiated in terms of the credentials they obtain (high-school diploma, college degree), which are not directly linked to particular kinds of jobs (with some exceptions, e.g., graduate and professional degrees). Linkages between schools and employers are less formal and structured than in other industrial societies. In fact, in the United States, employers pay scant attention to recent school leavers' academic performance, and schools have few resources to respond to requests for transcripts and other records, even when employers want them (Borman, 1991, p. 41). Specific job skills are acquired, for the most part, after leaving school. In the United States there is a notable absence of transition supports of any kind for a staggering 75% of youth: the non-college bound, constituting approximately half the cohort, which includes high-school dropouts (who no longer have a viable place in our increasingly technical occupational system), and for those who enter, but do not complete, a four-year college (these constitute one out of four youth). What few counsellors there are focus their energies on assuring that those who have the potential for college succeed in getting into a school of their choice. Many college dropouts and about half of high-school graduates acquire some further vocationally-relevant education in community colleges and technical institutes, but their credentials have little national currency (Kerckhoff, 1994). Clearly, the U.S. system as it is now configured is not addressing the needs of many young people.

Thus there may be important structural underpinnings of the much-heralded U.S. weaknesses in educational performance and economic productivity. Non-college youth, in the years immediately after high school, drift between jobs whose skill levels are the same, or quite similar to, the jobs they were able to obtain when they were still in high school (Osterman, 1980, 1989). Kerckhoff (1994) suggests that the closer the institutional connections between school and work, the more structured and patterned is the early career line. American youth who enter the labor force directly after high school hold jobs in the secondary sector of the economy and experience high unemployment, underemployment, and job instability. High-school graduates in the National Longitudinal Survey of Youth, who were not college bound, held, on the average, almost six jobs and experienced between four and five unemployment spells between the ages of 18 and 27 (Stern, et al., 1994). Most of the 1980 cohort of high-school seniors in the High School and Beyond study held jobs during the six years following graduation that lasted less than 2 years, even after temporary jobs, lasting less than 4 months, were excluded from the analysis (Koenigsberg, et al., 1994). Less than half the job exits led directly to new jobs; others preceded school enrolments or other activities. High job turnover fosters unemployment, as youth seek to relocate. In 1993, unemployment among 18- and 19-year-olds was more than three times the rate of persons aged 25 to 54—19% vs. 5.7 % (Stern, et al., 1994). Moving from job to job may in some cases improve the fit of worker and job, but it is more likely to result in quite similar, low-level employment. Unemployment, especially if it becomes chronic, also tends to have negative implications for subsequent wage attainment (Evans, 1986; Stern, et al., 1994).

Delay in entering jobs with career potential prolongs the ability of many young people who do not attend college to continue to enact a highly valued youthful life style. Osterman (1989) has characterized such youth as lacking career orientation, instead emphasizing peer relationships, travel, adventure, and short-term jobs to satisfy immediate consumption needs. Accordingly, employers express preference for low-wage workers who do not require fringe benefits and are not likely to unionize. When filling adult-like primary jobs, such employers seek evidence of stability or settling down, something that may not occur for several years after young people leave high school. Educators and societal leaders bemoan the loss of these years, with respect to the development of skills which would be productive of a highly qualified labor force. Furthermore, lengthy unemployment has serious implications for future employability and life chances (Petersen & Mortimer, 1994). While there is now much interest in the United States in developing apprentice-like school-to-work transition programs to remedy these problems (U.S. Department of Education, 1994; Stern, et al., 1994), issues of employer incentives for participation, the nature of training to be offered, and equity issues remain unresolved (Bailey, 1993; Hamilton, 1993). In the absence of institutionalized transition supports, American youth who do not attend college have become increasingly disadvantaged economically and socially, and the wage gap between high school and college graduates has widened (W.T. Grant Foundation, 1988; Stern, et al., 1994).

American society may no longer be able to afford an extensive youthful moratorium, particularly on the part of non-college youth. There has been a steep decline of well-paid manufacturing jobs that do not require post-secondary degrees, the technological complexity of work has increased, and the economy has become increasingly dynamic as competition in world markets increases. These changes necessitate a highly skilled and flexible work force, ready to be retrained and reallocated as the need arises. The growing demand for highly educated personnel is indicated by the fact that three-fourths of American job growth from 1990–1993 consisted of professional and managerial positions; they accounted for less than half the new jobs between 1983 and 1993 (Nasar, 1994). Moreover, the economic return for high-school graduates' mathematical proficiency increased from the 1970s to the 1980s (Stern, et al., 1994).

HISTORICAL DESTRUCTURATION OF THE EARLY LIFE COURSE

The process of transition to adulthood, and particularly, transition to the work role, varies across time, and is markedly influenced by factors such as cohort size, economic expansions and depressions, wars, and cultural shifts (Easterlin, 1980; Elder, 1974; Modell, 1989; Sanders & Becker, 1994; Mortimer, 1992). Shifts in the timing and ordering of transition events through historical time have been given considerable attention (Modell, et al., 1976; Mortimer, 1992), along with the implications of these patterns for attainment (Marini, et al., 1989). Historical studies of lives emphasize the increasing destructuration and individualization of the individual life course, as the duration, sequencing, and directionality of movement between historically aged-graded status positions are becoming increasingly diverse and subject to manifold contingencies (Modell, 1989; Buchmann, 1989; Rindfuss, Swicegood, & Rosenfeld, 1987). These trends make the linkages between school and work, as well as occupational career lines following completion of formal education, increasingly tenuous. Under such circumstances, it might be argued that social psychological factors become even more important in determining the achievement process, not only in the early stages of the life course, but throughout the socio-economic career. No longer can it be assumed that individuals, once securely placed on a lower rung of a success escalator, can ride smoothly toward the top, carried forward structurally via strong institutionalized career tracks.

Given the wide range of opportunities for later changes in direction—a wider array of branching points, more prevalent reversals in the directionality of movement, and movements between early attainment tracks (e.g., return to school for continuing training)—individual motivation, volition, and effort may become increasingly salient. The Youth Development Study indicates that adolescents' educational and family plans, while still in high school, have significant predictive capacity with respect to school attainment and living arrangements in the years immediately following (Pimentel, forthcoming). Moreover, the earlier study of Michigan graduates showed that self-confidence and values, measured in the senior year of college, predict occupational attainments over a period of ten years (Mortimer, et al., 1986). Clausen (1993) examined the attitudinal precursors of life-long attainment, finding planful competence, denoting self-confidence, intellectual investment, and dependability, measured in the adolescent years, to be especially predictive. These attributes imply planfulness, delayed gratification, and a sense of control over goal attainment (Jordaan & Super, 1974). Clearly, future researchers need to attend to both structural and psychological variability to fully understand the processes of attainment in the early life course.

References

Alexander, K.L., Eckland, B.K., & Griffin, L.J. (1975). The Wisconsin model of socioeconomic achievement: A replication. *American Journal of Sociology, 81*, 324–342.

Ahituv, A., Tienda, M., Xu, L., & Hotz, V.J. (1994). *Initial Labor Market Experiences of Black, Hispanic and White Men.* Unpublished manuscript, Population Research Center, University of Chicago.

Bachman, J.G., & Schulenberg, J. (1993). How part-time work intensity relates to drug use, problem behaviour, time use, and satisfaction among high-school seniors: Are these consequences or merely correlates? *Developmental Psychology, 29*, 220–235.

Bailey, T. (1993). Can youth apprenticeship thrive in the United States? *Educational Researcher, 22*, 4–10.

Bandura, A. (1988). Organizational applications of social cognitive theory. *Australian Journal of Management, 13*, 275–302.

Bidwell, C.E., Plank, S., & Muller, C. (1994, April). *Social networks and adolescent career development.* Paper presented at the Conference on Institutions and Careers, Duke University, Durham, North Carolina.

Borman, K.M. (1991). *The first real job: A study of young workers.* Albany: State University of New York Press.

Buchmann, M. (1989). *The script of life in modern society: Entry into adulthood in a changing world.* Chicago: University of Chicago Press.

Call, K.T., Mortimer, J.T., Lee, C., & Dennehy, K. (1993). *High risk youth and the attainment process.* Paper presented at the 1993 American Sociological Association Meeting.

Coe, R.D. (1978). Absenteeism from work. In G.J. Duncan & J.N. Morgan (eds.), *Five thousand American families—patterns of economic progress: Vol. VI. Accounting for race and sex differences in earnings and other analyses of the first nine years of the panel study of income dynamics* (ch. 5). Ann Arbor: Survey Research Center, Institute for Social Research, University of Michigan.

Corcoran, M., & Hill, M.S. (1980). Persistence in unemployment among adult men. In G.J. Duncan & J.N. Morgan (eds.), *Five thousand American families—patterns of economic progress: Vol. VIII. Analyses of the first eleven years of the panel study of income dynamics* (ch. 2). Ann Arbor: Survey Research Center, Institute for Social Research, University of Michigan.

Davis, J.A. (1964). *Great aspirations: The graduate school plans of America's college seniors.* Chicago: Aldine.

Dennehy, K., & Mortimer, J.T. (1993). Work and family orientations of contemporary adolescent boys and girls. In J.C. Hood (ed.), *Men, work, and family* (pp. 87–107). Newbury Park, CA: Sage Publications.

Duncan, O.D., Featherman, D.L., & Duncan, B. (1972). *Socioeconomic background and achievement.* New York: Seminar Press.

Easterlin, D. (1980). *Birth and fortune: The impact of numbers on personal welfare.* New York: Basic Books.

Elder, G.H., Jr. (1974). *Children of the great depression.* Chicago: University of Chicago Press.

Evans, Jr., R. (1986). The transition from school to work in the United States. In W.K. Cummings, E.R. Beauchamp, S. Ichikawa, V.N. Kobayashi, & M. Ushiogi (eds.), *Educational policies in crisis* (pp. 210–239). New York: Praeger.

Featherman, D.L., & Spenner, K.I. (1988). Class and the socialization of children: Constancy, change, or irrelevance? In E.M. Hetherington, R.M. Lerner, & M. Perlmutter (eds.), *Child development in life span perspective* (pp. 67–90). Hillsdale, NJ: Lawrence Erlbaum Associates.

Finch, M.D., Shanahan, M., Mortimer, J.T., & Ryu, S. (1991). Work experience and control orientation in adolescence. *American Sociological Review, 56,* 597–611.

Finch, M.D., Mortimer, J.T., & Ryu, S. (forthcoming). Transition into part-time work: Health risks and opportunities. In J. Schulenberg, J. Maggs, & K. Hurrelmann (eds.), *Health risks and developmental transitions during adolescence.* New York: Cambridge University Press.

Freeman, R.B., & Wise, D.A. (1979). *Youth Unemployment.* Cambridge, MA: National Bureau of Economic Research.

Gecas, V. (1979). The influence of social class on socialization. In W.R. Burr, R. Hill, F.I. Nye, & I.L. Reiss (eds.), *Contemporary theories about the family. Vol. I. Research-based theories* (pp. 365–404). New York: Free Press.

Gecas, V. (1989). The social psychology of self-efficacy. *Annual Review of Sociology, 15,* 291–316.

Gordon, C. (1972). *Looking ahead: Self-conceptions, race, and family as determinants of adolescent orientation to achievement* (Rose Monograph Series). Washington, DC: American Sociological Association.

Greenberger, E. (1988). Working in Teenage America. In J.T. Mortimer & K.M. Borman (eds.), *Work experience and psychological development through the life span.* Boulder, CO: Westview.

Greenberger, E., & Steinberg, L. (1986). *When teenagers work.* New York: Basic Books.

Hagestad, G. (1992). Assigning rights and duties: Age, duration, and gender in social institutions. In W.R. Heinz, (Ed.), *Institutions and gatekeeping in the life course* (pp. 261–279). Wannheim: Deutscher Studien Verlag.

Hallinan. M.T. (1994). *Educational processes and school reform.* Paper delivered at the annual meetings of the Eastern Sociological Association, Raleigh, North Carolina.

Hamilton, S.F. (1990). *Apprenticeship for adulthood: Preparing youth for the future.* New York: The Free Press.

Hamilton, S.F. (1993). Prospects for an American-style youth apprenticeship system. *Educational Researcher, 22,* 11–16.

Hauser, R.M. (1971). *Socioeconomic background and educational performance* (Rose Monograph Series). Washington, DC: American Sociological Association.

Hotz, V.J., & Tienda, M. (1992). *Gender and ethnic variation in the school-to-work transition.* Background Paper for testimony delivered before the Subcomittee on Census and Population.

Hutchison, R., & McNall, M. (1994). Early marriage in a Hmong cohort. *Journal of Marriage and the Family, 56,* 579–590.

Jordaan, J.P., & Super, D.E. (1974). The prediction of early adult vocational behaviour. In D.F. Ricks, A. Thomas, and M. Roff (eds.), *Life history research in psychopathology.* Minneapolis: University of Minnesota Press.

Kerckhoff, A.C. (1974). *Ambition and attainment: A study of four samples of American boys.* (Rose Monograph Series). Washington, DC: American Sociological Association.

Kerckhoff, A.C. (1990). *Getting started: Transition to adulthood in Great Britain.* Boulder: Westview Press.

Kerckhoff, A.C. (1994, April). *Building conceptual and empirical bridges between studies of educational and labor force careers.* Paper presented at the Conference on Institutions and Careers, Duke University, NC.

Kerckhoff, A.C. (1995). Social stratification and mobility processes: The interaction between individuals and social structures. In K. Cook, G. Fine, & J.S. House, *Sociological perspectives on social psychology* (pp. 476–496). New York: Allyn and Bacon.

Koenigsberg, J., Garet, M.S., & Rosenbaum, J.E. (1994). The effect of family on the job exits of young adults: A competing risk model. *Work and Occupations, 21,* 33–63.

Kohn, M.L. (1969). *Class and conformity: A study in values.* IL: Dorsey.

Kohn, M.L. (1981). Personality, occupation, and social stratification: A frame of reference. *In research in social stratification and mobility* (pp. 267–297). Greenwich, CT: JAI Press, Inc.

Kohn, M.L., & Schooler, C. (1983). *Work and personality: An inquiry into the impact of social stratification.* Norwood, NJ: Ablex.

Maccoby, E.E., & Jacklin, C.N. (1974). *The psychology of sex differences.* Stanford: Stanford University Press.

Manning, W.D. (1990). Parenting employed teenagers. *Youth and Society, 22,* 184–200.

Marini, M.M., Shin, H.C., & Raymond, J. (1989). Socioeconomic consequences of the process of transition to adulthood. *Social Science Research, 13,* 89–135.

McNall, M., Dunnigan, T., & Mortimer, J.T. (1994). The educational achievement of the St. Paul Hmong. *Anthropology and Education Quarterly, 25* (1), 1–22.

Meyer, R.M., & Wise, D.A. (1982). High-school preparation and early labor force experience. In R.B. Freeman & D.A. Wise (eds.), *The youth labor market problem: Its nature, causes, and consequences* (pp. 277–347). Chicago: University of Chicago Press.

Millham, S., Bullock, R., & Hosie, K. (1978). Juvenile unemployment: a concept due for re-cycling? *Journal of Adolescence, 1,* 11–24.

Modell, J. (1989). *Into one's own: From youth to adulthood in the United States, 1920–1975.* Berkeley: University of California Press.

Modell, J., Furstenberg, F., & Hershberg, T. (1976). Social change and transitions to adulthood in historical perspective. *Journal of Family History, 1,* 7–32.

Mortimer, J.T. (1991). Employment. In R.M. Lerner, A.C. Petersen, & J. Brooks-Gunn (eds.), *Encyclopedia of Adolescence. Vol. I.* New York: Garland Publishing.

Mortimer, J.T. (1992). Adulthood. In E.F. Borgatta & M.L. Borgatta (eds.), *Encyclopedia of Sociology.* New York: Macmillan.

Mortimer, J.T., & Finch, M.D. (1986). The effects of part-time work on self-concept and achievement. In K. Borman & J. Reisman (eds.), *Becoming a worker* (pp. 66–89). Norwood, New Jersey: Ablex.

Mortimer, J.T., Finch, M.D., Dennehy, K., Lee, C., & Beebe, T. (1994). Work experience in adolescence. *Journal of Vocational Education Research, 19* (1).

Mortimer, J.T., & Kumka, D. (1982). A further examination of the "occupational linkage hypothesis." *The Sociological Quarterly, 23,* 3–16.

Mortimer, J.T., Lorence, J., & Kumka, D. (1986). *Work, family, and personality: Transition to adulthood.* Norwood, NJ: Ablex.

Mortimer, J.T., & Shanahan M. (1991). *Adolescent work experience and relations with peers.* Paper presented at the Annual Meeting of the American Sociological Association.

Mortimer, J.T., & Shanahan, M. (1994). Adolescent work experiences and family relationships. *Work and Occupations, 21,* 369–384.

Mortimer, J.T., Ryu, S., Dennehy, K., Efron Pimentel, E., & Lee, C. (1994). *Part-time work: Occupational value formation in adolescence.* Revision of paper presented at the 1992 American Sociological Association Annual Meeting, Pittsburgh, PA.

Nasar, S. (1994, October 17). Statistics reveal bulk of new jobs pay over average. *New York Times* (pp. A–1, C–3).

Ogbu, J.U. (1989). Cultural boundaries and minority youth orientation toward work preparation. In D. Stern & D. Eichorn (eds.), *Adolescence and work: Influences of social structure, labor markets, and culture* (pp. 101–140). Hillsdale, NJ: Lawrence Erlbaum.

Osterman, P. (1980). *Getting started: The youth labor market.* Cambridge, MA: MIT Press.

Osterman, P. (1989). The job market for adolescents. In D. Stern & D. Eichorn (eds.), *Adolescence and work: Influences of social structure, labor markets, and culture* (pp. 235–256). Hillsdale, New Jersey: Lawrence Erlbaum.

Petersen, A.C., & Mortimer, J.T. (eds.). (1994). *Youth unemployment and society.* New York: Cambridge University Press.

Phillips, S., & Sandstrom, K. (1990). Parental attitudes toward "youthwork." *Youth and Society, 22,* 160–183.

Pimentel, E.E. (forthcoming). *Effects of adolescent achievement and family goals on the early adult transition.* In J.T. Mortimer and M.D. Finch (eds.), *Adolescents, Work and Family: An Intergenerational Developmental Analysis.* Newbury Park, CA: Sage Publications.

Rindfuss, R.R., Cooksey E.C., & Sutterlin, R.L. (1990). *Young adult occupational achievement: Early expectations versus behavioral reality.* Paper presented at the World Congress of Sociology, Madrid, July.

Rindfuss, R.R., Swicegood, C.G., & Rosenfeld, R.A. (1987). Disorder in the life course: How common and does it matter? *American Sociological Review, 52,* 785–801.

Rosenbaum, J.E., Kariya, T., Settersten, R., & Maier, T. (1990). Market and network theories of the transition from high school to work: Their application to industrialized societies. *Annual Review of Sociology, 16,* 263–299.

Rosenberg, M. (1957). *Occupations and values.* Glencoe, Illinois: Free Press.

Rutter, M. (1986). The developmental psychopathology of depression: Issues and perspectives. In M. Rutter, C.E. Izard & P.B. Read (eds.), *Depression in young people: Developmental and clinical perspectives* (pp. 3–30). New York: Guilford Press.

Sanders, K., & Becker, H.A. (1994). The transition from education to work and social independence: A comparison between the United States, The Netherlands, West Germany, and the United Kingdom. *European Sociological Review, 10,* 135–154.

Schwalbe, M.L., & Gecas, V. (1988). Social psychological dimensions of job-related disability. In J.T. Mortimer & K.M. Borman (eds.), *Work experience and psychological development through the life span* (pp. 233–271). Boulder: Westview Press.

Sewell, W.H., Haller, A.O., & Portes, A. (1969). The educational and early occupational attainment process. *American Sociological Review, 34,* 82–93.

Sewell, W.H., Haller, A.O., & Ohlendorf, G.W. (1970). The educational and early occupational status attainment process: Replication and revision. *American Sociological Review, 35,* 1014–1027.

Shanahan, M.J., Finch, M.D., Mortimer, J.T., & Ryu, S. (1991). Adolescent work experience and depressive affect. *Social Psychology Quarterly, 54,* 299–317.

Simmons, R.G., & Blyth, D.A. (1987). *Moving into adolescence: The impact of pubertal change and school context.* New York: Aldine.

Spenner, K.I., & Otto, L.B. (1985). Work and self-concept: Selection and socialization in the early career. In A.C. Kerckhoff (ed.), *Research in sociology of education and socialization. Vol. V* (pp. 197–235). Greenwich, CT: JAI Press.

Spenner, K.I., & Featherman, D.L. (1978). Achievement ambitions. *Annual Review of Sociology, 4*, 373–420.

Steel, L. (1991). Early work experience among white and non-white youths: Implications for subsequent enrolment and employment. *Youth and Society, 22*, 419–447.

Steinberg, L., & Dornbusch, S.M. (1991). Negative correlates of part-time employment during adolescence: Replication and elaboration. *Developmental Psychology, 27*, 304–313.

Steinberg, L., Fegley, S., & Dornbusch, S.M. (1993). Negative impact of part-time work on adolescent adjustment: Evidence from a longitudinal study. *Developmental Psychology, 29*, 171–180.

Stern, D., Finkelstein, N., Stone III, J.R., Latting, J., & Dornsife, C. (1994). *Research on school-to-work transition programs in the United States*. Berkeley, CA: National Center for Research in Vocational Education.

Stern, D., & Y. Nakata. (1989). Characteristics of high-school students' paid jobs, and employment experience after graduation. In D. Stern & D. Eichorn (eds.), *Adolescence and work: Influences of social structure, labor markets, and culture* (pp. 189–233). Hillsdale, NJ: Lawrence Erlbaum Associates.

Stryker, S. (1985). Symbolic interaction and role theory. In G. Lindzey & E. Aronson (eds.), *Handbook of social psychology. Vol. I* (pp. 311–378). New York: Random House.

Sullivan, M.L. (1989). *Getting paid: Youth, crime and work in the inner city.* Ithaca: Cornell University Press.

U.S. Department of Education. Office of Educational Research and Improvement. (1994). *School-to-work. What does research say about it?* Washington, D.C.: U.S. Government Printing Office.

Wilson, K.L., & Portes, A. (1975). The educational attainment process: Results from a national sample. *American Journal of Sociology, 81*, 343–363.

Wilson, W.J. (1987). *The truly disadvantaged: The inner city, the underclass, and public policy.* Chicago: University of Chicago Press.

W.T. Grant Foundation Commission on Work, Family and Citizenship. (1988). *The forgotten half: Pathways to success for America's youth and young families.* Washington, D.C.

5

Demographic and Career Issues Relating to Youth in Transition to Adulthood

Rosemary A. Venne

Canada has experienced fundamental demographic changes over the postwar period. This chapter will provide a demographic perspective as it relates to career paths in the postwar era. The experience of the immediate postwar career paths will be contrasted with the likely career patterns facing the youth of today. Driver (1985) noted that demographic boom and bust conditions (as well as economic boom and bust conditions) affect career mobility. More simply put, career patterns are affected by when one was born.

DEMOGRAPHIC PERSPECTIVE AND CAREER PATTERNS

Demography is the science of populations (Weeks, 1994); "Behind most news stories is a population story" (Haupt & Kane, 1991, p. 2). Population change has an impact on all facets of life. One of the central facts of the Canadian population is the extended postwar fertility boom, commonly referred to as the baby boom. This population pattern is shared with a few other industrialized countries, notably the U.S., Australia, and New Zealand. With the exception of the sustained postwar fertility boom, Canada's population trends are similar to that of other industrialized countries in that the country has a slowly aging population and a below replacement level fertility rate. Canada's fertility rate has been declining since confederation with the exception of the baby boom period. As a country becomes less agrarian and more industrialized, and as women become more educated and enter the labour force, family size becomes smaller (Novak, 1988). All of these trends have been effecting Canada.

Fertility rates (defined as the number of children per woman) declined over the depression and wartime years prior to the postwar fertility boom (Kerr & Ram, 1994). There is no firm consensus about the exact time span of the postwar fertility boom, but, in general, it is defined as a two-decade period from 1947 to 1966 with a peak around 1959 and 1960 (Foot & Venne, 1990; Galarneau, 1994). The baby boom accounted for slightly more than one-third of the Canadian population at the 1991 census. Following the baby boom, fertility rates declined over the late 1960s and 1970s. This period of low fertility and those born over this time (1967 to 1979) are often referred to as a baby bust. During the baby bust period women began to enter the labour force in unprecedented numbers. There has been a moderate increase in the number of births over the 1980s and 1990s as the baby boom women pass through their prime childbearing years. Even though, on average, these women are having less than two children per family, the baby boomers are such a large group that they account for the mini boom or the baby boom echo effect as it is sometimes called.

Moving from the baby bust of the depression and wartime era to the postwar baby boom and then to the most recent baby bust, represents a huge swing in the size of generations. This swing in generational size has tremendous implications for all facets of life in Canada. The baby boomers have been described as a tidal wave that has the power to disrupt society's institutions. For example, the educational system in Canada was small in size to accommodate the pre-boomers (depression and wartime era busters), then expanded to adjust to the baby boomers, and then had to shrink to fit the latest bust generation. Currently the baby boomers are in their mid-life decades while the current baby busters are in or entering their early adult years. This current baby bust group, who are in transition from youth to adulthood, are following on the heels of the large boom generation.

The career paths of the different demographic groups represent very contrasting experiences. Driver (1985) presents a classification of four career paths. The first one found in the immediate postwar period, is the steady state career concept, which defines a career as a lifelong commitment to a field with little actual job movement. A medical career or even a blue-collar job spent at one firm are examples. The second one is the linear career concept which is still the most familiar and most pervasive career concept in Canadian society. It is associated with upward career movement or climbing the career ladder. During the postwar years this promotion-centred career path became embedded in many people's minds as the norm. Driver's (1985) last two career concepts may not be as familiar. The third is the spiral career concept where there is significant career change in occupations over a lifetime and career movement consists of mainly lateral (horizontal) moves as opposed to only promotions. Occupational flexibility is emphasized along with lifelong education. There is constant and erratic job movement in the fourth, the transitory career concept. This career concept is characterized by the youth, part-time, and temporary work force (e.g., contract work or project work). Job movement is horizontal and job variety is an important employee motive. These latter two career concepts have become more familiar to young people over the 1980s and 1990s. Driver (1985) found that the linear career concept was widely held in North America in the 1980s. Driver's (1985) key premise is that demographic boom and bust conditions can affect career mobility—that is, career movement can be affected by when you were born. Of course career patterns can also be affected by economic boom and bust conditions and the interaction between these demographic and economic conditions.

The career experiences for the decades immediately following World War II contrast sharply with those that are more typical today. The depression and wartime baby bust generation was a small demographic group that came of labour force age during North America's economic heyday (Bardwick, 1986). This group was swept up in the tremendous interaction effect of being a small labour force (mainly male) during a sustained economic boom; it is not surprising that they had a strong linear career view. The postwar economic expansion led to disproportionate increases in white-collar and managerial positions and frequent promotions up the organizational hierarchy (Bardwick, 1986; A. Bennett, 1990). A. Bennett (1990) discusses how, during the economic boom, many companies added more middle management positions in their corporate structure (precisely those positions that were being cut in the recent and still ongoing flattening of corporate hierarchies). A recent article documents a typical pattern of a dizzying climb up the corporate ladder for the CEO of a large corporation where he experienced 20 job changes (many of them promotions) in 32 years (Farewell Fast Track, 1990). Morgan (1981) offers examples of linear career patterns in the Canadian federal public service. During the postwar period North American organizations coped with the economic boom and the small labour force by crash training and rapid promotion (Devanna, 1990). Pay systems were tied to advancement rather than performance in the present job. Even marginal employees, who lacked experience, were promoted, which gave rise to the popular 1960s term the Peter Principle (Bardwick, 1986).

North America's period of economic expansion lasted from approximately 1950 to the mid-1970s (Bailey, 1990; Bardwick, 1986). After the mid-1970s, rising fuel prices, the rise of other economic powers, and increasing global competition began to impact on North America's previously solo global empire. Competitive markets have become a fact of life for Canadian industry and more of that competition is coming from non-Canadian or global sources (Betcherman, et al., 1994). Economic boom conditions had continued for long enough that many people's expectations about careers became centred around promotions and climbing the career ladder—Driver's (1985) linear career concept. The depression and wartime era busters' experiences can be contrasted with those of the large demographic group of baby boomers. Boomers are such a large demographic group that they are said to face more within-group competition for educational opportunities and for jobs. Like the busters preceding them, the baby boomers face an interaction effect between demographic and economic conditions. The interaction, however, is that of a large demographic group and a slow growing economy, the reverse situation that the depression and wartime era busters faced. The baby boom spanned a two-decade long period; it is important to realize that different birth years within this boom generation will have different labour force experiences. The boom period can be broken down into early, middle, and late periods. Early boomers may have faced conditions similar to the wartime busters immediately preceding them; middle and later boomers have faced a changing economic climate when they entered the labour force.

From where are one's career expectations derived? It is likely that career aspirations are derived from parents, the preceding generation, and from societal norms. Thus, if the boomers and current busters get their career expectations from their parents and those groups that precede them, they will expect to have what the depression and wartime busters had in terms of careers. Bardwick contends that, "Their (depression and wartime busters') careers form the model for the expectations" (1986, p. 21) of the groups following them. The boomers and current busters are a more educated group than those who preceded them (Betcherman et al., 1994); thus, it is not unusual to suppose that these current groups, now mostly in their twenties and thirties, expect to surpass their parent's career successes. Current groups just entering the labour force, or in their early career stages, may not realize that part of the preceding group's career success was due to an interaction effect between being a small generation and enjoying an unprecedented period of economic expansion that lasted during a good part of their careers.

CHANGING FACTORS AFFECTING CAREER PATTERNS

Generally baby bust generations do well in their careers and earnings because they face less competition from fellow busters (Berger, 1989; Weeks, 1994). The caveat for the current busters is that they follow on the heels of a particularly large baby boom generation and they face economic conditions that are not as favourable as the ones that the depression and wartime era busters previously experienced. The baby boomers, especially the mid-to-late boomers, also face less favourable economic conditions as well as the typical generational crowding that accompanies large groups.

The factors of changing career patterns and the delayering thrust of firms are related. Linear career paths require tall organizational hierarchies. The standard linear career path of the postwar era has given way to more varied career patterns. The typical employment pattern for the postwar white-collar worker, the linear career path with regular promotions and stable employment (often with lifetime employment with one firm), is becoming less common (Bardwick, 1986; A. Bennett, 1990; Naisbitt & Aburdene, 1985). Flattening of the corporate structure results in a decline in mid-management positions and a related decline in promotions. The delayering thrust in organizations occurs due to technological change, increased global competition, and retrenchment during recessions. To cope with today's fast-paced economy the old style, rigid hierarchy has had to adapt to survive. Flatter organizational structures better suit today's fast-paced environment as they tend to have faster response time and more participatory management. Bardwick (1986) points out that the boomers are getting caught in this delayering thrust and are facing the end of promotions (plateauing) sooner because of their generational size. Careers today are more spiral careers with more horizontal movement (Egan, 1994).

Lifelong careers with one firm were quite common in many industries during the postwar decades. Currently this is rare for most firms. Egan (1994) acknowledges this in comparing the old and the new (largely unwritten) contracts that firms had with employees. While some may view the lack of lifelong careers with one firm as positive, others lament it as one more loss of employment stability. One positive point relating to today's firms is the workplace flexibility arrangements such as alternative worktime arrangements, leave programs, flexible benefit plans, and so forth. The increased flexibility on the part of firms reflects the fact that today's labour force is more diverse than the labour force of the 1950s and 1960s where a "one size fits all" benefits plan sufficed the mainly male work force. The recent attention to issues of work-family conflict addresses the fact that the work force now has a sizable female component (Higgins et al., 1992).

The depression and wartime era busters experienced a different rate of wage growth than today's boomers and busters. Real wage growth (changes in real or constant dollar wages) in Canada over the postwar period showed large gains especially in the 1950s and 1960s during the economic boom period (Rashid, 1994). Slower growth prevailed over the 1970s while the 1980s were largely stagnant years for a real wage growth rate of only two percent. In fact, Morisette (1995) points out that the real hourly wages of young workers have fallen substantially over the 1980s. Thus, those who worked in the immediate postwar decades experienced large wage increases and a general increase in the standard of living. The 42.5 percent wage increases over the decade of the 1950s (Rashid, 1994) is one reason why people look back fondly on this decade as a time of prosperity.

Another recent factor is rising skill requirements. Compared to a few decades ago, the "transition from school to work has become a more prolonged and complex process" (Krahn et al., 1993, p. 171). Almost every profession now requires more education, or a degree where none was required before. Fewer and fewer jobs require only high school (Dolan & Schuler, 1994). This is a key factor that is affecting youth today, and one main reason why they are slower to leave home (Boyd & Norris, 1995). Bellamy (1993) notes that high-school students realize that escalating credentialism would severely limit their futures if they did not participate in post-secondary education. Post-secondary enrolment soared among youths during the recent recession of the early 1990s as young people attempted to increase their credentials (Sunter, 1994). K. Bennett (1994) proposes that rising skill requirements are needed because of technological change, but others (O'Hara, 1993) view it as inflated credentialism mainly due to increased competition in the labour force (due to the large group of baby boomers). Both factors likely play a part. O'Hara (1993) gives the example of a psychologist now requiring a doctoral degree where before a master's degree was sufficient. The trend of rising skill requirements and the fact of spiral career paths have turned people into lifelong learners (Naisbitt & Aburdene, 1985).

People find these facts frightening and prefer to look forward to the future and say that things will get better for themselves and especially for their children. Ricard (1994) documents the tremendous optimism of Canadians in the early postwar period. Today, with increasing job insecurity, the recent recession, and the fact that wages are no further ahead after a decade, people are understandably not as optimistic as their postwar counterparts. But, Driver (1985) notes that people still cling to the ideal of the linear career path. A statement from a young graduate is informative. This 23-year-old woman, who after a cycle of unsatisfying jobs has just returned to school, stated her expectations following completion of her first degree (a bachelors): "I always believed that with my degree I would work my way up the corporate ladder of a large company, be taken care of in the way of a pension and benefits and then leave with a golden handshake" (Bacigalupo, 1993). Her expectations are for a linear career path, yet thus far she has experienced a transitory one. In her parents' early working days, any university degree was a ticket to a great job. Now with generational crowding (affecting the baby boomers and in some ways the recent busters too as they find the large group ahead of them seems to have taken all the jobs), rising credentialism, and more people than ever receiving post-secondary education, a degree is no longer a guarantee of a job. Her parents' career and life patterns came to be viewed as the norm, and became the expectations of young people. Bardwick (1986) points out that today's expectations are based on that extraordinary period in recent history of postwar economic expansion. Today's economic and demographic conditions do not allow those expectations of wage gains and upward mobility to be realized. The young graduate expects what her parents had, if not more, since she has more education that her parents. What her parents had was due, in part, to a unique combination of factors that are not present today. The careers that resulted from the interaction effect between economic and demographic factors of the postwar decades is perhaps an anomaly in this century.

CONCLUSIONS

Despite slower labour force growth with the work force entry of the baby bust generation, earlier predictions of a coming sellers' market for labour or a coming labour shortage have largely not materialized (Naisbitt & Aburdene, 1985). Current economic conditions (e.g., recent recession) are not the favourable ones of the immediate postwar decades in North America's so called heyday. Thus the current baby busters face much less buoyant economic conditions than their bust counterparts of the depression and wartime era. Current youth, though part of a bust group, follow on the heels of a very large boom generation. This often overlooked point will have an effect on the busters for most of their working lives. The school-to-work transition is becoming more complex in a more complicated and global workplace. Expectations of linear career paths and of rising standard of living (through rising real wages) need to be readjusted. Today's career paths will likely lead to more than one occupation over a working lifetime, challenging jobs at several workplaces, and lifelong learning.

References

Bacigalupo, N. (1993). Community-college enrolments booms. *Globe and Mail.* September 11, A4.

Bailey, T. (1990). Jobs of the future and the skills that they will require. *American Educator,* Spring, 10–15, 40–44.

Bardwick, J. (1986). *The plateauing trap.* New York: Amacom.

Bellamy, L.A. (1993). Life trajectories, action and negotiating the transition from high school. In P. Anisef & P. Axelrod (Eds.), *Transitions: Schooling and employment in Canada* (pp. 137–157). Toronto: Thompson Educational Publishing Inc.

Bennett, A. (1990). *The death of the organization man.* New York: William Morrow.

Bennett, K. (1994). Recent information on training. *Perspectives, 6 (1),* 22–24.

Berger, M.C. (1989). Demographic cycles, cohort size, and earnings. *Demography, 26* (2), 311–322.

Betcherman, G., McMullen, K., Leckie, N., & Caron, C. (1994). *The Canadian workplace in transition.* Kingston, ON: Industrial Relations Centre, Queen's University.

Boyd, M., & Norris, D. (1995). The cluttered nest revisited: Young adults at home in the 1990s (Working Paper). Centre for Study of Population, Florida State University, Tallahassee.

Devanna, M.A. (1990). Human resource management: Competitive advantage through people. In E.G. Collins and M.A. Devanna (eds.), *The portable MBA* (pp. 219-237). New York: John Wiley and Sons.

Dolan, S.L., & Schuler, R.S. (1994). *Personnel and human resource management in Canada* (2nd ed.). New York: Nelson.

Driver, M.J. (1985). Demographic and societal factors affecting the linear career crisis. *Canadian Journal of Administrative Studies, 2* (2), 245–263.

Egan, G. (1994). Hard times contract. *Management Today*, January, 48–50.

Farewell Fast Track. (1990). *Business Week.* December 10, 192–200.

Foot, D.K., & Venne, R.A. (1990). Population, pyramids and promotional prospects. *Canadian Public Policy, 16 (4)*, 387–398.

Galarneau, D. (1994). *Female baby boomers: A generation at work.* Ottawa: Statistics Canada and Prentice Hall.

Haupt, A., & Kane, T.T. (1991). *Population handbook: International edition* (3rd ed.). Washington, DC: Population Reference Bureau, Inc.

Higgins, C., Duxbury, L., & Lee, C. (1992). *Balancing work and family: A study of Canadian private sector employees.* London, ON: National Centre for Management Research and Development, The University of Western Ontario.

Kerr, D., & Ram, B. (1994). *Population dynamics in Canada.* Ottawa: Statistics Canada and Prentice Hall.

Krahn, H., Mosher, C., & Johnson, L.C. (1993). Panel studies of the transition from school to work: Some methodological considerations. In P. Anisef & P. Axelrod (Eds.), *Transitions: Schooling and employment in Canada* (pp. 169–187). Toronto: Thompson Educational Publishing Inc.

Morgan, N. (1981). *Nowhere to go? Possible consequences of the demographic imbalance in decision making groups of the federal public services.* Montréal: Institute for Research on Public Policy.

Morisette, R. (1995). Why has inequality in weekly earnings increased in Canada? Research Paper Series, No. 80, Analytical Studies Branch, Ottawa: Statistics Canada.

Naisbitt, J., & Aburdene, P. (1985). *Re-inventing the corporation.* New York: Warner Books.

Novak, M. (1988). *Aging and society: A Canadian perspective.* Scarborough, ON: Nelson Canada.

O'Hara, B. (1993). *Working harder isn't working.* Vancouver, BC: New Star Books.

Rashid, A. (1993). Seven decades of wage changes. *Perspectives, 5* (2), 9–21.

Ricard, F. (1994). [The Lyric Generation: The Life and Times of the Baby Boomers]. (D. Winkler, trans.). Toronto: Stoddart Publishing Company. (Originally published 1992).

Sunter, D. (1994). Youths—waiting it out. *Perspectives, 6 (1)*, 31–36.

Weeks, J.R. (1994). *Population: An introduction to concepts and issues* (5th ed.). Belmont, CA: Wadsworth.

PART II

Facilitating Transitions to Adulthood

6

Facilitating Transitions to Adulthood: Research and Policy Implications

Bryan Hiebert and Barbara Thomlison

Few would argue that adolescents today face a very different world than their parents faced when they were growing up. Nevertheless, in moving from adolescence to adulthood, young people are still expected to finish school, gain independence from their parents, and establish themselves as contributing members of society (Arnett & Taber, 1994; Chadsey-Rusch, Rusch, & O'Reilly, 1991; Mitchell & Gee, 1996). This involves simultaneous transitions in several domains: post-secondary education (or other work preparation training), labour force participation (or unemployment), independent living, marriage or cohabitation, and community living. Transition success is affected by many factors, including personal characteristics, gender, family influences, exposure to role models, economic status, cultural influences, and the economic viability of the community in which the person functions. Youth with unique characteristics, such as physical disabilities, learning disabilities, and differing cultural background, experience very different influences on their transitions (Arnett & Taber, 1994; Johnson, Bruininks, & Thurlow, 1987). This chapter overviews research regarding factors involved in adolescence-to-adulthood transitions, policy and program development implications for fostering successful transitions, and a research agenda for advancing the understanding of transition experiences.

SUMMARY OF THE RESEARCH

Transition from adolescence to adulthood is not an event. It is a repetitive, cyclical process, enacted across time, involving multiple domains, and subject to many environmental and individual influences. Chadsey-Rusch and colleagues (1991) identify employment, residence, and relationships as three primary domains in transition to adulthood. Employment transitions include school-to-work, as well as post-secondary, apprenticeship, other training experiences, and in some cases unemployment. Residential transitions involve gaining independence from parents and establishing a self-supporting abode. This transition often is delayed, especially for youth with handicaps; recent years have seen increases in boomerang children who return to their parent's home after a period of trying to make it on their own (Mitchell & Gee, 1996). Relational transitions involve establishing a social network which can offer companionship, encouragement, and support, in addition to courtship and marriage or cohabitation. Successful relational transitions require well developed social skills, which often are taken for granted, but seldom taught explicitly. Typically, transition is occurring in all domains simultaneously and difficulty in any one domain is likely to impact the others.

Adolescence occurs in a context (Spencer, Swanson, & Cunningham, 1991). Factors such as race, ethnicity, cultural customs, language, social views and practices, gender, sexual orientation, and physical or learning disabilities all combine to make the transition experiences of some adolescents very different from others. For example, Hill (1996) documents the multitude of transition barriers faced by youth with handicaps that do not exist for able-bodied young people. Chadsey-Rusch and colleagues (1991) report substantial differences in the factors promoting successful transitions for handicapped and nonhandicapped youth. Gabor, Thibodeau, and Manychief (1996) illustrate how native youth are torn between establishing their own cultural identity and integrating into the majority culture. Perron (1996) found that different ethnic groups experience transitions to post-secondary education in very different ways. There is no one pathway that is best for all youth; young people in differing contexts have very different transition experiences that require very different transition skills.

Gender is one over-arching contextual factor affecting adolescent transitions. Young men and young women in Canadian society have very different experiences (Martin, 1996). Adolescent boys and girls have diametrically different attributions for success and failure (Sayer, 1993) and considerable discrepancy exists between the career aspirations of young women and their career expectations (Geller, 1996; Sayer & Ellis, 1986). As a result, the skills needed to promote successful transitions to adulthood are likely to be different for adolescent males and females. However, there are few published reports documenting the differing skill sets young men and young women need to promote successful transitions. Instructional programs have been developed to sensitize high-school boys and girls to the restrictive effects of stereotyping on both sexes (Freeman & Balanchuk, 1994) and to expand the impact of positive role models on young women (Cahill, 1994). Alternately, some advocate judicial use of segregated programs to foster developing the strengths of young women (Varpalotai, 1996). Policy which supports the use of gender-related programs is needed to provide equal opportunity to both sexes.

A recent longitudinal study of Canadian young people (Amundson, Borgen, & Tench, in press) found that they were optimistic about leaving high school, entering the career area of their choice, and taking on adult roles that were challenging and personally satisfying. Follow-up 9 and 18 months after graduation, however, indicated that young people believed high school did not prepare them for the current labour market reality and both their career and personal lives were in a state of change and uncertainty. They reported that supportive family and friends, success in school, satisfying leisure activities, personal achievements, and having some opportunity to earn money all assisted the transition from high school (Borgen & Amundson, 1995). Factors that hindered post-high-school transitions were relationship problems, financial difficulties, lack of career direction, being unemployed, lack of satisfying work, being unable to enter their chosen post-secondary program, and trouble adjusting to demands of post-secondary education (Borgen & Amundson,

1995). Furthermore, youth from disadvantaged or poor families were less likely to experience successful transitions (Roberts & Parsell, 1992). The labour force attachment of youth and young adults was particularly affected by parent educational level and aspirations (Perron, 1996), employment status, and employment-related role modelling (Geller, 1996; Martin, 1996). The transition experiences of youth are embedded in the social and personal contexts in which they live and attempts to facilitate youth transitions need to address a broad array of factors.

POLICY IMPLICATIONS

Youth can not be categorized as an age group (Arnett & Taber, 1994). Therefore, transition needs to be viewed from a life-course perspective. There is much individual variation in the speed and pace of transition processes. Intervention needs to take into account the people factors and the contextual factors—different kinds of interventions are needed for different kinds of people in different kinds of contexts. Moreover, intervention needs to be developmental, proactive, and preventive, not just remedial. It needs to look at people's capacities and to let people know when they are doing OK. Interventions need to begin early because adolescent-to-adult transitions begin pre-youth. To be preventive, intervention needs to begin before the onset of the problem. Multidisciplinary, multisectoral, and multidimensional approaches need to be developed in order to embrace the broad range of personal and contextual factors involved in successful transitions. Policy needs to allow for diversity and to support multi-component programming at the community level where unique experiences and contextual factors can be addressed adequately. Communities need to be seen as cultural, not necessarily geographic, and communities need to be inclusive, seeing the strengths of all people, even those in the margins. Furthermore, programs need to be planned, supported, and managed in order to succeed.

Some specific policy themes have been advanced. Powers (1994) suggests that social policy aimed at creating jobs, training programs, and encouraging school enrolment are important for all youth, but especially for nonwhite young people. Spencer and others (1991) point to the need for revisions in school curricula that offset socioeconomic disadvantages. They also emphasize the importance of constructing social networks and support systems for minority youth, especially minority males, and for support for minority parents to help them assist children with the dual transition from adolescence to adulthood and minority to majority culture. Chadsey-Rusch and others (1991) focus on the need for policy to support increased services, advocacy, and social support for youth with disabilities, and for revised school curriculum with greater emphasis on attitude development, teaching social skills, increasing self-esteem, and empowering youth with disabilities.

Schools are seen as playing a central role in adolescent transitions. Career planning in schools must begin at an early age, so that students can explore alternatives, discuss their aspirations and expectations, and so schools might collaborate more closely with families to help youth and their families develop realistic plans for today's job market (Johnson et al., 1987). Non-academic training routes, such as vocational training, need to be valued as honourable and desirable, not as second-class alternatives to an academic career path. Business is calling for a broader range of employability skills where personal management and teamwork are just as important as academics (Conference Board of Canada, 1993). Good Canadian program resources have been developed (Hutchinson & Freeman, 1994; Jamieson, Paterson, Krupa, MacEachen, & Topping, 1993; Robb, 1995) and field test results are promising (Hutchinson, 1995; Jamieson & Paterson, 1995), but there needs to be more incentives for using such teaching approaches in the schools (Spencer, et al., 1991).

Entering adulthood is a complex process that requires a coherent, consistent, and integrated policy framework that spans schools, families, and the adult service delivery system (Johnson, et al., 1987; Turcotte & Assogba, 1996). Such a framework needs to set clear policy goals, establish explicit eligibility criteria, articulate consistent standards for service delivery, develop a shared language across jurisdictions, and obtain consensus on the type and scope of service provided at each level. This will require more than a simple fine-tuning of existing services and programs. A coherent policy framework that incorporates greater consistency across public programs in philosophy, goals, standards, and practices is necessary if greater coordination and more effective delivery of services is to be achieved.

RESEARCH AGENDA

The approach in policy, program, and research needs to be refocused to study the factors contributing to success, resiliency, an internal locus of control, a sense of inclusion, and community spirit. Present policy, program, and research has been primarily problem centered, dealing with individual risk factors and societal risk conditions that are barriers to successful transition. Instead, more attention needs to be paid to solutions in order to determine what works. Most youth are doing OK, many youth could use some help, some youth need very little help, and a small number of youth need intensive help. The research focus should be on how to facilitate success, keeping in mind that there are multiple levels of success and success may look quite different to different people. The approach needs to be iterative to discover how influences change across time.

Multiple measures should be encouraged and collaborative evidence gathering should be fostered, including biographical, ethnographic, critical incidence methods, self-monitored data, and client logs and check lists, in addition to survey data. Informal data gathering techniques need to be legitimized to capture the experiential processes involved. Research should be interdisciplinary, multisectoral, and collaborative across all people with a stake in the conduct or the outcome of the research (researchers, consumers, practitioners, policy makers, funders) keeping in mind that the most important consumers are the youth themselves.

Several areas of study are important for future research. First is a need to study self-as-subject, in order to better understand how people learn, cope, and survive; how some people develop a strong sense of personal agency (a sense that they have a strong influence on the future course of events in their lives) while others do not, and the role of spirituality in helping people develop a sense of meaning in life. Research needs to do a better job of hearing individual voices and then building a choir to amplify the message. Second, more research in basic human development is needed to better understand the factors contributing to positive transition outcomes and how people tell their own stories and in doing so construct their own identities. Both prospective and retrospective studies are needed and longitudinal studies are especially important in understanding these factors. Third, there is a need for research directed at model development in the area of career interventions. There is a substantial body of research attesting to the effectiveness of career guidance (Spokane & Hawks, 1990) but there is very little research identifying the factors contributing to that success. Fourth, the preparation of service providers needs to become a legitimate focus of research, in order to develop more effective ways to prepare counsellors, social workers, and others working with youth in transitions. Finally, program evaluation needs to be an integral part of program implementation. What is needed is longitudinal program evaluation research that extends beyond determining that participants believe they have been positively affected by the program, to display evidence that the program in question is responsible for the change in participants, and to determine what components of the program are responsible for that change (Chadsey-Rusch, et al., 1991). Policies supporting the type of research outlined above will greatly assist in identifying the factors and influences involved in facilitating successful youth-to-adulthood transitions.

Research, policy, and practice need to better inform each other. There are gaps in policy, research, and practice, as well as gaps between policy and research, research and practice, and practice and policy. Research frequently does not get expressed in policy, policy does not always get translated into practice, and modes of practice often are not considered when developing policy and planning research. There is a need for greater coherence and continuity across sectors and departments primarily responsible for youth, namely, health, social services, education, and career development. There is a need for evidence-based decision making and therefore a need to identify what supports are necessary to conduct research that informs policy.

Research results must be marketed to policy makers, funders, practitioners, consumers/clients, employers, and the general public, as well as other researchers. Researchers, practitioners, and policy makers must be involved in political action that will inform and influence social legislation. This will involve disseminating research results in places read by stakeholder groups and in meaningful and practical terms that readers can understand. For academics, this may involve educating administrators and tenure committees regarding the need for creative dissemination, collaborative multi-disciplinary research, marketing research results, the difficulty of writing for a nontraditional audience, and the difficulty and importance of writing for a lay audience.

CONCLUSION

It is necessary to create a milieu where society values youth for who they are (not just their revenue potential) and provides a supportive environment that creates a sense of belonging for all youth—one that helps young people have meaning and purpose in life, a sense of identity and pride in themselves and their communities, and personal aspirations and a belief in self that fosters success. The educational, social, recreational, health, and economic sectors need to be partners in providing training, counselling, job opportunities, and other meaningful opportunities for self-fulfilment and support. This will help provide access to human and financial resources which help youth make the multiple transitions involved in moving to adulthood in a way that is congruent with their bio-cultural and spiritual potential and develops autonomy, freedom, and interdependence.

Transitions are complex processes that are non-linear and last a lifetime. They are mediated experiences, therefore, amenable to influence. Individual and social factors contribute positively and negatively in optimizing transition experiences. We need to strengthen and reinforce individual and community resources, while minimizing the threats, barriers, and impeding forces. This can only be done if we recognize the new societal context and develop comprehensive approaches that meet individual and group needs. The pay off for helping youth make successful transitions to fulfilling and productive lives is worth the investment.

References

Amundson, N.E., Borgen, W.A., & Tench, E. (in press). Personality and intelligence in career education and vocational guidance counselling. In D.H. Saklofske & M. Zeidner (Eds.), *International handbook of personality and intelligence*. New York: Plenum.

Arnett, J.J., & Taber, S. (1994). Adolescence terminable and interminable: When does adolescence end? *Journal of Youth and Adolescence, 23,* 517–537.

Borgen, W.A., & Amundson, N.E. (1995). Models of adolescent transition. In B. Hiebert (Ed.), *Exemplary career development programs and practices: The best from Canada.* Greensboro, NC: ERIC/CASS Clearinghouse.

Cahill, M. (1994). *Shaping your future: Towards the occupational integration of Women.* Toronto: Lugus.

Chadsey-Rusch, J., Rusch, F.R., & O'Reilly, M.F. (1991). Transition from school to integrated communities. *RASE: Remedial And Special Education, 12* (6), 23–33.

Conference Board of Canada. (1993). *Employability skills profile: What are employers looking for?* Ottawa, ON: The Conference Board of Canada.

Freeman, J.G., & Balanchuk, M.L. (1994). *CareerWorld.* Toronto: Trifolium Books.

Gabor, P., Thibodeau, S., & Manychief, S. (1996). Taking flight? The transition experiences of native youth. In B. Galaway & J. Hudson (Eds.), *Youth in transition: Perspectives on research and policy.* Toronto: Thompson Educational Publishing.

Geller, G. (1996). Educational, occupational, and family aspirations of women: A longitudinal study. In B. Galaway & J. Hudson (Eds.), *Youth in transition: Perspectives on research and policy.* Toronto: Thompson Educational Publishing.

Hill, J.L. (1996). Adults with disabilities: Barriers to post-secondary education. In B. Galaway, & J. Hudson (Eds.) *Youth in transition: Perspectives on research and policy.* Toronto: Thompson Educational Publishing.

Hutchinson, N.L. (1995). Career counselling of youth with learning disabilities. In B. Hiebert (Ed.), *Exemplary career development programs and practices: The best from Canada.* Greensboro, NC: ERIC/CASS Clearinghouse.

Hutchinson, N.L., & Freeman, J.G. (1994). *Pathways* (5 volumes). Toronto: Nelson Canada.

Jamieson, M., & Paterson, J. (1995). Career counselling for young people with physical disabilities: An introduction to thresholds In B. Hiebert (Ed.), *Exemplary career development programs and practices: The best from Canada.* Greensboro, NC: ERIC/CASS Clearinghouse.

Jamieson, M., Paterson, J., Krupa, T., MacEachen, E., & Topping, A. (1993). *Thresholds: Enhancing the career development strategies of young people with physical disabilities.* Ottawa, ON: Canadian Guidance and Counselling Foundation.

Johnson, D.R., Bruininks, R.H., & Thurlow, M.L. (1987). Meeting the challenge of transition service planning through improved interagency cooperation. *Exceptional Children, 53,* 522–530.

Martin, F.E. (1996). Tales of transition: Leaving public care. In B. Galaway & J. Hudson (Eds.), *Youth in transition: Perspectives on research and policy.* Toronto: Thompson Educational Publishing.

Mitchell, B.A., & Gee, E.M. (1996). Young adults returning home: Implications for social policy. In B. Galaway & J. Hudson (Eds.), *Youth in transition: Perspectives on research and policy.* Toronto: Thompson Educational Publishing.

Perron, J. (1996). Ethnicity and educational aspirations of high-school students. In B. Galaway & J. Hudson (Eds.), *Youth in transition: Perspectives on research and policy.* Toronto: Thompson Educational Publishing.

Powers, D.A. (1994). Transitions into idleness among white, black, and Hispanic youth: Some determinants and policy implications of weak labour force attachment. *Sociological Perspectives, 37,* 183–201.

Roberts, K., & Parsell, G. (1992). Entering the labour market in Britain: The survival of traditional opportunity structures. *Sociological Review, 40,* 726–753.

Robb, M. (1995). ENGAGE: A career development-based, learning-to-learn program for youth, parents, & teachers. In B. Hiebert (Ed.), *Exemplary career development programs and practices: The best from Canada.* Greensboro, NC: ERIC/CASS Clearinghouse.

Sayer, L.A. (1993). *The a cappella papers: Careers and future plans of young women in Canada.* Ottawa, ON: Canadian Teachers' Federation.

Sayer, L., & Ellis, D. (1986). *When I grow up … Career expectations and aspirations of Canadian school children.* Ottawa, ON: Women's Bureau, Labour Canada.

Spencer, M.B., Swanson, D.P., & Cunningham, M. (1991). Ethnicity, ethnic identity, and competence formation: Adolescent transition and cultural transformation. *Journal of Negro Education, 60,* 366–387.

Spokane, A.R., & Hawks, B.K. (1990). Annual review: Practice and research in career counselling and development, 1989. *The Career Development Quarterly, 39,* 98–128.

Turcotte, D., & Assogba, Y. (1996). Range and limits of employability programs for youth: A case study of Québec's Outaouais. In B. Galaway & J. Hudson (Eds.), *Youth in transition: Perspectives on research and policy.* Toronto: Thompson Educational Publishing.

Varpalotai, A. (1996). Canadian girls in transition to womanhood. In B. Galaway & J. Hudson (Eds.), *Youth in transition: Perspectives on research and policy.* Toronto: Thompson Educational Publishing.

7

Young Adults Returning Home: Implications for Social Policy

Barbara A. Mitchell and Ellen M. Gee

The transition to adulthood encompasses a number of important life events including school completion, departure from the parental home, labour force entry, and marriage. Not all of these life changes, of course, are prerequisite for adult status attainment (Hogan & Astone, 1986). Furthermore, these transitions do not occur simultaneously; considerable individual variation has been found in the relative timing of these life course transitions (Marini, 1984). Nevertheless, they contain a common thread—movement from a situation of economic dependence on one's family of origin to economic independence apart from one's parental family. Considerable research has been performed on home-leaving as an important aspect of the transition to adulthood (Aquilino, 1991; Avery, Goldscheider & Speare, 1992; Goldscheider & DaVanzo, 1985, 1989; Goldscheider, Thornton & Young-DeMarco, 1993; Mitchell, 1994; Mitchell, Wister & Burch, 1989). The initial impetus for this research originated from the development of a period of independent living prior to marriage in the post-World War II years (Goldscheider & Goldscheider, 1987). In the last decade, however, it has become apparent that departure from the parental home is not necessarily a discrete, all-or-none phenomenon. Children may leave home and then return, sometimes several times. Children are not necessarily gone for good.

This is part of a general trend toward an increasing ambiguity or disorderliness in life course transitions in western societies. Delayed marriage within the last generation has played an important part in the overall loosening of what has been considered a tight package of transitions (Skolnick, 1987). Furthermore, increasing cohabitation, especially among younger persons, makes the transition to and from married status less clear, and retirement is no longer necessarily a one-time-only event (McPherson, 1990). Thus, many life course transitions, including the transition to adulthood, are taking on the quality of a process, rather than an event. On the other hand, the phenomenon of adult children returning home represents an exception to an overall trend of increasing non-family living arrangements among the unmarried (DaVanzo & Goldscheider, 1990).

Research on home-leaving focuses on the timing of departure from the parental home and on characteristics of both children and parents. For example, Aquilino (1991) found that family structure affects the timing of home-leaving, especially for young women. Family income affects home-leaving differentially depending on route out of the home (marriage versus premarital independent living) and on age (Avery, et al., 1992); further, sex of the child, religiosity and ethnicity are related to home-leaving behaviour (Goldscheider & Goldscheider, 1988; Mitchell, et al., 1989). In contrast, the research on young adults returning home tends to focus on characteristics of children only, such as age, sex, marital status, personal income, labour force status, educational attainment, and ambivalence about capacity to play adult roles (DaVanzo & Goldscheider, 1990; Grigsby & McGowan, 1986; Schnaiberg & Goldenberg, 1989). Little is known about the relative importance of the constellation of factors associated with boomerang living arrangements, and no research on the Canadian situation has been undertaken. According to the 1991 Canadian census, about 40% of unmarried men and 30% of unmarried women aged 25–29 lived at home in the 1980s, an increase of about 10% from the 1970s. It is impossible to know the proportions of young adults who return home because Statistics Canada data do not distinguish between those who do not leave home until later ages, and those who leave and then return.

The determinants of returning home among a sample of Canadian young adults are examined in this chapter. Three questions are addressed. What is the distribution of number of returns by sex, age, and marital status? What is the distribution of reasons and the relative importance of economic versus non-economic factors in returning-home behaviour? What are the determinants of economic versus non-economic reasons for returning to the parental home? Finally, implications of the findings for social policy in light of increasing residential dependency among Canada's young adults are considered

RESEARCH METHODS

This research is based on a sub-sample of 420 Greater Vancouver area families in which both a parent and a child were interviewed, separately, by telephone. Eligibility criteria for inclusion in the study were ability to communicate in English and age (19–35 for children and 35–60 for parents). The interviewed child had to have left home for at least six months and returned to live at home for at least six months, with the last return occurring within the last five years. The returner sample includes persons both currently residing (n = 120) and no longer residing (n = 98) in the parental home (total n = 218 returners). This chapter is based solely on the boomerang sample.

Random-digit dialling (RDD) was primarily used to recruit participants for the study. Interviewers used a table of random numbers to select phone numbers from the Greater Vancouver telephone directory. Snowball referrals from random recruits and replies to local newspaper advertisements (constituting less than 10% of the overall sample) were also used. A response rate of approximately 50% (of all contacted eligible households) was achieved (two family members had to participate in the study). The research instrument was an interview consisting of differing versions. Each respondent was asked the identical set of demographic and socio-economic questions. Variants of the interview were needed for parents and children and for the differing living arrangement histories. The interviews ranged from 30 to 45 minutes in duration.

The sample includes more females than males. Among the boomerang children, 70% (135) are female and 35% (83) are male. Similarly, more mothers (n = 156, 72%) than fathers (n = 62, 28%) participated in the study. The mean duration of time (in years) between first home-leaving and first return was approximately two years. The mean age at returning was 21.2 years and did not differ by sex. The average current age of the respondent parent was 53.1 years. Representativeness of the sub-samples is not known since national data on the distribution of the two types of children in the general population are not available. American research has reported, however, that young men are more likely to return home than young women (Schnaiberg & Goldenberg, 1989; DaVanzo & Goldscheider, 1990). If that is the case in Canada as well, this sample of adult children over-represents females.

RESULTS

Seventy-two percent of the young adults had returned home only once (a minimum six-month period after leaving home); 6% had returned home twice, 13% three times, 6% four times, and 3% had five returns home. The number of returns was examined controlling for sex, age group, and marital status. The only statistically significant relationship was between number of returns to the parental home and age (Tau b = .38, p < .01). Adult children who are currently aged 30–34 are more likely to be multiple returners than those aged 18–24. Age-related selectivities are likely involved here, however, given that the sample of returners includes persons whose last return was as much as five years ago. Statistically significant relationships were not found between number of returns and sex and between number of returns and marital status.

Table 7.1 presents the distribution of the main reason for the last return home. Economic reasons clearly take precedence over non-economic reasons. Economic reasons account for about 81% of the total reasons for returning home; 26% reported that they had boomeranged because of financial problems, 19% returned to save money, 13% stated that they returned due to transitional or temporary reasons such as finished travelling, and 13% returned for school-related reasons such as to attend university. Only 17% of all reasons for returning fall into a non-economic category. Nine percent reported that they returned home because of psychological factors; examples include wanting the companionship of parents or being "not ready to live on their own." Only 4% returned home because their parents needed help, and 4% stated that the most important reason for returning home was their own health problems.

Logistic regression was used to examine the determinants of economic versus non-economic reasons for returning home. Non-economic reasons are coded as 0, and economic ones are coded as 1. Table 7.2 shows the results of the logistic regression for two models: parental variables (Model 1) and both parental and child variables (Model 2). Regression coefficients, their standard error, a Wald statistic, and the level of statistical significance are given for each contrast of the independent variable. The coding and frequencies of all independent variables is in the Appendix.

Youth returning home to a single-parent family are less likely (odds ratio = .38) to state economic reasons than those from biological families (B = –0.96, Wald = 4.53, p < .05). The other family type contrast (step/biological) is not

Table 7.1: Primary Reason for Returning Home Last Time

Economic Reasons

Go to School	28	12.8%
To Save Money	42	19.3%
Financial Problems	57	26.1%
Housing Costs	10	4.6%
Relationship Ended	11	5.0%
Transitional/Temp. Reason	29	13.3%
Sub-Total	177	81.2%

Non-Economic Reasons

Psychological	20	9.2%
Health of Child	8	3.7%
Parent Need	9	4.1%
Sub-Total	37	17.0%
Missing Observations	4	1.8%
Total	218	100.0%

Reasons in each category include: Go to School (wanted to go to school, close to school); Save Money (save money, close to work); Financial Problems (unemployed, poor salaried job, business failure, roommate problems, needed more space); Housing Costs (housing costs too high); Relationship Ended (needed a place to stay because of an abusive relationship, after spouse died or because of a relationship break-up); Transitional/Temporary Reason (finished travelling, school or work, temporary until job starts or until accommodation available, temporary no other place to go); Psychological (wanted companionship of parents, not ready to live on own, comforts of home); Health of Child (illness/disability/injury of child); Parent Need (parent's marriage/relationship broke-up, illness/injury of parent, parent(s) needed help [general] and with care of other children).

statistically significant. Also, fathers' and mothers' occupational prestige, the responding parent's education, and parental household income are not statistically significant. In addition, the overall model is not statistically significant. When the child variables are entered into the second model, the single/biological contrast is no longer statistically significant. However, youth who return to a step-family environment are about 7.6 times less likely (odds ratio = .13) to have done so for economic reasons than those returning to a biological configuration ($B = -2.06$, Wald = 6.19, $p < .01$). The other parental variables are not statistically significant.

Previous research finds earlier ages at home-leaving in step-families than in two-parent, still-married households (White & Booth, 1985; Mitchell, Wister, & Burch, 1989). Furthermore, Bianchi (1987) finds that step-family environments are less likely to support the residential dependence of step-children past the age of 18, possibly because the presence of stepchildren at home can create stress, conflict or uneasiness. Step-parents may not support returning home in one's twenties to save money or to attend school (economic reasons) which

Table 7.2: Logistic Regression of Reasons for Returning Home and Parental (Model 1) and Child (Model 2) Variables

	MODEL 1				MODEL 2			
	B	**SE**	**Wald**	**Odds Ratio**	**B**	**SE**	**Wald**	**Odds Ratio**
PARENTAL VARIABLES								
Family Type	-	-	6.13*	-	-	-	6.78*	-
Single	-0.96	0.45	4.53*	0.38	-0.81	0.58	1.92	-
Step	-1.14	0.68	3.28	-	-2.06	0.83	6.19**	0.13
Bio. (ref)	-	-	-	-	-	-	-	-
Father's Prestige	-	-	0.56	-	-	-	0.55	-
Low	0.45	0.68	0.44	-	-0.41	0.79	0.26	-
Medium	0.28	0.46	0.38	-	0.12	0.55	0.04	-
High (ref)	-	-	-	-	-	-	-	-
Mother's Prestige	-	-	0.43	-	-	-	0.07	-
Low	-0.31	0.99	0.96	-	-0.31	1.16	0.07	-
Medium	0.18	0.43	0.19	-	-0.06	0.55	0.01	-
High (ref)	-	-	-	-	-	-	-	-
Parental Education	-	-	1.24	-	-	-	2.07	-
Less H.S.	0.70	0.76	0.84	-	1.15	1.01	1.30	-
H.S./ some P.S	0.40	0.44	0.84	-	0.74	0.59	1.60	-
P.S. (ref)	-	-	-	-	-	-	-	-
Household Income								
<= $39,000	-	-	1.15	-	-	-	1.64	-
$40,000	-0.43	0.60	0.52	-	-0.96	0.80	1.43	-
$80,000+ (ref)	-0.52	0.49	1.14	-	-0.79	0.68	1.32	-
	-	-	-	-	-	-	-	-
Constant	1.28	0.41	9.80*					

Model Chi Square = 9.12, p = .52

	B	SE	Wald	Odds Ratio	B	SE	Wald	Odds Ratio
CHILD VARIABLES								
Gender								
Female					-0.89	0.54	2.69	-
Male					-	-	-	-
Religiosity					-	-	3.34	-
Rarely					-	-	-	-
Sometimes					-1.15	0.63	3.34	-
Regularly					-0.30	0.77	0.15	-

Table 7.2: Logistic Regression of Reasons for Returning Home and Parental (Model 1) and Child (Model 2) Variables— _Continued_

	MODEL 1				MODEL 2			
	B	**SE**	**Wald**	**Odds Ratio**	**B**	**SE**	**Wald**	**Odds Ratio**
Ethnic Orgin					-	-	0.85	-
Other Eur.					0.37	0.61	0.37	-
Other					-0.44	0.75	0.34	-
Commonwealth (ref)					-	-	-	-
Age Group					-	-	7.56*	-
18-24					-	-	-	-
25-29					-0.85	0.59	2.09	-
30-34					-1.82	0.66	7.56**	0.16
Marital Status					-	-	3.02	-
Never Married					-0.81	0.96	0.71	-
Ever Married					-2.17	1.25	2.99	-
Married/C.L. (ref)					-	-	-	-
Reason Leaving					-	-	2.72	-
Form Relationship					-0.63	0.83	0.56	-
Work					-0.28	0.79	0.12	-
Conflict					-1.22	0.77	2.47	-
School					-0.65	0.78	0.69	-
Other					-0.19	0.85	0.05	-
Independence (ref)					-	-	-	-
Main Activity					-	-	5.08	-
Looking for Work					1.09	1.18	0.83	-
Student					-0.38	0.54	0.49	-
Other					-1.42	0.73	3.70*	0.24
Employed (ref)					-	-	-	-
Constant					2.17	1.27	2.92	-

Model Chi Square = 35.83, p < .05

*p < .05
**p < .01
***p < .001
B = Regression Coefficient, SE = Standard Error, Bio. = Both Biological Parents,
H.S. = High School, P.S. = Post-secondary, C.L. = Common Law Union

may not be viewed as legitimate reasons for prolonged dependency. Conversely, step-families may approve of returning situations if the young adult had left home unexpectedly at a young age after a stormy departure and was not psychologically prepared to be launched as an adult (Gee, Mitchell & Wister, 1995). Children aged 30–34 are also less likely (odds ratio = .16) to provide an economic reason for returning home than boomerang kids aged 18–24 (B = –1.82, Wald = 7.56, p < .01). As young adults enter into their thirties, they complete more of the transitions which mark the passage to adulthood—they finish school, start full-time jobs, and begin to earn enough money to support themselves. Thus, it is not surprising that age, which proxies the likelihood that school has been completed and that the work force has been joined, is related to returning home for non-economic reasons.

Finally, youths who reported that their main activity was other than being a student, working, or looking for work at the time of their return were less likely to return home for economic reasons than the employed reference category (B = –1.42, Wald = 3.70, p < .05, odds ratio = .24). Other types of main activities probably relate to non-economic reasons for returning. For example, a youth who was ill or injured (and unable to work) would be classified as doing something other than working, going to school, or looking for work. He or she would probably return home to receive parental care or to enjoy the comforts of home while recuperating. No other relationships are statistically significant. The overall model is statistically significant.

SUMMARY AND POLICY IMPLICATIONS

Most young adults who return home to live with their parents for a period of six months or more do so only once. Not surprisingly, multiple returners tend to be older in age. The vast majority of boomerang kids return home for economic reasons. A number of these young adults have experienced economic hardship directly as the result of a tough economic climate, but a substantial number returned home to advance financially or to attend school. A surprising number of young adults indicate that they could afford to live independently of their parents by renting an apartment. They prefer, however, to live at home and save money for the future. Many of these children express a desire to continue maintaining a comfortable standard of living; living at home is viewed as a means to facilitate this goal. The family home appears to serve as a valuable resource or home base for many young adults who require a place to stay after completing transitional or temporary roles, such as travelling. This supports previous American research on this topic (DaVanzo & Goldscheider, 1990).

Current socio-economic conditions may be largely responsible for the increased propensity of young adults to return to the parental home. The common presumption that high youth unemployment, poverty, and high housing costs are largely responsible for the increased co-residence of parents and their children is overly-simplistic. Demographic changes, such as delayed marriage and family formation, educational inflation, current economic conditions, and youths' attempts to conserve resources all appear to contribute to increasing numbers of refilled nests. Multivariate analysis was used to investigate the association between returning home for economic versus non-economic reasons and the characteristics of both parents and children. Child characteristics are more important than parental characteristics. Young adults under 30 are more likely to return for economic reasons compared to older returners. Stating a main activity other than working, going to school, or looking for work is also based primarily on non-economic reasons. Returns to non-intact families are motivated predominantly by non-economic needs.

These findings have implications for social policy. The family home appears to represent an increasingly utilized type of safety net at this stage of the life course. Many young adults cannot establish themselves in independent residences—a transition which, over the past few decades, has been widely considered to be one of the major tasks of normal adult development (Schaie & Willis, 1986). Previous research finds that children from poorer homes (as operationalized by father's occupational prestige) are more likely to return home than children from more well-off families (Gee, Mitchell, & Wister, 1995). Specific types of family environments, however, may also play an important role in returning home, regardless of factors such as family material resources. Returning home for economic reasons may be supported (even welcomed) by some families, but not by other family types. This finding points to the potency of the family in prescribing how and when children achieve full adult status. Families may establish their own social scripts or normative guidelines regulating the entry of children in and out of the household. For some, a revolving door simply does not exist. Some young adults may face short- and long-term disadvantage in educational and labour markets if they do not have the opportunity to return home. An inability to co-reside in the parental home while attending university or to save money can widen the gap between groups of young adults, perpetuating social inequality. Not being able to return to the security and comforts of home could have a devastating effect on the lives of young adults who are not psychologically prepared to be launched as adults.

This study was limited to the Vancouver area; the differential ability of families to take in their adult children may have a regional dimension. Looker (1993) highlights how the transition to adulthood in rural areas is quite different than in urban cities. Youth living in rural areas may not have the option of residing at home after high school, either to work or while attending post-secondary institutions. Thus, economically depressed areas will become even more economically stagnant if their young adults are unable to benefit from the advantages in launching into adulthood experienced by their counterparts in other areas. Conversely, for those who do return, " ... forced financial and emotional dependency and a concomitant erosion of rights and social status" can blur the distinction between adult and young adult (Côté & Allahar, 1994, p. 64–65). Children must wait longer before they are fully recognized as adults, and " ... must spend more time in a homelife over which they exert less than full control" (Boyd & Pryor, 1989, p. 19). This change in the way young people come of age contributes to a process whereby youths have become disenfranchised, and socially and economically marginalized (Côté & Allahar, 1994). A delay in the transition to independence can create feelings of frustration and a sense of failure (Norris & Tindale, 1994).

The trend toward privatization in the Canadian welfare state affects youth in transition. Policy inattention to young adults contains an implicit assumption that their families will and should look after them. Rhetoric and assumptions are that the family is a private institution that should be shielded from state intervention. The reality, of course, is that the state has a substantial investment in the way that families operate (Ursel, 1992). If families do not care for their own, the state is left to deal with the costs. With rising federal and provincial deficits, and ongoing and anticipated cuts in social spending, it is convenient for the state to leave the problems surrounding transition to adulthood to the older generation of family members. The privatization of an already private institution seems eminently defensible in the current economic and ideological climate. However, families vary in their ability and willingness to assist in the early adult life of their children. The result is a widening gap in social and economic advantage in early adulthood, a differential that tends only to get larger with the passage of time. Thus, the seeds of increasing social inequality are being planted.

Both youth who experience prolonged dependency on their families and those who face economic disadvantage because they are unable to reap the benefit of parental assistance run the risk of economic marginalization. They can easily come to be at the mercy of employers offering low-paying, dead-end jobs with minimum benefits. Labour policy that fails to recognize the changed (and varied) family circumstances of today's young adults will feed into this economic marginalization and could reinforce it if the connections between family and labour for young adults remain invisible.

Legislation and programs must be adjusted to more equitably meet the needs of young adults. What kinds of policies are needed to help young adults? Approaches include alleviating youth poverty and unemployment; widespread creation of work programs, including job counselling, training, and placement; a fair distribution of national income to ensure that employed young adults receive a sufficient wage, job security, and benefits; providing government-sponsored student incomes, loans and grants for students to live independently of parents, and the creation of affordable housing. Community-based organizations are also needed to provide information, resources, and socio-cultural activities to young adults. Implementation of these measures could have a large-scale positive impact on the lives of today's young adults in ways that would benefit them, the local community, and Canadian society as a whole.

References

Aquilino, W.S. (1991). Family structure and home-leaving: A further specification of the relationship. *Journal of Marriage and the Family, 53,* 999–1010.

Avery, R., Goldscheider, F., & Speare Jr., A. (1992). Feathered nest/gilded cage: Parental income and leaving home in the transition to adulthood. *Demography, 29,* 375–388.

Bianchi, S.M. (1987). Living at home: Living arrangements in the 1980s. Paper presented at the Annual Meeting of the American Sociological Association, Illinois.

Boyd, M., & Pryor, E.T. (1989). Young adults living in their parents' homes. *Canada Social Trends,* Summer, 17–19.

Côté, J.E., & Allahar, A.L. (1994). *Generation on hold: Coming of age in the late twentieth century.* Toronto: Stoddart.

DaVanzo, J., & Goldscheider, F.K. (1990). Coming home again: Returns to the parental home of young adults. *Population Studies, 44,* 241–255.

Gee, E.M., Mitchell, B.A., & Wister, A.V. (1995, March). Returning to the parental "nest:" An examination of Canadian data. Paper presented at the Warren Kalbach Conference on Current Issues and Research in Population, University of Alberta.

Goldscheider, C., & Goldscheider, F.K. (1987). Moving out and marriage: What do young adults expect? *American Sociological Review, 52,* 278–285.

Goldscheider, C., & Goldscheider, F.K. (1988). Ethnicity, religiosity and leaving home: The structural and cultural bases of traditional family values. *Sociological Forum, 3,* 525–547.

Goldscheider, F., Thornton, A., & Young-DeMarco, L. (1993). A portrait of the nest-leaving process in early adulthood. *Demography, 30,* 683–699.

Goldscheider, F.K., & DaVanzo, J. (1985). Living arrangements and the transition to adulthood. *Demography, 22*, 545–563.

Goldscheider, F.K., & DaVanzo, J. (1989). Pathways to independent living in early adulthood: Marriage, semiautonomy, and premarital residential independence. *Demography, 26*, 597–614.

Grigsby, J., & McGowan J.B. (1986). Still in the nest: Adult children living with their parents. *Sociology and Social Research, 70*, 146–148.

Hogan, D., & Astone, N.M. (1986). The transition to adulthood. *Annual Review of Sociology, 12*, 109–130.

Looker, E.D. (1993). Interconnected transitions and their costs: Gender and urban/rural differences in the transitions to work. In P. Anisef and P. Axelrod (Eds.), *Transitions: Schooling and employment in Canada* (pp. 43–64). Toronto: Thompson Educational Publishing, Inc.

Marini, M.M. (1984). The order of events in the transition to adulthood. *Sociology of Education, 57*, 63–84.

McPherson, B.D. (1990). *Aging as a social process* (2nd. Ed). Toronto: Butterworths.

Mitchell, B.A. (1994). Family structure and leaving the nest: A social resource perspective. *Sociological Perspectives, 37*, 651–671.

Mitchell, B.A., Wister, A.V., & Burch, T.K. (1989). The family environment and leaving the parental home. *Journal of Marriage and the Family, 51*, 605–613.

Norris, J.E., & Tindale, J.A. (1994). *Among generations: The cycle of adult relationships.* New York: W.H. Freeman and Company.

Schaie, W.K., & Willis, S.L. (1986). *Adult development and aging.* Boston: Little, Brown.

Schnaiberg, A., & Goldenberg, S. (1989). From empty nest to crowded nest: The dynamics of incompletely-launched young adults. *Social Problems, 36*, 251–269.

Skolnick, A. (1987). *The intimate environment* (4th ed.). Toronto: Little, Brown.

Ursel, J. (1992). *Private lives, public policy: 100 years of state intervention in the family.* Toronto: Women's Press.

White, L., & Booth, A. (1985). The quality and stability of remarriages: The role of stepchildren. *American Sociological Review, 50*, 689–698.

This research was supported by a grant from the Social Sciences and Humanities Research Council of Canada. The authors thank Doug Talling for his assistance with computer runs.

Appendix A: Coding and Frequency Distribution for Independent Variables in the Logistic Regression

Variable	Categories	Frequency	Percent
(1) Parental Characteristics			
Family Type*	1. biological (ref)	150	68.8
	2. single	45	20.6
	3. step	20	9.2
	missing	3	1.4
Father Prestige	1. low (values 62 through 93)	29	13.3
	2. medium (values 32 through 61)	123	56.4
	3. high (values 11 through 31)	66	30.3
Mother Prestige	1. low (values 62 through 93)	7	3.2
	2. medium (values 32 through 61)	138	63.3
	3. high (values 11 through 31)	73	33.5
Parental Education	1. some high school or less	21	9.6
	2. high school grad or some post-sec.	109	50.0
	3. post-secondary or degree (ref)	88	40.4
Household Income	1. <= $39,999	41	18.8
	2. $40,000 - 79,999	120	55.0
	3. $80,000 +	57	26.1
(2) Child Characteristics			
Sex	1. Males = 1	83	38.1
	2. Females = 2	135	61.9
Religiosity of Child	1. never/rarely	141	64.7
	2. sometimes (ref)	49	22.5
	3. once a week	28	12.8
Ethnic Origin	1. Commonwealth (ref) - Canadian, American, British	143	65.6
	2. Other European - including French Canadian	49	22.5
	3. Other	20	9.2
	missing	6	2.8
Marital Status*	1. married/common-law (ref)	17	7.8
	2. never married	188	86.2
	3. ever married	9	4.1
	missing	4	1.8
Age Group	1. 18-24	88	40.4
	2. 25-29	92	42.2
	3. 30-34	38	17.4
Primary Reason for Leaving	1. form a relationship**	25	11.5
	2. went to work	40	18.3
	3. independence (ref)	67	30.7
	4. conflict at home	28	12.8
	5. school	34	15.6
	6. other (e.g., travel)	23	10.6
	missing	1	0.5
Main Activity*	1. employed	119	54.6
	2. looking for work	16	7.3
	3. student	57	26.1
	4. other (ref)	18	8.3
	missing	8	3.7

* These variables are time-embedded. Family type and marital status are constructed at the time of first return. Main activity is the main activity reported at the time of the last period of co-residence. All other variables are measured at the time of the survey.
** Includes leaving to marry or to live with a boy/girlfriend.
Missing values were recoded as the middle-category for all ordinal variables.
(ref) = reference category.

8

Range and Limits of Employability Programs for Youths: A Case Study in Québec's Outaouais

Daniel Turcotte and Yao Assogba

Unemployment among youths is a worrying problem in several industrialized countries. The consequences go beyond the people affected
and are a danger for the economic and social future of the whole
community. A society should not expect any progress when a large part of the
potential labour force cannot be part of the labour market. The unemployment
rate for youths under 25 in Canada is 23% and the activity rate is 43%, compared
to 56% in 1989 (Statistics Canada, 1993). Moreover, even youths with a job are
not safe from insecurity because most of them have precarious or short-lived
jobs; they go through alternating periods of unemployment, work, and
education (Gauthier, 1994). The phenomenon of exclusion from labour market
is even more worrying for youths who drop-out of school without any
professional qualifications. Those young people are the main victims of the
economic and technological changes that occurred in the last twenty years in
the industrialized societies of Western Europe and North America. Youths with
only an elementary level of education are current victims of unemployment
(Organization de coopération et de développement économique, 1989) and
when they do have a job, it usually is a precarious one (Langlois, 1986). Those
youths are often prematurely excluded from school, with limited financial
resources, and often confronted with serious family and personal problems;
they are a disturbing reflection of the education system and the labour market's
inability to adapt to the development of technology and socioeconomic
structures (Gauthier, 1988; Sauvage, 1987).

Professional integration is a process that defines the transition between
school and labour market. Wanous (1977) believes that the process begins at
school, when the student chooses an educational establishment, education
degree, and career; for most authors, the process of integration begins at the
end of full-time education and the beginning of a job search. This process
comes to an end when the person with a steady job does not plan to change
his professional situation (Dossou, 1980; Remion, 1988; Tanguy, 1986; Trottier
& Hardy, 1988). Dupaquier (1986) identifies two approaches in the study of
professional integration: integration as a process and integration as a socially
structured phenomenon. The combination of the two approaches suggests that

research on socioprofessional integration must take into account both structural variables and individual variables and take notice of the position of the youths' original family, internalized aspirations, and the opportunities offered after they drop out of school (Dupaquier, 1986). Integration is a logical procedure in which the youth, considered as an intentional social actor, makes choices following a logic that comes from both personal characteristics and social context (Assogba, 1990). This study tries to define the logic by studying the social, academic and professional trajectories of youths who have participated in a program of employability offered through Option Travail Outaouais (OTO).

The OTO program is offered by the Carrefour Jeunesse-Emploi, a community organism that works on the development of employability for youths from 16 to 30, for the region of Québec's Outaouais. Drop-out (Ministère de l'Éducation du Québec, 1991) and unemployment rates for youths (Lamothe, 1987) in the region of Outaouais are among the highest in the province. The program has three main goals: (1) to help the youth choose a job that is in line with tastes, abilities, and qualifications; (2) to help youths get the tools needed for an efficient job search; and (3) to develop behaviour and attitudes that will help keep jobs. This program has been offering twelve-week courses on self-knowledge and job research techniques as well as training in a working environment. This program services youths from 16 to 25, who have not completed high school and who have been out of work for at least six months. Participants to this program receive a financial allowance equal to minimum wage.

This chapter presents the results of a research aimed at describing the social, academic, and professional paths of youths who have received the services of this organization as well as defining the logic which underlies the strategies used by youths to enter the labour market. The methodology was in line with a hypothetico-inductive procedure based on the actors' experience. A sample of 30 youths were selected and 19 were followed from the beginning of the program to follow-up—three months after the end of the training. Various sources of information were used including semi-directed interviews with each youth, summaries of evaluations made by those in charge of the program at the time of the youth's registration, observations noted in files, and evaluation reports from the employers. Eight youths were contacted a second time, a year after their participation in the program, to complete information and validate the initial observations. All data were the object of an interpretative-descriptive analysis (Tesch, 1990). Interview recordings were transcribed in full and submitted to a thematic content analysis following a procedure suggested by Van der Maren (1987). Professional integration is a socially structured process; the youth is active in this process but the nature of the actions is influenced by family, academic, and professional history and by available opportunities.

TREACHEROUS TRAJECTORIES

Family history of most of the youths was characterized by instability; economic instability in some cases but mostly emotional instability. The latter was manifested by conjugal tensions between parents, conjugal violence, and repeated ruptures of the parents. Most of the parents of those youths occupied an unspecialized job, although some hold specialized occupations or management positions. Most of the siblings had left school before getting their high-school diploma and, when they worked, their jobs were unspecialized and badly-paid. The youths tended to develop conflicting relations outside the family. Their friends also confronted problems of socioprofessional integration and their love affairs were tinged with dependency and victimization. Several had been battling psychosocial problems such as unwanted pregnancy, abuse of drugs and alcohol, and delinquent behaviours.

Their academic experiences were very limited; most had not made it through junior high school and those who had completed ninth grade did so with a lightened school program. Their academic paths were characterized by repeated failures from primary school and, for some, behavioral problems. School for these youths was a very frustrating period when they started questioning the relevance of their efforts and were often confirmed in their belief by the attitude of some teachers. One youth, for example, noted, "Once, a teacher told me, you have no future here; I don't know why you come to school." Dropping out appeared as the only acceptable solution to get out of a frustrating situation devoid of any foreseeable positive prospect. They knew about the importance of school since many brought up the hypothesis of choosing adult education, but they could no longer stay in an education system where they felt marginalized. One illustrative comment was, "I wanted to succeed, but finally, I had to drop out because I just couldn't make it anymore. My grades were going down the drain and there was no more progress." Another youth stated, "I was 16 and I was with 12- or 13-year-old kids. I had nothing to do there. Maybe it will be more fun if I go to adult education."

After school, employment is viewed as a symbol: one has to rebuild an image, after the negative experiences in school, and prove that it is possible to earn one's living without a high education level. Almost every youth succeeded in getting a job after quitting school. But these were badly-paid jobs, often part-time, and for very short periods (from a few days to a few months). The jobs often ended abruptly; this contributes to the youth's insecurity and feeling of incompetence. Thus, entry to the labour market does not make up for the negative consequences of an academic trajectory marked by failure and feelings of inadequacy; instead, it contributes to worsen those consequences. Further, some may feel self-actualized when they find a job but this feeling is often lessened by the fact that the jobs are often obtained with the help of family members or relations rather than on their own initiative. If they are not responsible for getting the job, they feel like they have even less control over what happens to them afterwards. Thus, loss of a job is usually imputed to external factors such as lack of work, labour surplus, firm closure, and unacceptable working conditions. The youths felt incompetent when confronted with academic requirements and helpless when faced with labour market regulations. This situation is even more dramatic since working is the access road to financial autonomy and self-fulfilment. Working means "feeling no different from anybody else" or "being proud of yourself;" in short, "it feels good."

The description given by youths of their social, academic, and professional trajectories reflect two common traits: accumulation of depreciating experiences and lack of control over one's reality. Their problems of socioprofessional integration are in line with a development which had its roots in the family circle and which persists and becomes more pronounced with events in school and on the labour market.

OTO'S CONTRIBUTION TO YOUTHS' SOCIOPROFESSIONAL INTEGRATION

The OTO program is presented as a springboard towards labour market though development of knowledge behaviour and attitudes that are likely to help in obtaining and keeping a job. Youths register with the objective of getting a job in the end; they also view it as a chance to improve their life condition. "I was desperate, totally desperate. I had done everything I possibly could to find myself a job, like go and check to the Employment Center, but I couldn't find anything." Another youth commented, "I came here when I heard that I would get paid. At the same time, I told myself that I would have money to pay for the bus and I can save some money." The youths registered with some anxiety despite the attraction of the immediate and more distant gains of the program. Several decided to participate at the suggestion, even under the pressure, of members from their circle. At first, they feared that the courses part will be like what they went through in school, "a kind of class where you sit and listen to what the other has to say and that's it." They appreciated that things were not that way and found the program was different from what they experienced at school. The courses were concrete and relevant, activities took place in a climate of respect and trust where they could learn at their own pace, and the group normalized their situation since they were in contact with people who were going through the same reality. "At least, you know there are still people on Earth who also want to make it, who want to find a job. You're not the only one, it's more encouraging. I can't find myself a job, but I'm not the only one."

Expectations regarding training were related to the observations expressed about the courses. The youth want to receive relevant knowledge in a climate of acceptation and respect. But they also wanted to contribute to where they were working and wanted this contribution to be acknowledged. They were not paid by the employer during the training and felt easily exploited if their tasks were different from those of the other employees. The training was perceived as positive if they were considered as real employees; if not, they tried to change their training place or dropped out. Staff in charge of the program often considered that those youths show little persistence when confronted to obstacles. Self-confidence and perseverance at work are two important consequences that youths attributed to participating in the program; they start feeling that they have better control over their reality. "I learned that if I really want to, I can make it …. They taught me that I'm really able to go for it and keep going. I became more ambitious." Several also reported that they had acquired a more precise idea of "the tough reality of labour market" and the importance of school. Finally, the program leads to significant learnings such as writing a resume and presentation during interviews. The comments of youths about the personal development and learning benefits they gained from participation in the program confirm the relevance of such a program, although it comprises some risks.

The program, however, can create new disappointments and add to the feelings of failure and helplessness that are already present if the results of training are negative or the hope of getting a job does not materialize. "Here, during the program, you get money. It's okay, you've got money, but then you go out and you don't have a job anymore. You lost four months and you're still without a job. But I would have liked getting out of here with a job." At the end of the program most of the youths find themselves faced with the same reality of a difficult professional integration marked by an alternation of activities and wavering between attending school, precarious jobs, and special programs. How long will the acquisition of self-confidence and feeling of control over reality resist to the new disappointments, since participating in a program of employability will not modify a labour market of which those youths are the first victims?

Youths adopt a behaviour that shows that they are aware of the precariousness of their situation even if they do not express it orally. They warily accept the opportunities offered to them and they readily retire if they are confronted with frustrating situations. At first sight, their attitude seems to reveal a lack of perseverance, a search for easiness, or an instability in commitments. But it can also be interpreted as a way to protect themselves from new disappointments. The actions of those youths to realize their professional integration fit with a logic that is related to the dilemma of risky investment. If they do not show initiative, they can be sure of getting nothing; however, if they give their all for a project, they could lose what they have left of confidence, pride and hope. Their social, academic, and professional trajectories show that the youths have often invested in relations and activities from which they gained very little, except for disillusions. To avoid new disappointments, they are suspicious; but at the same time, they know they cannot remain passive in the face of an unsatisfying situation. "People see me as a bum because my hair is long. If I show up for a job, they're going to say, Get a haircut and I'll take you after that. Come on! If you listen to them, you get your hair cut and then you show up again and they're going to say, I don't want you anyway!"

Their reality presents a negative attitude directed towards oneself, the accumulation of negative experiences in social interactions, and the presence of environment obstacles which limit the possibilities of action. These are all the elements of a process that leads to the development of a feeling of helplessness (Solomon, 1976). The firm belief that they have little control over what happens to them means that the youths will participate in activities which require a minimum of investment and which bring immediate benefits, but they will hesitate to get involved in actions for which results are uncertain. Many are inactive in their search for a job; they wait to receive offers or to be introduced by relatives. Thus, they avoid moves that could not only be useless, but could also contribute to their view of self as incapable and inefficient. Those youths seek to avoid failure and they try to protect the aspects of their life over which they can still exert a certain control. A program such as OTO can appear particularly appealing given this logic. It brings immediate gains, the climate of acceptance and respect in which it is conducted contributes to the realization of significant learnings, and it can give access to labour market. This program is an opportunity to obtain significant gains with a minimum of risk. The main stumbling block is that youths will not persist if they do not feel recognized and respected. They are ready to get involved but they remain careful, especially since many feel that they are subject to external events over which they have little control.

CONCLUSION

The problem of unemployment becomes even more dramatic when it affects youths whose social, academic, and professional trajectories have contributed to undermining self-confidence and developing a feeling of helplessness. Difficulties of professional integration lead to withdraw into themselves and create a tendency to self-depreciation. A program such as OTO is both enriching and appealing for those youths; enriching because it allows them to learn usefully in an environment which favours the development of self-confidence, and appealing because it both brings immediate gains and allows them to go through a self-actualizing working experience. But this program also has some limits. The program has no effect on the reality of employment; thus, at the end of the program, several youths are back to their starting point. Moreover, this program can give the impression of explaining exclusion in an individual way, thus putting aside the numerous structural factors which contribute to socioprofessional exclusion. Professional integration is a complex phenomenon that requires global and coordinated actions.

Are there real, medium- or long-range benefits of educational interventions directed essentially to the technical aspects of the job search? The interventions would be much more influential if they were more constant with a perspective of empowerment where the youths' abilities would be used to contribute to the development of their communities. A self-actualizing experience would also increase realization of how the social system is influencing their functioning. Youths need to distinguish the factors contributing to the maintenance of their situation that have to do with social organization and those that have to do with themselves. Youths could then detect the control they can exert over their reality. They could better plan their future if they used their abilities for the development of their community.

References

Assogba, Y. (1990). Théorie systémique de la rationalité de l'acteur et aspirations. *Recherches sociologiques, 19* (1), 55–77.

Dossou, F. (1980). Un bilan des mécanismes et des modes d'insertion professionnelle des jeunes à 20–22 ans. In G. Balazs, J.P. Faguer & F.S. Dossou (Eds.), *Jeunes et premiers emploi* (pp. 257–287). Paris: Presses Universitaires de France.

Dupaquier, M. (1986). L'insertion professionnelle. In L. Tanguy (Ed.), *L'introuvable relation formation/emploi* (pp. 35–95). Paris: La documentation française.

Gauthier, M. (1988). *Les jeunes chômeurs, une enquête.* Québec: Institut québécois de la recherche sur la culture.

Gauthier, M. (1994). *Une société sans les jeunes?* Québec: Institut québécois de la recherche sur la culture.

Lamothe, B. (1987). *Le contexte de vie des jeunes de l'Outaouais. Un aperçu de leurs caractéristiques sociales et économiques.* Hull: Département de santé communautaire.

Langlois, S. (1986). Les rigidités sociales et l'insertion des jeunes dans la société québécoise. In F. Dumont (Ed.), *Une société des jeunes?* (pp. 301–323). Québec: Institut québécois de la recherche sur la culture.

Ministère de l'Éducation du Québec (1991). *Indications sur la situation de l'enseignement primaire et secondaire.* Québec: Ministère de l'Éducation, Direction générale de la recherche et du développement.

Organisation de coopération et de développement économiques. (1989). *Perspectives de l'emploi.* Paris: Organisation de coopération et de développement économiques.

Remion, G. (1988). *Jeunes et exclusion—l'avenir reconstruit.* Bruxelles: Fondation Roi Beaudoin.

Sauvage, P. (1987). *Insertion des jeunes et modernisation.* Paris: Économica.

Solomon, B.B. (1976). *Black empowerment: Social work in oppressed communities.* New York: Columbia University Press.

Statistics Canada. (1993). *Moyennes annuelles de la population active 1993* (catalogue 71–220). Ottawa: Statistics Canada, Household Survey Division.

Tanguy, L. (1986). *L'introuvable relation formation/ emploi.* Paris: La documentation française.

Tesch, R. (1990). *Qualitative research: Analysis types & software tools.* New York: Falmer Press.

Trottier, C.R., & Hardy, M. (1988). *La transition du système éducatif au monde du travail. Problématique, cadre d'analyse et méthodologie.* Québec: Université Laval.

Van der Maren, J.M. (1987). *Méthodes qualitatives de recherche en éducation.* Montréal: Centre interdisciplinaire de recherches sur l'apprentissage et le développement en éducation.

Wanous, J.P. (1977). Organizational entry: Newcomers moving from outside to inside. *Psychological bulletin, 84,* 601–618.

This study was made possible with the help of a joint grant from the Ministère de la Santé et des Services sociaux du Québec (Health and Social services) and from the Régie régionale de la santé et des services sociaux de l'Outaouais in the framework of a program of grants in community health.

9

Taking Flight? The Transition Experiences of Native Youth

Peter Gabor, Steven Thibodeau and Santanita Manychief

Leaving adolescence and moving into adulthood is a significant transition in the lives of most young people. Critical challenges during this period include the assumption of responsibilities for independent living as well as the re-definition of relationships with family and peers (Dumbbrill, 1994). Individuals must successfully negotiate a series of new and unfamiliar developmental issues (Mech, 1994). Several factors have been identified. Educational attainment (Aldgate, 1994; Biehal et al., 1994; Samuda, 1985) and employment opportunity play an important role in a successful transition process. Living skills including both hard skills such as budgeting and self care and soft skills such as self-awareness, dealing with feelings, and interpersonal skills (Cook, 1994; Iglehart, 1994; Lammert & Timberlake, 1986; McFadden et al., 1989) also relate to a successful transition. A variety of program models are available to assist youth with the transition process (Barth, 1986). Services, however, are often concentrated in the period immediately preceding and following the move into independence (Dumbrill, 1994). Some matters can be addressed by programs concentrated around the emancipation event, but others require a longer term approach (Cook, 1994).

Native youth face additional transition challenges resulting from the loss of important caring figures. Most native children, by the age of six, will have lost two significant people in their lives (Edwards & Egbert-Edwards, 1990); this has a negative impact on social and emotional maturation as well as personal development. Native youth, in common with other minority youth, face special difficulties in identity development and psychological adjustment associated with the fact that their ethnic and racial status are often subject to pervasive negative stereotypes projected by the majority culture. They often find conflicts between their ethnic values and those prevalent in the mainstream culture (Phinney et al., 1990). Ultimately, all native youth encounter this challenge; those who move away from reserves are faced with it more directly. Phinney, Lochner and Murphy (1990) indicate that, for the best adjustment, individuals need to develop their own sense of the meaning of their ethnicity. There are a variety of ways of dealing with this issue, ranging from relatively dysfunctional responses to more positive ones. Achieving a sense of ethnic identity can be a struggle, but youth who succeed show better psychological achievement and higher self-esteem then those who do not (Phinney et al., 1990).

The prevalence of substance abuse provides another challenge for native youth in their transition to independence. Data from a U.S. study indicate that over 80% of native adolescents report having used alcohol at least once (Beauvais & Laboueff, 1985) and much of the use of alcohol is characterized as heavy, leading to incidences of blackouts. Many native adolescents have witnessed drinking or substance use among the people around them and early experimentation with sniffing, smoking, and drinking are common (Edwards & Egbert-Edwards, 1990). Compounding the problem is that many peer group activities revolve around drinking; the lack of employment opportunities and the limited commitment to education often result in experimentation with substances to relieve boredom (Edwards & Egbert-Edwards, 1990). The abuse of substances, particularly early experimentation, in turn interferes with the development of personal and interpersonal skills and attainment of educational objectives.

METHODOLOGY

The process of transition to adulthood has attracted considerable research interest but little attention has been paid to the transition process faced by native youth. This study explores key issues and challenges of this transition process by describing the perceptions and experiences of 26 native youth. The youths had been involved in an independent living situation within the preceding two years and were interviewed in 1994–95. Participants were recruited through a high school and a counselling services office, both located on a large reservation in Western Canada. Individuals who were thought to be good sources of information were asked to participate in the study by attending an interview. Participants were paid an honorarium of twenty dollars. Interviews were carried out by a senior mental health clinician on the reserve and by a M.S.W. social worker. A detailed interview protocol helped focus the interviews around topics of interest but respondents were encouraged to add any other issues and themes they thought were relevant. The interviews were taped and then transcribed. The main objectives of the interviews were to obtain a description of the first independent living experience and to ask respondents to reflect on that experience. Specifically, the interviews covered:

- The young person's background, including the living situation from which he or she moved into independence,
- A detailed description of experiences in the first independent living situation,
- The young person's perception about his or her own preparation for independent living,
- The supports and services that were available, and,
- Suggestions and advice that the young person had for others moving out into independent living.

The youth were between the ages of 17 and 21 at the time of the interview. Their ages, at the time of entry into their first independent living situation, ranged from 15 to 19. There were 9 females and 17 males. Only about a third were in their final year of high school or had completed high school at the time of moving into independence; two thirds had less educational attainment. Approximately half of the respondents made their move into independence on the reserve while the other half moved away from the reserve into an urban location. Close to 90% indicated that they had received social assistance at some point during their first independent living situation. The findings were reviewed by native elders and youth workers, who were asked to consider the implications of this research.

The selection process resulted in a study population that was composed of young people who had returned to the reserve since their initial move into independence; this may indicate that they had encountered some problems and difficulties in the transition process. Youth not currently residing on the reserve had no chance of being selected for this study. This group likely included individuals who were successful in the transition process and were, at the time this study was carried out, away from the reserve pursuing their education or other opportunities.

GEORGE'S STORY

> The first little while I wanted just to get away and I went to the city and got into that whole life of drinking and stuff and doing drugs. I started trying to go to school and to find jobs and all that but I just didn't do it. So, for the first while there was no plan just getting out of here. As time went on my plans started to take off a little. I guess subconsciously there was a plan all along. I enjoyed the freedom for a while and then the stuff that was deep in my mind about bettering myself finally came out once I got all that stuff out of my system.

Ultimately, George cut down on the parties and began to pursue employment. Although he had few job search skills, he managed to talk himself into a position as a youth recreational worker, an area that had always interested him. "Once I got that first real job, ever since then, there have been no worries. From the time they hired me it seemed to get better and people wanted to pay me more for doing what I loved." George is now back on the reserve, pursuing further education, with the hope of making youth work his career. George has met with some success in his move to independence, but realizes that, for some youth, the transition process is much more complicated.

> You are just another kid and you might have all these big dreams in your head and even a plan set out but once you are actually involved in carrying out your plan everything changes. Your whole outline of what you are going to do is not going to follow. There are going to be many things that will interfere, and many problems.

Indeed, for many youth, the barriers and problems prove insurmountable. George's story, although encouraging, is not typical—most native youth meet with little success in the first few years after their move into independence.

REASONS FOR MOVING INTO INDEPENDENCE

"I wanted to be on my own."
"I wanted a change and to get out and do something."
"I was hoping for more freedom and privacy too."
"I didn't get along too well with [my father's] wife."
"I just wanted to get away."
"I wanted to get off the reserve and try to start a new life."
"I wanted to find out how it feels to be on your own."
"I didn't want to depend on my mom or grandma anymore."

These quotes reveal a variety of reasons for moving out but some common themes can be identified. One is a normal adolescent yearning for freedom and independence. People, as they approach young adulthood, want to attain a higher degree of autonomy; for many of the respondents this translated to the ability to make their own decisions and to be free from parental authority. Young people yearn for a sense of independence, the ability to stand on their own feet, and to be responsible for their own well being. They no longer want to impose on their parents or other caregivers. They begin to feel that it is appropriate for them to take full responsibility for their own needs and requirements. The young people also responded to a kind of wanderlust that is often associated with youth. They simply wanted a change of scenery and an opportunity to explore beyond their immediate environment.

Some respondents wanted to get away from their current family situation. In a few cases, the relationship between the young person and adult caregivers had deteriorated to the point where there was constant conflict and the youth simply felt that he or she could not stay any longer. Some youth indicated that there was no conflict but that few emotional bonds tied him or her to the family situation; "There was no relationship. It was just empty." Some reported warm, supportive relationships with their families even though conflicts and arguments were common and the opportunity for privacy limited. Perhaps this was due to the crowding that exists in many residences on the reserve; this increases demands on individuals to accommodate themselves and to coordinate their activities with others in residence. Many young people felt pressured in such circumstances and decided to get away from the arguments, day to day responsibilities, and the lack of privacy. The lack of privacy was a key issue for those young people who are attempting to start a family. Often several nuclear families, representing two or three generations, shared the same household. There are advantages to such arrangements, including the availability of support, advice, help, as well as child rearing assistance. Nevertheless, young couples often find it difficult to develop and establish their own distinctive family unit and view moving away as the best solution. A participant commented, "After a while we moved away to get to know each other better and to build our own family."

Some respondents come to the conclusion that opportunities on the reserve were limited. Suitable housing is in short supply and there were few employment opportunities. One commented, "when you are on the reserve it is harder to move forward then when you are in the city." In reality, young people moving to the city are likely to encounter a different set of barriers and obstacles which also limit their opportunity, but these are not evident as they contemplate the lack of possibilities on the reserve. Few of the respondents had specific plans for the move into independence. Most noted the immediate goal of continuing or resuming their education, very few described any occupational objectives, and none related a longer term plan. For most, the move into independence represented a move away from where they are rather than a move to something more attractive.

THE INDEPENDENT LIVING SITUATION

I was nineteen when I first moved to [a small city] with a room mate. This went about seven months and then I moved back to my mom's. After a while I moved to [a large city] with my sister. I stayed with her about three months and then I moved down to my grandma's on the reserve for six months. Then I moved back to my sister's for a couple of months and last month I moved to this hotel [on the edge of the reserve] with my boyfriend.

Not all young people moved as often or experienced as many different living situations after their initial move into independence. Some experience only a few different living situations but a sizable percentage of the respondents did enter a variety of different living situations in the initial period after moving into independence. The move into independence is not as much an event as a process. It is sometimes difficult to decide whether a particular living situation represents a move into independence. For example, for some young people, a move to a relative's house simply signaled a change in caregiving responsibilities whereas for others a similar move provided the young person with an initial independent living experience. Ultimately, independence is related not to a type of living but to the arrangements and relationships. A common initial move for young people was to the household of a grandparent, an uncle or aunt, or other older relative. Such moves almost always took place within the reserve. Typically, the young person gained some independence and responsibility. However, he or she also remained under the care of a family member from a preceding generation. Family guidance, support and assistance were still available; thus, such situations offered a graduated step into independence by providing an opportunity for the young person to develop skills and experience over a period of time.

A slightly different situation arises where a young person decided to move in with a boyfriend or girlfriend. They often moved into the existing home of one of the couples, usually that of the female. There appeared to be a tacit understanding that this move represented a move into independence, even though one member of the couple has remained in his or her existing family situation. The couple assumed increasing responsibility and autonomy, but advice and support were still readily available. Often, such a couple had a child relatively quickly, creating a new set of issues relating to child care and child rearing. Again, the extended family often provided considerable help, both teaching about child rearing as well as participating in the care of the child.

A very different pattern emerged when a young person decided to move in with friends or relatives of his or her own generation. Such situations usually involved a move away from the reserve. Such living situations are often unstable, lasting only a short while and involving a variety of people who moved in and out of the household. In these circumstances the young person experienced a full measure of responsibility and autonomy. He or she had a complete range of choices available regarding lifestyle, social interactions, school, employment, and family. There was a decline of parental involvement and the influence of peers increased. Often this influence was not a positive one as many peers are involved in self-destructive lifestyles and there may be few positive role models available. A number of the study participants found that their living situation quickly went out of control, their home acquired a reputation for being a party house.

Most young people moved into an already established household upon their move into their first independent living situation. Consequently, skills related to locating housing and setting up a household were not immediately required.

Because the household was already functioning (although in some cases not very well), the young people had the opportunity to gradually acquire the skills required to operate a household. In subsequent moves, young people may attempt to acquire their own housing. It is in this connection that a sizable minority reported experiencing prejudice. Landlords were often reluctant to rent to them. Alternatively, unreasonable conditions were sometimes imposed, apparently with the hope of deterring the young person from renting the unit. If they did rent the unit, landlords often kept an unreasonably close watch on the unit.

Typically most young people experienced a series of living situations immediately after their move into independence. The situations varied from living with relatives on the reserve to living with friends in the city; the level of independence also varies from situations where the young person was semi-autonomous to others where he or she was fully independent. Most young people experienced several moves, some of short-term duration. A variety of people may be involved in the various living situations, with the composition of the household changing as people moved in or out. During this period, many young people also returned home for a short while, before moving into independence once again.

EDUCATION AND EMPLOYMENT

"I have set some long-term goals I am still working on. Finishing school for one and then furthering my education. Right now I am in school." This twenty-one-year-old male came from a close-knit family where the parents emphasized the importance of a good education. Unfortunately, many of the study participants did not have the benefit of such role models; they were more likely to see family members, relatives, and friends who had abandoned their education early. Edwards and Egbert-Edwards have pointed out, "Indian children have not incorporated high-school graduation into their lifestyles as a realistic, attainable goal" (1990, p. 287). Many of the young people in this study left school around the time they moved into independence. Many were receiving poor grades, found it difficult to accept the constraints of school discipline, and had grown tired of school.

Nevertheless, most of the respondents understood the importance of a good education. A large majority indicated that it was their intention to upgrade or complete their schooling. However, returning to school, after having left, proved to be a difficult challenge for most. One commented, for example, "When I moved away from home I was only in grade nine. I went back to school when I was seventeen but it just didn't work out." Only a third of the study participants were in their final year of high school or had completed high school. Lack of educational attainment posed a great barrier to employment; virtually any good position required a high-school diploma and, indeed, many positions called for post-secondary education.

Several of the respondents had found casual or part-time employment, often working for a relative; only one succeeded in finding career oriented employment. For most, the issue was not to locate career oriented employment but to find any job. One young man commented, "I am looking for any job just to keep myself going money wise." The respondents also found themselves deficient in the area of job search skills. As one put it, "It was something new, I wasn't used to it. I never had to go out and find a job before." Another said, "As far as knowing how to do a resume and that stuff, I didn't know anything about that." Ultimately, he succeeded in obtaining a position and commented, "Getting my first job, I didn't have a resume, it was all just talking." Some young people sought help from organizations and a few were referred to a native job finding club. One commented, "I went there and they taught me a little bit of the basics, like working in a store or something. They didn't teach me how to get a meaningful career." Transportation was often identified as a barrier to finding employment. Very few of the young people participating in this study had their own transportation which limits both their ability to search for positions as well as the positions they can realistically hold.

Attending school or finding employment were the only constructive alternatives available for many young people upon their move into independence. Problems arose when they were unable to successfully pursue either of these options. A twenty-year-old male, who had moved out at the age of eighteen commented, "I had plans to go to school but they just never came through because I was too late to register. So those fell through and then I fell into the welfare rut. After that it was just parties." About 90% of the respondents ended up receiving some type of social assistance. A study participant pointed out that there is the real danger that young people will develop a dependency on welfare, "They rely on that cheque every month. Then they see that cheque as free money and they have no incentive to do anything else. They just fall into a rut."

PROBLEMS, SUPPORTS, AND SERVICES

"I was pretty grown up but I wasn't ready for it all." Few of the young people felt that they were prepared for the move into independence. Most reflected that they were unprepared for the many challenges of independent living. For many, the move to independence was very sudden. The young people found themselves, from one day to the next, in a totally new situation. This was particularly true in the case of young people who had moved away from the reserve. One respondent recalled, "Emotionally I wasn't prepared. To me it was happening so fast." Another expressed a sense of shock at being away from his family, "It is tough to get used to being on your own. It think I sometimes felt depressed."

A few of the respondents had had the opportunity to learn daily living skills by watching their parents or caregivers. One respondent commented, "I used to watch my mom and dad so I probably just learned from them how to do it [budgets and housekeeping]." Most of the respondents, particularly the males, had few such opportunities as their parents or caregivers took care of everything at home. Thus, they lacked any knowledge of daily living skills. Money management and budgeting were particular skill areas in which many respondents reported themselves to be lacking skills. Typical comments were. "I didn't know about bills; I never saw a bill. I guess you could say it was always paid for me" and "Money was a problem. I spent it foolishly."

Alcohol and drug abuse proved problematic. Almost every study participant indicated that, at some point, a family member or a close relative had had a major problem with alcohol or drugs. In addition, about three quarters of the respondents indicated that they themselves had had problems with alcohol or drugs prior to leaving home. Young people who already had a problem with alcohol or drugs indicated that these got worse after moving into independence, while many of those who had not reported a problem previously, indicated that they began abusing these substances. Comments included, "The fact was I partied a lot more;" "I just drink to not think about the other problems;" and "I would drink a little on the weekends but then, as time went on, I started going into the week."

Did the youth make ample use of supports and services? Those who remained on the reserve continued to receive help and support from their network of family and friends. However, these sources of support were less available to those who moved off the reserve. Ironically, even though these young people faced the most jarring transition experience, they were also the most reluctant to seek help. Many seemed to regard asking for help, even from family members and relatives, as a sign of failure or weakness. One young man summarized this situation, "Most youth think they know everything but once they are there, they realize [how hard it is]. Then they turn to drugs or alcohol because they are too ashamed and proud to say they were wrong." The young people found it even more difficult to seek help from formal organizations and made comments such as, "I am not the type of person to go talking to anybody;" "I felt I did not need anyone's help;" and "Having to ask for help was a hit to my pride." Many of the young people felt alone and tried to persevere on their own. In fact, several indicated that they had learned the most from their own experience. As one said, "Things get better each time. The first time you don't know much but the second time you know more and now it gets to the point where I know all about the skills that I need." Experience was an effective teacher but, judging by the experiences of many of the study participants, it was also a hard teacher.

The young people who reported receiving help indicated that the main sources of help were family and friends. For those who had left the reserve, the family was less available as a source of support and guidance and, correspondingly, the influence of peers increased. Many respondents commented on the fact that family members had been a relatively positive influence in their lives while peers often exerted a negative influence. They said that their problems, including drinking, got worse after they moved into independence and attribute this to negative peer influence. "My [drinking] problems got worse because my parents weren't there to tell me to quit." Another commented, "At home my parents settle me down a little bit but on my own I give in to people more easily, like drink and stuff like that." A common remark was that their peers held them back from making progress in their independent living situation. "People kept coming over all the time knowing it was a place you could come over and drink."

Financial help was most frequently sought (and obtained) from formal organizations. The young people had little faith in the ability of formal organizations, including native organizations, to provide effective psycho-social support. A twenty-year-old male commented on his experience, "I tried to go to some of the native organizations. I thought that when I went there I would get some sort of support but now I think they are over rated—they don't help you out very much." Study participants were asked about other sources of strength and comfort. Specifically, they were prompted about the impact of native traditions on their lives. About half of the young people confirmed that this had, indeed, helped them cope. One young woman summed up this issue by saying, "It gave me inner strength."

RESEARCH, POLICY AND PROGRAM IMPLICATIONS

Some native youth succeed in their transition to independence, although many experience significant problems in the process. It is difficult to generalize from these findings due to the manner in which the respondents were selected. But it is possible to identify the nature of the difficulties experienced by these native youth and to describe related issues. Key findings are:

- Lack of economic development resulted in pressure on young people to leave the reserve in order to find employment.
- Lack of educational attainment by native youth represented a major barrier to finding career oriented employment.
- Many native youth perceived themselves to be unprepared for the transition to independence and lacking in personal development as well as in life skills.
- Many young people encountered serious personal and social problems in the initial period after moving into independence, particularly when the move was from the reserve to the city.
- Parental support and guidance decreased once young people leave the reserve; peer influence, which is often negative, increased correspondingly.
- Once in the city, young people felt that they had few sources of help and support available to them, particularly since they were reluctant to access formal helping organizations.

Initial experiences with independent living can have a major impact throughout a young person's life. A successful transition to independence can result in a lifetime of contribution as a successful, productive citizen whereas difficulties at that point can lead to dependence and personal distress that may extend into the next generation. Society might wisely invest more heavily to help native youth successfully negotiate the transition process. The higher the proportion of young people who are successful at this stage, the more likely that effective leadership will be available to native communities in the future.

Many young people do not have the option to remain on their reserve and feel compelled to leave because of lack of employment opportunities. They must make a dramatic break with their past and move from the reservation to the city. Economic development is vitally needed to provide long-term employment opportunities to young people and to provide the option to stay on the reserve or to delay the move away until they are truly ready. Education is a cornerstone; without educational development, other measures are unlikely to be successful. The young people were virtually unanimous in acknowledging the need to complete their education prior to moving into independence. The problem of dropping out early requires further study to develop policies and practices that can result in better student retention. Programs can be designed that focus on development of personal preparation and inadequate life skills. These programs should be available well before the young person has moved into independence. Different program models should be tried to determine the best configuration and best auspices for such programs.

Parents have key responsibilities for preparing young people for independence but many parents lack an appreciation of the importance of teaching independent living skills to their children and may lack the parenting skills required to adequately prepare their children. Family support schemes are needed to assist parents to more effectively prepare their children for independence. Tribal elders also have an important role to play in helping to adequately prepare young people. Elders can be involved in programs aimed at preparing young people for independence as well as in programs designed to develop the ability of parents to prepare their children. For example, elders could help to provide the youth with a strong sense of native traditions. Several young people found this to be a source of strength in the transition process. The involvement of elders would serve to provide programs with legitimacy and credibility as well as to ensure their cultural authenticity.

Finally, more effective assistance and support should be made available to young people during the transition process itself. Most young people moving from the reserve to the city face formidable challenges and can use help and support regardless of their level of preparation for independent living. Young people are unlikely to turn to passive programs, that await individuals to contact them. Active outreach models are more likely to be successful. Such programs can employ transition workers who take the initiative to contact young people, provide them with necessary information, and help to link them to the resources and services they require. Such programs can also be instrumental in developing in-city support groups involving native young adults who have succeeded in the transition process. Successful role models can provide inspiration, hope, as well as tangible support.

This was a small, qualitative study. Larger studies using representatiave samples would be desirable. Some native young people succeed in their move into independence; studying the experiences of those who succeed would help to further understand of the transition process. The greatest problems and challenges arise when the move to independence also involves a move away from the reserve. Future research should attempt to identify measures that can better prepare and support youth in this transition.

References

Aldgate, J. (1994). Graduating from care: A missed opportunity for encouraging successful citizenship. *Children and Youth Services Review, 16,* 255–272.

Barth, R.P. (1986). Emancipation services for adolescents in foster care. *Social Work, 31,* 165–171.

Beauvais, F., & Laboueff, S. (1985). Drug and alcohol abuse intervention in American Indian communities. *International Journal of Addiction, 20,* 139–171.

Biehal, N., Clayden, J., Stein, M., & Wade, J. (1994). Leaving care in England: A Research perspective. *Children and Youth Services Review, 16,* 231–254.

Cook, R.J. (1994). Are we helping foster care youth prepare for their future? *Children and Youth Services Review, 16,* 213–229.

Dumbrill, G.C. (1994). Preparing children in care for independence: A developmental process. *Journal of the Ontario Association of Children's Aide Societies, 38,* 15–19.

Edwards, E.D., & Egbert-Edwards, M. (1990). American Indian adolescents: Combating problems of substance use and abuse through a community model. In A.R. Stiffman & L.E. Davis (Eds.), *Ethnic issues in adolescent mental health* (pp. 285–302). Newbury, CA: Sage.

Iglehart, A.P. (1994). Adolescents in foster care: Predicting readiness for independent living. *Children and Youth Services Review, 16,* 159–169.

Lammert, M., & Timberlake, E.M. (1986). Termination of foster care for the older adolescent: Issues of emancipation and individuation. *Child and Adolescent Social Work, 3* (1), 36–37.

McFadden, E.J., Rice, D., Ryan, P., & Warren, B. (1989). Leaving home again: Emancipation from foster family care. *Child and Youth Services, 12,* 133–148.

Mech, E.V. (1994). Foster youths in transition: Research perspectives on preparation for independent living. *Child Welfare, 73,* 603–623.

Phinney, J.S., Lochner, B.T., & Murphy, R. (1990). Ethnic identity development and psychological adjustment in adolescence. In A.R. Stiffman & L.E. Davis (Eds.), *Ethnic issues in adolescent mental health* (pp. 53–72). Newbury, CA: Sage.

Samuda, R.J. (1985). Comparative immigration patterns in the U.S., Australia and Canada. In R.J. Samuda & A. Wofgang (Eds.), *Intercultural counselling and assessment: Global perspectives* (pp. 5–17). Lewiston, NY: C.J. Hogrefe.

The authors express their appreciation to Jennifer Thibodeau for conducting some of the interviews and to Patti-Jo Aiken for transcribing the resulting tapes.

10

Canadian Girls in Transition to Womanhood

Aniko Varpalotai

Schooling is widely recognized as the major social institution for the socialization and education of Canadian youth. The role of the community in this enterprise is increasingly being recognized and advocated. The Ontario Report of the Royal Commission on Learning (1995) identifies community education as one of the key partners among the "four engines" constituting the driving force behind the education system. One of the school's tasks is to take into account the diversity and needs of the student body and to facilitate learning in an equitable fashion. Schools cannot address gender, race, social class, and other inequalities alone, particularly when these inequalities are reflected and reproduced throughout society. This chapter will focus on gender inequities, and the ways in which the schools can work in partnership with the community to enhance girls' opportunities in their transition to womanhood. Implications will be drawn from four case studies: single sex schools for girls, the Girl Guides, girls' sports, and family studies classes.

THE ALL-GIRLS' SCHOOL: THE REVIVAL OF AN OLD IDEA?

The all-girls' school may appear to be a throwback to an era when girls and boys were educated separately for very different roles in life (Riordan, 1990; Tyack & Hansot, 1990). The coeducational school was perceived to be a move towards greater educational and gender equity, but the new girls' schools are recognizing that coeducation is not the answer to gender equity. Girls may have suffered from even greater inequalities in the presence of boys while boys have benefitted from the presence of girls in their classrooms. Boys receive significantly more attention from both male and female teachers, girls are sexually harassed by boys even in early elementary grades, and some degree of sex-role division of curriculum options continues despite the apparent availability of all options to both boys and girls. The curriculum, both in content and delivery, continues to be geared toward boys (Gaskell et al., 1989; Canadian Teachers' Federation, 1990; Holmes & Silverman, 1992). Some school jurisdictions have attempted to rectify these problems by introducing single-sex classes in areas identified to be of most concern, such as mathematics and science where female attrition rates in secondary school are particularly high. The bigger issue encompasses the social context of schools and societies where girls are sometimes overtly and sometimes very subtly undermined and silenced as they become adolescents and young women (Gilligan et al., 1990).

Canadian, American, British, and Australian studies have documented the erosion of girls' self-confidence and future aspirations as they proceed through their schooling. At the same time, single-sex schools for girls have shown significantly better results in the academic and extra-curricular accomplishments of their students—even after self-selection and socio-economic factors have been taken into account (Riordan, 1990; Kenway & Willis, 1990; Orenstein, 1994). Girls have attested to their experiences in single-sex groups and classrooms. Most do not want to live in a separate world, and most prefer a coeducational school if that school was more responsive to their interests and valued their contributions. The Linden School in Toronto was founded in 1993 to provide female students with an overtly feminist approach to education; the experience of this school may help to understand what girls and women find in such a place that is apparently missing from most coeducational public schools (Duffy, 1994). It will be a sad commentary on public schools if girls can find safety and equitable educational opportunities only in all-girls' schools. The revival of the all-girls' school speaks to the need to educate both girls and boys, as well as male and female teachers, differently if the coeducational classroom is to provide a welcoming, inclusive, and fertile learning environment for all students.

GIRL GUIDES: MEDIATING THE TRANSITION AND DILEMMAS OF GIRLHOOD

According to Carol Gilligan and her associates, "By fifteen, more than twice as many girls located powerful learning experiences outside of the school than inside" (1990, p. 14). Girl Guides is one of those rare organizations that is run by and for girls and women. The Girl Guides of Canada, however, has been challenged in courts, through human rights commissions, and the media to allow the participation of boys and men. The public debate about the Girl Guides' single sex membership and leadership policy has politicized the organization, requiring it to clearly articulate the rationale for its position. The question of its location and role within the women's movement, and a reluctance on the part of some members to align themselves with feminism, continues to create tensions as the organization strives to keep itself up to date and relevant to the needs of girls and young women (Varpalotai, 1994). A statement issued in 1990 clarifies the reasons for its single sex mandate:

> ... We believe strongly that the girls of Canada are best served by a program designed specifically for girls, and led by women. Although it is recognized that society is changing, it does not treat males and females equally. There is still a sexist approach to the development of girls and to the contributions that females can make to society ... [Guiding] inspires an ethic of co-operation while encouraging leadership potential, it fosters in girls a sense of pride in their own gender and equips them to function as persons in their own right in these complex competitive times ... All-female organizations provide women with the opportunity to take executive and leadership positions and thus provide role models for girls ... (Girl Guides of Canada National Council, 1991, p. 30).

Some callers to a radio talk show debating this issue questioned whether it was "natural for a lot of girls to just be with other girls," and suggested that "kids should be shown the real world—not put in a bubble." Margaret Ringland, Executive Director, Girl Guides of Canada, responded by saying:

… almost all situations that girls are thrown in today are co-ed … we offer the one place where girls can in fact exist in a single sex situation and learn and develop and grow in their formative years … it gives them an alternative opportunity to be just with girls and they strive and are encouraged to develop some skills that they may hold back on when they are in co-ed situations. (CFRB, 1991).

A cross-section of 63 Canadian Girl Guide leaders and youth members were interviewed. Friendship is a key motivator for continuing membership in Girl Guides, as well as for maintaining the all-female organization. A majority of the girls interviewed felt that it was important for Girl Guides to remain a single sex organization. Despite their inability to clearly articulate why it is so important, there is a strong belief that the value of Girl Guides lies in its all-female membership. Juliet (17) explained, "Is it important that it stay all girls? I think it is. It is kind of a support thing and encouragement. Like we said before, it's girls, you can really empathize with each other because you know somebody has been through that same situation as you, but with guys it's different … "

The Girl Guide movement is frequently referred to as an educational organization. The Canadian government recognized its educational value as early as 1919 and voted to provide a grant valued at $3,000 per year. The Girl Guides are unlike traditional forms of education and try to make the program as different from school as possible. Nonetheless, the program is explicitly aimed at personal and skill development and is frequently cited as a valuable contribution to a woman's education. The leaders are adamant that they are not teachers, but rather Guiders or facilitators; much of the learning is achieved through experiential methods and personal challenges (Varpalotai, 1992). Clear differences are noted between Girl Guides and school. Juliet observed that in school "you are required to learn what they want you to learn," whereas in Girl Guides there is more input from the members. Melissa (16) explained that in Girl Guides there was an opportunity to discuss women's issues for which there was no forum in school. Each of these girls stated that Girl Guides would be the last activity they would give up. It's been a part of their lives for ten years or more! Melissa said, "Girl Guides has given me a lot of confidence … it showed me that I can do anything I want even if somebody says girls aren't supposed to do that. It gives you self-confidence in order to say I can do anything I want." All of the other girls, in their own ways, supported the maintenance of the all-female organization using words such as, "it just clicks better," "It is a great support group for girls," and "you need time away from them because you are not the same as when you are with guys."

Each of the girls interviewed had an awareness of the tensions and contradictions facing girls and women in a society that continues to discriminate against women. In Girl Guides they have found a safe and comfortable haven to support one another, develop a respect for girls and women, value female friendship and role models, and learn more about their own strengths and abilities. Girl Guides had enabled them to develop their self-confidence in the face of male teasing and dominance at school, and with respect to non-traditional career aspirations, independence as adults, and as active participants in their communities. Each of the girls had found the single sex environment of Girl Guides to be of particular value in comparison to the co-educational situation at school and where their self-expression and confidence was undermined by both the boys and the teachers who rarely intervene. The girls were sensitive to gender equity, to the point of apologizing for their need and desire to maintain their organization for girls and women only; they also had a sense of its importance in helping them to mediate the transitions and dilemmas of girlhood.

GIRLS' SPORTS AND ROLE MODELS: RINGETTE

In a nation where ice hockey reigns supreme, it is not surprising that some girls would want to participate in it alongside their male counterparts. Ringette was invented (significantly, by men) as a girls' substitute for what was considered to be the masculine and inappropriate sport of ice hockey. Women's ice hockey has become one of the fastest growing sports in recent years, but ringette continues to serve the purpose of broadening participatory opportunities for girls, and provides a measure for the changes that have (and have not) occurred in women's sport since its inception.

Most of the ringette players interviewed for this study (Varpalotai, 1987) expressed satisfaction with the sport and preferred to play on all-girls teams. Some of the reasons given included the fact that boys become rougher as they get older and that they resent a girl who is a better player. The relative status of the sexes had been internalized by most of these successful female athletes and was not questioned. The gender role stereotypes were reinforced by both the attitudes and the actions of the players. Limited integration of males and females during pre-adolescence was considered acceptable, and perhaps even good, but the preference on the whole was for single-sex sporting opportunities regardless of the sport.

The girls recognized the limited opportunities available to them in sports like hockey, but knew of girls who had proven their exceptional abilities on boys' hockey teams and in other sports. Ironically, the girls all stated initially that ringette had been their own choice and that they had not experienced discrimination in sport—that is, until they were asked why they had not chosen to play hockey. Every one of the girls reported a desire to play hockey when they were younger, but recalled being redirected by parents or others to a more suitable sport for girls, usually figure skating. Their participation in ringette frequently evolved from both a dissatisfaction with figure skating and peer encouragement. It is this subtle, often unrecognized, hidden curriculum of conformity to socially-constructed norms of femininity (and masculinity) that needs to be addressed by sports leaders, policy makers, educators, coaches, and parents. These pervasive attitudes transcend the sport milieu and carry over into attitudes and aspirations beyond the gym or the arena.

A common belief is that female role models provide the necessary leadership and *entrée* into non-traditional areas for younger women. Several inherent problems with the issue of female role models must also be recognized despite some of the positive examples that a successful, powerful female role model may provide. First, there are very few visible female role models, particularly in sport. Second, successful women are often portrayed as simply hardworking individuals, obliterating the very real social barriers which negate the efforts of so many women (Overall, 1987). Thus, female role models are often portrayed as exceptional individuals, particularly in relation to members of their own gender. Furthermore, a blame-victim response is easily created when a girl or woman is unable to achieve the success of her role models, masking the social inequalities that continue to limit women's choices. The role model approach, in and of itself, is inadequate as a means to achieving social change.

The documented under-representation of female coaches at all levels of sport is a serious problem, even though it is not always interpreted as such, even by the young women who are themselves leaders in their sport (Macintosh & Whitson, 1990, p. 59–80). Ringette originated as an exclusively female sport, yet the majority of coaching and administrative positions are still held by men. Recent Ontario Ringette Association figures indicate that women now account for almost 80% of coaches in the Level I Coaching clinics, but their numbers decline to approximately 50% in the Level II clinics. These numbers are still significantly higher than the actual male/female active coaching ratio in Ontario at the present time.

Many ringette associations now have a rule that there must be a female on the bench. In practice, the woman often acts as team manager rather than coach, and is responsible for the team's administrative work. She is therefore not a visible presence on the ice as an athletically-skilled woman. Interestingly, most of the athletes in this study did not distinguish between the relative status of the male and female leadership of the team, which may be obscured by the female on the bench rule. Tracey, age 15, describes why the male/female combination is seen to be the most desirable, "I like having a male and a female there … the male can be the more strict type because women tend to be the mother type and they get to be soft … and with the male there you can always be guaranteed that there is going to be some kind of strictness behind it. And I think every team should have some of that discipline and firmness."

Again, there is an ongoing acceptance of male authority and blatant sex-role stereotyping. Only a few of the athletes were critical of the status quo, citing the need for more women coaches, female leadership, role models, and the need to encourage more women to become qualified. But there seemed to be little understanding of the barriers standing in the way of women. The issue of participation of girls and women in sport is not simply one of equal access to sport opportunities, a handful of exceptional role models, or even policies legislating equality, although these are all important. It goes beyond that to social and cultural constraints, ranging from the more subtle prescriptions of femininity to the sanctions surrounding sexuality, which effectively control and inhibit women's activities from a very early age. The status quo may remain unchanged simply by default; women do not have the leisure time or the opportunity to challenge it.

The findings of the ringette study indicate that physical activity is potentially empowering for women, both individually and collectively. They learn a great deal about themselves, their new-found abilities, strengths and talents, and the abilities of other girls and women. They need ongoing support if they are to remain active as women helping to re-engage the many more girls and women who are alienated from physical activity in the face of overwhelming social pressures. An all-female activity or organization allows girls to experiment with a variety of skills and interests and provides the opportunity to interact with female leaders and instructors who enjoy a diverse set of activities, careers, and skills. This interaction encourages them to develop leadership skills of their own.

THE ROLE OF THE FAMILY

The family continues to be the foundation for youth socialization, education, and gender relations. It can be argued that substantive gender equity will only be achieved when both men and women share equally in the work of both the public and private domains. The subject areas subsumed under Family Studies/Home Economics continue to be perceived (and devalued) as traditionally female domains. This has been exacerbated by the encouragement of girls to pursue non-traditional (male dominated and valued) subject areas. Gender equity will not be achieved by changing women alone, while further devaluing what has been viewed traditionally as women's work. There has been little attention paid to the socialization of, and non-traditional opportunities for, boys. This fourth study examines gender equity from the perspective of young men enroled in secondary school optional courses in Foods, Parenting and Family Studies.

In 1970 the Royal Commission on the Status of Women noted,

> Family life education should teach boys how to care for children, to cook and sew, and should encourage girls to acquire manual skills. We believe that family life education classes should be co-educational and should begin at kindergarten level. Therefore, we recommend that, where they have not already done so, the provinces and territories set up courses in family life education, including sex education, which begin in kindergarten and continue through elementary and secondary school, and which are taught to girls and boys in the same classroom (p. 185).

Girls have continued to be expected to contribute to the household in ways that boys are not. It could even be argued that girls do not need formal classes in this subject area at all (Attar, 1990). But what about the boys? In our enthusiasm for making life better for girls and women have we forgotten about the role that men and boys need to play in creating a more equitable society? The family seems most resistant to social change, yet it is where the gendered education and socialization of both girls and boys begins. Unlike girls, boys don't automatically get taught, nor do they learn and model, family and domestic skills. Some fathers are becoming more involved in parenting, but boys generally do not grow up in households where parents share the domestic labour equitably even when the mother holds a full-time job outside of the home. Statistics Canada data shows that women continue to carry a double burden of work in and out of the home, while men divide their time between work and leisure, with household chores still split (inequitably) along stereotypical lines (Devereaux, 1993).

Boys are rarely, if ever, exposed to home economics or family studies, beyond their introductory Grade 7 and 8 classes. The few that do, pursue this subject for very specific reasons, most of which do not concern their future role as parent or partner in a family. Boys are interested in this subject because they think it's an easy high-school credit, because they want to pursue a career as a chef, or for temporary survival purposes (to learn the basics to be able to look after himself temporarily during university/pre-marriage days, after which it will no longer be necessary), or because they like to eat and the cooking course is fun. Rosemary Brown remarks on the absolute dependence of men on women for their everyday needs (National Film Board, 1989). This dependence can be viewed as a male inadequacy; however, most men are either looked after by women, in an unpaid capacity, or they can afford to pay someone to clean their homes, cook their meals, and launder their clothes. There are relatively few single fathers who are solely responsible for childcare. The results of men's non-involvement are women's double workday, stress, career constraints, and lack of leisure.

What is the potential role of family studies and home economics for boys? The boys in this exploratory study had all taken family studies voluntarily at the secondary school level. They were few in number (16 boys out of a school population of 700). None had chosen the course because of a sense of the importance of family and domestic skills, although these had been the outcomes. Girls may be attracted to the girls-only spaces offered in family studies classes, but for girls this may be less a reflection on the content of the course than the safety to be found there from the harassment and intimidation experienced in co-ed classrooms (Orenstein, 1994). This cannot be a justification for maintaining these courses while neglecting the reasons that girls feel uncomfortable in the rest of the school. The existence of a girls' subject has "distracted attention for too long from the overdue task of ensuring that they do not find themselves in such need of a retreat, and can see the whole curriculum as legitimately theirs" (Attar, 1990, p. 52). Boys have more fun in home economics than girls and need to be challenged both directly and indirectly about their attitudes, stereotyping, and masculinity (Eyre, 1991). Boys appear to be accommodated and praised to make them comfortable in the home economics classroom; Attar wonders if this is once again at the expense of the girls and concludes that "unless we seriously believe that men have left the burden of most domestic chores to women because they do not know how to do them, there is little point in concentrating educational resources on boys instead of girls … educating boys to equal roles they can still refuse is a less urgent task than empowering girls, who still have far less choice" (1990, p. 135).

This brings us back full circle to the study of girls and their educational needs. Are we in fact wasting our time, and theirs, trying to reinvent home economics and family studies to suit boys? This is not to argue that family studies has no place in the school curriculum for girls or boys. On the contrary, family studies should be everywhere in the curriculum—an unavoidable, intrinsically interconnected part of every subject—but this implies a fundamental, curriculum transformation (Smith, Olin & Kolmar, 1990). Family and home, in one form or another, are among the most common experiences shared by students. The artificial separation of family from all else in the curriculum, as well as the ghettoization of what is perceived to be women's work, ensures the knowledge and power gap, reproduces the public and private male and female spheres of society, and only very rarely does it make a difference in changing the attitudes and behaviours of the few students who opt to learn about the family. We need to pay attention to the way boys are socialized and educated and to intervene for the sake of the girls, as well as the boys, on issues of sexual harassment, violence, and other overt and subtle forms of sexism and manifestations of inequalities. A proactive, anti-sexist approach is necessary in all classrooms and activities. Girls' and boys' interests and aptitudes must be equally validated whether the boy is a skilled baker or the girl is an outstanding athlete (Askew & Ross, 1988). Only such systematic, daily intervention will interrupt and breakdown the stereotypes and attitudes that have made family studies so problematic for both girls and boys.

SUMMARY

Girls and women in Canada continue to be constrained by limitations imposed on them through socially constructed gender roles and expectations. They seek safe places for learning and leisure. They cannot continue to juggle paid work, unpaid domestic work, and volunteer work, to say nothing of leisure time. Girls in Canada are hearing that they must either become skilled jugglers, or make difficult choices about what they can and cannot do. Opting out of certain subject areas in school, leadership roles in the community, leisure and sports, coeducational settings, and taking on more than their fair share of household work are some of the choices and limitations imposed on young women in Canada. Gender equity policies are not enough. If Canadians are serious about gender equity, and concerned about the ramifications of gender inequities for both women and men, then the entire community must attend to the oft-repeated findings of research in this area.

References

Askew, S., & Ross, C. (1988). *Boys don't cry: Boys and sexism in education*. Buckingham: Open University Press.

Attar, D. (1990). *Wasting girls' time: The history and politics of home economics*. London: Virago Press.

Canadian Teachers' Federation. (1990). *A cappella: A report on the realities, concerns, expectations and barriers experienced by adolescent women in Canada*. Ottawa: Author.

CFRB. Jan 7, 1991. The Wayne Maclean Show: Male leaders. (Transcript of Radio Program), Toronto.

Devereaux, M.S. (1993). Time use of Canadians in 1992. *Canadian Social Trends*, 30, 13–16.

Duffy, M.A. (1994). Linden lore: Images of a new educational model for young women. *Resources for Feminist Research*, 23 (3), 32–36.

Eyre, L. (1991). Gender relations in the classroom: A fresh look at coeducation. In J. Gaskell & A. McLaren, (Eds.), *Women and education* (2nd edition). Calgary: Deselig Enterprises Limited.

Gaskell, J., McLaren, A., & Novogrodsky, M. (1989). *Claiming an education: Feminism and Canadian schools*. Toronto: Garamond Press.

Gilligan, C., Lyons, N.P., & Hanmer, T.J. (Eds.). (1990). *Making connections: The relational worlds of adolescent girls at Emma Willard School*. Cambridge, MA: Harvard University Press.

Girl Guides of Canada National Council. (1991). Fostering female leadership: Statement on the Girl Guides of Canada as a single sex organization. *Canadian Guider*, January/February, p. 30.

Holmes, J., & Silverman, E.L. (1992). *We're here, listen to us! A survey of young women in Canada*. Ottawa, ON: Canadian Advisory Council on the Status of Women.

Kenway, J., & Willis, S. (Eds.) (1990). *Hearts and minds: Self-esteem and the schooling of girls*. London: The Falmer Press.

Macintosh, D., & Whitson, D. (1990). *The game planners: Transforming Canada's sport system*. Montréal and Kingston: McGill-Queen's University Press.

National Film Board of Canada. (1987). "No Way, Not Me!" Feminization of Poverty Series.

Ontario Royal Commission on Learning. (1995). *For the love of learning*. Toronto: Author.

Orenstein, P. (1994). *School girls: Young women, self-esteem and the confidence gap*. New York: Doubleday.

Overall, C. (1987). Role models: A critique. In K. Storrie (Ed.), *Women: Isolation and bonding.* Toronto: Methuen.

Royal Commission on the Status of Women (1970). Report of the Royal Commission on the Status of Women in Canada. Ottawa: Author.

Riordan, C. (1990). *Girls and boys in school: Together or separate?* New York: Teachers College Press.

Smith, C.H., Olin, F., & Kolmar, W. (1990). *The New Jersey project: Integrating the scholarship on gender, 1986–1990.* Rutgers: Institute for Research on Women, The State University of New Jersey.

Tyack, D., & Hansot, E. (1990). *Learning together: A history of coeducation in American schools.* New Haven, CT: Yale University Press.

Varpalotai, A.T. (1994). Women only and proud of it! The politicization of the Girl Guides of Canada. *Resources for Feminist Research, 23* (1 & 2), 14–23.

Varpalotai, A.T. (1992). A "safe place" for leisure and learning: The Girl Guides of Canada. *Society and Leisure, 15* (1), 115–131.

Varpalotai, A.T. (1987). *Sport, gender and the hidden curriculum in leisure: A case study of adolescent girls.* Unpublished doctoral dissertation, University of Toronto.

11

Tales of Transition: Leaving Public Care

Fay E. Martin

Youth leave child welfare care in a more abrupt, depersonalized, decontextualized and irreversible way than most youth leave their families (Stein & Carey, 1986; Fisher et al., 1986; Clough, 1988; Parker et al., 1991; Garnett, 1992; Beihal et al., 1992; National Children's Homes, 1993; Raychaba, 1988; Meston, 1988; Cook et al., 1993). There has, however, been little exploration of the nature and extent of the differences. This may be because there is no consensus about goals for youth for whom the state assumes parental responsibility until emancipation, and therefore no consensus about to whom they should be compared. Are they expected to become normal youth? Poor youth? A clinical population? There is further confusion about when a comparison is warranted, since the adolescent transition is a process that spans at least a decade. It is intuitively evident that 18, the age at which Ontario and most other provinces discontinue wardship, is a much earlier emancipation than is normal, but the impact of this policy on the transitional experience of youth is largely unexplored. Much of the care-leaving research focuses on the impact of extended care, an optional package of counselling and/or financial support, and post-care programs. Such programs may ameliorate the effects of abrupt emancipation, but they are unavailable or unacceptable to a proportion of care-leavers, often including the most vulnerable.

This chapter reports findings of the first data-collection session with 29 youths who turned 18 in 1994 and were in child-welfare care in Toronto after their 16th birthday. These ages were selected because they are legal markers. Sixteen is the age at which a youth can live independently, can be legally responsible for him or herself, and cannot enter or re-enter care; 18 is the age at which wardship ends and youth are expected to vacate child welfare facilities. The research reports the perspective of youth, and includes the full range of youth who left care to be on their own, from those who left at 16 to those who receive extended care.

METHOD

The Children's Aid Society of Metro Toronto (CASMT) provided computer-generated information on all children born in 1976 who had either left care since 1992 or were still receiving service, a population of 165. CASMT is the largest child welfare agency in North America, serving the population in Metropolitan Toronto that does not fall within the jurisdiction of the Catholic, Jewish, or Aboriginal child welfare agencies. Its clientele reflects the multicultural nature of the Toronto population. The CASMT computerized information system was used to secure data on sex, date of birth, date of last admission to care, date of discharge (where applicable), and for calculating time in care to discharge or age 18. Some evidence was found that suggests differences between males and females in this population:

- Males slightly outnumber females, 86 to 79.

- Males come into care earlier than females. This reaches statistical significance at the.01 level (2-tail t-test for unequal variance). At last admission, the mean age for males was 11.25 years compared to 13 years for females.

- The frequency distribution of last admission to care is flatter for males than females. Males are over-represented among those who entered care as pre-schoolers; 15 of 20 in this category are male. Children who remain in care from a very early age may do so because they require specialized services. Among the 6 cases selected randomly from the population but rejected as inappropriate for participation in the qualitative study, 5 were males and, of these, 4 were severely developmentally delayed and in long-term institutional care. This is consistent with the greater vulnerability of males in early development (Jacklin, 1989).

- Males are more likely to receive extended care; 65% of males and 49% of females were not discharged at 18.

- Those of either gender who come into care late, leave early. Males who left care at or before age 18 were in care for an average of 46 months compared to 43 months for females. Males receiving extended care were in care for 89 months (to their 18th birthday) compared to 70 months for females receiving extended care.

- Youth of either gender who leave care do so earlier rather than later; 60% of those who left care did so at age 16, 14% at 17, and 24% at 18.

- Males use the care system more than females. Because they enter earlier and stay longer, they spend more time in care (excluding extended care, which they also use more). This gender difference reaches statistical significance at the.01 level (2-tailed t-test for unequal variance).

A sample of 15 youth of each gender was randomly selected from among this population to participate in a qualitative study. Social workers were approached for open cases to arrange contact with the youth. Closed files were examined for information to support a search to locate the youth. An initial interview was scheduled as each youth was located and agreed to participate. New random selections were made if a youth declined to participate, was deemed inappropriate, or could not be located. Thirteen males and 5 females did not participate; 5 males and 1 female were deemed cognitively inappropriate; 4 males and 2 females could not be located; and 4 males and 2 females refused to participate. Twenty-nine of a planned 30 initial interviews, 14 females and 15 males, were completed in early 1995; the thirtieth youth, a female, was in jail and not available for interview. Participants could choose to meet in the researcher's office, their home, or a neutral location; most opted to meet in their homes. After an introduction to the purpose and shape of the research, the questionnaire, a slightly adapted version of the Census '91 Long Questionnaire, was presented on a notebook computer to familiarize the participant with working with the researcher on the computer and the concept of direct scribing. The questionnaire contained 45 questions to be answered in relation to each person living in the same dwelling. The interview took from 1/2 to 2 hours depending on the number of people with whom the participant lived and his/her response style.

FINDINGS

Table 11.1 indicates that overall the sample did not differ significantly from the population from which it was drawn with respect to age at last admission to care, age at discharge, time in care, or proportion receiving extended care. The sample, although randomly selected, tends to exaggerate the gender differences evident in the larger population. That is, male participants came into care younger than males in the population (sample = 130 months; population = 135 months) while female participants came into care older (sample = 172 months; population = 155 months). Male participants were slightly more likely than males in the population to receive extended care (sample = 10 of 15, 66%; population = 65%), whereas female participants were less likely than females in the population to receive extended care (sample = 5 of 14, 36%; population = 49%). The overall tendency to greater time in care was also exaggerated in the sample, with males in the sample spending an average of more than twice as long in care than females (males = 81 months; females = 37 months). The 29 youth completed a Census '91 Questionnaire; thus comparisons are possible between the study group and responses of 47,883 18-year-olds in the Toronto Census Metropolitan Area (CMA) who answered the same questions in June 1991. Table 11.2 displays these comparisons.

The proportion of visible minority youth in the sample is similar to their age cohort, but they were Caribbean (all but one were of black Jamaican descent) which was probably an over-representation. Six of these 10 youth immigrated, all between ages 10–14, to families they did not know. A combination of developmental stresses within the family and overload on reception or settlement services may have played a role in the family breakdown that brought these youth into care. Six participants indicated aboriginal ancestry, although none had registered status or claimed the culture. Three males had no idea about their ethnic or cultural background. Several who claimed Canadian heritage specified Maritime or Newfoundland lineage.

Sixty-six percent (19) of the respondents reported attending school in the current academic year compared to 85% of the age cohort. Participants may not, however, be well-connected to the educational system because there are many reasons to enrol in school, such as qualifying for financial support or fulfilling court orders. None of the participants had a high-school certificate, compared with 45% of the cohort. Two participants claimed to be disabled; one is physically and mentally handicapped and resident in a special care foster home, and the other is being treated for a psychiatric illness.

The pattern of employment among participants is almost the converse of their age cohorts; 46% of the cohort worked more than half the previous year compared to 21% (6) of the participants. Forty-one percent (12) had worked less than one week. The cohort were reporting work in 1990 and the

Table 11.1: Comparison of Sample and Population

	Population	Sample	Test of goodness of fit	p
Age at last admission (months)	$\bar{x}$ = 142.7	$\bar{x}$ = 153.2	2 tail t-test for equal variance	.288
Age at discharge (months)	$\bar{x}$ = 199.1	$\bar{x}$ = 204.9	2 tail t-test for equal variance	.421
Time in care (months)	$\bar{x}$ = 67.0	$\bar{x}$ = 58.4	2 tail t-test for equal variance	.410
File closed at/by 18	yes: 41% no: 59%*	yes: 43% no: 57%*	Pearson chi-square	.852

* This excludes about 13% of the population whose birthdays were too close to the time data was obtained to have closures reflected in the computerized data base.

participants in 1994; conditions for youth employment may have changed; this is unlikely, however, given the persistent disadvantage of youth in employment. The participants tended to work at minimum-wage jobs in manufacturing, retail, clerical work, and child care, and to be employed briefly or as casual labour. One exception, a table dancer, averaged $1,570 per week in wages and tips. Only two other participants earned more than $10,000. Fewer females worked, and those who did were likely to work part-time, whereas the males were likely to work full-time but for a shorter period. Three participants reported that they worked the week prior to their interview; one worked part-time in candy retail, another did casual but profitable baby-sitting, and a male (who is planning to marry in the summer) worked 70+ hours as a cleaning products sales trainee. Illicit activity was more lucrative than employment; participants reported earning $1,000 to $2,000 for delivering a stolen car on order, an easy $100–150 per day on casual drug sales, and a more difficult $500 for extortion. In 1994, 17 participants, mostly males, received extended care, and 10, mostly females, received welfare. Either source covers about half the cost of living in Metro Toronto (Monsebraaten, 1995) and slightly more than the estimated annual cost (in 1991) of raising an 18-year-old in his or her family (Social Planning Council of Metro Toronto, 1992).

A high proportion of the participants were parents consistent with other studies on young people leaving care. Garnett (1992) reports 1 in 7 girls in her study was pregnant at discharge; Stein and Carey (1986) report 10 of about 45 youth were parents within 2 years of leaving care; Biehal and colleagues (1992) report that 13% of their sample were parents. A large American study found that 60% of the females in the study were mothers 2–5 years after leaving care, a rate equal to their age cohort who lived in poverty (Cook et al., 1993). In this study, 57% of females (8) and 33% of males (5) were or were imminently due

Table 11.2: Comparison of Sample with Toronto Census Metropolitan Area (CMA) Cohort

VARIABLES	PARTICIPANTS (1994) n = 29		CMA COHORT (1991) n = 47883
ETHNICITY:			
visible minority	34%	(10)	30%
immigrated	21%	(6)	26%
EDUCATION:			
attended school this year	66%	(19)	85%
has educational certifcate	-	(0)	45%
EMPLOYMENT:			
in '94 worked <1 week	41%	(12)	7%
in '94 worked 1-13 weeks	21%	(6)	21%
in '94 worked 14-26 weeks	17%	(5)	26%
in '94 worked 27-52 weeks	21%	(6)	46%
never worked*	17%	(5)	18%
INCOME IN '94: (individual may have more than one source)			75% = <$5000
legally earned income	59%	(17)	
received welfare	38%	(11)	
received CAS financial support	59%	(17)	
PARENTING:			
parents of 1 child (women only)	50%	(7)	3.5%
parents of 1 child (both men & women)	38%	(11)	not available
parents of 2 children (women only)	7%	(1)	.28%
parents of 2 children (both men & women)	7%	(2)	not available
MOBILITY:			
did not move in prior year	10%	(3)	82%
did not move in 5 years	3%	(1)	54%
CURRENT LIVING CIRCUMSTANCES:			
live alone	17%	(5)	not available
live with parents	3%	(1)	92%
live with surrogate family or other relatives	24%	(7)	7%
live with common-law spouse	29%	(8)	1%
live alone with children	3%	(1)	not available
in jail	7%	(2)	not available
in supported placements	17%	(5)	not available

* These are a subset of those who worked less than 1 week in 1994.

to become biological parents. Among the cohort, 4% of 18-year-old females had one child (the census does not ask males about procreation). One of each gender among the participants had a second child, as did.3% of the female age cohort. All but one mother were parenting (or planning to parent) their children, two biological fathers had never parented their children, and one male who was not a biological father was parenting his partner's child. The participants had produced 15 children. One child, conceived in an incestuous relationship and born to the participant when she was less than 14 years old, had been taken into care but had died of congenital defects. Two, perhaps 3, other children were being monitored by child welfare authorities. No participant had ever been married, but a much higher proportion than in the cohort were currently living common-law. All but one common-law couple cared for children. Male common-law partners tended to be older than the females, up to twice the partner's age. Although attached to the labour market, they saw their partners as self-supporting on welfare, and the females seem satisfied to receive an occasional gift. In one case, a male participant received welfare as head of the household, but perhaps only because his partner was too young to be eligible on her own.

Only three participants had not moved in the prior year; one was stably housed with her child, one was in jail, and another was in a special-care foster home. The latter is the only one who had been in the same place for five years. This is considerably more mobile than the age cohort. Participants were asked to identify all their living circumstances since leaving their last child welfare facility. The time covered ranged from 7 to 48 months, with a mean of 24 months. There is little gender difference although females leave care earlier. It may be that females felt they need to leave care to have age appropriate freedom, whereas males were given more latitude in care. Participants described from no moves to more than they could recall. Females were the most mobile; 7 females and 11 males had 1 to 5 moves, 4 females and 3 males had 6 to 10 moves, and 2 females moved more than 11 times. Females also reported having been homeless more frequently. It may be that males are more stable because of requirements of the justice system or the influence of their agency worker, and/or that females are destabilized by greater vulnerability. Previous research has reported that many youth return to family after leaving care. Beihal and others (1992) report 26% returned or remained at home, Little (1990) found that 56% of boys and 41% of girls returned to their parents after leaving residential care, Bullock (1995) sets the number at 87% of all ages within five years post-care, and Cook and colleagues (1993) found that 54% returned to family within 2–5 years after leaving care. In this study, 57% (8) of females and 27% (4) of males reported that one of their moves involved living with relatives, in most cases mothers. Usually this was the first move after leaving agency facilities. Independence is often defined in the care system as synonymous with living alone. Many participants found this difficult, even with several attempts. Others sought surrogate families, a friend's or partner's family and in one case an ex-foster family. Others tried to live with peers, often experiencing difficulty. Some established families by living with partners and/or children. The current living circumstances of the participants were atypical of their age cohort, 92% of whom lived with parents, 3% with other relatives, and 4% with others to whom they were not related.

DISCUSSION

The life circumstances of this small but random sample of 18-year-olds who have left child welfare care in Metropolitan Toronto were very different than that of their age cohort. They were poor, under-employed, and under-educated relative to their peers. They had little or no support from their families, although one-third of the females and two-thirds of the males received extended care. Many had experienced the justice system, and for some it may offer a more adequate and predictable living situation than they can provide for themselves. Almost half had moved into the next stage of the life cycle by establishing a family. It is difficult to see how, on this foundation, they can hope to build a good-enough future. And yet they do articulate this goal. The daunting challenge of the transition to adulthood for youth leaving care requires consideration of the following points:

- The usual age at which Canadian young people leave home is in the mid-twenties; how then can the state justify requiring children in care to leave home at 18?

- Why would 74% of this study population who were entitled to stay in care until they were 18 choose to leave early? Does this suggest a poorness of fit between what they want or need and what is offered?

- Are high-risk behaviours, such as early parenthood and illicit activity, among youth leaving care the result of rational and informed choices among the options reasonably available to them as they pursue accepted social goals? Should resources be used to reduce the transitional gap, or to support the capacity of young people to manage the reality they encounter?

- What conditions will motivate society to reconceptualize responsibility to youth during their decade of transition? Youth, with those who value their capacity to become good and caring adults, must collaboratively articulate a vision and market it to the public.

This was the first phase of a continuing study. Over an eight-month period, these youth will participate in two additional meetings to produce a narrative about the transition to independence, which will be scribed directly into a computer and collaboratively analyzed and edited. The youth will also meet in same-gender focus groups. The additional data is expected to further illuminate the interplay between the internal and external realities that determine the life courses of young people leaving care, as well as gender differences in the challenges they face and how they conceptualize and manage these.

References

Beihal, N., Clayden, J., Stein, M., & Wade, J. (1992). *Prepared for living?* London, England: National Children's Bureau.

Bullock, R. (1995). Return home as experienced by children in state care and their families. In B. Galaway & J. Hudson (Eds.), *Child welfare in Canada: Research and policy implications* (pp. 298–307). Toronto: Thompson Educational Publishing.

Clough, R. (1988). *Living away from home.* Bristol, England: University of Bristol.

Cook, R., Fleishman, R., & Grimes, V. (1993). *A national evaluation of title IV-E independent living programs for youth, phase 2, final report, volume 1.* Rockville, MD: Westat Inc.

Fisher, M., Marsh, P., Phillips, D., & Sainsbury, E. (1986). *In and out of care: The experiences of children, parents and social workers.* London, England: Batsford.

Garnett, L. (1992). *Leaving care and after.* London, England: National Children's Bureau.

Jacklin, C. (1989). Female and male: Issues of gender. *American Psychologist, 44* (2), 127–133.

Little, M. (1990). Specialized residential services for difficult adolescents: Some recent research findings. In Roger Bullock (Ed.), *Problem adolescents: An international view* (pp. 122–133). London, England: Whiting & Birch.

Looker, E.D. (1996). The transitions to adult roles: Youth views and policy implications. In B. Galaway & J. Hudson (Eds.), *Youth in transition: Perspectives on research and policy.* Toronto: Thompson Educational Publishing.

Meston, J. (1988). Preparing young people in Canada for emancipation from child welfare care. *Child Welfare, 67* (6), 625–634.

Monsebraaten, L. (1995). Pledges of welfare cuts strike fear in recipients. *The Toronto Star,* May 22, 1995 (A9).

National Children's Homes (1993). *A lost generation? A survey of the problems faced by vulnerable young people living on their own.* London, England: Author.

Parker, R., Ward, H., Jackson, S., Aldgate, J., & Wedge, P. (Eds). (1991). *Living away from home: Assessing outcomes in child care.* London, England: HMSO.

Raychaba, B. (1988). *To be on our own with no help from home.* Ottawa: National Youth in Care Network.

Social Planning Council of Metro Toronto (1992). *Guides for family budgeting '91.* Toronto: Social Planning Council of Metro Toronto.

Stein, M., & Carey, K. (1986). *Leaving care.* Oxford and New York: Basil Blackwood.

Varpalotai, A. (1996). Canadian girls in transition to womanhood. In B. Galaway & J. Hudson (Eds.), *Youth in transition: Perspectives on research and policy.* Toronto: Thompson Educational Publishing.

Wyn, J. (1996). Youth in transition to adulthood in Australia: Review of research and policy issues. In B. Galaway & J. Hudson (Eds.), *Youth in transition: Perspectives on research and policy.* Toronto: Thompson Educational Publishing.

This research has been funded by a Canadian Welfare Fellowship (1993-'96) and a Laidlaw Foundation Advanced Study Fellowship (1994-'96) and was undertaken with the active cooperation of Metro Toronto Children's Aid Society.

12

Educational, Occupational and Family Aspirations of Women: A Longitudinal Study

Gloria Geller

A considerable body of literature has developed on the aspirations and expectations of girls and women. Most studies are conducted with high-school students or with students in colleges and universities, and often include both males and females in order to compare differences in the aspirations of both sexes (Machung, 1989; Porter & Tasmin, 1987; Friesen, 1983; Aneschensel & Rosen, 1980; Anisef et al., 1980; Breton, 1972). A number of authors have focused their research on the aspirations of females of varying ages (Baker, 1985; Geller, 1984a, 1973; Poole & Low, 1985; Corder & Stephan, 1984; Maxwell, 1970; Baber & Monaghan, 1988; Holms & Esses, 1988). Authors of such studies recognize the need for longitudinal studies in order to find out to what extent aspirations held in high school or even in college are pursued, and to determine the reasons they may not have been pursued. Some efforts have been made to undertake longitudinal studies (Erwin, 1996; Harmon, 1989; Maxwell & Maxwell, 1984; Friesen, 1983; Porter et al., 1982; Anisef et al., 1980; Williams, 1972) but few longitudinal studies follow respondents into adult life (Anisef, 1996; Harmon, 1989). This chapter presents findings based on research conducted over a twenty-year period in which there have been profound changes in the lives of women, a time in which women's involvement in the paid labour force has grown in unprecedented numbers and proportions, and a time when the lives of women appear to have changed substantially from that of their mothers and grandmothers.

THE RESEARCH

In the spring of 1973 and again in 1983 diaries of the future were collected from female students in Grade 9, Grade 12 as a completing year, and Grade 13, from three high schools in the Toronto area. In 1983 three schools from Regina were added to the study (Geller, 1984a, 1984b, 1985). The schools located in Toronto included an inner city commercial high school (City School) that had large numbers of predominantly working-class female students, an elite upper-middle-class private girls' school (Private School), and a primarily middle-class suburban school (Suburban school) that was a composite school on the outskirts of the city. Regina students were from Regina North School, a predominantly working-class school, Regina South School, a predominantly middle-class school, and Regina Private School (a co-educational school), also a predominantly middle-class school.

The students were asked to write a diary of the future in which they discussed their hopes and dreams from the time they completed high school until they were old women in their 70s or 80s. Each of the respondents also completed a demographic questionnaire. There was an option on the questionnaire to fill in names and phone numbers if they would be willing to be interviewed. About 35 of the 241 respondents in 1973 did so. In 1983 all the students were asked to give the researcher their names, phone numbers, and addresses if they were interested in being found in ten years. At that time 216 gave this information.

A subsample of 18 respondents have been drawn from the larger sample of women interviewed in 1983 and 1993 (about 108 in all). The 18 consist of six respondents from the 1973 cohort and twelve from the 1983 group, all of whom were interviewed in 1993. Two respondents were randomly selected from each of the schools included in both studies. Comparisons were made between the respondents from the three Toronto area schools (six from 1973 and six from 1983) and the twelve respondents from the 1983 study that included six schools (three Toronto area schools and three Regina schools). The findings were compared by school, by social class, and by differences over the ten year time period. The research is presented in case study form and focuses on the personal experiences of a small group of women who were followed over a period of 10 or 20 years.

RESEARCH FINDINGS

The focus is on the educational, occupational, and family aspirations that the respondents wrote about in their diaries of the future and on what they have subsequently been doing in these areas. All 18 respondents are presented in Table 12.1. The first six are from the 1973 cohort and the remaining 12 are from the 1983 cohort. The women ranged in age from 14 to 19 when they wrote the diaries. Most of the respondents' parents were Canadian-born. None of the Regina respondents' parents were born outside of Canada. All Regina respondents were born in Canada and all but two of the Toronto-area respondents were born in Canada while one was born in Greece and one in East Pakistan. All the respondents had at least one other sibling; five was the largest number of siblings.

Parents' occupations and mother's employment status when the young women were students are presented in Table 12.2. Social class is an important factor in determining the future choices and opportunities of the next generation. Most of the working-class respondents' mothers were employed in both the 1973 and 1983 cohorts and half of the middle-class respondents' mothers were employed as well; the upper middle-class respondents' mothers were either pursuing further education or were primarily housewives while perhaps engaged in volunteer work.

Educational and Occupational Aspirations and Attainments

The educational and occupational aspirations and attainments of respondents are presented in Tables 12.3 and 12.4. Two of the respondents from the 1973 cohort indicated a desire to complete Grade 12 commercial high-school

Table 12.1:   Longitudinal Study of Women's Aspirations: A Subsample of Respondents

Pseudonym	Age in High School	Age 1993	School	Grade
Betty	16	36	City	9 - 4*
Joan	14	34	City	9 - 4
Ruth	14	34	Private	9 - 5
Melinda	15	35	Private	9 - 5
Theresa	19	39	Suburban	13
Frances	18	38	Suburban	13
Philomena	15	25	City	9 - 4
Robin	16	26	City	9 - 4
Trish	15	25	Private	9 - 5
Arun	15	25	Private	9 - 5
Roberta	14	24	Suburban	9 - 5
Barbara	19	29	Suburban	13
Katherine	17	27	Regina South	12
Olga	15	25	Regina South	9
Jane	14	24	Regina Private	9
Liz	14	24	Regina Private	9
Pearl	14	24	Regina North	9
Megan	15	25	Regina North	9

*The grades included were first-year high school, or Grade 9 students (4- or 5-year program in the Ontario school system) as well as a completing year, either Grade 12 or 13 in Ontario schools and Grade 12 in Saskatchewan schools.

programs while the other four respondents specified going to university. In 1983, university was aspired to by seven respondents, two aspired to high-school completion, and one wanted to go as far as Grade 9 or 10. Ten years later none of the working-class respondents from both cohorts had any post-secondary education leading to a diploma. Of the middle-class respondents, none of the Regina women completed university and only one completed a post-secondary diploma. The other three Regina residents indicated they were unable to pursue further education due to lack of funds. All Toronto Suburban and Toronto Private School respondents from both cohorts completed at least a first degree and some have gone on to further studies.

In 1983 and again in 1993, the two working-class City School women from the 1973 cohort were working in office jobs for which they had been prepared in high school. The woman who wanted to be a doctor while in high school practiced family medicine, while the other Suburban School respondent had worked for Bell Canada since graduating from university. The two Private School respondents from 1973 both worked for some time and subsequently decided to change their occupations which required returning to University for other degrees. Regina respondents from the 1983 cohort were not in occupations of their choice, with the possible exception of one of the respondents who had obtained a diploma in nursing. Suburban and Private School women

Table 12.2: Parents' Occupations and Mother's Employment Status

Pseudonym	Occupations		Mother's Employment Status*
	Mother	Father	
Betty	factory worker	factory worker	housewife - ft
Joan	makes jewelery	machine operator	employed - ft
Ruth	researcher	lawyer	housewife - ft grad student
Melinda	unknown	stockbroker	housewife - ft volunteer
Theresa	bookeeper secretary	warehouse manager	employed - ft
Frances	file clerk	tool designer	housewife - ft
Philomena	nurse	construction foreman (deceased)	employed - ft
Robin	store clerk family business	electrician own TV/radio store	employed - ft
Trish	restaurant owner	lawyer	employed - ft
Arun	none	self-employed	student - nursing
Roberta	teacher or aide	civil engineer	housewife - ft occasional employment
Barbara	manual labourer	plant manager	employed - ft
Katherine	office manager family business	interior decorator and home building business	employed - ft
Olga	physiotherapist's attendant	unemployed civil servant	employed - ft
Jane	secretary/dental nurse	engineer	housewife - ft
Liz	teller	vice-president corporation	employed - pt
Pearl	nurse	self-employed carpet cleaning	unemployed or retired
Megan	clerk	welder	employed - pt

* Mother's employment status as indicated when the respondents were in high school — specified as full-time housewife or as being employed on a full-time (ft) or part-time (pt) basis. Mothers identified as being employed either full-time or part-time are also recognized as being housewives.

Table 12.3: Educational Aspirations and Attainments

Pseudonym	Aspirations in High School	Attainments	
		10 years	**20 years**
Betty	Grade 12 Bible School	Grade 12 and Bible School	-
Joan	Grade 12	Grade 12	-
Ruth	University	Honours B.A. History, B.Ed.	M.Ed., Ph.D. in process
Melinda	University	B.A. - Art History, B.Ed.	Degree in Speech Pathology
Theresa	University - Pschology Theater	Junior College and University B.A.	-
Frances	University - Arts & Sciences and Medicine	University - Arts & Sciences and Medicine	Family Practice Courses
Philomena	Grade 12	Grade 11 and 1 Year Community College	N/A
Robin	Grade 9 or 10 and Hairdressing School	Grade 9	N/A
Trish	University	University B.A. in Fine Arts; Student in Architecture	N/A
Arun	University	University - B.A. in Modern Languages	N/A
Roberta	not stated	University - B.Sc. Honours; Law Student	N/A
Barbara	University	University - B. Music	N/A
Katherine	University	Grade 12	N/A
Olga	University - Languages	University - Arts - dropped out	N/A
Jane	University	University - PreAdministration Studies - One Semester - dropped out	N/A
Liz	University - Music	Technical Institute - Nursing and Student, University	N/A
Pearl	Grade 12	Grade 12 and Bible College	N/A
Megan	not stated	Grade 12 and Correspondence School	N/A

Table 12.4: Occupational Aspirations and Attainments

Pseudonym	Aspirations in High School	Occupation	
		10 Years	20 years
Betty	stewardess, airlines office worker	Manager - Bell	Manager - Bell
Joan	Secretary	Secretary	Secretary (same company)
Ruth	researcher	Outdoor instructor	Doctoral Student/Lecturer
Melinda	actress	Antique dealer	Speech Pathologist
Theresa	drama, theatre	Course developer - Bell	Manager - Bell - Computers
Frances	doctor	Doctor	Family practitioner
Philomena	social worker, teacher, stewardess, cruise director, model, own business	Desktop publisher	N/A
Robin	hairdresser	Day care worker - part-time	N/A
Trish	lawyer	Student -architecture	N/A
Arun	psychologist, architect, own business	Production sales coordinator in a film house	N/A
Roberta	veterinarian, physician	Student - law school	N/A
Barbara	teacher of music	Mother, wife - full-time; piano teacher	N/A
Katherine	social worker, guidance teacher, own business	Clerk - Crown Corporation	N/A
Olga	translator, model, stewardess	Customer service management - credit card company	N/A
Jane	lawyer, real estate	Cosmetic manager Drugstore chain	N/A
Liz	nurse, teach piano, actress	Nurse	N/A
Pearl	not stated	School bus driver	N/A
Megan	veterinarian, cook	Customer service cashier - large merchandising chain	N/A

had either continued their studies, were staying at home with children or were in an entry level position of at least some interest to them. Many of these women, especially those from the Regina 1983 cohort, were experiencing constraints in their abilities to seek out educational and occupational opportunities for themselves.

There appears to have been minimal career planning while in high school. Many of the women got into jobs without any planning or for very practical reasons; they needed to work and took what they could find. A few of the respondents seem to have pursued their interests and when no longer interested, they took further training or education. Others had interests they never pursued. Most of the 1983 Regina cohort either did not have aspirations to study beyond high school or were unable to do so for monetary reasons. Few appeared to have pursued options that lead to a specific career ladder. Several respondents have lowered their aspirations for economic reasons. The women either did not know about student loans or were reluctant to take out student loans to study nor did they appear to consider becoming parttime students while working fulltime as possible options. The effects of having children was to further circumscribe some of the women's educational and occupational opportunities. The situation of the 1983 cohort, especially those who are working class, as well as all the women from the Regina schools, seems to be considerably less favourable than that of the 1973 cohort (including the 1973 working-class women who have secure employment) and the Toronto respondents from both the 1973 and 1983 cohorts.

Family Aspirations and Attainments

All but one of the six 20 year respondents had indicated in high schools that they wanted to get married. Three of the women had been married by 1993. One of the three, a Suburban School respondent, was divorced. One of the six was engaged and planned to marry, while both Private School women were single and had not married. Among this group, all but one had written in their diaries that they wanted to have children. The three women who had married had children. The two City School graduates had both married at 23 years of age and started families shortly after they married, while the Suburban School respondent completed her medical education, married at 28 and started her family after she had established herself in her career. All but one of the twelve in the 1983 cohort had also indicated they wanted to marry. Ten years later two were married, two were engaged and planned to marry in the fall of 1993, two were in common-law relationships, and two had plans to marry. All but one of the women had stated she wanted to have children; three of the women had children in 1993.

Many of the women clearly expected in high school that they would remain at home with their children and be full-time mothers for at least several years. Four of the 1973 group made statements of this type. In fact both working-class women did not leave their jobs only taking time off for maternity leave; while the third stayed home with her first child for one and a half years and then set up an office in her own home and practised medicine parttime. While in high school the young women believed they would likely be at home with their children for some periods of time but there was little indication in the diaries that they would also be doing housework. Only one of the women mentioned that she would be a housewife; although one respondent made the point that she would not be a "typical mother/wife figure." When asked in 1983 and again in 1993 why they had not mentioned this role, the women generally indicated that their mothers (or grandmothers or paid help) did the housework, they did not do housework when they were in high school, or they said that doing housework is not an aspiration.

The respondents were asked about current housework and childcare arrangements, and whether or not they were satisfied with their partners' involvement with housework and childcare. Of the three women from the 1973 cohort with children, two had their children in day care while one woman's mother babysat the children in her home. In 1983, the two women who were employed and young mothers, were not satisfied with their husbands' involvement with housework and childcare; while in 1993 one stated that she and her husband both do housework on the weekend, although she wished he would spend more time with the children, and the second stated she was the "prime" person while "he does whatever needs to be done," and that she was satisfied with his involvement. The third respondent did not have children in 1983 but she was very satisfied with her husband's involvement in housework; in 1993 she was divorced.

Very few respondents from the 1983 cohort had mentioned in their diaries what they would do once they had children nor is there mention made of housework. As to why they had not mentioned housework, the respondents stated either that housework was not an aspiration or that it was something they took for granted that they would do. One of the three respondents who had children had her children in subsidized daycare, another's mother babysat and the third was a fulltime stay-at-home mom. Of those living with partners, four stated that they were very satisfied while one was not satisfied with the involvement in housework of their partners. There was a wide range of activities and time allotted to housework by the men, ranging from a couple of hours to eight hours a week.

The women who had married or were living in relationships were asked about how the roles of wife, mother, and housewife differed from what they had thought they would be like when in high school. The mothers all stated that they find their roles to be "demanding" and "a lot more work than they had expected." The two City School respondents from the 1973 cohort noted that they had not known about the "trials and tribulations" of being a wife, mother, and housewife. The divorced Suburban School respondent from the 1973 cohort indicated she had not expected to divorce. She noted that her job required more than a 9 to 5 commitment and she felt pulled by her job and her children, although both her practice and her children have kept her going. Most of the women from the 1983 cohort also found these roles to be very different from what they had expected in high school. One of the mothers stated she found it to be "completely different, being a parent is 24 hours a day" and that it is much more work than she had realized. The fulltime housewife indicated "being married takes more work and communication and cooperation and give and take than I thought. I thought things would fall into place a bit more easily." One of the Regina North respondents, a single mother of three, stated, "as a mother, it's more trying than I thought it would be, housework never ends, a lot more responsibility than I thought it would be."

The transition from youth to adult life was quite profound for these young women. This is especially true once they take on the responsibilities of a home and a family. The burden of caring for children and a home while holding down a job is especially onerous and many of the women have had to make decisions about how to balance their responsibilities. Some work parttime, at least one had decided to be a fulltime homemaker and mother, others hold down a fulltime job and come home in the evening to care for their children. Those who have children are less positive than the others about the involvement of their partners or husbands in doing housework. Few of the respondents who wanted to marry and have children had expected to work while their children were young and yet most are employed. Housework is work, and it is work that most women, especially women who have children, must do on top of any other paid employment they may hold down. The realities of young women's lives must be taken into account when considering young women's educational and occupational opportunities. The contrast between those women who married and/or had children at a young age and those from wealthier backgrounds who have continued their education, travelled, pursued careers and refrained from early marriage and motherhood, must be given serious consideration by policy makers and by educators.

CONCLUSION

Canadian society has changed. Young women and mothers of young children are in the labour force and will be expected, perhaps required, to be either employed or in some kind of training if they are single parent mothers (Vanier Institute of the Family, 1994; Blau & Ferber, 1986; Armstrong & Armstrong, 1984; Phillips & Phillips, 1983). Large numbers of women and children are living in poverty (Lero & Brockman, 1993; National Council of Welfare, 1990; Gunderson et al., 1990; Hochschild & Machung, 1989). Working-class women are not pursuing non-traditional blue-collar jobs or technical jobs but continue to fill the ranks of the service and clerical sectors (Gunderson et al., 1990; Statistics Canada, 1985; Armstrong & Armstrong, 1984; Phillips & Phillips, 1983). These are often the women who are at risk of living in poverty with their children. At the same time those born into the wealthier classes are able to take advantage of the changed climate in which more and more women are entering post-secondary education and find their way into professional and business occupations and careers (Norbert & McDowell, 1994; Guppy et al., 1987; Porter & Tasmin, 1987).

There is a need to consider the nature of social, economic and educational policy as it relates to the poor in this country. Many working-class women are being streamed out of the education system by the end of Grade 12 if not sooner (Gaskell, 1987; Jackson, 1987). Gaskell (1987) has pointed out that these young women tend to view the education system as irrelevant and opt for courses they believe have some practical application. Many of these young women must enter the labour force as quickly as possible as they do not have family support to continue their education beyond age 16 or Grade 12. The current situation must be changed if we are to ensure that considerable numbers of working-class women are not going to continue to raise their families in poverty. The things that must be done include:

- Gender-role education in elementary and high school.
- programs in high school that offer skills leading to adequately paid employment in which mobility is possible.
- Teachers and educational personnel offering encouragement and information to working-class women students and their families concerning the importance of education for their daughters.
- Availability of bursaries and scholarships to encourage working-class women students to remain in school and to go on to further education.
- Greater mobility from job to job within large organizations, such as bridging type programs which allow for upward mobility.
- Pay and employment equity.
- Universal 24 hour child care.
- Recognition of the value of the work of mothers staying at home to raise children.

References

Aneschensel, C., & Rosen, B. (1980). Domestic roles and sex differences in occupational expectations. *Journal of Marriage and the Family, 42* (1), 121–131.

Anisef, P. (1996). Transitions, the life course, and the class of '73: Implications for social policy. In B. Galaway & J. Hudson (Eds.), *Youth in transition: Perspectives on research and policy*. Toronto: Thompson Educational Publishing.

Anisef, P., Paasche, J., & Turrittin, A. (1980). *Is the die cast? Educational achievements and work destination of Ontario youth*. Ontario: Ministry of Colleges and Universities.

Armstrong, P., & Armstrong, H. (1984). *The double ghetto* (Revised Edition). Toronto: McClelland and Stewart.

Baber, K., & Monaghan, P. (1988). College women's career and motherhood expectations: New options, old dilemmas. *Sex Roles, 19*(3–4) 189–203.

Baker, M. (1985). *What will tomorrow bring? ... A study of the aspirations of adolescent women*. Ottawa: Canadian Advisory Council on the Status of Women.

Blau, F., & Ferber, M. (1986). *The economics of women, men, and work*. Englewood Cliffs, NJ: Prentice-Hall.

Breton, R. (1972). *Social and academic factors in the career decisions of Canadian youth*. Ottawa: Queen's Printer.

Corder, J., & Stephan, C. (1984). Females' combination of work and family roles: adolescents' aspirations. *Journal of Marriage and The Family, 46* (2), 391–401.

Erwin, L. (1996). "Having it all" in the nineties: The work and family aspirations of women undergraduates. In B. Galaway & J. Hudson (Eds.), *Youth in transition: Perspectives on research and policy*. Toronto: Thompson Educational Publishing.

Friesen, D. (1983). Changing plans and aspirations of high-school students. *The Alberta Journal of Educational Research XXIX* (4), 285–296.

Gaskell, J. (1987). Course enrolment in the high school: The perspective of working-class females. In J. Gaskell & A. McLaren (Eds.), *Women and education: A Canadian perspective*. Calgary: Detselig Enterprises Ltd.

Geller, G. (1985). The fairy tale syndrome: The aspirations of young women. *Briarpatch, 14*(2), 13–17.

Geller, G. (1984a). Aspirations of female high-school students. *Resources for Feminist Research, 13*(1), 17–19.

Geller, G. (1984b). Aspirations of adolescent women. Paper presented at the Canadian Women's Studies Association meetings, Learned Societies, Guelph, Ontario.

Geller, G. (1973). Role aspirations and life-style orientations of high-school women. Master's thesis, University of Toronto.

Gunderson, M., Muszynski, L., & Keck, J. (1990). *Women and labour market poverty*. Ottawa: Canadian Advisory Council on the Status of Women.

Guppy, N., Balson, D., & Vellutini, S. (1987). Women and higher education in Canadian society. In J. Gaskell & A. McLaren (Eds.), *Women and education: A Canadian perspective*. Calgary: Detselig Enterprises Ltd.

Harmon, L. (1989). Longitudinal changes in women's career aspirations: Developmental or historical? *Journal of Vocational Behaviour, 35* (1), 46–63.

Hochschild, A., & Machung, A. (1989). *The second shift: Working parents and the revolution at home*. New York: Viking Press.

Holms, V., & Esses, L. (1988). Factors influencing Canadian high-school girls' career motivation. *Psychology of Women Quarterly, 12* (3), 313–328.

Jackson, N. (1987). Skill training in transition: Implications for women. In J. Gaskell & A. McLaren (Eds.), *Women and education: A Canadian perspective*. Calgary: Detselig Enterprises Ltd.

Lero, D., & Brockman, L. (1993). Single-parent families in Canada: A closer look. In J. Hudson & B. Galaway (Eds.), *Single-parent families: Perspectives on Research and Policy* (pp. 91–114). Toronto: Thompson Educational Publishing, Inc.

Machung, A. (1989). Talking career, thinking job: Gender differences in career and family expectations of Berkeley seniors. *Feminist Studies, 15* (1), 35–58.

Maxwell, M. (1970). Social structure, socialization and social class in a Canadian private school for girls. PhD Thesis, Cornell University.

Maxwell, M., & Maxwell, J. (1984). Women and the elite: Educational and occupational aspirations of private school females 1966/76. *Canadian Review of Sociology and Anthropology, 21* (4), 371–394.

National Council of Welfare. (1990). *Women and poverty revisited*. Ottawa: Minister of Supply and Services.

Norbert, L., & McDowell, R. (1994). *Profile of post-secondary education in Canada* (1993 Edition). Ottawa: Minister of Supply and Services Canada.

Phillips, P., & Phillips, E. (1983). *Women and work: Inequality in the labour market*. Toronto: James Lorimer and Company.

Poole, M., & Low, B. (1985). Career and marriage: Orientations of adolescent girls. *The Australian Journal of Education, 29* (1), 36–45.

Porter, J., Porter, M., & Blishen, B. (1982). *Stations and callings: Making it through the school system*. Toronto: Methuen.

Porter, M., & Tasmin, G. (1987). *A profile of post-secondary students in Canada*. Ottawa: Department of the Secretary of State.

Statistics Canada (1990). *Women in Canada: A statistical report*. Ottawa: Minister of Supply and Services Canada.

Vanier Institute of the Family (1994). *Profiling Canadian families*. Ottawa: Author.

Williams, T. (1972). Educational aspirations: Longitudinal evidence on their development in Canadian youth. *Sociology of Education, 45* (2), 107–133.

Appreciation is extended to Linda O'Halloran in Regina and Barbara Mainguy in Toronto for tracing the respondents and conducting interviews with them, to Sharon Moryski for assistance in organizing the data and developing profiles of all of the respondents, to Debbie McLeod for her secretarial assistance, and to Jan Joel for reading the paper and giving feedback to me. The President's Fund of the University of Regina has given financial support to this project.

13

Adults with Disabilities: Barriers to Post-Secondary Education

Jennifer Leigh Hill

The Health and Activity Limitation Survey (HALS) conducted between 1986 and 1987 by Statistics Canada (1990a) provides a wealth of information on the estimated 3.3 million persons with disabilities residing in households and health-related institutions in Canada. Of particular interest are the data related to the educational attainment of the 1.5 million females (14.7% of the total population) and 1.3 million males (13.9%) over the age of 15 who resided in non-institutional settings (see Table 13.1). The amount of education obtained by men and women with disabilities was similar (Statistics Canada, 1990b). However, when the educational attainment of individuals with disabilities was compared to those without, significant variations were found. Regardless of gender, those with a disabling condition were "heavily concentrated in the lowest educational category and significantly under-represented in the highest educational categories"(Statistics Canada, 1990b, p. 11). Not all students who graduate from high school will enter a post-secondary educational settings. Continuing one's education, however, may be more important for individuals with disabilities than for persons who are non-disabled; "in the employment arena, educational credentials attest to skills, knowledge, and a work ethic that can help focus an employer on a person's abilities rather than disabilities" (Marder, 1992, p. 3–1). Fichten (1988) found that individuals with disabilities who have completed a course of post-secondary studies are more likely than those who have not to be employed, to have spent less time seeking employment, and, once employed, were more satisfied with their jobs and remained for a longer period of time.

The rise in the number of students with disabling conditions in post-secondary institutions has been described as meteoric (Wilchesky, 1986) but a gap remains between the number of students capable of pursing a program of higher education and those who actually do (Gajar et al., 1993). Students with disabilities vary greatly on several dimensions that must be considered when discussing possible barriers to post-secondary education. For some, the nature of the disability may prevent the students from continuing education beyond the high-school level, for others the degree of severity of the impairment may limit participation. This chapter will explore some of the reasons why students who have the necessary cognitive skills and the physical ability to compete with their non-disabled peers may choose not to continue their schooling. Only

Table 13.1 Persons with Disabilities, Aged 15 and Over, Residing in Households, by Sex by Education

Education	Females (%)		Males (%)	
	With Disabilities	Without Disabilities	With Disabilities	Without Disabilities
0-8 years	38.8	13.9	35.9	14.0
Secondary	36.4	45.3	36.5	41.8
Some Post-secondary	11.2	16.6	16.2	20.9
Certificate/ Diploma	10.2	15.5	6.2	11.4
University Degree	3.4	8.7	5.2	11.9

Source: Statistics Canada (1990b). Tables 5 (p. 9) & 6 (p. 10).

those barriers that are unique to the population under discussion will be examined. Obstacles that are common to youth in general (e.g., cost) will not be addressed unless the presence of a disabling condition has a particular effect on the student's educational aspirations. Many of the barriers to the pursuit of a post-secondary education have their roots in the elementary and secondary school years and are less evident than barriers in the post-high-school years.

BARRIERS TO POST-SECONDARY EDUCATION ENCOUNTERED IN ELEMENTARY AND SECONDARY SCHOOL SETTINGS

Attitudinal Barriers and Lack of Role Models

One of the greatest barriers to the pursuit of higher education may be the false, patronizing, and stereotypical attitudes of others. Carpenter (1992), a parent of a severely handicapped young adult, described the biases held by many able-bodied individuals:

> Our beliefs about disability fall into the category of things our society takes for granted. Like sexism, which until relatively recently was unconsciously accepted by almost everyone, ableism is rarely recognized for what it is: the oppression of the socially weak by the socially strong. The ableist regards allowances society makes for the special needs of disabled persons—designated parking places, wheelchair ramps, sign language interpreters, special-needs classes in school—as accommodations granted, even as gifts given, to people with disabilities rather than as what they are: obligatory rights (pp. 27–28).

Attitudinal barriers take many forms and have a variety of roots. Teachers, not fully cognizant of the impact of a specific disabling conditions on future work plans, may not have the necessary information to help students make realistic post-school choices. Parents may undermine the child's confidence in his or her own ability by exercising a tremendous amount of control of the life of their child (Michaels, 1994). Grandparents may excuse children with disabilities from being required to carry out routine household chores, thereby weakening the foundation of the work personality and competencies that normally develop in the early years (Szymanski, 1994). Employers may assign tasks that do not reflect the students' strengths but rather their weaknesses and/or the disability label assigned to the students (Gajar et al., 1993). These attitudes contribute to lack of self-esteem, self-confidence, and self-determination to pursue a program of higher education, even though the students may be competitive. Many students with disabilities, particularly those with learning disabilities, have significantly lower aspirations for future educational opportunities than their non-disabled peers (White, 1992; Reiff et al., 1995).

Stereotypical attitudes held by others can be offset by the presence of positive role models. Students with disabilities may have had contact with persons without disabling conditions who have pursued a program of higher education. Rarely, however, will they have had contact with a person with a disability following a career path similar to the one they are considering. Szymanski (1994), in tracing the early development of children with disabling conditions, has suggested that sparse exposure to credible role models, along with the lack of encouragement to engage in career-related fantasy, a normal activity of childhood, may result in a restriction of the range of career objectives that the children may aspire to in their school-age years.

Poor Academic Preparation

Students with disabilities are often poorly prepared to enter a post-secondary program (Burbach & Babbitt, 1988). A common practice in the school system is to develop an individualized educational program (IEP), a document that "spells out just what teachers plan to do to meet an exceptional student's needs" (Hallahan & Kauffman, 1994, p. 35). Students with disabilities (particularly those with learning disabilities) may be innocent victims of the IEP process (Michaels, 1994); IEPs generally include one of three variations on the theme of changing academic demands to enable the student to succeed. The first is the provision of less work (e.g., the student has to read one short story instead of two); the second is the provision of easier work (e.g., the student is provided with an abridged version of a novel); and, the third is the provision of extra time (e.g., the student is given an extra hour to complete a test) (Michaels, 1994). Unfortunately, "rather than empowering students, these interventions only provide students with the covert message that 'we do not think that you are as capable as your peers'" (Michaels, 1994, p. 16) and fail to prepare students for the competitive environment in which they will be required to compete with students who do more work, harder work, and complete the work in a prescribed period of time. Rather than efforts to change the learning demands for students with disabilities, Michaels (1994) has suggested that teachers must focus on changing the learner. In many cases this can be accomplished by teaching a variety of cognitive strategies (e.g., problem solving skills, note taking skills, study skills) that are "designed to enhance an individual's ability to successfully function with grade-appropriate material in the mainstream environment" (Michaels, 1994, p. 16).

Many students with disabling conditions also experience a change in academic setting. An increasing number of students with special learning needs are being educated in the regular classroom setting, but it is still a common practice to find students with special needs in resource rooms for a significant part of the school day (U.S. Department of Education, 1994). The traditional resource room model for the provision of services has been denounced by many in the field (Brinckerhoff et al., 1993; DuChossis & Michaels, 1994). Emphasis on tutoring specific content subjects, reinforcement of work previously completed in the regular classroom, and provision of assistance with homework and other required assignments may be detrimental to some special needs students because there is the potential for students to develop the conviction that "it is help from others that gets them through their classes" (DuChossis & Michaels, 1994, p. 85).

Consequences of Dropping Out or Being "Pushed Out"

Students without disabilities who drop out of high school are greatly disadvantaged, compared to students who remain until graduation (e.g., have fewer jobs; suffer from a lower level of personal health; experience decreased cultural enjoyment) (Human Resources & Labour Canada, 1993). Only recently, however, has the plight of students with disabilities who drop out of school prior to graduation been examined. An obvious consequence of dropping out is the inability to continue one's post-secondary education without returning to school to obtain a high-school diploma or General Education Development certificate. Information about the number of Canadian students with disabilities who drop out of high school is lacking. Data from the United States has shown that students with disabilities drop out of school significantly more frequently than their non-handicapped peers (37% vs. 21%) (Marder, 1992). Wolman, Bruininks, and Thurlow (1989) discuss the many factors that contribute to students with disabilities leaving school prior to graduation (e.g., negative attitudes; low achievement measures), and raise the rhetorical question, "Why do some children in special education drop out of school while others do not?" (p. 18). They also have provided a possible answer, "Although it may be obvious that these students [special education students who drop out of school] are ones who have difficulties adapting themselves to the educational system, it may be less obvious that the educational system also has difficulties adapting to students who need a special approach" (p. 18). Cohen and DeBettencourt (1991) note, "Clearly, the population with mild handicaps … is leaving the system at an alarming rate. One could argue that if schools were meeting the needs of students with mild handicaps, the number of special education dropouts would not be so great" (p. 264). Some have predicted that the dropout problem in special education will be exacerbated by a pushing out of students with disabilities in response to the pressure being exerted on schools to return to programs that promote academic excellence (Semmel, 1987, cited in Diem & Katims, 1991).

Lack of or Inadequacy of Transitional Support

The importance of adequate planning to facilitate the transition of students with disabilities from secondary school to post-school activities (e.g., work, further education) has been reported by many (Halpern, 1994; Hill, 1996). However, current emphasis on the attention placed at or near the time the student is about to leave school and on specialized curriculum developed to address transitional needs of students (generally emphasizing work related skills) with disabilities has been criticized. Most school-based transitional programs focus on movement from school to work; students with disabling conditions often need assistance in transitioning from school to school. College career days and the provision of catalogs on post-secondary programs may not be sufficient to meet the unique needs of students with disabilities who may also need information on special financial aid opportunities or on special arrangements for modified college admission tests. Transition services such as activities which promote the movement from school to post-school activities and the development of appropriate transitional plans are mandated in the United States by Public Law 101–467, the Individuals with Disabilities Education Act; no similar law exists in Canada.

Dalke (1991) has suggested that the transition to the post-secondary environment is particularly dramatic for students with disabilities as a result of the number of changes that may lead to unforeseen obstacles that they will have to face, "Adjusting to these changes can be so overwhelming for students that they may, in fact, find themselves failing almost as soon as they have begun" (p. 119). Probably the greatest and most difficult problem that students face is that fact that "special education does not exist at the post-secondary level" (Michaels, 1994, p. 93). No longer is the standard support system readily available to students and without charge. Students with disabilities in post-secondary settings must disclose the nature of their disability to staff, advocate on their own behalf, and request specific accommodations or modifications that they may need in order to overcome the effects of their disability.

Most post-secondary institutions have a specific person responsible for providing services to students with disabilities. One would assume that students with disabilities would contact the person prior to applying to ensure that the services they might need would be available. However, such is not always the case. Fifty-two percent of the respondents in a recent study of 264 students with disabilities attending universities across Canada stated that they learned about services available from the Office of Students with Disabilities subsequent to their arrival on campus (Hill, 1994; 1995a). It is unknown how many of these students knew that they would need to contact the service provider, but failed to do so, perhaps out of fear of the possible negative consequences (real or imagined) that might result from prior self-identification.

BARRIERS TO POST-SECONDARY EDUCATION ENCOUNTERED IN POST-SECONDARY SETTINGS

Lack of written policies regarding students with disabilities

Policies need to be developed to ensure that students with disabilities are treated fairly and equitably at the time of admission as well as during their course of studies. Brinckerhoff (1985, cited in Michaels, 1994) has suggested that post-secondary institutions should not be able to (a) limit the number of students with disabilities admitted, (b) make preadmission inquiries as to whether or not an applicant is disabled, (c) use admission tests or criteria that inadequately measure the academic level of applicant who are disabled because special provisions were not made for them, (d) exclude a student with a disability from any course of study solely on the basis of his or her disability, (e) counsel students with disabilities toward a more restrictive career than students without disabilities, unless such counsel is based on strict licensing or certification requirements in a profession, (f) measure student achievement using modes that adversely discriminated against the student with a disability, and (g) institute prohibitive rules that may adversely affect disabled students, such as the baring of tape recorders from the classroom.

Few universities in Canada reported having written policies that dealt specifically with the needs of students with disabilities; some reported that they were in the process of developing such policies (Hill, 1992). Some post-secondary institutions stated that their policies only addressed issues related to admission; others reported having more comprehensive policies, covering areas such as the provision of services and the institution's duty to accommodate students with diverse learning needs. Institutions with written policies have often set up mechanisms by which students, who feel that they have been discriminated against, can appeal decisions that they feel are discriminatory; in institutions without written policies, the student has to rely on the Charter of Rights and Freedoms which guarantees Canadians with disabilities equality before and under the law without discrimination based on a mental or physical disability and/or the human rights legislation of the province in which they reside. Lepofsky has made the point that "many persons with disabilities have neither the resources nor the willingness to undertake the formidable ordeal of mounting protracted constitutional litigation" (1994, p. 3).

Institutional Inflexibility

It would be exceptional to find an institution that discriminated solely on the basis of a disability (e.g., setting a quota on the number of students with disabilities being admitted to an institution). But it is not uncommon to find regulations and practices that hinder a student with a disability from successfully pursuing a program of further studies. Examples of strict regulations or inflexible practices include:

- Admission to the university may be jeopardized by the lack of a second language course (e.g., French, Italian) especially for students with a hearing impairment. Rarely, however, do post-secondary institutions accept American Sign Language as a second language, even though it is recognized as a distinct and true language by most linguists.

- Attendance in all lectures in courses for which they are enroled may be difficult for students with a chronic health problems. It is not uncommon for instructors to establish very strict attendance requirements and fail students who miss more than a preset number of classes.

- Scheduling of classes may be problematic for students with mobility problems. In many institutions a 10-minute break between classes and/or a 15-minute break during a 3-hour class is common. There may not be enough time to get to the next class on time, particularly if they have to go to the bathroom, have a snack, and/or take their medication.

- Many institutions require students to provide documentation outlining the nature of the disability and the functional impact of the disability on the pursuit of further studies. However, it is rare for the same institutions to provide diagnostic services; consequently students may have to pay for an assessment that costs $800.00 or more.

- The additional costs required for the students with a visual impairment to pursue a program of studies (e.g., for transportation, for persons to function as readers) may be prohibitive. Bursaries may be available to assist in meeting the education-related costs associated with their disabilities but the amount varies widely among the provinces, and some provinces have no such provisions.

Physical barriers that limit accessibility

Students with disabilities must be able to travel with ease around the campus to pursue a program of post-secondary studies. The ability to travel freely on a campus that consists of many buildings, spread over a wide geographic area with varying types of terrain, may present a formidable challenge for the student who has only had to navigate one building during his or her high-school studies. When considering accessibility, most individuals tend to think about the obstacles faced by persons with mobility impairments (e.g., persons in wheelchairs or on crutches) who need designated parking spaces, curb-cuts, ramps, and elevators. It is equally important to consider the unique needs of those with other types of disabilities, such as persons with a visual impairment who may require braille or large-print labels on doors and elevators, and those with a hearing impairment who may need amplification systems in lecture halls, auditoriums, and gymnasiums. Similarly, it is important that all buildings be accessible to students. Libraries, athletic facilities, and residences, as well as other buildings containing food service areas, stores, the chapel, and the faculty club often need to be altered in order to accommodate the diverse needs of students with disabilities.

Retrofitting buildings is a costly endeavour and staff at most universities have reported that they are attempting to alter buildings as funds are made available (Hill, 1992). A new type of problem, "segregation by design," is emerging to make a building accessible in order to get to class, students with disabilities are required to travel a different route than their classmates in order to by-pass a set of stairs or an inaccessible door. The British Columbia Educational Association of Disabled Students (1992) has suggested that consultation be "sought early and on a continuous basis throughout the design and building process" with persons who are knowledgeable about all types of disabling conditions, in order to prevent the "expensive and avoidable mistakes [that] are invariably made" (p. 2). The same recommendation should be heeded for the renovation of existing buildings.

Lack of Services and Faculty Accommodation

Services (e.g., obtaining taped texts) must be available for students with disabilities to succeed in post-secondary settings. Michaels (1994) has suggested that in the United States some colleges and universities offer only the basics (i.e., a minimum level of services in order to comply with the law), whereas others have developed an extensive package of services. The situation in Canada appears to be similar (Hill, 1992). Some services are widely available (e.g., arranging for special test options), whereas others are provided less frequently (e.g., providing special materials), particularly at the smaller institutions. On the whole, students with disabilities have reported that services are adequate (Hill, 1995) but some have reported difficulty in finding out about services, accessing services in a timely manner, and procuring services that they required. Due to lack of services, some students have reported that they have had to withdraw from certain courses or have had to change their program of studies.

Many students may have difficulty completing their studies without the willingness on the part of instructors to accommodate students with special needs. Fichten (1988) commented that professors, in general, have "moderately favourable attitudes toward disabled students on campus ... their attitudes are somewhat less positive about having such students in their own department" (p. 177). Many students rate the willingness of instructors to modify their instructional techniques in order to accommodate their specific learning needs as being in the good to excellent range (Hill, 1995). In the minds of the students, it appears that faculty have a hierarchy of preference for certain students (i.e., faculty members were more accepting of some students, such as those with chronic illnesses compared to those with learning disabilities) and a hierarchy of accommodation (i.e., some modifications are more readily provided, such as allowing the student to tape record a lecture compared to providing the student with copies of board notes). Some faculty are unwilling to provide certain accommodations, such as extended time for the completion of an exam, fearing that it gives the student with a disability an advantage over their non-disabled peers (Higher Education and Disability Law, 1995) even though the student's disability may require such an adjustment.

CONCLUSION

Students with disabilities face a number of unique barriers that may prevent them from pursuing a program of higher education. This chapter examined some of these obstacles in elementary and secondary school years as well as post-secondary education. Without consideration of their unique learning needs, many students with disabilities may be doomed to fail, even before they put their foot inside the door that may offer them the opportunities to be successful and to achieve in the competitive world that faces them in the future.

References

Brinckerhoff, L.C., Shaw, S.F., & McGuire, J.M. (1993). *Promoting post-secondary education for students with learning disabilities: A handbook for practitioners.* Austin, TX: Pro-Ed.

British Columbia Educational Association of Disabled Students (1992). *Barrier-free design supplement to the Canadian Standards Association barrier-free design 1990 manual.* (Available from BCEADS, 2158-West 12 Ave., Vancouver, BC, V6K 2N2).

Burbach, H.J., & Babbitt, C.E. (1988). Physically disabled students on the college campus. *Remedial & Special Education, 9* (2), 12–19.

Carpenter, V. (1992). Who is welcome here? *The World* (September/October), 26–29.

Cohen, S.B., & DeBettencourt, L.V. (1991). Dropout: Intervening with the reluctant learner. *Intervention in School & Clinic, 26,* 263–270.

Dalke, C.L. (1991). *Support programs in higher education for students with disabilities: Access for all.* Gaithersburg, MD: Aspen Publishers.

Diem, R., & Katims, D.S. (1991). Handicaps and at risk: Preparing teachers for a growing populace. *Intervention in School & Clinic, 25,* 272–275.

DuChossis, G., & Michaels, C.A. (1994). post-secondary education. In C.A. Michaels (Ed.), *Transition strategies for persons with learning disabilities* (pp. 79–117). San Diego, CA: Singular Publishing Group.

Fichten, C.S. (1988). Students with physical disabilities in higher education: Attitudes and beliefs that affect integration. In H.E. Yuker (Ed.), *Attitudes toward persons with disabilities* (pp. 171–186). New York: Springer.

Gajar, A., Goodman, L., & McAfee, J. (1993). *Secondary school and beyond: Transition of individuals with mild disabilities.* New York: Merrill.

Hallahan, D.P., & Kauffman, J.M. (1994). *Exceptional children: Introduction to special education* (6th ed.). Boston: Allyn & Bacon.

Halpern, A.S. (1994). The transition of youth with disabilities to adult life: A position statement of the Division on Career Development and Transition, The Council for Exceptional Children. *Career Development for Exceptional Individuals, 17,* 115–124.

Hill, J.L. (1992). Accessibility: Students with disabilities in universities in Canada. *Canadian Journal of Higher Education, 22,* 48–83.

Hill, J.L. (1994). Speaking out: Perceptions of students with disabilities at Canadian universities regarding institutional policies. *Journal of post-secondary Education and Disability, 11,* 1–14.

Hill, J.L. (1995). Speaking out: Perceptions of students with disabilities regarding adequacy of services and willingness of faculty to make accommodations. Manuscript submitted for publication.

Hill, J.L. (1996). Promoting post-school educational opportunities for students with diverse needs. In J. Andrews (Ed.), *Secondary classrooms: Teaching students with diverse needs* (pp. 275-306). Toronto: Nelson.

Human Resources & Labour Canada (1993). *Leaving school: Results from a national survey comparing school leavers and high-school graduates 18 to 20 years of age.* Ottawa: Minister of Supply & Services.

Lepofsky, M.D. (1994). Brief to the Ontario Standing Committee on the Administration of Justice of the Ontario Legislature regarding Bill 168—The Ontarians with Disabilities Act. (Available from the Advisory Group on Employment Equity for Persons with Disabilities, 720 Bay Street, 3rd Floor, Toronto, Ontario, M5G 2K1).

Marder, C. (1992). Education after secondary school. In M. Wagner, R. D'Amico, C. Marder, L. Newman, & J. Blackorby (Eds.), *What happens next? Trends in postschool outcomes of youth with disabilities.* Menlo Park, CA: SRI International.

Michaels, C.A. (1994). Transition, adolescence, and learning disabilities. In C.A. Michaels (Ed.), *Transition strategies for persons with learning disabilities* (pp. 1–22). San Diego: Singular Publishing Group.

Reiff, H.B., Ginsber, R., & Gerber, P.J. (1995). New perspective on teaching from successful adults with learning disabilities. *Remedial & Special Education, 16,* 29–37.

Statistics Canada (1990a). *The health and activity limitation survey highlights: Disabled persons in Canada* (Cat. 82–602). Ottawa: Minister of Regional Industrial Expansion.

Statistics Canada (1990b). *Selected socio-economic consequences of disability for women in Canada* (Cat. 82–615, Vol. 2). Ottawa: Minister of Supply & Services.

Szymanski, E.D. (1994). Transition: Life-span and life-space considerations for empowerment. *Exceptional Children, 60,* 402–410.

U.S. Department of Education (1994). *Sixteenth annual report to Congress on the implementation of the Individuals with Disabilities Education Act: To assure the free appropriate public education of all children with disabilities.* Washington, DC: Author.

Wilchesky, M. (1986, March). *Post-secondary programs and services for exceptional persons.: North American trends.* Paper presented at the Canadian Symposium on Special Education Issues, Toronto, Ontario. (ERIC Reproduction Service No. ED 194 389).

White, W.J. (1992). The postschool adjustment of persons with learning disabilities: Current status and future projections. *Journal of Learning Disabilities, 25,* 448–456.

Wolman, C., Bruininks, R., & Thurlow, M.L. (1989). Dropouts and dropout programs: Implications for special education. *Remedial & Special Education, 10* (5), 6–20, 50.

This research was supported in part by a grant from the Social Sciences and Humanities Research Council of Canada.

14

Ethnicity and Educational Aspirations of High-School Students

Jacques Perron

Pursuing post-secondary education represents an important aspect of the transition from adolescence to adulthood and significantly improves the probability of integrating the workplace (Boileau, 1986). Thus, it is relevant to examine the potential factors that explain how adolescents aspire at pursuing post-secondary education. The work of Hossler and his associates (Hossler et al., 1989; Hossler & Gallagher, 1987; Hossler & Stage, 1992; Stage & Hossler, 1989) is helpful in four ways. First, they consider four types of predicting models: econometric, consumer, sociological, and mixed. Second, they present a thorough synthesis of the writings about variables to be considered in the prediction of aspirations to pursue post-secondary education. Third, they describe the process of educational choice according to three stages: *predisposition* refers to decisions and aspirations related to post-secondary education; *research* consists in examining post-secondary institutions to determine where to apply; *choice* corresponds to the selection of a specific institution. Fourth, they propose and test a structural model for the prediction of the predisposition to pursue college education. This model (Hossler & Stage, 1992) stipulates that parents' education, familial socio-economic level, and the student's sex and ethnicity influence student's educational aspirations either directly or indirectly through parents' expectations towards their child, academic achievement, and extracurricular activities. Analyses performed with 2,497 9th graders show that the proposed model explains 36% of the variance in aspirations to pursue post-secondary education.

Hossler and Stage conclude that their model is theoretically sound but that it can be improved. There are several promising avenues to explore. One avenue is to add student's interest for subject matters and the time devoted daily to homeworks to the variables of GPA and extracurricular activities already in the model. By doing so, concepts like motivation and commitment to education (Vallerand, 1993) would be better represented. In addition, the number of paid working hours during school time (Greenberger & Steinberg, 1986) could also be linked to the academic variables. The construct of ethnicity can be improved. Hossler and Stage (1992) define ethnicity as belonging to a minority or to the majority. Phinney and Rosenthal (1992) have drawn from research about identity formation during adolescence (Adams et al., 1992; Marcia et al., 1993) to define ethnic identity development as the result of exploration and commitment processes towards one's own ethnic group. The Multigroup Ethnic Identity Measure (MEIN; Phinney, 1992) is a 20-item instrument assessing ethnic identity (14 items) and other-group orientation (6 items). Such an instrument would diversify the construct of ethnicity used by Hossler and Stage (1992). Finally, as shown by Coallier (1992), life-events in adolescence as well as personal and social identity are significantly related to career planning attitudes. The Identité Personnelle et Événements de Vie [Personal Identity and Life Events] (IPEV; Massonnat & Perron, 1985) measure consists of two five-item scales respectively assessing identity towards oneself and identity towards others. It can be used to examine the role of these two variables in the prediction of educational aspirations. The present research was designed to complement Hossler and Stage's (1992) model by adding academic and psychological variables to improve understanding of the predisposition to pursue post-secondary education.

METHODOLOGY

A longitudinal study was conducted with a sample of 1,748 French-speaking students from grades 8 to 12 and their parents. Three sets of data were collected—fall 1993, spring 1994, and winter 1995. This chapter is based on data collected during the fall of 1993. The subjects were from five schools in the Montréal area—one private and one public school (n = 902) with small multicultural representation (3.5%) and three public schools (n = 846) with large multicultural representation (59.3%). Students who identified themselves with an ethnic group other than Québécois or Canadian were from 98 ethnic groups. They had learned and were still speaking one of 39 different languages. They were classified according to their countries or origin: Western Europe (11.3%), Asia (7.7%), Eastern Europe (5.3%), French Caribbeans (5.2%), Latin America (3.8%), and Arab countries (3.3%). Parents (n = 1,329) also participated to the research with a participation rate of 76%.

Data was collected in the classroom. Subjects completed a battery of eight assessment instruments with the assistance of a team of researchers composed of previously trained psychology students. They were also given a questionnaire to take to their parents and to return to school a week later. The study takes into account one criterion variable, Student Educational Aspirations (SEA) and three sets of predictors defined as socio-biographical, psychological, and academic variables.

The SEA score was obtained by treating the subject's answers to three pairs of questions related to the importance (1 = no importance; 7 = the greatest importance) and the perceived probability (1 = extremely improbable; 7 = extremely probable) of completing high school (HS), college (C) and university (U) education. For each level of education, a 7 X 7 matrix of the frequencies of subjects having answered both questions was divided into four areas. In quadrant A, importance and probability answers varied from 1 to 4; in quadrant B, the importance answers varied from 1 to 4 and the probability answers from 5 to 7; in quadrant C, the importance answers varied from 5 to 7 and the probability answers from 1 to 4; in quadrant D, the importance and probability answers varied from 5 to 7. The SEA score = 4 when a subject was in quadrant D for the university, the college, and the high-school levels. When in quadrant

D for college and high-school levels but in another quadrant for university, the SEA score = 3. The SEA score = 2 when in quadrant D for the high-school level but in another quadrant for levels university and college. SEA = 1 if the subject was in a quadrant other than D for the three education levels.

The socio-biographical variables used as predictors of student educational aspirations were:

sex	(male = 1; female = 2)
grade level	(8th = 1; 9th = 2; 10th = 3; 11th = 4; 12th = 5)
paid work during school time	(no = 1; yes, from 0 to 5 hours per week = 2; yes, from 6 to 10 hours per week = 3; yes, from 11 to 15 hours per week = 4; yes, from 16 to 20 hours per week = 5; yes, from 21 to 25 hours per week = 6)
reference group	(majority = 1; minority = 2)
mother's & father's education	(elementary = 1; high school = 2; college = 3; university = 4)
parents' civil status	(separated, divorced, single, widow = 1; married = 2)
working parents	(father only = 1; mother only = 2; father and mother = 3)
family status	(father and children, mother and children, blended = 1; father, mother, and children = 2)
student's perception of family financial condition	(poor = 1; modest = 2; moderate = 3; wealthy = 4; very wealthy = 5).

Students also completed the Échelle d'Identité Ethnique (Perron, 1993) a French translation of the MEIM (Phinney, 1992) as well as the IPEV [Personal Identity and Life Events] (Massonnat & Perron, 1985). The Échelle d'Identité Ethnique (MEIM) consists of 20 items which the subjects answer using a 4 point Likert-type scale (1 = completely disagree; 4 = completely agree). Two dimensions are assessed by the instrument. Ethnic identity is represented by items relating to affirmation of beliefs (e.g., "I feel a strong attachment towards my own ethnic group"), exploration and commitment (e.g., "I have a clear sense of my ethnic background and what it means for me"), and behaviour (e.g., "I am active in organizations or social groups that include mostly members of my own ethnic group"). Other-group orientation is measured by items eliciting how the subject defined self in relation to other ethnic groups (e.g., "I like meeting and getting to know people from ethnic groups other than my own"). In both the English (Phinney, 1992) and the French (Perron et al., 1994) versions, the two scales are characterized by acceptable internal consistency coefficients (ethnic identity: alpha = 0.81 and 0.86; other-group orientation: alpha = 0.71 and 0.75).

The IPEV is designed to assess the perceived effect of life-events on personal and social identity. Subjects are asked to take into account what they have experienced in the last three months, choose one of two antonyms (e.g., organized or disorganized) and, using a 7-point scale (1 = very poorly; 7 = very well) indicate to which degree the adjective applies to themselves. The scale is transposed on a continuum varying from 1 to 14 points on which, for example, very disorganized = 1 and very organized = 14. The instrument consists of 10 pairs of antonyms; five assess personal identity (organized-disorganized; valued-devalued; proud-ashamed; stable-unstable; motivated-unmotivated) and five others measure social identity (autonomous-dependent; respected-despised; close-distant; similar-different; accepted-rejected). Coallier (1992), using a sample of 565 high-school students, reported internal consistency coefficients (apha) of 0.63 and 0.62 for each of the two scales respectively.

Four academic variables were considered. The most recent grade point average served to measure school achievement on a 6-point continuum (less than 50% = 1; from 50% to 60% = 2; from 61% to 70% = 3; from 71% to 80% = 4; from 81% to 85% = 5; 86% and over = 6). Interest for eight subject matters (arts, English, French, human sciences, mathematics, moral or religious education, natural sciences, physical education) was measured by a 4-point scale (1 = very little interested; 4 = very much interested). The total score varied from 8 to 32. Homework was distributed on a five-point continuum according to the number of minutes devoted per day by the student at home (from 0 to 30 minutes = 1; from 31 to 60 minutes = 2; from 61 to 90 minutes = 3; from 91 to 120 minutes = 4; more than 120 minutes = 5). Finally, parents' educational aspirations (PEA) for their child were computed like the SEA and were characterized by a score varying from 1 to 4.

Three multiple regression analyses were performed to predict students' educational aspirations (SEA). The first series of analyses successively described the relationships with SEA of the socio-biographical, the psychological, and the academic variables. Then, the academic variables were factor analyzed and represented by a factor score to be predicted by the socio-biographical and the psychological variables. After these two series of multiple regression analyses, the socio-biographical and the psychological variables which significantly predicted the SEA score (direct relationships) and the academic factor score (indirect relationships) were selected; they were finally grouped with the academic variables in a block multiple regression analysis to predict the SEA score.

RESULTS

Students belonged to the majority in 70% of the cases while 30% came from diverse ethnic groups; there were no differences according to sex and grade level. Fifty-three percent had a paid job requiring 10 hours or less per week. Mother education (median = high school) was lower than father education (median = college). Seventy-five percent were married and 70% of the students lived in intact families, but for 59% both parents were working outside the home. Finally, 77% of the students described the financial condition of their families as comfortable living. Students showed positive scores on the scales assessing ethnic identity and other-group orientation (means = 2.99 and 3.11 on a maximum of 4) as well as personal and social identity (means = 53.81 and 55.48 on a maximum of 70). Internal consistency coefficients (ethnic identity = 0.86; other-group orientation = 0.76; personal identity = 0.72; social

Table 14.1: Multiple Regression Analyses of Three Groups of Predictors of Students' Educational Aspirations

Predictors	R	R^2	ß
Academic			
Parents' aspirations	0.39226	0.15387	0.343732
GPA	0.42177	0.17789	0.146433
Interest for subject matters	0.44018	0.19169	0.127338
Socio-biographical			
Grade level	0.10627	0.01129	-0.120161
Mother education	0.14578	0.02125	0.103114
Sex	0.16098	0.02592	0.068316
Reference group	0.17292	0.02990	0.081079
Work outside the home	0.18556	0.03443	0.071026
Psychological			
Ethnic identity	0.13873	0.01925	0.119072
Other-group orientation	0.16341	0.02670	0.088557

identity = 0.68) were higher for the MEIM and generally acceptable for the IPEV.

The students had high educational aspirations; 65% considered both important and probable to pursue education at the university level, 87% expected to complete college level education, and 94% aspired at finishing high-school education. GPA scores were normally distributed; 44% of the subjects were in the 71% to 80% category. Students were nearly equally divided in terms of time devoted to homework, 53% spent 60 minutes and less per day and 47% spent more than 60 minutes per day. Interest for subject matters (mean = 23.20; standard deviation = 3.43) was positively skewed. Parents' educational aspirations (PEA) and students' educational aspirations (SEA) were similarly distributed.

Some measures (PEA, civil status, mother education, etc.) were obtained from their parents; thus, only students whose parents filled a questionnaire were retained in the analyses on the prediction of SEA scores. The mean of SEA scores of students whose parents returned the questionnaire (3.5135) was significantly higher than that of students whose parents did not return the questionnaire (3.3010) (t = 4.24; df = 1640; p = 0.000). Results in Table 14.1 show that three academic variables (PEA, school achievement, and interests for subject matters) contribute to predict SEA scores (R = 0.44018; R^2 = 0.19169; p < 0.01). Socio-biographical variables characteristic of the students (grade level, sex, and reference group) and of the parents (father education and work outside the home) also present a direct relationship (R = 0.18556; R^2 = 0.03443; p < 0.01) with students' educational aspirations. Finally, two psychological variables (ethnic identity and other-group orientation) have a direct relationship with SEA scores (R = 0.16341; R^2 = 0.02670; p < 0.01). Academic variables are predominant in predicting SEA scores; they were combined into a single

Table 14.2: Multiple Regression Analyses of the Predictors of the Academic Factor

Predictors	R	R^2	ß
Socio-biographical			
Mother education	0.14869	0.02211	0.118519
Reference group	0.21128	0.04464	0.181906
Sex	0.25541	0.06255	0.150507
Father education	0.27205	0.07401	0.119390
Parents' civil status	0.29079	0.08456	0.103559
Grade level	0.30433	0.09262	-0.090414
Work outside the home	0.31312	0.09804	0.077575
Psychological			
Other-group orientation	0.24851	0.06176	0.227290
Personal identity	0.28937	0.08373	0.203320
Social identity	0.30768	0.09467	-0.121883
Ethnic identity	0.31334	0.09818	0.061710

variable to examine its relationships with socio-biographical and psychological variables. A principal components factor analysis showed that the four academic variables composed a single factor (eigen value = 1.52132) explaining 38.0% of the variance. GPA (0.65917) and homework (0.65632) had the highest loadings followed by parents' educational aspirations (0.58738) and by interests for subject matters (0.55772). A factor score derived from this analysis was used to define a single academic variable.

Data in Table 14.2 show that socio-biographical variables characteristic of the parents (mother's education, father's education, civil status, and work outside the home) and of the students (reference group, sex, and grade level) contribute to predict (R = 0.31312; R^2 = 0.09804; p < 0.01) the academic factor. On the other hand, the four psychological constructs (ethnic identity, other-group orientation, personal identity, social identity) also predict (R = 0.31334; R^2 = 0.09818; p < 0.01) the academic factor. A last prediction analysis of SEA scores consisted of treating as blocks of predictors the four academic variables (GPA, homework, interests for subject matters, and PEA), the five socio-biographical variables (sex, grade level, reference group, mother education, and working parent(s)), and the two psychological variables (ethnic identity and other-group orientation) previously identified as significant predictors of both the academic factor and the SEA scores. The entry order of blocks that explained the most significant variance was: academic variables (R = 0.45163; R^2 = 0.20397; p < 0.01) + psychological variables (R = 0.46397; R^2 = 0.21527; p < 0.01) + socio-biographical variables (R = 0.48082; R^2 = 0.23119; p < 0.01).

DISCUSSION

This study aimed at analyzing high-school students' educational aspirations by taking into account academic and socio-biographical predictors and by introducing additionnal psychological variables in the prediction analyses to confirm and improve Hossler and Stage's (1992) mixed causal model. Students' educational aspirations were directly related to those of their parents and to their own academic achievement. SEA scores were also correlated with the level of interest the subjects had for subject matters. This variable seems to play the role of a motivational factor which has been shown to be associated with academic behaviours (Vallerand, 1993; Vallerand et al., 1989) and also with the preparation of vocational projects (Perron, 1994). Second, girls who belonged to minorities and whose mother educational level was higher also tended to have higher SEA scores. Moreover, students in the lower grade levels and whose father and mother worked had higher educational aspirations. Hossler and Stage (1992) did not take into account these two variables because their subjects were all 9th graders. On the other hand, the fact that both parents are working is significantly related to the mother's education ($r = 0.22$; $p < .01$) and the father's education ($r = 0.14$; $p < .01$) and thus represents an additional contribution in terms of socio-biographical variables in the prediction model. Ethnic identity and other-group orientation were directly related with educational aspirations, meaning that the more students explored their own cultural group, affirmed their beliefs about it, and showed openness towards members of other cultural groups, the more they aspired to pursue post-secondary education. The developmental aspect of these two psychological variables brings a new perspective to the prediction of educational aspirations and may even be more explanatory than the mere fact of belonging to a majority or a minority group.

The preponderance of academic variables ($R^2 = 0.1917$) over socio-biographical ($R^2 = 0.0344$) and psychological ($R^2 = 0.0267$) variables in the prediction of educational aspirations led to an analysis of the indirect relationships of predictors with SEA scores. Socio-biographical ($R^2 = 0.0980$) and psychological ($R^2 = 0.0982$) variables are more closely related to the academic factor than to educational aspirations. These predictors have a higher impact on the immediate reality of the student's current environment than on his or her vision of the future. More specifically, father education and parents' civil status predicted only the academic factor. Such was also the case for personal and social identity. These data again show possibilities, particularly in adding psychological variables, to improve Hossler and Stage's (1992) prediction model of the predisposition to pursue post-secondary education.

Students whose parents did not participate in the research had lower educational aspirations than their counterparts. Considering that the complete study is based on three collections of data, it will be possible to determine if the difference will again be observed and to relate it with SEA scores as well as with other variables. Repeated abstention on the part of the parents could indicate a lesser commitment to the education of their child and might have an impact on certain aspects of his or her development.

In conclusion, this research supports a mixed model for the prediction of educational aspirations of high-school students and shows that the refinement of socio-biographical and academic predictors as well as the addition of psychological predictors can improve the validity of the model. This conclusion is derived from data analyses (multiple regressions) which differ from those (structural equations) used by the authors of the original model. Upon completion of the longitudinal study, the three sets of collected data will be analyzed with structural equations which will allow for an examination of the reproductibility of the causal model and to take into account changes occurring in the assessment of variables. Finally, further research on the model should include English-speaking subjects both from Québec and other Canadian provinces in order to extend its validity and generalization.

References

Adams, G.R., Gullotta, T.P., & Montemayor, R. (Eds.). (1992). *Adolescent identity formation.* Newbury Park, CA: Sage Publications.

Boileau, G. (1986). *Les jeunes au Québec et le marché du travail. Volet IV: Le chômage.* Québec: Direction des services économiques, Commission de l'emploi et de l'immigration du Canada, Emploi et immigration Canada.

Coallier, J.C. (1992). *Étude des déterminants de la maturité vocationnelle à l'adolescence dans une perspective multidimensionnelle.* Thèse de doctorat inédite, Université de Montréal.

Greenberger, E., & Steinberg, L.D. (1986). *When teenagers work: The psychological and social costs of adolescent employment.* New York: Basic Books.

Hossler, D., & Stage, F.K. (1992). Family and high-school experience influences on the post-secondary educational plans of ninth-grade students. *American Educational Research Journal, 29,* 425–451.

Hossler, D., Braxton, J., & Coopersmith, G. (1989). Understanding student college choice. In J. Smart (Ed.), *Higher education: Handbook of theory and research* (vol. 5, pp. 231–288). New York: Agathon Press.

Hossler, D., & Gallagher, K.S. (1987). Studying student college choice: A three phase model and the implications for policy makers. *College and University, 2,* 207–221.

Marcia, J.E., Waterman, A.S., Matteson, D.R., Archer, S.L., & Orlofsky, J.L. (1993). *Ego identity: A handbook for psychological research.* New York: Springer-Verlag.

Massonnat, J., & Perron, J. (1990). Pour une approche multidimensionnelle de l'identité de la personne. *Psychologie française, 35,* 7–15.

Massonnat, J., & Perron, J. (1985). *Identité personnelle et événements de vie.* Document inédit, universités d'Aix-en-Provence et de Montréal.

Perron, J. (1994, Septembre). *Valeurs de travail et motivations aux études: Prédiction de la réussite et de l'orientation scolaires.* Présentation au Congrès international de psychologie du travail de langue française, Neuchâtel.

Perron, J. (1993). *Échelle d'identité ethnique.* Document inédit, Université de Montréal.

Perron, J., Coallier, J.C., & Tremblay, C. (1994, Novembre). *Multiculturalisme et identité ethnique d'adolescents québécois.* Communication présentée au congrès de la Société Québécoise de Recherche en Psychologie.

Phinney, J.S. (1992). The multigroup ethnic identity measure: A new scale for use with diverse groups. *Journal of Adolescent Research, 7,* 156–176.

Phinney, J.S., & Rosenthal, D.A. (1992). Ethnic identity in adolescence: Process, context, and outcome. In G.R. Adams, T.P. Gullotta, & R. Montemayor (Eds.), *Adolescent identity formation.* Newbury Park, CA: Sage Publications.

Stage, F.K., & Hossler, D. (1989). Differences in family influences on college attendance plans for male and female ninth graders. *Research in Higher Education, 30,* 301–314.

Vallerand, R.J. (1993). La motivation intrinsèque et extrinsèque en contexte naturel: Implications pour les secteurs de l'éducation, du travail, des relations interpersonnelles et des loisirs. In R.J. Vallerand et E.E. Thill (Eds.), *Introduction à la psychologie de la motivation* (pp. 533–581). Laval (Québec): Éditions Études Vivantes.

Vallerand, R.J., Blais, M.R., Brière, N.M., & Pelletier, L.G. (1989). Construction et validation de l'Échelle de Motivation en Éducation (ÉMÉ). *Revue canadienne des sciences du comportement, 21,* 323–349.

This research was supported by a grant (RS–2037) from the Conseil Québécois de la Recherche Sociale.

PART III

Preparing for the
World of Work

15

Preparation for the World of Work: Research and Policy Implications

E. Dianne Looker and Graham Lowe

The academic literature closely links education and training to economic prosperity. Recent policy reports from government and non-government organizations (Canadian Labour Market and Productivity Centre, 1993; Economic Council of Canada, 1992; New Brunswick Commission on Excellence in Education, 1993; Ontario Premier's Council, 1990) signal a rethinking of how Canada can best develop the full potential of individuals, especially youth, at school and at work. Two key assumptions underpin this public policy thrust: (1) many graduates are not finding suitable employment and (2) there is a poor fit between outputs of the educational system and changing employer needs. The research suggests that these assumptions should be questioned and that the school-work transition is central to human resource development policy.

There are four core research questions that are directly relevant to understanding youth transitions to the world of work. They are:

- What are the consequences of an individual's educational achievement for her or his chances of success in the labour market, and how do these trajectories vary by key socio-economic characteristics (e.g., gender, class background, race/ethnicity) (Furlong, 1992; Gaskell, 1992; Kerckhoff, 1993; Looker, 1993)?

- What are the social and psychological consequences of transition difficulties, as expressed in the image of a lost generation of unemployed or marginally employed youth who may stray into deviant activities (Hartnagel, 1995; Tanner et al., 1995)?

- How has economic and labour market restructuring transformed employment opportunities for youth (Anisef & Axelrod, 1993; Ashton & Lowe, 1991; Ashton et al., 1990; Evans & Heinz, 1994; Krahn & Lowe, 1993; Redpath, 1992)?

- In what ways is the educational system not serving those who drop out, who have disabilities, or who have literacy deficiencies (OECD, 1991; Tanner et al., 1995)?

School-work problems are linked to the rise of an increasingly polarized service economy. Education levels for entry-level jobs are increasing on average, yet many new jobs require no post-secondary education. The result is a growing gap in job rewards and skills. Surveys of recent college and

university graduates find pervasive underemployment and a growing prevalence of temporary and part-time work. These trends signal a contradiction in
the Canadian labour market; well-educated youth may be unable to make
meaningful economic contributions due to limited job opportunities, and their
problems may be exacerbated by the lack of effective school-work bridging
mechanisms.

The ten chapters in this section capture the diversity of issues addressed in
school-work transition research. The chapter by Anisef on life-course transitions
among members of the class of 1973 and Looker's analysis of how the transition
to adulthood is shaped by gender and rural/urban context exemplify longitudinal research that has illuminated the complexities of youth transitions. These
studies document that the process of moving through educational institutions
and into the labour force occurs within the constraints imposed by specific
social, cultural, and economic conditions. But individuals do make choices,
thereby introducing variability and uncertainty into transition patterns. King's
research draws on a cross-national comparative study of elementary and
high-school students to argue that the Canadian educational system is more
university-oriented and provides fewer vocational preparation opportunities
than in Europe. King also uses an Ontario study to show that difficulties arise
because many parents, schools, and employers tend to favour university
education, a path only a minority of high-school students will follow. Sharpe's
research tracks the transitions into the labour market of a large sample of
Newfoundland youth, underscoring the barriers young people often encounter
in attempting to pursue further education or find decent employment. Echoing
Looker, Sharpe points to gender as well as rural-urban differences in plans and
opportunities. McGrath's article also focuses on Newfoundland and provides
a detailed analysis of the extent to which social-psychological characteristics,
features of the educational system, and the larger socio-economic context
influence participation in post-secondary education. McGrath emphasizes the
barrier to participation created by the rising costs of post-secondary education.

The chapters by Donaldson and Erwin document the experiences and
attitudes of university undergraduate students. These two studies caution
against assuming that it is smooth sailing once youth reach college or university.
Donaldson suggests that negative experiences can drive talented students away
from certain programs, although her case study offers a model for how to rectify
this institutional drift. Erwin, also examining student experiences at a large
Canadian commuter university, offers a gendered analysis of how women's
career aspirations are converging with those of men. She argues, however, that
the reality of having to balance career and family responsibilities will make it
far more difficult for the women to reach their career goals.

The chapters by Kennett, by Bourassa and Tardiff, and by McCarthy shift
the focus to disadvantaged youth. These chapters offer case studies of the
multiple difficulties marginalized youth can face in obtaining adequate education, training, and employment. Kennett's study of disadvantaged youth at a
Peterborough employment centre highlights the importance of counselling,
especially counselling aimed at increasing motivation. Bourassa and Tardiff's
evaluation of a recent Québec program designed to provide at-risk 16- to 18-
year-olds with employability skills illustrates the problems such youth have
keeping a job once they find one. They suggest that school-business partner-

ships could be a useful mechanism for addressing this problem. Finally, McCarthy's study of homeless adolescents dispels any misconceptions that these youth, as a group, tend to be deviant or criminal. With alternative schooling, training, and employment programs homeless youth can become self-supporting and independent.

The complexity of transition processes and the diversity of the youth cohort requires different approaches to illuminate specific issues in transitions. The chapters in this section demonstrate the importance of approaching transition questions using a variety of research methodologies, both qualitative and quantitative. Longitudinal studies are useful to document the process of life transitions and enable researchers to answer a variety of transition questions. Most follow the same group of individuals over a time period to document their changing life experience. Depending on the specific research questions and the target group, the length of these panel studies ranges from a few months to several years to decades. Sample characteristics vary from small, specialized groups to large regional and national samples. The studies reported in this section also utilize a variety of data collection techniques, ranging from structured mail questionnaires to in-depth, face-to-face interviews. Data are collected from a range of sources, mostly from youth themselves but also from parents, teachers, employers, educational institutions and government agencies.

POLICY IMPLICATIONS

The chapters in this section all underscore the importance of looking at the school-to-work transition as a process that has become increasingly complex, non-linear, and uncertain. The meaning of being an adult has changed. There is growing recognition of the complex challenges that face youth in the world of work, both paid and unpaid. The economic transformation Canadians have experienced since the late 1970s has redefined the relationship between education and work. The new economic environment requires re-thinking the policies that shape school-to-work transitions. No longer can we take for granted that the transition will be smooth and predictable. Canada has lagged behind some other industrialized countries in responses to school-to-work concerns, although the openness of the Canadian educational system has been a strength. It will be important to seek a balance between structured transition mechanisms and more flexible school-work linkages that continue to offer individual choice as new school-to-work initiatives are developed. Helping people, especially youth, find jobs that match their education and skills must be a central goal of public policy. This requires locating school-work transitions at the centre of any national or provincial human resource development strategy.

Canadians need to understand the importance of youth issues to maintaining and renewing Canada as a society. Youth are particularly vulnerable and need attention, especially in today's rapidly changing social and economic environment. Ignoring their needs now could have dire consequences in terms of rising costs of youth crime, loss of human capital, and erosion of citizenship. New policies and programs need to be developed and implemented to improve the transition process in general and to ensure equal access to members of disadvantaged groups. Policy initiatives should take into account that transitions to adulthood in the 1990s are more complex, prolonged, and non-linear than in previous decades. Policy makers must recognize that a young person's immediate social context (region and rural or urban location) and personal characteristics (gender, race/ethnicity, and social class) directly influence transition patterns and outcomes. Changing patterns of education, employment, family formation, and retirement behaviour require a focus on the variety of school-work transitions.

Persistently high unemployment and increasing polarization in job rewards mean that many school-work transition problems cannot be solved by additional training or counselling. Policy responses must address both supply and demand factors that affect transitions from school to work. Focusing exclusively on the education and training of youth, and their general preparedness for the world of work, is inadequate because it ignores a wide range of employer and labour market-related influences on the demand for young workers. Canadian youth need an increased supply of skilled, challenging jobs that will provide a decent livelihood and a high quality of life. Job creation strategies are central elements of school-work transition policy.

The definition of success must be broadened to help young people understand that fulfilment is not solely linked to economic status and participation in the full-time labour force. There are linkages between the different transitions to adulthood, transitions between school and work, out of the parental home, to post-secondary institutions, and those involving marriage and parenting. A program designed to deal with one transition is unlikely to be effective if it ignores the relevance of the other transitions. Family and community ties are important to the transitions for young people. Government programs should help to nurture support and resources available from families and community, and provide active backup in communities where naturally occurring supports are inadequate. Efforts should be made to ensure that programs are not concentrated solely in large urban centres, ignoring the needs of youth in rural and remote areas. It is important for youth to feel that they belong and are in control of their lives; intervention programs should build on the skills that young people have, rather than focusing on their academic, social, physical, or psychological inadequacies.

There are a number of important, innovative directions being taken by various levels of government and public agencies. It is important to extend the move to more coordination among different government initiatives at the federal, provincial, and local levels. A coordinated approach will reduce costs and increase efficiency by making programs more accessible to communities and individuals, and by reducing duplication of effort or agencies working at cross-purposes. Programs developed at the community level may be more effective since they can be fine-tuned to local school and employment situations. However, policies at the provincial and federal levels are needed to encourage, coordinate, and monitor such local initiatives.

Government agencies need to balance the demand for innovation with the need for stability and predictability in programs. Frequent reorganization of programs and changes in funding priorities undermine commitment and are wasteful of developed expertise. Partnerships need to involve multiple partners, reflecting the multiple stakeholders in youth and their transitions. Broadly-based partnerships are more effective than initiatives in which business sets the agenda. An expanded definition of partnerships would facilitate the involvement of community groups, unions, and small as well as large businesses. Community groups should include both the immediate geographic community as well as specific social communities (native and ethnic groups, support groups for those with disabilities, and so forth).

Mechanisms are needed to facilitate the transferability of credentials nationally. Portability of credentials (such as that encouraged by the recent protocol involving universities and community colleges) is a pre-requisite for the flexibility needed in today's labour market. Schools need to recognize that there are different kinds of career success, spanning the range of vocational, technical, and academic educational programs. Students and their parents should be encouraged to think in terms of parallel tracks rather than viewing these choices as organized hierarchically from less successful to more successful.

In Canada, skilled trades and technical (vocational) training have generally received less attention than academic education. Current efforts to broaden apprenticeship programs are beginning to address this problem. Specific job skills and more general employability skills which help a young person move out of the student labour market into full-time employment are important. Also important is how work experience contributes to a young person's personal development. The federal government's sector councils may be able to use these insights to encourage businesses to complement educational objectives by providing transferable skills and high quality work experience for youth. Work experience components are a necessary component of senior high, and perhaps even junior high, education. This is especially true for the many young people who are not going to enter post-secondary education. School-based programs which include a workplace learning component may be more effective. Out-of-school programs targeting non-students are more useful if they address problems of finding (satisfactory) employment as well as skills acquisition. Schools could make use of student's part-time work experiences as a basis for increasing students' critical understanding of the larger issues of working life.

Career and life skills counselling need to be refocussed in light of the transformations occurring in economic life. The innovative approaches that are now being developed to bring more comprehensive career and life skills counselling to the schools need to be extended. Mechanisms are needed to link high-school counselling with counselling provided in government programs, in the community, and in post-secondary institutions. Employment and career counselling services should strive for a more pro-active approach. Peer counselling may be one option for helping students develop work and life skills. Governments should explore the use of tax incentives to generate high quality jobs for young people. Employers could be given tax incentives to invest in relevant research, provide flexible working conditions, and provide access to full-time career paths for youth. Job creation strategies aimed at youth should target small business, given that this sector has generated most of the employment growth in recent years. Self-employment is also a growing option for which young people require preparation.

FUTURE RESEARCH AGENDA

There are several program evaluation research priorities. Programs focused on school-work transitions must be systematically monitored and evaluated. Evaluation criteria should be defined at the outset of the project, incorporated into the design of the program and the research conducted by independent researchers. Mechanisms (e.g., a central clearing-house, use of Internet) should be established to disseminate the results from program evaluations. Confidentiality requirements should not prevent dissemination of key findings for comparative purposes. Research should identify the attributes of successful business-education and other partnerships. A broad set of criteria is needed to assess the benefits accruing to youth, schools, and the community. Such research would be able to identify model partnerships that promote the quality of education. Research is also required to identify how employers and schools can better cooperate and collaborate in order to foster the complementarity of education and work. How can schools and employers work together to reduce the negative effects of part-time student employment, and to enhance work experience so that it has beneficial learning outcomes? To what extent, and how, do existing work experience programs in high schools contribute to students' overall education and job preparedness? Research should develop a definition of employability skills (i.e., transferable, generic work skills). This definition could then be used to identify where such skills are being taught, with a view to assessing the ingredients of effective employability skills teaching.

There are additional key policy-relevant research issues that go beyond program evaluation. Research should compare what students, parents, teachers, counsellors, employers, unions, community groups, and policy makers perceive to be the major issues and problems in the school-work transition. Research in this area should be community-based and action-oriented, in the sense that it should aim to involve community members in addressing transition difficulties. Cross-national research could critically analyze existing national data, provide a broader context for assessing the effectiveness of Canada's educational system, and consider alternative approaches. Research could improve understanding of how particular members of vulnerable or marginal youth populations are able to overcome multiple barriers, while others are not. Conversely, research could address why some seemingly advantaged youth have difficulty capitalizing on the opportunities available to them. Research on the various spheres of young people's lives will provide a more holistic perspective of how these individuals construct their lives. By studying the diversity of work performed by young people—paid and unpaid work in the labour market, the household, and the volunteer sector—researchers could assist policy makers and educators to understand how these forms of work are interconnected.

Existing major research initiatives, such as Brighter Futures, could provide an opportunity for youth transitions researchers to piggy-back focused studies of youth. The Council of Ministers of Education in Canada (CMEC) should expand their measures of school-work transitions outcomes to include measures such as preparedness for work and citizenship. Further, provinces often conduct valuable research which is now beginning to be nationally shared. An important link is between government departments and agencies on the one hand, and the researcher community on the other. Practitioners should be encouraged to hold research-based workshops and to attend research conferences. Grants and contracts to researchers should require that findings be directly communicated to practitioners. A solid research component (including program evaluation) should be a funding requirement of any project on school-to-work transitions. Such structures would create even better links than currently exist between policy and research.

Finally, six specific research questions warrant serious consideration:

- What is the impact of the current restructuring of the teaching profession throughout the country on educational outcomes?

- What are the major gender differences in transitions to adulthood, and what individual, institutional, and cultural factors account for such variations?

- What are the key employment and educational equity issues in youth transitions?

- What are the most effective methods of communicating to young women and men the realities of balancing work and family?

- In what ways, and how, are different labour market experiences related to alternative and/or deviant lifestyles among youth?

- How do universities, community colleges, and technical/vocational institutes coordinate and communicate with high schools in order to ease the transition for students? How can these institutional links be strengthened?

References

Anisef, P., & Axelrod, P. (Eds.). (1993). *Transitions: Schooling and employment in Canada*. Toronto: Thompson Educational Publishing.

Ashton, D., & Lowe, G. (Eds.). (1991). *Making their way: Education, training and the labour market in Canada and Britain*. Toronto: University of Toronto Press.

Ashton, D.N., Maquire, M., & Spilsbury, M. (1990). *Restructuring the labour market: The implications for youth*. London: Macmillan.

Canadian Labour Market and Productivity Centre (1993). *Canada: Meeting the challenge of change. A statement by the economic restructuring committee*. Ottawa: Canadian Labour Market and Productivity Centre.

Economic Council of Canada (1992). *A lot to learn: Education and training in Canada*. Ottawa: Supply & Services Canada.

Evans, K., & Heinz, W.R. (Eds.). (1994). *Becoming adults in England and Germany*. London: Anglo-German Foundation.

Furlong, A. (1992). *Growing up in a classless society? School-to-work transitions*. Edinburgh: University of Edinburgh Press.

Gaskell, J. (1992). *Gender matters from school to work*. Milton Keynes: Open University Press.

Hartnagel, T.F. (1995). Labor market problems in the transition from school to work and illegal drug use: A panel study of Canadian youth. *Current Perspectives on Aging and the Life-Cycle, 4*, 61–90.

Kerckhoff, A.C. (1993). *Divergent pathways: Social structure and career deflections*. New York: Cambridge University Press.

Krahn, H., & Lowe, G.S. (1993). *The school-to-work transition in Edmonton, 1985—1992*. Edmonton: Population Research Laboratory, University of Alberta.

Looker, E.D. (1993). Interconnected transitions and their costs: Gender and urban/rural differences in transitions to work. In P. Anisef & P. Axelrod (Eds.), *Transitions: Schooling and employment in Canada*. Toronto: Thompson Educational Publishing.

New Brunswick Commission on Excellence in Education. (1993). *To live and learn: The challenge of education and training*. St. Johns, NB: Author.

OECD. (1991). *Disabled youth: From school to work*. Paris: Centre for Educational Research and Innovation.

Ontario Premier's Council (1990). *People and skills in the new global economy*. Toronto: Queen's Printer for Ontario.

Redpath, L. (1992). Education-job mismatch among Canadian university graduates: Implications for employers and educators. *Canadian Journal of Higher Education, 24*, 89–114.

Tanner, J., Krahn, H., & Hartnagel, T. (1995). *Fractured transitions from school to work: Revisiting the drop-out problem*. Don Mills, ON: Oxford University Press.

16

Transitions, The Life Course, and the Class of '73: Implications for Social Policy

Paul Axelrod and Paul Anisef

The role of personal decisions and actions in determining what happens to individuals in the course of their lives is one of the most common themes in literature—the proverbial crossroads; the door not opened; the road not travelled. To what extent do people determine their future through decisions made at crucial moments? To what degree are they subject to circumstances and forces beyond their control? The Class of '73 explores such questions with respect to a generation of Ontario residents who graduated from Grade 12 in 1973. The panel project, begun more than twenty years ago and consisting of six distinct research phases, recreates the world of the early 1970s in which those youth faced the future, examines their educational and occupational experiences in the late 1970s, follows their vocational and career pathways during the subsequent decade, and searches for patterns in their personal and family lives through the late 1980s and early 1990s (Anisef et al., 1980, Ashbury et al., 1994). The study draws from life course theory to explore the impact of "context..time ... and interactive processes" on the ways in which individuals make important decisions about their lives (Elder, 1987; Poole, 1989, p. 65).

This chapter is a preliminary account of the histories of a small section of the Class of '73. It is a qualitative analysis based on conversations with twelve individuals who were interviewed in 1979 and again in 1994. The small numbers allow for a detailed analysis of the recollections, the patterns of behaviour, and the comparative experiences of people from different environments who came of age in a period characterized by distinct social and economic challenges. The chapter examines the interviewees' perceptions of the importance of their backgrounds on educational and vocational choices, the sources of occupational satisfaction, and the link between gender, family life, and work. Implications for future research agendas and social policy are discussed.

Six women and six men participated in in-depth interviews in 1979 and 1994; four had graduated from university, six from college, and two from high school only. All of the subjects had changed occupations or positions within their fields since 1979. Ten claimed that difficult economic circumstances in the 1980s and early 90s had affected them or their spouses in terms of occupational selection, unemployment, choice of residence, or standard of living. All were married and ten participants had at least one child.

SUBJECTIVE PERCEPTIONS: CLASS AND SCHOOLING

Social stratification and status attainment literature indicate that level of education is linked to one's socioeconomic position and that parents play both a passive and active role in influencing their children's educational pathways (Looker, 1994). This tendency was identified in previous surveys of the Class of '73 (Anisef, 1980). How did the individuals interviewed in 1979 and 1994 perceive the relationship between their socioeconomic backgrounds and their subsequent educational and vocational choices? R., whose father was a chartered accountant, grew up in a "generally middle-class neighbourhood" in Scarborough, and recalls having "general exposure to the professions as opposed to blue-collar labour." He had decided early in high school, without explicitly discussing the matter with his parents, to attend university. "There was never any decision to be made as to whether you would go to post-secondary education or university. It was more a function of when you [would] go ... " He entered Scarborough College, dropped out after second year, but resumed his studies full-time in 1979, and obtained a degree with a specialization in economics and computer science. C.'s father was a District Fire Chief in a Toronto suburb, and her mother was a full-time secretary in a public school. Neither had a post-secondary educational degree, but her father had taken some university courses later in his career. C. always wanted to attend university, something she attributes to her parents' influence. "I guess they wanted us to do better than what they had done themselves," and they "implanted" [that idea] "in us." J. grew up in a middle-class Toronto suburb, and was always encouraged to attend college or university. Her father was an alumnus of the University of Toronto and Harvard, and eventually began an oil company that was bought out by a large firm in the industry. J. was unhappy in high school, deeply self conscious of a weight problem, and uncertain about her plans for higher education. She obtained a summer job in a resort, which introduced her to the hospitality industry and led her to enrol in Hotel and Institutional Administration at Ryerson. She thoroughly enjoyed the program, and has worked in the industry since graduation.

Parents' influence, expectations, and support, directly or indirectly, played an important role in directing these individuals to university. Those from middle-class backgrounds came to understand the cultural or economic value of higher education. If they attended high schools where it was expected that most students would enrol in university, as was the case with R., this too influenced their decision making. Yet, as the experience of J. indicated, the link between the status of one's social class and occupational pathway was not invariably direct or inevitable. Unique events in a young person's life, or complicated family dynamics during the child's adolescence, might alter one's expected educational course.

The experiences of three of the college trained students, M. and G. (both females), and of a high-school graduate, B. (male), were different than these middle-class encounters. All three grew up in farming families and attended schools where the majority of students did not pursue post-secondary education. M. enjoyed high school, and performed well; G. was a somewhat indifferent student. B. found high school easy, and succeeded without ever having to do homework. None had any interest in university. M. and G. both entered college programs, one training as an x-ray technician, and one as a nurse. From the outset they were fulfilled by their vocations and never regretted their choices. B. briefly considered becoming an electrical engineer, but resolved instead to take over the operation of his father's farm. His desire to work outdoors was one important factor in his choice. Another was the strong influence of his father, who hoped to keep the farm in the family. Though he has struggled financially over the years, he too had no regrets about his vocational selection.

K. was consumed by regrets. She completed high school in a small community, and soon left home, where her relations with her parents had broken down. Supporting five children, her father, the owner of a nursery, struggled financially. "There were too many mouths to feed," and the possibility of K's pursuing post-secondary education was never raised. She worked for three years in Europe, returned home, felt unwelcomed in her parents' house, and took up a variety of clerical positions before settling for one in the freight forwarding business. Over the years, she experienced periodic financial difficulties, which helped tie her to jobs she has found unchallenging. She has considered continuing education, though has not pursued it.

Being exposed to an environment at home, and at school, which promoted university education, enhanced a youth's chances of obtaining one. Yet none of the subjects, including those who attended community college, or who only graduated from high school, saw themselves as merely the product of their backgrounds. While they appreciated family support when it was received, and while acknowledging the negative impact of personal problems, they took full responsibility for the decisions they made in charting their futures. Interestingly, three of those from the lowest socioeconomic strata (G., B., and M.)—and who in the literature on stratification might be portrayed as comparatively disadvantaged—had the clearest aspirations, the most positive outlooks, and the fewest regrets about their educational or vocational choices.

OCCUPATIONAL PATHWAYS: REWARDS AND STRESSES

The mid-to-late 1970s was a period of uneven economic development in Canada. The unemployment rate for males aged 15 to 24 rose from 16% to 17% from 1971 to 1981 and for women from 13.5% to 15.5% (Baker, 1989; p.20). Underemployment was a greater challenge for post-secondary graduates in this sample; 41.8% were underemployed in 1979 but eight years later, the rate decreased to 29.5%. These economic realities were reflected in the early employment experiences of most of the interviewees. Only M., who graduated from the x-ray technician program in 1976, moved directly into a rewarding full-time position in her field. All of the others found themselves in jobs for which they were over-qualified, employed part-time, or dissatisfied with for various reasons. Z. had a B.A. in English and worked first in a music store and then in a secretarial position with the Ontario government. C. had completed the business administration course at the University of Western Ontario only to find work as a secretary-receptionist. G. was hired as a nurse in her own community but only on a part-time basis. R. left university after two years and found work as a computer operator and programmer, but was unhappy with his advancement prospects in this position and eventually returned to university. Although they were displeased to varying degrees with their situations, all of the subjects were optimistic about their futures, and determined to take the steps they believed would lead to more fulfilling employment.

By the early 1980s, most had made significant strides in this direction, though labour market and economic undulations continued to pose significant challenges for some. R. obtained a position as an information centre consultant with a large insurance company after completing his degree in economics and computer science. This enabled him to draw both on his experience in computing and his economics training. He was pleased with the autonomy he had in this middle income position, and believed that there was a good fit between his education and work. Corporate downsizing in the insurance industry led to major layoffs throughout the 1980s. R. held on to his own position but he continued to look elsewhere for new opportunities. In 1992, he joined the partnership of a small reinsurance facilitation company from which he has derived considerable satisfaction. C.'s first continuing position was with a bank where she subsequently worked for ten years. She developed expertise in the interest rate swap area, but the eventual decline of the housing market led her to consider other positions within the bank. In the early 1990s, she took a new bank job arranging loans for small firms. She has found her work stimulating, felt well compensated, but has been frustrated by the bank industry's failure to promote many women to managerial positions. B. has continued to run the farm he took over from his father in the mid-1970s. But various problems—difficulty getting bank loans, conflict with a marketing board, low prices for his products—led him to take on a contract to deliver mail to 500 residences and businesses in his community. He has been doing this for seven years, while simultaneously farming part-time. He hopes to pass the farm on to his only son, the youngest of his three children. Extending farm ownership through male lines is a family tradition which he intends to uphold. If his son does not want to farm, he will attempt to sell his property to any "fool crazy enough to buy it." S., an accountant and manager for a small manufacturing company, has nowhere to move in the organization, and is clearly bored by his work. He expressed frustration at the company's failure to employ new computer technologies. "It's incredible … They are using the same books and ledgers that were used thirty years ago." Q., who works with emotionally disturbed adults, is also deeply unsettled. His job is physically exhausting, and the provincial facility he works in is scheduled to close, leaving him with uncertain employment prospects.

Common themes run through these experiences with respect to sources of satisfaction. Merely having a job fulfilled no one. Even earning a good income was insufficiently rewarding if the job itself lacked challenge or prospects for advancement. Positions without flexibility or humane employment conditions also earned the subjects' disdain. By contrast, they valued work in fields for which they felt equipped and/or highly motivated. Employment which combined the elements of relative security, improved status, significant autonomy, and a flexible schedule elicited much enthusiasm. Income also mattered but was seldom emphasized. Some interviewees, like C. and J., appreciated the standard of living their positions helped provide; others like B. and G. had sacrificed money for a preferred way of life. Living in the country, spending more time with one's family, being one's own boss in a small company instead of an employee subject to the whims of an employer in a large firm, explained these choices, for men and women alike. The matter of family income was stressed with greater urgency in circumstances where financial pressures were particularly severe, as in the case of Z., who was not employed but wanted to be.

GENDER, FAMILY AND WORK: RECONCILING ROLES

The Class of '73 completed high school at a time when family life and the role of women were in a state of transition and the subjects of considerable public discussion. The feminist movement, which exposed and challenged the discriminatory treatment and subordinate role of women in the work force, in politics, in education, and within the family, was a prominent presence by the early 1970s (Prentice et al., 1988). Divorce laws had been liberalized in 1968, the labour force participation of women had risen from 24% in 1952 to 37% in 1971, and women constituted 45% of university students in 1976 compared to 38.5% in 1961 (Baker, 1989, p. 18). Magazine and newspaper articles highlighted the accomplishments of professional women, and debated the merits of the role of feminism itself. While feminist writers encouraged women to pursue their rights vigilantly (Greenglass, 1973, p. 55; Thompson, 1971, p. 7), a psychiatrist denounced the movement and labelled its promoters "libchicks" who were blind to the problems of men (Rich, 1971, p. 31).

The Class of '73 grew to maturity in an era when the ideal of gender equality competed for legitimacy with traditional values about women's place in the family, in the community, and in the workplace. Women were pursuing post-secondary education in increasing numbers in the 1970s but were concentrated in programs that led to professions and vocations offering lower status and incomes than those dominated by men. A survey of 1976 graduates of Canadian universities found that, two years after graduation, men earned on average $2,000 per year more than women (Clarke & Zsigmond, 1981). This gap reflected the early employment experiences of the Class of '73 (Anisef & Ashbury, 1989). For men, starting salaries in first jobs averaged $12,627 in 1978–79 while women averaged $9,959 (Anisef et al., 1980, p. 258).

Interviews with the twelve subjects reveal ways in which family dynamics and evolving gender roles affected and were affected by occupational experiences. Nine of the interviewees were part of two-income households. In two of the other families, Z. herself and G.'s husband were involuntarily unemployed. S.'s wife was a homemaker by choice. The mothers of the subjects had generally not worked outside the home; most women from the Class of '73, however, expected and sought continuing employment, though the problematic economic conditions of the late 1980s and early 90s impeded the prospects of some.

Male roles and attitudes were changing within the household as well. J. who married a man ten years her senior, saw him, reluctantly at first, and then more enthusiastically, take responsibility for their two children's preschool morning activities. J.'s own job as a cafeteria administrator takes her out of the house by 5:30 a.m.; to some degree, this forced her husband to take more responsibility for the children. She is home every afternoon to greet her children when they return from school; from her point of view, this is the ideal working arrangement. In general, women retain the majority of household responsibilities, while men do more of this work than did their own fathers. The most traditional view with respect to gender roles was that of B. who asserted that "the man of the house is the person to look after what's to happen. I was brought up [on the farm] that way and I live that way. If my wife didn't have a job, we'd survive." He claims that he would never go on welfare. He is certain that he would always find a way to provide for his family. Judging from the experience of another rural interviewee, women's roles do change, though not necessarily radically. G., a part-time nurse aspiring to return to work full-time, grew up on a farm where education for girls was not especially valued. She had always disliked the city, and lives with her husband and two children in a modest country home. She refused, however, to marry a farmer because she did not want the onerous life of a "farmer's wife … farm women work too hard and they get no credit for it." Her husband, now unemployed, is very involved in child-rearing, though she does most of the housework. She sometimes wishes he did more, but she is better at it than he, and the issue is not a source of household dissension.

Children are a major priority, and their presence, where possible, has influenced parental occupational arrangements and practices in urban and rural families alike. C. would like to have advanced more quickly in a banking industry that is still very conservative in its promotion of women. But not at any cost. Her impression is that women in management are generally not married and that they "sacrifice everything for the bank. I'm not prepared to do that. I have a [family] life as well." K. has yet to achieve her vocational goals, and is now exploring more spiritual concerns, hoping soon to open a plant nursery in the country. Z., the mother of four children and expecting a fifth, struggles with the challenge of reconciling her occupational aspirations, her personal values, and her family life. Growth and change continue for the Class of '73.

CONCLUSIONS

Previous surveys of the Class of '73 and recent interviews confirm the importance of one's socio-economic origin, gender and place of residence to the life course. The research shows that class advantage, being male and living in a city generally foster greater social and economic advantage. Individuals, however, tend not to perceive the unfolding of their own lives through these sociological lenses. To do so would be to assign control of their fate to impersonal, external forces. Instead, the subjects assumed personal responsibility for educational, occupational, and family-related decisions. The value of a university education had not been emphasized in every household, but, rather than bemoaning their fate, most selected occupational pathways that required alternative forms of training and education. Not all had yet found their preferred calling—something that was also true of a number of the university educated— but their search was essentially a private or family matter, and would be engaged by them in that way.

This is not to imply that they were unaware of or unaffected by larger social issues, only that they personalized the strategies employed to face them. They criticized the educational system while arming themselves with additional credentials, looking for new opportunities, and making occupational moves at what they hoped would be an appropriate moment. Economic difficulties and the changing social role of women touched the lives of most interviewees. Women, including those with young children, were far more likely than the previous generation to be employed outside the home. But they were not deeply philosophical about the issue of women's place in society. They believed in fairness, they were at times frustrated by gender barriers to advancement on the job, and they often experienced the stress of reconciling family and occupational responsibilities. They chose paid work, and they required it, for the sake of securing an adequate household income. They believed their future would depend upon their ability to plan and prioritize according to their needs and values. By privatizing these decisions, both at the time, and in retrospect, the subjects gained a sense of control over their environment.

All of the interviewees appreciated employment which enhanced their autonomy and resented that which did not. Here too, the themes of flexibility and control mattered most. If the experiences of the subjects are typical, employers and supervisors who provide employees with flexible schedules, decision-making authority, prospects of advancement, regular encouragement, as well as reasonable remuneration will contribute to the quality of the working environment, and in all probability, to the productivity of the employee. A number of the subjects became self-employed in order to secure these conditions. Policy makers should be cognizant of the degree to which the restructuring of the economy enhances or diminishes the worker's sense of satisfaction and self worth, and employers would be well advised to consider flex-time arrangements for employees with family responsibilities.

Policy makers should improve the quality of school guidance, not for the purpose of channelling young people prematurely into specific vocations, but with a view to demonstrating options, encouraging the most competent to pursue their schooling, and allowing young people an outlet to talk about their interests and their goals. Quick fixes of the educational system, designed to make it more efficient or market-responsive, are unlikely to succeed. Several individuals from the Class of '73 changed their minds about the value of their schooling. What influenced their opinions was the availability of rewarding employment. Once they obtained it, they tended to recast previous schooling, including "irrelevant" subjects, in a more positive light. Their problem initially was less that of over-education or mis-education than of underemployment. Improving occupational opportunities, not forcing schools to follow the fickle trends of an undulating economy, should be another aim of policy makers.

The context in which future graduates make the transition from schooling to employment will differ from that of the Class of '73. Continuous schooling or re-training, already experienced by some of the subjects, will increase (Thomas, 1993; Livingstone, 1993). Researchers might explore the degree to which this phenomenon diminishes the traditional impact of class origins on educational and occupational pathways. If the influence is positive, and if society remains committed to generating equality of educational opportunity, perhaps more resources should be directed to facilitating the education of mature students. Attention should also be devoted to the relationship between multiculturalism, schooling, and employment. The Class of '73 was more ethnically homogenous than is the current Ontario population, 13% of which is now of racial minority or Aboriginal origin. Do ethnic and racial factors shape the ways in which young people chart their futures? Do minority groups, as did women of the previous generation, encounter a "glass ceiling" in the forging of their vocations and careers (James, 1993)? And to what degree do young people today privatize the process of decision-making? Research on the Class of '73 provides interesting insights and provokes new questions about the transition from youth to adulthood.

References

Anisef, P., & Ashbury, F.D. (1989). *The transition from school to work: Educational and occupational attainment of youth.* Toronto: Ontario Ministry of Skills Development.

Anisef, P., Paasche, J.G., & Turritin, A.H. (1980). *Is the die cast?: Educational achievements and work destinations of Ontario youth.* Toronto: Minister of Colleges and Universities.

Ashbury, F.D., Anisef, P., Zeng, L. & Bischoping, K. (1994, August). The causes and consequences of mismatches between post-secondary education and employment: A longitudinal study of a baby boom cohort in Ontario, paper presented at the 16th Annual European Association of Institutional Research Forum, Amsterdam, The Netherlands.

Baker, M. (1989). *Canadian youth in a changing world.* Ottawa: Library of Parliament, Research Branch.

Clark, W., & Zsigmond, Z. (1981). *Job market reality for post-secondary graduates: Employment outcomes by 1978, two years after graduation.* Ottawa: Statistics Canada.

Elder, G.H. (1987). Adolescence in historical perspective. In H.J. Graff (Ed.), *Growing up in America: Historical experiences.* Detroit: Wayne State University Press.

Greenglass, E. (1973). Issues affecting women's rights get low government priority. *Toronto Star,* July 17.

James, C.E. (1993). Getting there and staying there: Black's employment experiences. In P. Anisef & P. Axelrod (Eds.), *Transitions: Schooling and employment in Canada* (pp. 3–20). Toronto: Thompson Educational Publishing, Inc.

Livingstone, D.W. (1993). Lifelong education and chronic unemployment: Exploring the contradiction. In P. Anisef & P. Axelrod (Eds.), *Transitions: Schooling and employment in Canada* (pp. 89–102). Toronto: Thompson Educational Publishing, Inc.

Looker, D.E. (1994). Active capital: The impact of parents on youths' educational performance and plans. In L. Erwin & D. MacLennan (Eds.), *Sociology of education in Canada, critical perspectives on theory, research & practice* (pp. 164–187). Toronto: Copp Clark Longman Ltd.

Poole, M.E. (1989). Adolescent transitions: A life-course perspective. In K. Hurrelmann & U. Engel, (Eds.), *The social world of adolescents: International perspectives* (pp. 65–85). Berlin: Walter de Gruyter.

Prentice, A., Bourne, P., Cuthbert, B., Light, B., & Mitchinson, N. (1988). *Canadian women: A history.* Toronto: Harcourt Brace Jovanovich.

Rich, J. (1971). Watching all the liberated girls go by. *Chatelaine, 44* (4), 34, 85, 86, 88.

Thomas, A.M. (1993). Transitions: From school to work and back: A new paradigm. In P. Anisef & P. Axelrod (Eds.), *Transitions: schooling and employment in Canada* (pp. 117–128). Toronto: Thompson Educational Publishing.

Thompson, N.K. (1971). Women's rights: Two perspectives. *Canada and the World, 37* (3), 13.

This research was made possible by the Social Sciences and Humanities Research Council of Canada under the Strategic Grants Program, Education and Work in a Changing Society. We also acknowledge Gottfried Paasche for organizing and facilitating the in-depth interviews in 1979 and the assistance of Etta Anisef, Carl James, and Marshall Abecassius who helped with follow-up interviews in 1994.

17

The Transitions to Adult Roles: Youth Views and Policy Implications

E. Dianne Looker

There is a growing body of research on youth transitions in Canada (Anisef & Axelrod, 1993; Institute for Social and Economic Research, 1985) that documents the complexity of the transition process and the fact that there is not one pattern that all or most youth follow. Understanding these complexities requires information about the meaning of transitions to youth and linkages between different transitions. This chapter looks at youths' transitions to adulthood. The emphasis is on factors which can be influenced by social policy and practice. What are youths' own reasons for pursuing certain options? How do youth perceive the links among transitions?

METHOD

Data come from a longitudinal study of 1200 youth born in 1971; data were collected in 1989, 1992, and 1994. Four hundred youth were interviewed in each of three areas: Hamilton, Ontario, Halifax, Nova Scotia and rural Nova Scotia (Looker, 1993, 1994). Random samples of youth were drawn from lists of those in school, graduates, and drop outs provided by school boards. Response rates were 78% for Hamilton, 71% for Halifax, and 72% for rural Nova Scotia. In 1992 respondents completed a one page questionnaire. In 1994 the youth (then 23 or 24 years old) were sent a detailed questionnaire asking about their educational, occupational, and marital/family histories, their aspirations, and their attainments. At this stage information was obtained from 794 respondents. The interviews used both pre-coded and open-ended questions (Looker, Denton & Davis, 1989), and provided quantitative and qualitative data. Most of the information on transitions reported in this chapter relies on data from the 1989 interviews and the 1994 questionnaires.

The 1994 questionnaire asked about positive and negative influences in the youths' decision about how much education to obtain. Potential influences included courses taken in high school, high-school grades, distance from the nearest post-secondary institution, availability of student financial assistance, cost of tuition, knowledge of post-secondary program offerings, entrance requirements for post-secondary education, availability of accommodation on campus, attitudes towards school, childbearing or fathering, availability of child care, marriage, lack of available jobs, parents' expectations, and friends' expectations. Two sets of questions got at the role of school counsellors in the transition decisions of these youth. The first (asked in both 1989 and 1994) involved the youth agreeing or disagreeing that their school provided counselling that was useful in their educational and occupational decisions. The second set deals with who goes to school counsellors. The youth were asked (in 1989) how often in the last school year they had a talk with various school officials, including the guidance counsellor. In 1989 a closed ended question asked the youth what path they would most like to take after completing high school. The responses were coded as no post-secondary, non-university post-secondary, and university. An open ended question asked the highest level of education the youth realistically expected to attain. In 1994 the respondents were asked the highest level of education they had attained by that point.

In 1992 and 1994 the youth were asked whether or not they had yet experienced a series of transitions, specifically whether they had held a full-time job (30 or more hours a week), drawn unemployment insurance, gotten married, had any children, attended and/or graduated from a community college or a university or some other post-secondary institution, taken a formal apprenticeship, or moved out of their parents' home.

Finally, there were questions that deal with the ways that the youth see different transitions fitting together. They were asked their reaction to having a child before they are married, getting married before finishing their education, getting married before getting a full-time job, and living with their parents after getting married. Response categories were: very much or somewhat prefer this, not care, and be bothered a bit or a great deal. Another set of items asks about their views about paid employment at different life stages: before marriage, after marriage but before children, when there were preschool aged children, when all children are in school, and when all children have left home. The response categories differed slightly between 1989 and 1994 for this set of questions. In 1989 respondents indicated that they definitely or probably would or wouldn't work. In 1994 the question asked how good an idea working at each life stage would be—really or fairly good, really or fairly bad, or neither a good nor a bad idea.

FINDINGS

Table 17.1 shows that half of the youth had undertaken some full-time work by 1992; two thirds of them have done so by 1994. A quarter of the respondents report having drawn on unemployment insurance by the time they were twenty-one; the figure is 33% two years later. The men report higher rates of unemployment in both years than the women. Even more striking is the difference by region; many more rural Nova Scotia respondents than those in the urban areas have used unemployment insurance. As many as 50% of the rural youth used unemployment insurance by 1994, reflecting higher unemployment rates in rural areas. A third of the youth had moved out of their parents' home by 1992, and 61% by 1994. Mitchell (1995) argues that prolonging one's time under the parental roof is, for most youth, an asset. However, the viability of staying home is severely reduced for rural youth who have to leave their home communities in order to pursue either post-secondary education or the ever more elusive jobs (Looker, 1993). Table 17.1 also shows the percentage of youth who, by 1994, say they have finished all their formal education or

Table 17.1: Transitions 1992, 1994

Path/transition	Total	Males	Females	Hamilton	Halifax	Rural N.S.

A. TRANSITIONS EXPERIENCEBD BY YOUTH 1992 AND 1994 BY GENDER AND AREA

1992

Path/transition	Total	Males	Females	Hamilton	Halifax	Rural N.S.
Full-time job	**52%**	54%	51%	52%	55%	50%
Drawn U.I.	**25%**	30%	21%	22%	16%	37%
Moved out	**35%**	32%	38%	28%	28%	50%
Married	**5%**	1%	8%	3%	2%	10%
Had a child	**7%**	2%	11%	5%	4%	12%

1994

Path/transition	Total	Males	Females	Hamilton	Halifax	Rural N.S.
Full-time job	**67%**	67%	67%	64%	75%	62%
Finished all educ	**46%**	41%	50%	39%	41%	56%
Drawn U.I.	**33%**	38%	28%	21%	24%	50%
Moved out	**61%**	53%	66%	52%	58%	71%
Married	**11%**	4%	16%	9%	4%	19%
Had a child	**11%**	6%	15%	6%	8%	18%

B. LEVEL OF EDUCATION ATTAINED 1992 AND 1994 BY GENDER AND AREA

1992

Path/transition	Total	Males	Females	Hamilton	Halifax	Rural N.S.
Graduated high sch	**85%**	81%	88%	88%	85%	82%
Apprenticeship	**5%**	9%	2%	6%	4%	6%
Trade ticket	**1%**	0%	1%	1%	0%	1%
Some non-univ.	**46%**	48%	44%	55%	34%	49%
Non-univ. diploma	**14%**	14%	15%	13%	10%	20%
Some university	**50%**	47%	53%	41%	65%	43%
University degree	**4%**	4%	5%	0%	9%	3%

1994

Path/transition	Total	Males	Females	Hamilton	Halifax	Rural N.S.
Graduated high sch	**96%**	96%	96%	96%	97%	94%
Apprenticeship	**1%**	3%	0%	2%	1%	1%
Trade ticket	**2%**	3%	1%	0%	3%	2%
Some non-univ.	**22%**	17%	26%	27%	10%	29%
Non-univ. diploma	**12%**	9%	14%	14%	5%	18%
Some university	**57%**	57%	57%	56%	72%	44%
University degree	**36%**	33%	37%	30%	48%	28%
Some post-graduate	**7%**	7%	7%	8%	7%	5%
Post-grad. degree	**2%**	2%	3%	3%	3%	2%

schooling. Almost half of all youth, and more women than men, gave this response. In rural Nova Scotia 56% say they have completed their education.

Only a minority of the youth had made the transitions to marriage and childbearing by either 1992 or 1994. More women than men had married (16% versus 4% in 1994) and had had a child (15% versus 6%). Marriage and childbearing have quite different impacts on males as compared to females. Young men say that marriage would push them into the labour force; they still see themselves as the primary economic provider for a family (Looker, 1993). It is motherhood, more than marriage, that is expected to have an impact on the young women. The women say they expect to stay home and look after young children despite the fact that 90% of the women and 75% of the men say that responsibility for child care should be shared equally by fathers and mothers.

Table 17.1 provides information on the educational paths taken by the youth. The 1992 questionnaire provides information on who attended and graduated from different educational institutions. In 1994 the youth were asked the highest level of education they had completed to date. Fifty-seven percent had attended university (21% had some university, 29% had a degree, and 7% pursued post-graduate education). By 1994, almost all of the respondents say they had graduated from high school. Many of those who had not graduated directly after Grade 12 or 13 had taken their high-school equivalence examination. The level of participation in apprenticeship programs was low, particularly for women. The pattern of male dominance of apprenticeships has been long noted (Burns, 1995) but little has been done to change it. Young women who said that they wouldn't go into male dominated jobs mentioned the physical demands of the jobs and the sexual harassment that they would encounter. Women have slightly higher educational attainment than men, consistent with their outperforming their male counterparts throughout their schooling. These differences in attainment are a lot lower than the differences in aspirations and expectations—mostly because fewer women than men expect to go on to university (Looker, 1995).

There were striking differences by sample area. Halifax had a lot more youth attending university than either Hamilton or rural Nova Scotia. By 1994 almost half of the Halifax youth had university degrees. Slightly more than half of Hamilton youth had attended university, but only a third had a degree by 1994. Only 44% of rural Nova Scotia youth attend university, less than 30% had a degree. The attendance figures for the urban areas increase between 1992 and 1994 but there was not a similar increase for rural Nova Scotians. If they were not in university by 1992, the rural Nova Scotians were unlikely to enter later. More youth from the urban rather the rural areas have pursued post-graduate education; not only are there more options available to urban youth, their options stay open longer.

Why do these differences exist? Table 17.2 provides an overview of the reasons offered by the youth. The reasons are listed in rank order starting with the most frequently given. The first section presents the negative influences that youth said they face. At the top of the list is the cost of tuition. Over a third of the youth—both those who do go on and those who don't—saw cost as an active disincentive. Cost is one of those issues which can be addressed by public policy. Caps on tuitions, access to bursaries and loans and subsidies for

Table 17.2: Influences on Decisions about Pursuing Post-Secondary Education

NEGATIVE INFLUENCES		POSITIVE INFLUENCES	
Overall	*Those with no post-sec.*	*Overall*	*Those with post-sec.*
1. Cost 2. Attitudes to schooling 3. Lack of jobs 4. Student assistance 5. Entrance requirements 6. Grades in high school 7. Knowlegdge of programs	1. Cost 2. Attitudes to schooling 3. Lack of jobs 4. Entrance requirements 5. Grades in school 6. Student assistance 7. Knowledge of programs	1. Attitudes to school 2. Parental encouragement 3. Courses taken 4. Grades in high school 5. Knowledge of programs 6. Friends' encouragement	1. Attitudes to school 2. Parental encouragement 3. Courses taken 4. Grades in high school 5. Knowledge of programs 6. Friends' encouragement

those with low income can all affect the cost of attending university and other post-secondary programs. Nevertheless, public policy seems to be moving in the direction of providing *less* public money for post-secondary education, and relying more on individuals and their families to foot the bill. Further, many scholarships, bursaries and loans are not available to part-time and/or distance education students. Those who try to work to finance their education run into other problems. As one young women said: "I couldn't get a student loan in my third year. I tried to work full-time to pay for school, but then my grades started suffering because I worked late and was too tired to get my schoolwork done." Income dependent loan repayment programs are a positive option to many policy makers, but many youth were reluctant to take on a heavy debt load that would influence not only their finances, but their credit ratings for loans on a house, or costs associated with starting a family. Lack of student assistance was also cited as a negative influence on post-secondary plans. The second highest ranked disincentive, by the youths' own admission, was their attitude to schooling. Negative attitudes are particularly strong among the young men, especially rural men.

The lack of available jobs is the next item on the list. High levels of unemployment may induce some to further their education. This can only operate as an incentive, however, if the youth saw post-secondary graduates getting jobs. Many saw just the opposite. As one youth said: " ... I was discouraged at how bleak the chances of getting a job were when I graduated; I watched my friends draw unemployment with their diplomas shoved in a drawer." Another who did go on reinforced this image that an education may not, in fact, be a job ticket. "It is frustrating to get an education then not be able to use it. Being unemployed makes you unable to do anything. You can't get married, buy a house, or start your own life. You are in limbo." These youth send a message to their contemporaries that education may not have the expected pay off.

Table 17.3: Reported Usefulness of School Counselling, by Area

Counselling Useful To:	Stongly Agree	Agree Somewhat	Neither	Disagree Somewhat	Strongly Disagree
			1989		
Education					
Total	**16%**	**33%**	**19%**	**17%**	**15%**
Hamilton	20%	36%	19%	17%	15%
Halifax	12%	33%	18%	20%	17%
Rural N.S.	16%	31%	19%	16%	17%
Job					
Total	**11%**	**28%**	**23%**	**19%**	**18%**
Hamilton	15%	30%	29%	15%	13%
Halifax	7%	24%	22%	24%	23%
Rural N.S.	12%	31%	19%	18%	20%
			1994		
Education					
Total	**5%**	**23%**	**21%**	**24%**	**27%**
Hamilton	4%	28%	24%	26%	19%
Halifax	2%	22%	23%	24%	29%
Rural N.S.	9%	19%	18%	22%	33%
Job					
Total	**3%**	**14%**	**25%**	**26%**	**33%**
Hamilton	3%	18%	28%	27%	24%
Halifax	2%	9%	27%	37%	36%
Rural N.S.	4%	15%	19%	23%	39%

Knowledge about post-secondary program offerings was an asset to those who pursued further education and its lack was a barrier for others. Providing access to knowledge about program offerings is one of the tasks that public policy can address and is one that is supposed to have already been addressed through the offices of guidance counselling in the public schools. Are those who are most in need of the resources that guidance counselling can provide receiving this service? Table 17.3 presents data on how the youth viewed the counselling provided by their schools. A sizable number of the youth (a third in 1989) indicated that counselling was not useful to them—either to their educational decisions or to their decisions about job choice. Almost half agreed in 1989 that counselling was useful, but by 1994 this figure drops to less that 30% for educational counselling, and less than 20% for job counselling. Even more youth were critical of school counselling when they look back on it. By 1994 over half of the youth were responding in the negative to these questions. Fifty-one percent said the school did not provide counselling that was useful to their educational decisions; 59% said this with respect to occupational decisions.

Who goes to the counsellor? The question focused on contact in the past year (for dropouts, their last year in school) but can be used as a general

Table 17.4: Contact with Counsellor

Percentage Who Say They _Never_ Saw Counsellor Last Year by School Performance and Attitudes

Marks % Never	< 50% 22%	50 - 59% 18%	60 - 69% 11%	70 - 79% 10%	80% + 6%
Chance of University _% Never_	**Very good** 6%	**Good** 13%	**Fair** 12%	**Poor** 24%	
Ever Failed _% Never_	**Yes** 15%	**No** 6%			
Ever Repeat _% Never_	**Yes** 24%	**No** 8%			

% Who Never Saw Counsellor

Attitudes:	Agree	Neutral	Disagree		
School is boring	13%	10%	8%		
Could do better	11%	11%	5%		
Discipline problems	15%	14%	9%		
School is difficult	14%	10%	10%		
Hard to adjust	14%	14%	8%		
Good study habits	9%	11%	13%		
Educational:	**No Post-sec.**	**Non-univ.**	**University**		
Aspirations 1989	21%	14%	6%		
Expectations 1989	26%	13%	7%		
Attainments 1992	20%	13%	5%		
Attainments 1994	17%	14%	7%		

measure of contact. Table 17.4 presents the relevant results. The overall pattern is that those who did well in school were more likely to go to the school counsellor than those who are not doing well. Those who had low marks, had failed a course or repeated a grade, found school boring, difficult, hard to adjust to, and had discipline problems were more likely than others to say they had never went to the counsellor in the last year. Those who said they had good study habits and those who were university bound were more likely to have gone to see the counsellor. The image is one of counsellors playing a relatively passive role by providing specific information to those who take the initiative to request it. Those who need counselling the most were the least likely to have accessed these resources. These results were discussed with school boards; there was agreement that counsellors tend to leave the initiative for contact to the student and most schools agreed that more pro-active counselling is needed. The irony is that schools are becoming less and less likely to provide this service in light of a shift of funding away from non-teaching positions to teaching positions.

Table 17.5: Transitions' Links

A. Attitudes to Ordering of Certain Transitions by Gender, 1989 and 1994

	1989					1994				
	VM perf.	*Pref. sw.*	*Not care*	*Bit both.*	*VM both.*	*VM pref.*	*Pref. sw.*	*Not care*	*Bit both.*	*VM both.*
Live with parents	**0%**	**1%**	**4%**	**22%**	**73%**	**0%**	**0%**	**7%**	**23%**	**70%**
Males	0%	1%	5%	26%	68%	0%	0%	7%	24%	68%
Females	0%	1%	3%	18%	78%	0%	1%	6%	22%	71%
Child before marriage	**1%**	**2%**	**10%**	**33%**	**54%**	**1%**	**2%**	**30%**	**32%**	**35%**
Males	1%	3%	9%	33%	55%	1%	2%	28%	33%	36%
Females	2%	2%	11%	34%	52%	1%	2%	32%	31%	35%
Marriage before education	**1%**	**2%**	**15%**	**40%**	**43%**	**1%**	**2%**	**39%**	**24%**	**35%**
Males	0%	2%	12%	40%	46%	1%	1%	29%	26%	43%
Females	1%	2%	18%	39%	40%	1%	2%	46%	23%	29%
Marriage before job	**0%**	**3%**	**23%**	**47%**	**27%**	**1%**	**1%**	**38%**	**32%**	**28%**
Males	0%	2%	14%	47%	37%	1%	1%	21%	37%	41%
Females	1%	4%	31%	47%	17%	1%	1%	50%	29%	19%

B. Attitudes to Paid Work at Different Life Stages by Gender, 1989 and 1994

	1989				1994					
	Def. yes	*Prob. yes*	*Prob. not*	*Def. not*	*Really good*	*Fairly good*	*Neither*	*Fairly bad*	*Really bad*	
Before marriage	**79%**	**20%**	**1%**	**1%**	**84%**	**10%**	**6%**	**0%**	**0%**	
Males	82%	17%	1%	0%	82%	11%	7%	0%	1%	
Females	76%	22%	2%	0%	85%	9%	6%	0%	0%	
Married before children	**84%**	**15%**	**1%**	**0%**	**76%**	**13%**	**8%**	**2%**	**1%**	
Males	89%	11%	0%	0%	73%	15%	8%	2%	1%	
Females	80%	18%	1%	1%	78%	13%	8%	2%	0%	
With preschoolers	**47%**	**31%**	**18%**	**4%**	**39%**	**27%**	**19%**	**12%**	**3%**	
Males	80%	15%	4%	1%	58%	21%	14%	5%	2%	
Females	18%	45%	30%	7%	25%	31%	22%	17%	5%	
With children in school	**77%**	**21%**	**1%**	**1%**	**57%**	**31%**	**10%**	**2%**	**1%**	
Males	91%	8%	1%	0%	68%	20%	10%	1%	1%	
Females	64%	33%	2%	1%	49%	38%	11%	2%	0%	
After children leave	**70%**	**24%**	**5%**	**1%**	**70%**	**22%**	**6%**	**1%**	**1%**	
Males	71%	24%	4%	1%	67%	23%	8%	1%	1%	
Females	69%	24%	7%	1%	73%	21%	4%	1%	1%	

Response categories: 1989 -- "Definitely work," "Probably work," "Probably not work," "Definitely not work." 1994 — "Really good idea," "Fairly good idea," "Neither good nor bad idea," "Fairly bad idea," "Really bad idea."

How did youth see various transitions as being linked? Were there norms about which events should happen before which others? The first section of Table 17.5 looks at the ways the youth saw marriage and four other transitions: living with parents after marriage, having a child before marriage, marriage before completing one's education, or getting a full-time job. The strongest norm is the one relating to the timing of marriage and leaving home. Over 70% of the youth in both 1989 and 1994 said they would be very much bothered if they and their spouse lived with their parents after marriage. More women than men would object to this arrangement. Few of the youth said they would prefer to have a child before being married but they were less opposed to this than living with their parents after marriage. By 1994 close to one-third said they would not care one way or the other about having a child before marriage. It is interesting that there was no gender difference in the response patterns, given the stigma that has traditionally attached to unwed mothers.

It was more important to the men than to the women that they finish their education and get a full-time job before getting married. This is consistent with the persistence of the image of the male as the family provider. A third of the women in 1989 and fully a half in 1994 say they did not care one way or the other if they marry before getting a full-time job. Childbearing, not marriage, influenced the young women's transitions to work. Table 17.5 addresses the way the youth saw marriage and childbearing influencing their plans to work. There was little gender difference in plans to work prior to marriage. Slightly more men than women in 1989 said they definitely plan to work at this stage. With the shift in time to 1994 (and the change in question wording), this difference disappeared. In 1989 almost 90% of the men and 80% of the women said they would definitely work after they were married, but before they had children. The gender difference in plans to work was most pronounced when there were preschool aged children. Only 18% of the women said they definitely would work at this point in their lives and over a third said they would not. Two thirds of the women who would work with preschool aged children said they would work part-time rather than full-time. The 1994 question asked whether or not they think it was a good idea to work at this life stage. Over half of the women were willing to say that it is a good idea, but many more of them than the men said it was not a good idea. The neutral category allowed them to sit on the fence. The next life stage, which was still very much in the future for most of the youth, still had a gender difference. More women than men were either neutral or less definite about the possibility of working. It was not until one talks about the empty nest phase, when all children have left home, that the responses for the women again parallelled those for the men. The figures for those who definitely plan to work were very low for both men and women. Either they planned to be retirement age by the time all the children had left or, as one respondent put it, "I figure I deserve a rest by then."

CONCLUSIONS

A number of policy relevant conclusions can be drawn from the analyses. Marriage and parenting have a dramatic effect on other transitions, but the effects of these family transitions are quite different for women than for men. Gender differences must be taken into account to ensure that those with the requisite talent and skill are active in the labour force. The responsibilities women face for child care must be recognized to increase their labour force participation. Provision of affordable, flexible quality child care will go a long way to opening up options to qualified women. The expectations that women should care for young children and men should earn a living are pervasive. So long as these gender stereotypes persist one cannot talk of transitions to adulthood without recognizing the gendered nature of those transitions.

Any policy initiatives should recognize that there is not one set of variables that affects the timing of and linkages between the transitions to adulthood. These transitions vary both by area of the country as well as by gender.

Rural-urban differences, in particular, need to be recognized. Relying solely on an accounting scheme that calculates number of clients served by dollars spent, will continue to concentrate resources in the urban areas. Rural youth, however, will benefit more from government interventions since they have fewer options from other sources. Cost issues affect access to post-secondary education. Do available programs of student assistance ensure that the needs of a diverse population are being met? There may be a need to extend financing to part-time and distance education. Perhaps some of the young men who are pushed into the labour force by marital responsibilities would continue their studies if they could be assured of financing. The section on school counselling documents a need for change. The current system is not meeting the requirements of many youth. There is a need for more pro-active counselling within the public school system.

There is a fundamental need for more jobs. Youth are not likely to continue to invest in time consuming and expensive post-secondary education if there is little hope of a pay off in terms of employment. Young adults will not be able to support a family if they cannot find regular work. The crisis facing Canada is less a skills crisis than a lack of jobs for the highly educated youth who are entering the labour force (Davies et al., 1994; Osberg, 1995). The issue of access to jobs is central to policies that hope to facilitate the transition of youth to adult roles.

References

Anisef P., & Axelrod, P. (Eds.). (1993). *Transitions: Schooling and employment in Canada*. Toronto: Thompson Educational Publishing.

Burns, D. (1995). The New Brunswick journeyperson follow-up survey. Paper presented to the Canadian Employment Research Forum (CERF) Workshop on Retooling the Work force, Fredericton, NB.

Davies, S., Mosher, C., & O'Grady, B. (1994). Trends in labour market outcomes of Canadian post-secondary graduates, 1978–1988. In L. Erwin & D. MacLennan (Eds.), *Sociology of Education in Canada*. Mississauga: Copp Clark Longman.

Institute for Social and Economic Research. (1985). *Transitions to work*, Winnipeg, MB: University of Manitoba.

Looker, E.D. (1993). Interconnected transitions and their costs: Gender and urban-rural differences in the transitions to work. In P. Anisef & P. Axelrod (Eds.), *Transitions: Schooling and employment in Canada*. Toronto: Thompson Educational Publishing.

Looker, E.D. (1994). Active capital: The impact of parents on youths' educational performance and plans. In L. Erwin & D. MacLennan (Eds.), *Sociology of education in Canada*. Mississauga: Copp Clark Longman.

Looker, E.D., Denton, M.A., & Davis, C.K. (1989). Bridging the gap: Incorporating qualitative data into quantitative analysis. *Social Science Research, 18*, 313–330.

Looker, E.D. (1995). Preparing for tomorrow. Paper presented to the CERF Workshop on Retooling the Work force, Fredericton, NB.

Mitchell, B. (1995). Home-leaving among Canadian youths. Ph.D. dissertation, McMaster University.

Osberg, L. (1995). Case studies of Atlantic Canada firms. Paper presented to the Canadian Employment Research Forum (CERF) Workshop on Retooling the Work force, Fredericton, NB.

18

Factors Inhibiting the Transition of Youth to Work and to Adulthood

Alan J.C. King and Marjorie J. Peart

The purpose of this chapter is to identify school-related factors that act to inhibit the effective transition of young people both to work and into adulthood. The focus is on youth who enter the labour market after dropping out of or graduating from secondary school. These youth have been consistently targeted by provincial educational reviews as lacking in preparation for the labour market. Reviews in Ontario (1994) and British Columbia (1988) both made recommendations designed to improve the transition to work, but the recommendations are cosmetic and do not respond to the real forces contributing to the problem. What aspects of school curriculum and organization as well as society contribute to this weak transition to work in Canada? Are there models of preparation for work that exist in other countries that are more effective in facilitating the transition? The chapter is organized into two major sections: the first identifies the problems in school-to-work transition; and, the second is concerned with the factors that influence the process.

Two large-scale studies were employed for this analysis. The first is a survey of 11-, 13- and 15-year-old students conducted in 24 countries (King et al., 1996). National samples of at least 1500 students in each of three age groups (11, 13, and 15 corresponding to grades 6, 8 and 10) were drawn from 24 countries; in Germany and France only one large region was sampled. The surveys were administered by teachers according to specific requirements. These data are used to examine the relationship between school structure and student aspirations. This survey includes items related to school performance, school adjustment, student aspirations, and relationships with parents and peers. Three other developed countries, each with its own specialized educational systems, were selected to compare with Canada. Germany represents the model of an early sorting, highly structured, formal preparation for work system. Sweden represents a late sorting, informally structured preparation for work system. Scotland represents what may be seen as an intermediate sorting system with particular attention given to preparation for university.

The second study was undertaken in Ontario and involved surveys of teachers, students, parents, employers and university and college officials (King & Peart, 1984). Secondary school marks, secondary school course enrolments and first-year university and college course marks and enrolments were also analyzed. The Ontario survey was undertaken in 1992–93 in 11 secondary schools and 11 elementary schools; 466 teachers were surveyed and 75 were interviewed; 6,660 students from grades 8 to OAC (grade 13 equivalent) were surveyed and 40 were interviewed; 518 parents from the 12 secondary schools were surveyed and 12 were interviewed. In addition, interviews were conducted with 36 employers and 12 university and college officials. The Ontario Ministry of Education provided mark information for all secondary school students for the school years 1991–1992. In addition, mark information was collected for the years 1992–93 from 60 schools. This was done to provide information on failed courses which was not available from the Ministry of Education. Provincial enrolment patterns in all courses were also examined.

THE PROBLEM

In this section, the structure of education in the four countries is examined with particular emphasis on students' preparation for post-secondary school destinations. The systems in Sweden, Germany, and Scotland were selected for analysis and comparison to those in Canada because they differ on critical parameters. Factors involved in the analysis include the stage at which formal decisions are made by students regarding post-secondary alternatives, the use of external examinations to facilitate the sorting process, the relationship of schools with business and industry, and the degree of formalization of the preparation programs. The nature of the problem of work preparation for those students who do not go on to post-secondary education is illustrated using Ontario as an example. This is followed by a discussion of student aspirations in the four countries within the context of the situation in Ontario.

Characteristics of the educational systems of the four countries

In Canada, the responsibility for educational programming rests with each of the provinces. As a result, while there is much in common across the country, there are some significant differences. Most systems are organized in a 6–3–3 format with one or two years of kindergarten available (see Figure 18.1). In many provinces, the junior and senior high schools are often integrated into the same school. Ontario is organized into two panels—an elementary (junior kindergarten to Grade 8) and a secondary (grade 9 to OAC) but the curriculum is organized into a 6–3–3 format. Québec's system also is divided into elementary and secondary panels with the elementary going to Grade 6 and the secondary ending at Grade 11. The 11- and 15-year-olds tend to be in comparable situations across the country (i.e., in elementary and secondary schools) but the 13-year-olds could be in junior high school, secondary school or elementary school, and faced with different kinds of decisions and different kinds of stresses. For the most part, Canadian Grade 6s and Grade 8s take a common program. The Canadian model is one of a comprehensive secondary school. There is some course choice in Grade 10 and some differentiation of courses according to level of difficulty, but rarely are there specialized schools. At the present time, students are relatively untouched by external examinations except for Québec students. Exams, where they exist, tend to be used for post-secondary admission decisions and occur in the senior grades of secondary school. The instructional program tends to be offered in the direction of

Figure 18.1: Canada's Educational System

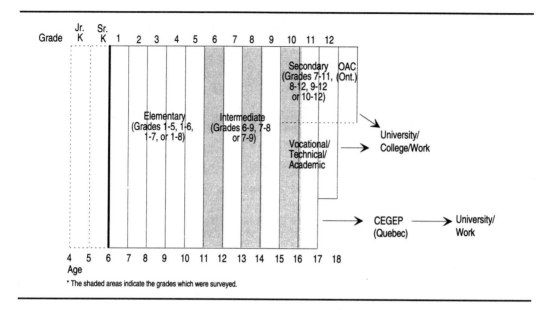

* The shaded areas indicate the grades which were surveyed.

Figure 18.2 Germany's Educational System

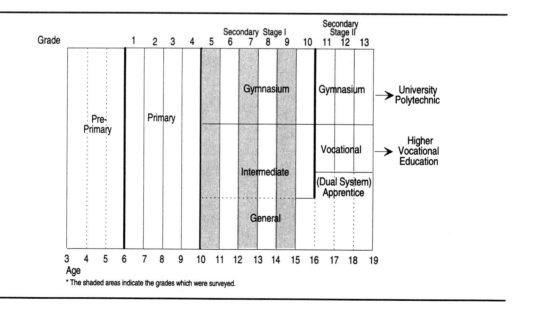

* The shaded areas indicate the grades which were surveyed.

Figure 18.3: Scotland's Educational System

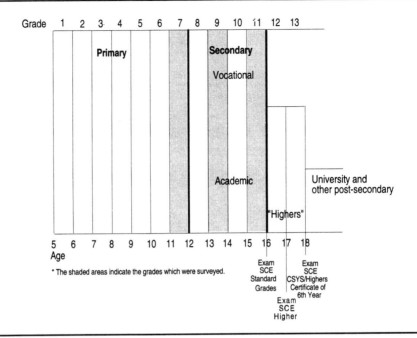

* The shaded areas indicate the grades which were surveyed.

student-centredness with cooperative learning encouraged. There are many school-to-work programs in Canada. The most popular is cooperative education, typically offered to students in grades 11 and 12. These initiatives are school-based and require the cooperation of business and industry in a climate where there is no tradition of collaboration. Overall, the system can be characterized as being very flexible, encouraging students to recover, re-enter, and maintain aspirations to complete post-secondary education.

Germany's educational system has long been recognized as one of the most successful in the world in terms of producing well-educated and well-trained people to meet the needs of the German economy. The system is characterized by very early differentiation (Figure 18.2). Students are divided at age 10 into four general streams, each one with program and status differentiation implications. The sample of students drawn for this study was taken from this highly differentiated part of the program where students were enroled in four different types of schools. The students in all four types took different programs depending on their career direction and school. The 15-year-olds in the HBSC study will be required to make another decision with regard to type of school they attend the following year, but for most the decision will have already been made (King et al., 1996). While curriculum and some testing is centralized, considerable freedom is given to the region and the school to adapt programs and, as a result, there is a student-centred orientation to the instructional programming. Many critical career decisions will already have been made for

Figure 18.4: Sweden's Educational System

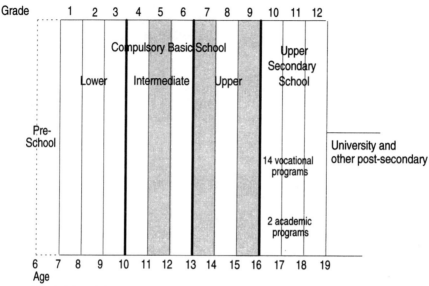

* The shaded areas indicate the grades which were surveyed.

these three groups of students. Germany has a long tradition of formal collaboration between school and the world of work, particularly in the area of apprenticeships, but is experiencing some strain in adapting this system to current conditions. Germany represents the best example of early, formal sorting.

Scotland's educational system requires students to be in school from age 5 to age 16, with primary school lasting for seven forms (see Figure 18.3). The 11-year-old HBSC sample was drawn from the last year of the primary school—a critical transition point for students. The 13- and 15- year-olds could be in either vocational schools or academic schools, and the 13-year-olds were facing a major decision to determine whether they were to go on to take more academic courses. The 15-year-olds in the study were drawn from a greater range of programs. All three of the Scottish age group samples were facing important career-related decisions. Exams play an important role in the Scottish system for 16-, 17-, and 18-year-olds and determine who will proceed to university. The vocational programs tend to be specific in terms of preparation, but do not ensure an easy transition into the world of work.

The Swedish system has recently been reviewed and major structural changes are being implemented for the upper three years of secondary school. The programs were of varying length and have now been standardized to three years. The 15-year-old Swedish student sample from Grade 9 has to make career-related selections from 14 vocational programs and two academic programs (see Figure 18.4). There is still considerable flexibility in terms of

Figure 18.5: Students' Response to "How do you feel about school at present?" (%)

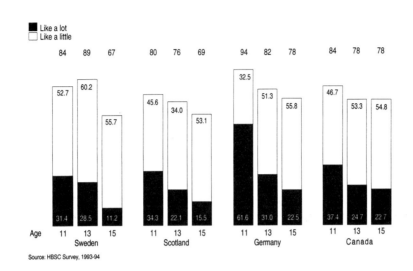

Source: HBSC Survey, 1993-94

program selection and program change, although not all programs are offered at every school and, therefore, a student may be required to travel to a school not necessarily attended by his or her former Grade 9 peers. The three age groups take relatively common programs with some course choice and level of difficulty of choice in years 7 to 9. Although the programs selected after Grade 9 are career-related, there is some flexibility in course selection and changing goals. Up to that point, students take essentially the same program in an instructional atmosphere emphasizing their broad personal and social growth. The Swedish educational system might be considered oriented towards the personal growth of its students. There has, however, been a strong relationship between school and the world of work; this tradition is reinforced by legislation and funding that encourages youth to stay in school.

Students' responses to their educational systems

The students were asked, "How do you feel about school at present?" in order to determine if structural differences in the school systems produced different responses across the four countries (see Figure 18.5). The most structured system, Germany, produced the most positive responses in the early grades although by Grade 10, Canadian students were as positive about school as their German peers. Fifteen-year-olds in Sweden were faced with critical choices related to program and they were less likely to like their schools.

Responses to the question, "I feel stressed at school" (see Figure 18.6) were consistent with these findings. Stress seemed to be related to forces influencing decision making in the middle years of secondary school. Relatively low stress

Figure 18.6: Students' Response to "I feel stressed at school." (%)

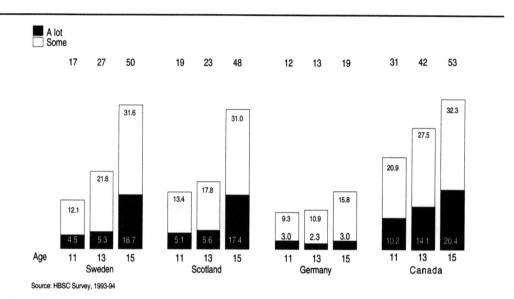

Source: HBSC Survey, 1993-94

was found among German youth, where critical decisions had already been made, but was high in Scotland and in Sweden where exams and program decisions had to be faced. Stress levels increased as the implications of academic performance for careers became more important. Evidence of pressure was most pronounced in Canadian students at all three grade groups.

It was not possible to compare the different marking systems in each of the countries; consequently students were asked to estimate how they thought their teachers viewed their school work. Four alternatives were provided—very good, good, average or below average. The German students were less likely than those from the other countries to see their work as good or very good (see Figure 18.7). Canadian students were the most likely to see their work as good or very good. This is, in part, related to the weaknesses of the sorting mechanisms in Canadian schools and, in part, to the encouragement provided by Canadian teachers which had the indirect effect of encouraging far more students to remain in university-bound courses than will later attend university.

Figure 18.8 represents the Ontario educational system in terms of student progress through secondary school and to post-secondary school destinations. Ontario's post-secondary institutions' enrolments indicated the flexibility of the system; 40% of college and 18% of university students had been out of school for at least one year or had come from other provinces or other countries. Over one-third (25% of the original Grade 9 cohort) of those who graduate from secondary school went directly to work. All these students were eligible to go to college, but not necessarily in the program of their choice. Of those who dropped out, nearly one-third would later obtain a secondary school graduation diploma. Of those who graduated from secondary school but did not go directly

Figure 18.7: Students' Response to "What do your teachers think about your school work" (%)

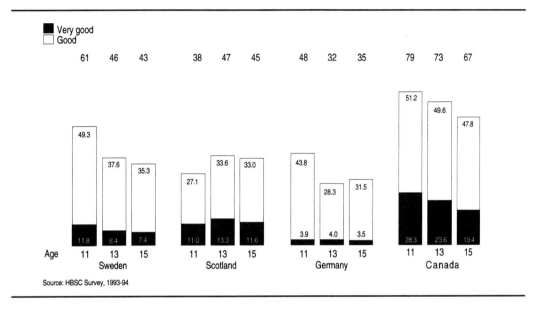

Source: HBSC Survey, 1993-94

Figure 18.8: Secondary School to Post-Secondary Destinations (Ontario)

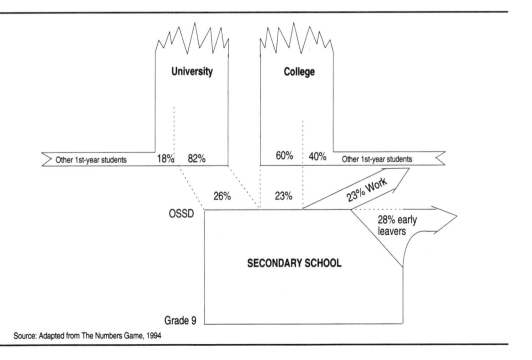

Source: Adapted from The Numbers Game, 1994

Figure 18.9: Aspirations of Ontario Students Enrolled in Grades 9, 10 and 11 Taking Advanced-Level Courses (%)

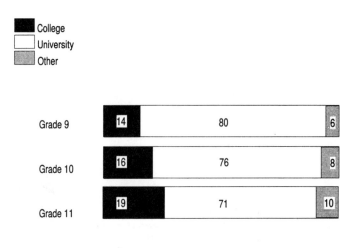

Source: The Numbers Game, 1994

Figure 18.10: Aspirations of Ontario Students Enrolled in Grades 9, 10 and 11 Taking General-Level Courses (%)

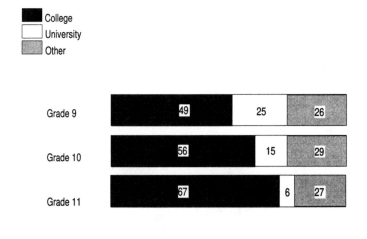

Source: The Numbers Game, 1994

to post-secondary education, over one-half would later attend university or college. The system might be described as manipulative in a gentle, soft way, always leaving open opportunities for recovery. At the same time, it has the effect of encouraging the majority of students to remain in university-bound courses; very few took concentrations in business and technological studies. The relatively small numbers of students who were not enroled in university-bound courses were not in sufficient numbers to allow most schools to develop program-related sequences of courses designed to prepare students for work or college. Surprisingly, few students who took their courses at the general level of difficulty attempted to specialize in vocationally-oriented courses. Their goal tended to be graduation from secondary school by the easiest possible sequence of courses.

Student aspirations

How students interpreted their achievement in schools affected the extent to which they believe they can achieve their goals. Goals for the future emerge in the midst of powerful influences. Young people weighed what their parents think and expect and considerations about the social status of various jobs against what they believed will appeal to them. They began to question what employment opportunities would be available and whether they would be able to impress potential employers and get the job they wanted. They are aware of what their friends are doing and many of them begin to ask themselves "Will my marks and the courses I am taking get me where I want to go?" Post-secondary aspirations of students taking advanced-level courses are summarized in Figure 18.9. Eighty percent of the Grade 9 students planned on attending university. About one-half of this group actually will attend university and many others will seek entry into a college. Over half of the 14% who planned on college will not attend and will end up as early school leavers. Even by Grade 11, the proportion of students planning on university was far greater than would ultimately attend. This illustrates the weakness of the information provided to students regarding the sorting process and explains why so few take courses that will prepare them for a direct transition to work. Even students taking mainly general courses had an ill-defined notion of what their post-secondary destination might be. Very few of the 49% who planned on college will actually reach college and virtually none of the 25% who planned on university will ever reach it (see Figure 18.10). This inability of students to develop clear career aspirations was the major inhibiting force in the development of effective school-to-work programming.

The aspirations of students across the four countries are compared in Figure 18.11. Canadian youth had a far more exaggerated view of their future than youth from the other countries and were far less likely to be considering vocational education. Apprenticeships played a much bigger role in Germany and vocational education a bigger role in Sweden.

Factors influencing youth transitions

Students from Ontario who went directly to work from secondary school were not well prepared for the transition to work or to adulthood. What factors contribute to this situation? Most parents encourage their children to attend

Figure 18.11: Aspirations of 13- and 15-Year-Old Students, By Country %

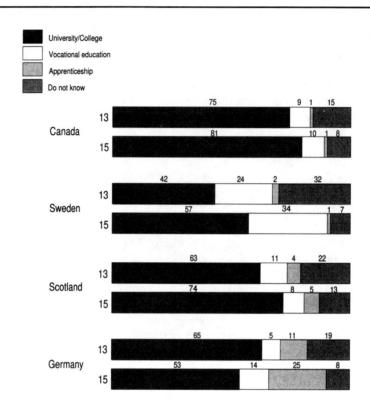

Source: HBSC Survey, 1993-94

university. Parents encourage their children to sustain this motivation, even when school marks indicated that such a goal is not likely to be realized. Teachers, in some instances, provide support for this goal by indicating poor achievement is a function of a lack of effort. Parents then assume that with the necessary increase in effort their children will succeed. A number of analyses were conducted with the parent sample from the Ontario study to explore the dynamics of this process. More specifically, parents were asked to indicate what advice they would give to a son or daughter who obtained each of two sets of marks—one with an average of 82% and one with an average of 62%. In every case, the parents assessed the marks in terms of their implications for future career decisions, the most important being admission to university and, to a lesser extent, admission to a community college. The 82% average marks were favourably regarded by most of the parents because they believed such marks would allow the student to move ahead on any of a number of possible career paths: "all options are open;" "all goals still available." Alongside these positive comments from parents, however, were negative ones from parents who know that competition for places in universities is strong and a student's access to a particular program, such as engineering, occupational therapy, or architecture, was not guaranteed by marks in the low 80s; "short of your target" and "these marks will not get you into the university of your choice." The vast majority of parents viewed an average in the low 60s as unacceptable for their child; comments indicated that their child should "try to do better; " or "look into tutoring." Some parents tended to blame someone or something else, "could be teacher's fault" or "part-time work?" Very few suggested a change in aspirations. None of the parents looked at the marks from the point of view of determining what the child had or had not learned. They saw the marks as indicators of their child's overall academic potential and, more specifically, as indicative of his or her eligibility for university. Parents were asked about current report cards and the information they would like to receive, they were particularly concerned about the kind of information needed to make career decisions, including the relationship between marks obtained and effort, and how the child was doing in comparison with his or her peers.

The influence of universities on secondary school further dilutes attention given to students who go directly to the work force. Universities cannot admit all who would choose to attend, criteria must be established to distinguish between those who are eligible and those who are not. Secondary school marks were the biggest determinant of whether students will be admitted to university programs. The admission procedures and the subject-structured organization of universities determine, to a great extent, how students are taught and evaluated, especially in senior grades. There have been significant increases in the number of applicants to universities while the actual marks obtained by students have been increasing. This makes differentiation among students by marks for admission decisions more difficult and less valid. The required admission mark for entry into oversubscribed programs has increasingly become a moving target. As a result, universities further contribute to the lack of precision of the sorting process. This uncertainty encourages many students to repeat courses to get the necessary average required for entry into particular programs. Since university was the goal of most students, secondary school courses and sequences of courses must be viewed as direct preparation for university courses and programs. These courses do little for those students who will go directly to work after completing secondary school.

The marks assigned to students at secondary school are the building block of the sorting process and determines who will or will not attend university or college. However, while marks are an incentive to some, they act as a disincentive to others to follow certain career paths. Different subjects contribute to this sorting process to a greater extent than others. The mark distribution for advanced-level English courses in Ontario schools approximated a normal distribution. The distribution for general-level marks was skewed with a substantial portion of students receiving below average or failing marks. Five English credits are required for graduation. The loss of credits in English throughout secondary school represents a fundamental barrier to higher education. The loss of key credits for some students discourages them from continuing in school. Significant numbers of both advanced and general-level students received near failing or failing marks in Grade 10 mathematics. Mathematics, a required course, plays a large role in the sorting process by encouraging some students to continue on in mathematics, but it also discourages those who receive average or below average marks from continuing in mathematics, and continuing to take applied courses, apprenticeships and technology programs at college. Mark assignment procedures have the effect of discouraging the most likely candidates from these areas of interest. Marks in science tend to follow a similar pattern and have the same effect, that is, discouraging students from careers that involve math and science skills. Subjects like physical education, music and drama play very little role in the sorting process. Students frequently took these courses instead of others in which they had failed to perform (e.g., math and science).

Teachers felt uncertain about the marks they assigned and most would have raised marks given certain situations (e.g., a final credit for a diploma, a mark raised to reach scholarship level). This uncertainty and teachers' tendency to explain low achievement by students in terms of a lack of effort contributes to the maintenance of unrealistic aspirations. On the other hand, marks assigned in subjects such as mathematics and science tend to spread students out, rewarding students at the one end and discouraging students at the other. This process may work well in sorting out students who will attend university, but it has a discouraging effect on the selection of alternative careers for the remaining students.

THE SCHOOL-TO-WORK INTERFACE

Employer interviews were used to determine how information from schools was used for employment decisions. The employers hired very few young people without an Ontario secondary school diploma. Dropouts working for them tended to have low-paying service jobs such as grocery store clerks, general labourers, or work in maintenance, or retail sales. Employers were more interested in the applicants' previous job experience than in their educational level or ability. In some businesses, even low-paying jobs required a diploma. Figure 18.12 indicates what employers consider when hiring secondary school graduates. Fewer than half of employers of secondary school graduates required proof of graduation. Employers' reasons for not asking to see a candidate's diploma varied. Many assumed that qualified applicants will respect that requirement since the job qualifications were listed in the advertising for the position. Most added that they trusted applicants to tell the truth during interviews. Several employers indicated that they questioned applicants about their education more to learn about their interests and personality than to test their educational qualifications.

Even fewer employers asked to see transcripts than asked to see diplomas when making employment decisions. Some employers mentioned that they asked to see the certification papers of tradesmen, journeymen, and technicians. One employer wanted the certificates and diplomas for display and promotion in the office. Clearly, employers used the diploma and transcripts more as a very general screening device than as the main criterion in their decisions to hire certain candidates. Since few employers requested transcripts, it was not anticipated that many would consider marks when hiring secondary

Figure 18.12: Factors Employers Consider When Hiring Secondary School Graduates; Percent Indicating Very Important

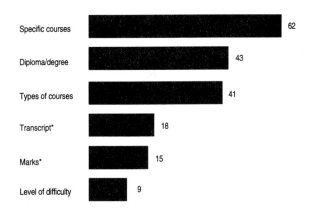

* % very important
Source: The Numbers Game, 1994

school graduates. Only 15% said they considered marks to a great extent. Some were not interested in secondary school marks at all and others relied on job applicants' descriptions of how well they did in school. Some looked at marks for evidence that a candidate was capable of consistent effort; gaining an understanding of what he or she learned in school was not mentioned. Although well over half of employers said that they considered the level of difficulty at which candidates took secondary school courses to some extent, the majority did not feel this would influence their final decision. Employers were not familiar with the current reporting procedures, particularly at the secondary level, and this may be one reason they expressed a lack of interest in level of difficulty of courses.

Secondary schools in Ontario have a variety of formal and informal programs in place to ease the transition of students from school to work and create a higher level of communication with local businesses. The most widespread of these is cooperative education in which students divide their time between attending school and working at a job related to a course they are taking. There were several models of the program, but, typically, students received two work-related credits and one course credit in a cooperative education placement. Full-time cooperative education coordinators were in place in many schools. The program has become quite popular among students in advanced-level courses although originally aimed at students in general-level courses. Employers who were involved in co-op education felt that it helped to prepare students:

The student finds out what the real world is all about. It is a very sheltered world in academia. You make that transition and it's like, "Oh, I didn't realize that's what I had to do when I was out there working." And we feel that every opportunity we have to bring students in is going to make them better students and help them bear down a little more in school; and when they finally come to the job market they are going to be a much better asset to the organization.

The availability of job placements in cooperative education courses depends in great part on the size of the local community and on the willingness of employers to participate. Some programs limit enrolment to students at certain grade levels and admit only students who had acquired a certain number of credits. The placements available do not always match students' interests. They are frequently low-paying jobs and tend to be in relatively safe, easy-to-access areas such as social services and small business. Many businesses are not prepared to devote the time or resources involved in these programs, for example, to do the paperwork and the evaluation for students placed with them. There may also be sensitivity about union issues that act to inhibit both schools and employers. There is little evidence that cooperative education has facilitated the transition of youth from school to work.

Does part-time work during school facilitate direct transition into the work force? Nearly two-thirds of Ontario students in grades 11 and above were working part-time. In addition, 22% were actively seeking part-time work. Part-time work was a new universal phenomenon among adolescents. The range of part-time jobs was substantial but the most common element was that they were low-paid, service industry jobs. They effectively represent a band of employment opportunities for young people that contribute to the economy by making service-oriented operations viable. They also are characterized by few opportunities for advancement. Personal spending money was the primary reason students offered for working. Very few saved for the future and only small numbers of them contributed to the family income or were self-supporting. The money was spent on clothes (probably with the tacit approval of parents who appreciated the saving), compact discs and cassettes, entertainment, and visits to fast-food emporiums. Students were enthusiastic and flexible in terms of work time. They can generally be available at the busiest hours in the evenings and on weekends. They represent an extremely valuable and low cost labour resource.

CONCLUDING COMMENTS

Canada's educational systems are university-driven in curriculum content and in career directions. The powerful influence of the universities is reinforced by parents' ambitions for their children. Canada has a competitive economic system and university graduation offers financial advantage and status. Young people cannot adequately develop the skills and knowledge required for an effective transition to work in the secondary school system. The lack of direction in the schools and parental pressure encourage Canadian youth who do not go on to university to take university-bound courses to the point where they either have too many failed courses and drop out or they do not have enough courses left before graduation to specialize. Other countries provide more opportunities for vocational preparation in the secondary school years. Very realistic work experiences are offered in Germany, Scotland, and Sweden.

The door to university can be kept open and still provide functional preparation for careers is effectively demonstrated in the Swedish model.

Canadian educational systems serve a heterogeneous population and matters of discrimination and equity are often raised by members of minority groups. Formal tracking and program specialization tend to highlight achievement differences among ethnocultural groups. Provincial governments have responded to these pressures by trying to provide all students with common programs. This approach has the effect of delaying decision making and weakening the preparation for work and life for those who do not go on to post-secondary education.

References

Bégan, M., & Caplan, G.L. (1994). *For the love of learning: Report of the Royal Commission on Learning.* Toronto: Queen's Printer.

King, A.J.C., Tudor-Smith, C., Wold, B. and Harel, J. (1996). *The health of youth: cross-country perpsectives.* Copenhagen: World Health Organization.

King, A.J.C., & Peart, M.J. (1994). *The numbers game: A study of evaluation and achievement in Ontario schools.* Toronto: Ontario Secondary School Teachers' Federation.

Sullivan, B.M. (1988). *Legacy for learners: Report of the Royal Commission on Education.* Victoria: Government of British Columbia.

19

Perceptions of Work and Education Transition Problems Encountered After High School

Dennis B. Sharpe

Completion of senior high school marks one of the major transition points in most peoples lives. It is the beginning of a new life style, increased responsibility, and entry into post-secondary education or the workplace. This initial transition is part of a broader developmental process into adulthood. Choices made at this time are heavily influenced by developing aspirations and goals that form and coalesce during the latter years of schooling. The transition process is not necessarily an easy one. Many problems are encountered as adjustments to work and further education are made. Success in transition is not easy to define, but it is generally accepted, especially under the rubric of human capital and status attainment theory, that the goal is economic independence of the individual. Achieving this may involve combinations of further education and work. Increased years of education beyond high school tends to increase employment prospects for young adults (Secretary of State, 1991). Numerous recent federal and provincial documents also concur on the importance of continued education (especially lifelong learning) and its effects on the individual, the economy, and in the development of a well educated work force (Canadian Steering Group, 1992; Economic Council of Canada, 1992; Government of Newfoundland, 1992; Porter, 1991). The context in which the transition process is taking place is likely to influence the aspirations and goals of youth as well as place some of the problems encountered into perspective. For example, in a province such as Newfoundland and Labrador, unemployment has often been double that of other provinces (Economic Research and Analysis Division, 1992; Statistics Canada, 1991). Economic difficulties in the province have been exacerbated by dramatic fluctuations in the primary resource industries and on a high dependence on income support programs (Royal Commission, 1986). The recent closure of much of the fishery have further impacted on the economic context (Economic Research and Analysis Division, 1993).

This chapter will focus on education and work related transition problems identified by a group of Newfoundland youth as they proceeded from high school and followed various transition pathways. The analysis of data from three different groups examined their career plans and aspirations, work experiences, and some of the problems identified within the first two to three years after school.

THE YOUTH TRANSITION STUDY

Four comprehensive surveys have been made of a large cohort of New-foundland youth as part of a longitudinal study of youth transition into the labour market. The initial data collection was conducted in the spring of 1989 at a point when most students were about to complete senior high school and were making decisions regarding further education, work, and other options (Sharpe & Spain, 1991a). The graduating class of 1989 was surveyed again in the fall of 1989, between December 1990 and January 1991, and a fourth time about one year later. In 1989, 7,390 questionnaires were returned via home-room teachers from the approximately 9,600 students in Grade 12. Successive follow-ups used a combination of mail questionnaires and phone interviews and yielded 6,807, 5,429, and 5,664 returns respectively. Attempts were made to contact the original group of respondents in each follow-up to reduce overall sample mortality; 59% (4,329) of the cohort participated in all four surveys. The study addressed a wide range of variables pertinent to the transition process, and, in particular, concentrated on education and work related issues and decisions. The overall intent was to track this group of young adults over several critical decision making years to a point where most would be about 25 years of age and would have had an opportunity to complete post-secondary education programs and enter the labour market. Sixty-three percent of the initial respondents had entered some kind of post-secondary program within 18 months of leaving high school. This participation rate had increased by another 11% a year later. However, not all remained in education. Some left after a period of time to take up employment; a few returned to high school; some left and re-entered a program; a few engaged in home making full-time; and others engaged in combinations of part-time or full-time work and education. Such varied pathways are becoming the norm rather than the exception, and tend to develop into increasingly complex and circuitous routes over time (Bellamy, 1991; Campbell et al., 1984; Krahn & Lowe, 1990; Ontario Teachers Federation, 1983; Rosenthral & Pilot, 1988). Groups of youth can be tracked and compared within these various pathways, especially where a particular group is considered to be successful or unsuccessful in terms of the transition process from school to work. Comparisons of participation and non-participation in education beyond high school, for example, can poten-tially yield information pertinent to policies and programming that could assist large numbers of youth to at least make the initial years of transition more successful and contribute to satisfying lives and long-term employment.

This analysis examines and contrasts three groups of youth based on their education status following the transition from high school. One group (n = 698) consisted of those who had not engaged in any kind of education or training program since leaving high school in 1989. Another group (n = 1702) were continuously engaged in post-secondary programs after high school and a third group (n = 185) had completed a post-secondary program by January 1992. A general profile of these groups revealed several demographic and educational differences, especially between the further education participants and non-participants. The latter group were mostly (72%) from rural areas, more likely to be male (54%), older than average for the total sample, and, as of the last survey, mostly living at home with their parents. Their age profile could be explained in part by the fact that 32% had repeated grades while in school. About 45% had considered dropping out, but only 2% had actually done so and then eventually returned to school. Their academic high-school perform-ance was the lowest of the three groups with an average mark of 63.2% for all courses taken and 59.5% for Grade 12 courses only. By contrast, those in post-secondary programs were mostly women (61%), had graduated high school, and were the group with the highest average (77%) high-school marks. Almost none had repeated grades in school and few (7%) had considered dropping out. The largest number (84%) were in university programs, mostly in Newfoundland, 14% were in Diploma of Applied Arts or Technology programs, and the remaining 2% were in pre-employment or pre-apprentice-ship programs. Their home living status was less easy to determine since many were attending different educational institutions typically within the Province, but not necessarily in their home community. Rural and urban differences in this group were not apparent. The third group, the post-secondary graduates, exhibited some similar characteristics to those continuing with more lengthy programs, although more (68%) were from rural areas. The larger number (60%) were women, had done fairly well in high school with an average mark for the group of 70.2%, and had a high-school diploma. About 20% had considered dropping out of school at some point. They had completed post-secondary programs of two years or less in the areas of Applied Arts or Technology diplomas, or in pre-employment or pre-apprenticeship certificates.

CAREER PLANS

Developing aspirations and plans are an integral part of the transition process for youth and, according to Gottfredson (1981), are one of the most significant determinants of success or eventual attainment. They help to provide direction and focus efforts for educational and job searches and establishment in programs, jobs, and eventually careers. Higher aspirations were likely to result in post-secondary qualifications and thus potentially a more successful transition (Campbell et al., 1984). Several questions addressed career aspira-tions, including intent to pursue education sometime after high school; 98% of the post-secondary groups intended to pursue post-secondary education, while only 75% of the non-participants indicated they would do so. Table 19.1 displays information about the high-school seniors plans for the year immedi-ately after high school. Only 20% of the non-education group compared to 92% of those in post-secondary education and 76% of the post-secondary graduates said they had definitely planned to continue their education. Many more of the non-education group had plans that involved work or taking the year off. More of this group also declared they did not have any plans. Differences by gender and rural and urban location were minimal for the most part, although those with definite work plans in the non-education group were more likely to be rural men. Another question in the initial survey addressed reasons for not planning to continue with education beyond high school. Responses given by the non-education group revealed an anticipated lack of money for education

**Table 19.1: Transition Status and Grade 12 Student Plans for the Year
after High School**

Plan	Transition Status 1989-92 (%)[1]		
	No Post-Secondary (N = 676)	In Post-Secondary (N = 1645)	Post-Secondary Graduates (N = 185)
Do not have a plan	6.2	0.4	0.6
Plan to take a year off	18.9	0.7	2.8
Like to continue education, but may have to work	21.4	3.8	10.1
Probably continue education, but rather work	8.7	1.3	8.4
Definitely plan to work	22.5	1.6	2.8
Definitely plan to continue education	19.5	92.1	75.4
Plan to return to high school	2.7	0.2	-

[1]No responses excluded from analysis.

(21%), wanting to start supporting themselves (21%), problems deciding on a program (9%), and doubts about their ability to do well in post-secondary education (8%); about one third of this group did not give any reasons.

Aspirations of those in post-secondary education remained high and consistent from point of departure from high school through the follow-up surveys with most anticipating a future that involved full-time work and little or no involvement with seasonal work and unemployment cycles. Fewer in the non-education group anticipated full-time work (54% versus 80% of those in education) and more anticipated dependence on unemployment insurance in their futures (18% versus 4%). At least one-third of this group simply did not know what their status might be in the future even 18 months out of high school. This was an increase from 20% who did not know while in high school. Such uncertainty also increased in the other groups (from 5% to 15%) over the same period. A worsening economy and job market in the Province may have been a contributing factor to the uncertainty. Forty-two percent of the non-education group, compared to about 25% of the other groups, expected to be pursuing their career plans in their home communities (typically rural areas). However, another 30 to 40% of each group also indicated that their career plans would take them out of the Province. The latter perspective was probably realistic given the changing and shrinking job market, especially in rural areas.

Within six months of finishing high school, 75% of the non-education group, compared to only 5% of those still in programs and 23% of the post-secondary graduates, considered their career plans not on track. Reasons could be categorized into those who said their career plans were on hold (25%), their academic qualifications inadequate (24%), and institutional constraints such as course waiting lists or courses not being available (18%). Similar reasons were also evident in the graduate group. Overall, gender and rural and urban differences were not significant except that there were more women in a small group that cited family and personal reasons for their career plans not being on track. Two years later, more of the non-education group were satisfied with their career plans being on track, but 59% who considered otherwise was still the highest of the three groups. Reasons varied, but the most commonly cited were career indecision (18%), lack of money (17%), not enough jobs available (14%) and not having the right education (11%). Forty-four of the post-secondary graduates also responded negatively to this question with the most pressing issue being the lack of jobs (36%) and indecision about a career (19%). Far fewer (17%) of those still in programs were dissatisfied with their career plans; the main problem with this group (mostly those in university) was career indecision, especially by the women. Real or perceived barriers to further education had emerged and were being voiced by the group that had not entered an educational program since high school. Yet 93%, at the time of departure from school, had said that taking courses would help them in obtaining employment. They had realized the value of further education but were not disposed or able to overcome obstacles or change a lifestyle to which they were becoming accustomed.

WORK EXPERIENCE

Involvement in work was not a new experience for the majority of this group of youth. Many had held full-time (typically summer) and part-time jobs while in high school. Eighty-two percent of the total youth transition study cohort had worked during the summer of 1989 right after high school (Sharpe & Spain, 1991b). This finding was similar to findings from a study of Ontario youth that documented substantial work experience by students while they were in high school and concluded that the transition to work was in fact a "transition in the nature of work, not just a transition to work for the first time" (Walsh, 1989, p. 23). Data from the second follow-up survey showed that 92% of the non-education group and about 85% of the other groups had worked sometime during 1990. Typically the job was full-time, especially for the non-education participants of whom about two-thirds were employed through the year. The full-time work experience of the group in education peaked during the summer months and only involved 18 to 22% of the group through the year. Less than 10% in any of the groups expressed any concerns or identified any specific problems encountered while working at a job. Similar patterns of employment participation were documented the following year. The types of jobs were also similar and were dominated by lower skill, low paying insecure jobs. Typical examples listed by both groups were sales (including cashiers), labouring, babysitting, factory worker, waiter or waitress, and fishing. The group in post-secondary education were engaged in a wider range of jobs including some in recreation and coaching. Over 80% of each group was generally satisfied with the kind of job they had although less satisfaction was expressed by the non-education group. Only 40% of the latter group indicated that the employment they had was related to their overall career plans; many were in jobs intended to satisfy their basic needs, but were not part of longer range goals and aspirations. Very few (5% of those in education and less than 3% in the other groups) had not been employed since leaving school. Overall, the type of work reflected that of relatively young, inexperienced workers with minimally required education and training. The contrast in types of jobs held by those in post-secondary education compared to the non-education participant group will increase dramatically as more of the group graduate and enter jobs based on their preparation.

GETTING STARTED AFTER HIGH SCHOOL

Youth are faced with a variety of issues and problems related to employment and or further education as they begin the transition from school. Perceptions of problems, whether real or not, are important in decision making and the resultant pathways followed. The more negative the perceptions, the greater likelihood of resistance to change or to seek ways to overcome problems, thus resulting in potentially less desirable or successful pathways. The degree to which the youth transition study respondents considered several work related issues to be problematic are shown in Table 19.2. Some changes were evident between the two surveys, but overall, there was a remarkable degree of consistency particularly in relation to the scarcity of jobs, a factor which at least three-quarters of the sample, regardless of educational status, considered to be a problem. The majority indicated it was a serious and increasing problem. Those not in post-secondary education and the group of program graduates, especially those in rural areas, found this issue particularly troublesome. Most had found employment, however, despite their concerns about the scarcity of jobs. The stability of that employment may be the real issue. The second most problematic work related issue for about two-thirds of the sample concerned their lack of work experience. This was especially considered a problem by the post-secondary graduate group and by those in rural areas. Except for the graduates, the concern did lessen over time as many in the sample gained work experience for periods of time since leaving high school.

Finding jobs they liked was perceived as a problem area for about 60% of both non-education participants and the post-secondary graduates. Such responses were predictable given the job market situation faced by youth. Knowing how to look for jobs was considered somewhat problematic for approximately one-third of the sample, but decreased as a problem over time, especially for the post-secondary graduates. It remained as a problem for about 25% of the others. Almost one-third of the sample also considered their youth to be somewhat of a problem in obtaining employment. About half of the non-education and graduate groups and approximately a third of those in education said that money to look for work was also a problem within the first year of finishing high school. The concern lessened the following year. Expanding job searches to other locations (especially when most considered

Table 19.2: Perception of Career Related Issues Associated with Getting Started after High School

Item	Perceived problem in 1990 (%)			Perceived problem in 1991 (%)		
	No Post-Secondary (N=670)	In Post-Secondary (N=1675)	Graduated Post-Sec. (N = 175)	No Post-Secondary (N = 670)	In Post-Secondary (N=1675)	Graduated Post-Sec. (N=175)
Work related						
Finding a job you liked	61.0	51.2	61.2	62.3	45.0	56.8
Knowing how to look for a job	38.7	35.1	40.2	26.2	24.8	19.3
Being too young to get jobs	36.8	38.6	43.9	30.2	27.9	35.5
Scarcity of jobs	76.2	74.8	82.7	82.1	73.4	80.1
Not having enough job experience	66.4	61.3	72.1	58.1	49.6	71.4
Having money to look for work	52.6	34.4	53.8	43.4	28.6	42.2
Education related						
Finding time to go to school	45.2	3.5	10.0	-	-	-
Finding courses near home	61.9	36.9	41.4	-	-	-
Meeting entrance requirements	45.8	9.0	12.9	35.5	10.4	7.7
Working to support self/family	43.1	17.8	24.7	-	-	-
Getting information about courses	26.0	19.7	22.1	20.1	16.7	15.0
Getting money for education	69.7	46.6	54.7	56.7	43.1	40.8
Having to go away from home	-	-	-	26.9	21.3	19.4
Getting first choice of programs	-	-	-	39.8	26.6	16.6

Note. The total N for each group varies slightly by item. Not all items were included in each survey. Items were assessed using a three point scale: not, somewhat and serious problem. Percentages based on collapsing the somewhat and serious categories.

personal contact a prime way to obtain employment) will be costly for most young adults living in their home community.

The group who had not started any post-secondary program since leaving high school were much more concerned about education. They perceived many barriers to entry into education, the most prominent being funding, lack of courses available near home, meeting entrance requirements, and finding time to attend (see Table 19.2). Their chosen lifestyle (typically work) and commitments were no doubt impacting on possible re-entry into the educational system. Over 40% indicated that having to work and support themselves was a problem. Obtaining information about courses was less of an issue. Funding and available courses near home were concerns of about one-third to one-half of those in education. The funding concerns tended to diminish slightly with time, but still remained the most dominant of the perceived problem areas for all groups in the survey. Gender differences concerning these problem areas were slight; educational funding and finding courses close to home were significantly more of a concern to rural students. The youth not in education were becoming accustomed to a life-style that included some independence with work as a means of supporting themselves. To start into an educational program would disrupt this newly achieved independence. Additionally, giving up some or all of their income might well compound their problem of funding courses.

DIFFICULTIES WHILE IN PROGRAMS

Post-secondary program students indicated that several areas were problematic to them while taking courses (see Table 19.3). The adjustments from a high-school program to that of a post-secondary environment were difficult ones for many of these young adults, especially in terms of experiencing different teaching approaches, academic expectations, grading practices, and planning the use of time. These were more of a problem initially for those still in programs, mostly university and college diploma students. Forty-one percent of these young adults also identified their high-school preparation, especially in maths, as a problem. Funding issues and finding summer employment were additional concerns of about 40% of both groups; planning the use of time was problematic to even more of those in programs. Rural students were more likely to be concerned about jobs, funding, and high-school preparation issues. The problems were greater in the initial transition period from high school, except for money to live on which remained a consistently high concern through each follow-up survey. Reflecting back on their high-school days, the students identified a number of things that could be improved, including offering more appropriate courses (especially in rural areas), offering better preparation for post-secondary education, and not babying students but rather helping them to develop more independent learning styles required for college and university (Sharpe & White, 1993). Very few students in either group identified the atmosphere of the post-secondary institution as being a problem, especially the graduate group who had taken mainly college pre-employment and pre-apprenticeship programs. The literature on student retention in post-secondary suggests that a supportive environment is an important factor in terms of students positively integrating into an institution and developing a sense of belonging (Byrne, 1991; Dietsche, 1990; Gilbert & Gomme, 1986; Pascarella et al., 1986).

SUMMARY AND DISCUSSION

Each of the three groups exhibited different characteristics and helped to identify several areas of concern related to work and education. The large group still in post-secondary education and the college program graduates had more in common compared to the non-education group. All youth identified concerns about the labour market and finding suitable jobs; those in education were also concerned about funding and support. Most of these issues are not new ones for youth as they make their way through the first few years after school.

Table 19.3: Extent to Which Education Related Issues Were Problematic While in Courses

Item	Problem in 1990 (%)		Problem in 1991 (%)	
	In Post-Secondary (N = 1675)	Graduated Post-Secondary (N = 175)	In Post-Secondary (N = 1675)	GraduatedPost-Secondary (N = 175)
High school preparation	40.9	17.3	34.2	14.8
Finding a place to stay	15.8	16.5	19.3	15.2
Getting a job last summer	42.0	32.4	-	-
Money for tuition and books	39.2	39.1	31.7	18.4
Money to live on	41.3	42.3	45.3	41.9
Planning use of time/enough time	46.9	28.9	43.2	27.4
Adjusting to teachers	49.3	18.8	29.1	24.0
Teachers expecting too much	55.1	32.8	-	-
Teachers marking too hard	55.5	23.0	-	-
Math	42.9	17.5	34.2	20.6
Reading	8.4	6.3	9.8	5.6
Science	-	-	14.5	8.7
Work was too hard	-	-	20.3	5.1
Atmosphere of school	-	-	13.4	6.1
Really preferred to be working	-	-	12.1	17.4

Note.The total N for each group varies slightly by item. Not all items were included in each survey. Items were assessed using a three point scale: not, somewhat and serious problems. Percentages based on collapsing the somewhat and serious categories.

There is a need to identify high-school students with low aspirations and ambitions after high-school completion. One indicator of this would be the lack of plans, or plans that excluded further education. Ways and processes to develop appropriate aspirations and plans to help students continue some form of education needs to be addressed even recognizing that to graduate from high school is a challenge for a number of them. Many in this group realized the value of education, but for various reasons did not engage in it. The changing nature of the workplace, living in an increasingly technological environment, and realizing ambitions will require engagement in further studies. A recent analysis of school leavers and high-school graduates, concluded that "much more education and training is required for decent jobs, incomes and life-chances. Anything less than the minimum may restrict youth to long hours, tedious jobs with little opportunity for advancement, and a low quality of life" (Gilbert, et al., 1993, p. 47). More articulation is required across the educational system to reduce the impact of entry into post-secondary education (especially into degree and diploma programs) and to align the college and high-school environments (Cargill, 1994). Mutual, cooperative efforts are required by both parts of the educational system to accommodate and help students in transition to adjust and become more independent, self-reliant, and satisfied as learners.

Funding concerns were consistent problems faced by youth in post-secondary education; current budgetary constraints at all levels in the educational system means that the concerns are likely to increase. Funding (and finding time) for post-secondary education is reduced for students who can access courses and programs within commuting distance of their homes. The advantages of satellite campuses, transferability of credits, and components of programs being available through distance delivery could help in this regard.

Perceptions of issues related to securing employment were a problem for many in the survey. The perceptions may well reflect the typical difficulties encountered by youth who have traditionally experienced more problems, less success, and overall greater levels of unemployment compared to other groups in the labour market. Some of the areas of concern might be addressed through appropriate programming both within the high-school context and in initial post-secondary education; work and co-op experiences that place students in business and industry will enable the accumulation of experience and perhaps confidence. Job seeking skills are critical in an era of growing uncertainty about employment, widely fluctuating job market, and job searches that need to extend beyond the local home areas.

References

Bellamy, L.A. (1991). Transitions from high school: Determinants, decisions, and destinations. Paper presented at the Canadian Sociological and Anthropology Association Conference, Queen's University, Kingston, Ontario.

Byrne, M. (1991). *Attrition at Cabot Institute: Causes and proposed remedial measures.* St. John's: Cabot Institute of Applied Arts and Technology.

Canadian Steering Group on Prosperity. (1992). *Inventing our future.* Ottawa: Author.

Campbell, P.B., Gardner, J.A., & Winterstein, A. (1984). *Transition patterns between education and work.* Columbus, OH: The National Center for Research in Vocational Education, Ohio State university. (Eric Document Reproduction Service No. ED 240 272)

Cargill, U.B. (1994). Transition experiences of high-school students planning to attend college. In A.J. Paulter (Ed.), *High school to employment transition: Contemporary issues.* Ann Arbor, MI: Praaken.

Dietsche, P.H.J. (1990). Freshman attrition in a college of applied arts and technology of Ontario. *The Canadian Journal of Higher Education, 20,* 34–46.

Economic Council of Canada (1992). *A lot to learn: Education and training in Canada.* Ottawa: Minister of Supply and Services Canada.

Economic Research and Analysis Division. (1992). *Newfoundland and Labrador: The economy 1992.* St. John's: Government of Newfoundland and Labrador, Cabinet Secretariat.

Economic Research and Analysis Division. (1993). *Newfoundland and Labrador: The economy 1993.* St. John's: Government of Newfoundland and Labrador, Cabinet Secretariat.

Gilbert, S., Barr, L., Clark, W., Blue, M., & Sunter, D. (1993). *Leaving school: Results from a national survey comparing school leavers and high-school graduates 18–20 years of age.* Ottawa: Human Resource and Labour Canada, Government of Canada.

Gilbert, S.N., & Gomme, I.M. (1986). Future directions in research on voluntary attrition from colleges and universities. *College and University, 61,* 227–238.

Gottfredson, L.S. (1981). Circumscription and compromise: A developmental theory of occupational aspirations. *Journal of Counselling Psychology, 28,* 545–579.

Government of Newfoundland and Labrador. (1992). *Change and challenge: A strategic economic plan for Newfoundland and Labrador.* St. John's: Author.

Krahn, H., & Lowe, G.S. (1990). *Young workers in the service economy* Working paper No. 14). Ottawa: Economic Council of Canada.

Ontario Teachers Federation. (1983). *The school-to-work transition.* Toronto: Author.

Pascarella, E.T., Terenzini, P.T., & Wolfe, L.M. (1986). Orientations to college and freshman year persistence/withdrawal decisions. *Journal of Higher Education, 57* (2), 155–175.

Porter, M.E. (1991). *Canada at the crossroads.* Ottawa: Minister of Supply and Services Canada.

Rosenthral, N.H., & Pilot, M. (1988). Information needs for initial and ongoing work transition. *Journal of Career Development, 15* (1), 20–41.

Secretary of State. (1991). *Profile of higher education in Canada.* Ottawa: Minister of Supply and Services Canada.

Royal Commission on Employment and Unemployment. (1986). *Building on our strengths.* St. John's: Queens Printer.

Sharpe, D.B., & Spain, W.H. (1991a). *The class of '89: Initial survey of level iii (grade 12) high-school students.* St. John's: Centre for Educational Research and Development, Memorial University of Newfoundland.

Sharpe, D.B., & Spain, W.H. (1991b). *Six months after high school: Class of '89 follow-up survey one.* St. John's: Centre for Educational Research and Development, Memorial University of Newfoundland.

Sharpe, D.B., & White G. (1993). *Educational pathways and experiences of Newfoundland youth.* St. John's: Centre for Educational Research and Development, Memorial University of Newfoundland.

Statistics Canada. (1991). *Labour force annual averages* (Cat. 71–220). Ottawa: Minister of Supply and Services Canada.

Walsh, J. (1989). Managing the transition from school to work. *A.C.F.P. Journal, 25* (2), 23–25.

Correlates of Post-Secondary Participation

Samuel J. McGrath

The public media, government publications, and the sociological literature have all given considerable attention to the demographic, economic, and labour market realities of the 1990s and to their projected
changes into the 21st century. Some reports (Curtis, 1989; Organization for
Economic Cooperation and Development, 1986) have suggested that restructuring in industry is becoming the norm rather than the exception on a
worldwide scale. Others (Feather, 1983; Picot, 1987) have referred to the intense
competition for and the shortage of highly skilled workers in many industries
and of a growing need for both a higher level of employment skills and for
different kinds of skills. The general message has been that modern industry
was in a state of flux, the outcome of which would have serious implications
for the traditional competitiveness of industrialized countries. The linkage
between education and training and the labour market has become increasingly
important. Education and training have been traditionally perceived as primary
instruments for determining labour market outcomes for youth. Education
beyond high school was considered an assured means of improving opportunities to obtain employment, of increasing the range of opportunities for the
type of employment obtained, of providing for higher salaries, and for assisting
the worker to become more adaptable to occupational and industrial changes
(Sharpe & Spain, 1991). Education was also considered one of the most
important means for resolving some of the difficulties which youth experience
in making the transition from high school to work (Ashton, 1988).

Generally, the notion of transition refers to the changes which occur in
personal status as youth leave high school and eventually enter the labour force
full-time. The transition period may be considered to extend from age 16 to
24. Mason (1985) considered the experience to be strongly influenced by the
acquisition of education and work skills even though the patterns of transition
were often individualistic. Some youth make a decision to delay entry into the
labour force by continuing their education at a vocational school, technical
institute, or university. In this way, they tend to prolong the transition period.
Other youth make a decision to seek full-time employment immediately after
high-school graduation, or before completing high school. The latter stream of
youth generally seem to encounter more difficulty in finding employment than
do those who complete high school, and the kind of work the early leavers
obtain is often part-time, menial, low-paying, and cyclic (Samuelson, 1988).
High-school graduates were found to fare only a little better (Empson-Warner

& Krahn, 1990). The best chance youth had of obtaining full-time, better paying, and more meaningful work was to continue on to post-secondary education after high school (Krahn & Lowe, 1989).

Post-secondary participation rates across Canadian provinces have been low in absolute terms. For example, in 1990–91, the national rate for both university and public college participation among 18–24 year-olds, as a percentage of the total general population in Canada 18 years and over, was 30.9%. The comparable rate for Newfoundland was 21.9%, the second lowest rate in the country (Statistics Canada, 1991). Post-secondary participation in Newfoundland has not been extensively studied although provincial rates in comparison to national rates have been viewed as the most serious problem facing post-secondary education (Royal Commission on Employment and Unemployment, 1986). The differential prompted an exploratory study—on which this chapter is based—to examine factors that might influence the decision made by young people in Newfoundland about furthering their education beyond high school. The study was oriented to youth in transition into the labour market with a focus on post-secondary participation. Overarching assumptions were that post-secondary participation is a social issue which has its roots in the family and the school, and the dynamics between the relevant variables influencing participation are interwoven and complex (Hayden & Carpenter, 1990).

THEORETICAL FOUNDATIONS

Theory related to post-secondary participation specifically emanates from the literature on educational attainment which is usually encompassed in the general literature on occupational attainment (McGrath, 1993). The Canadian mobility study, an omnibus Statistics Canada occupational study, was the first national effort that indirectly examined educational attainment. Approximately 45,000 young people from all ten provinces who were 18 years old or over were surveyed in 1973. With reference to educational attainment, the study found that family origin was positively associated with attainment,that coming from a large family reduced attainment, and that the level of attainment was virtually the same for males and females although fewer females had gone to university (Boyd et al., 1985, pp. 207–519). A second national social mobility study was conducted in 1986 (Creese, Guppy, & Meissner, 1991). Educational attainment was examined in terms of its role in social mobility and status attainment among Canadian men and women. Among its findings was that educational attainment in Canada was rising—16% of parents in the study had some post-secondary education compared with 43% for their children (Creese, Guppy, & Meissner, 1991, p. 57).

Breton's survey of 145,817 high-school students (grades 9–13) found a direct association between student knowledge and use of guidance services and educational aspirations (1972, p. 391). Williams (1972) used longitudinal data from approximately 3,700 Grade 12 Ontario students enroled in general academic programs to study changes in educational aspirations over time. The sample was randomly selected from 25,000 Grade 12 students who were first surveyed in 1959–60 when they were enroled in Grade 9. The 1972 study compared the aspirations which the students held in Grade 10 with their aspirations in Grade 12. At both time periods, the influence of parents was substantially more effective on students' educational goals, both male and female, than the influence of peers; teachers' influence was moderate by comparison with that of parents (Williams, 1972, pp. 124, 130). O'Neill found that residential settings including rural-farm, rural non-farm, village, small-town, and large city accounted for only a small proportion of the variance (.013) in educational aspiration of 7,500 Grade 12 Ontario students who were surveyed during the 1975–76 school year (1981, p. 58). Looker (1993) compared gender and urban/rural differences in the educational and occupational plans of approximately 1,200 17-year-olds from Hamilton, Halifax, and rural Nova Scotia. Most of the respondents wanted and expected advanced education but their educational plans were interwoven into their occupational plans and their plans for marriage and a family (Looker, 1993, p. 64).

The model developed to guide the study followed conventions established in antecedent models in the Blau and Duncan (1967) and the Wisconsin model (Sewell & Shah, 1967) traditions. The study variables were grouped as follows:

Personal Variables	**Family Variables**
Gender	Value of Education in the Family
Career Plans	Family Size (number of siblings)
Well-being	
Learning Style	

School Variables	**Community Variables**
Guidance	Geographical Region
Career Information	Rurality (Rural/Urban)
Mathematics Program	Attachment

Intervening Variables	
Academic Achievement	Vocational Self-concept
Academic Attainment	Significant Others
Barriers	

Dependent Variable
Post-secondary Participation

The model assumes that personal status variables, selected family status variables, school resource variables, and community context variables are all independent variables. Academic achievement, high-school graduation, vocational self-concept, the influence of significant others, and barriers are all intervening variables that mediate the effects of the independent variables on the dependent variable—participation in post-secondary education. The model is a series of structural equations in which the parameters of the variables are estimated from correlational matrices or partial regression coefficients. It is additive in nature in that the effects of the independent and intervening variables combine directly and indirectly to affect the probability that a young person will participate in post-secondary education (Hayden & Carpenter, 1990). The selection and causal ordering of the variables is partly due to the patterns traditionally found in the literature and partly to hypotheses. As a consequence, the model displays characteristics of both convention and idiosyncrasy. The path model assumes linearity in the effects of the independent and intervening variables on the dependent variable and hypothesizes that the effects of the independent variables are both direct and indirect. That is, the independent variables independently influence participation in post-secondary education. At the same time, their effects are also transmitted through one or more of the five intervening variables so that the total effect on participation is due to a combination of the direct effects and the indirect effects.

The design of the research flowed from the conceptual framework. The independent and dependent variables were selected following a review of the youth transition and status attainment literatures, from a pilot study, and from a series of interviews undertaken as a preliminary to the main study (McGrath, 1993). Quantitative data for the study were obtained from a longitudinal study that began in Newfoundland in 1989 (Sharpe & Spain, 1991); qualitative data were from interviews with former students and with educators from the secondary and post-secondary education systems in the province. Other information was obtained from federal and provincial public documents and from the public examination database at the Newfoundland Department of Education. The data were organized and analyzed using factor analysis, multiple regression, and path analysis. Separate analyses were conducted for males and females.

FINDINGS

Both the correlational and regression analyses of the survey data revealed that six of the 17 independent variables were consistently related to post-secondary participation. In descending order, they were academic achievement, barriers, value of education, advanced mathematics, academic attainment, and well-being. Their correlation coefficients were comparable in all three matrices, i.e., the model for males, the model for females, and the total group model. In the regression analysis, the order of the effects of the six variables was generally consistent in all three models and the relative size of the effect of each variable on participation was generally comparable across the three models. However, while the relationships were statistically significant at the .01 level throughout, an artifact doubtlessly of the large sample size (n = 5420), they were weak in real terms and suggested that major shifts would have to occur in the effects of the independent variables for a movement from non-participation to participation to take place (See Table 20.1).

A profile of the most likely participant in post-secondary education in Newfoundland emerged, albeit opaquely, from the regression analysis for the integrated model. The participant could either be a male or female from a small family in any community—rural or urban—in the most populous region of the province (Region 1, the Avalon Peninsula). He or she would have graduated from high school with a high average in the provincial public examinations, and would likely have taken advanced mathematics in high school as well as attended a school where career information services were available. The person may not have formulated a career plan but her or his continuing sense of well-being would be high.

Table 20.1: Correlations, Direct Effects, Indirect Effects, Total Effects, and t-Values for the Effects of the Exogenous Variables and the Intervening Variables on Post-secondary Participation

OutcomeVariables	Independent Variables	Correlation (r)	Direct Effect	Indirect Effect	Total Effect	t-Value
Participation	Gender	.097	.048	.022	.070	3.823
	R-U	.099	.037	.008	.045	2.438
	Reg2	.022	.028	-.007	.022	1.166
	Reg3	-.079	-.047	.007	-.039	-2.133
	Reg4	-.033	-.031	-.016	-.047	-2.569
	Reg5	.006	.004	.008	-.004	-0.233
	Plans	.130	.044	.016	.060	3.261
	Famsize	-.123	-.047	-.013	-.061	-3.288
	Attach	-.071	-.022	-.027	-.048	-2.634
	Valued	.286	.128	.079	.208	11.525
	Guidance	.001	.028	-.004	.025	1.330
	Careinfo	.113	.067	.019	.086	4.694
	Advmath	.226	.071	.073	.145	7.933
	Wellbe	.153	.079	.021	.100	5.435
	Lstyle	.065	.019	.019	.040	2.161

Multiple R $= .4739$; $R^2 = .224$.
Note: The t-values are given for the total effect only. A t-value equal to or greater than ±2.00 is statistically significant at the .05 level.

Path analysis was utilized to determine if any of the independent background variables influenced post-secondary participation indirectly as a result of the influences of the intervening variables. Indirect effects showed if the influences were mediated or transmitted through the intervening variables. For example, attachment to home and community was not statistically significant as a determinant of participation in the extended integrated model. But, in both the male and female reduced models, attachment was statistically significant as a barrier to post-secondary participation with about equal effects on males and females. The object of examining the indirect effects and the direct effects of the attachment variable in a path model was to determine if the total effect was a predictor of or a detractor to participation. It was hypothesized that attachment was a factor in participation as a form of barrier which prevented young people from otherwise enroling in post-secondary education. Other independent variables were also examined for indirect effects.

Table 20.1 shows the estimated direct effects, indirect effects, and total effects for each of the background variables. A t-value was calculated for total effect only. All values found to be statistically significant at the .05 level included gender, value of education, rural/urban, regions 3 and 4, career plans, family size, career information, attachment, advanced mathematics, well-being, and learning style. Standardized regression coefficients (β) for independent variables that were shown in the extended integrated model to be statistically significant with participation were generally enhanced through the effects of indirect analysis. That is, the size of the total effects was in all cases but one—region 3—bigger than the β for direct effects indicating support for the general hypothesis that the independent variables were mediated by the intervening variables. The total effects of attachment, value of education, and advanced mathematics were substantially higher, relatively, than the direct effects. In the regression equation for the extended integrated model, the standardized coefficient for attachment, for example, was statistically significant with participation. Through the mediating effects of the intervening variables, however, the for total effect of the attachment variable was rendered statistically significant at the .05 level. The magnitude of the attachment-participation relationship was made twice as strong by the addition of the indirect effects.

Findings from the series of interviews with youth, principals, and guidance counsellors in the K–12 education system, principals and senior officials from the post-secondary system, and the Department of Education staff complemented the quantitative results from the survey data. Results from the interviews gave added weight to the influence of the variables found in the regression analyses to have statistically significant effects on post-secondary participation. For example, the importance of advanced mathematics to participation was confirmed by the principals and guidance counsellors, all of whom also said it was important for parents to have a high value for education because a positive attitude largely determined whether parents encouraged their children to attend university or one of the public colleges. The nature of the barriers to participation that were identified in the regression analyses was similar to the kinds of barriers the stakeholders identified; the main impediments, in their view, were lack of money, meeting academic prerequisites, inadequate access to programs, negative family influences, and an encumbering attachment to home and community.

CONCLUSIONS AND IMPLICATIONS

The main purpose of the study was to identify an inventory of variables that were believed to influence participation in post-secondary education. The independent variables were grouped into five categories—four background categories relating to personal, family, school, and community variables. One category of intervening variables was considered to mediate the effects of the background variables on participation. The conclusions can be summarized as follows:

- None of the effects of the personal variables was strongly associated with participation in post-secondary education. The effects of well-being were higher than the effects of gender, career plans, and learning style, but not to the extent where it could be generalized that a continuing sense of well-being is predictive of entry into post-secondary education.

- The extent to which family variables influenced participation in post-secondary education was contingent on the value held for education in the home. Family size had little effect, but value of education had the third highest effect on participation of the 17 independent variables in the study.

- School variables on average were moderately related to participation in post-secondary education. Guidance had a negligible influence, and both career information and advanced mathematics in the numerical analyses had small effects on participation. The interview results gave much more support to the impact of all three variables on participation.

- Community variables generally had little or no effect on participation in post-secondary education according to results from the survey data. Results from the interviews, however, indicated that the attachment variable was highly associated with participation for many students from small communities. Principals, counsellors, post-secondary administrators, and even several youth referred to the inhibiting effects on young people of not wanting to leave home. These respondents all regarded community attachment to be influential in detracting young people from participating in post-secondary education.

- The mediating effects of the intervening variables marginally enhanced the effects of the background variables on participation. While the boosting effects were small, the influence of the intervening variables was in the direction that was hypothesized and as was theorized in the literature.

- There were no substantial differences between males and females in the effects of the variables on participation.

In summary, the variables found to be most frequently associated with participation were academic achievement, barriers, value of education, advanced mathematics, academic attainment, and well-being. These six consistently had the biggest effects in the various analytical models used in the study. Results from the interviews held with various stakeholders supported the findings from the regression and path analyses and gave added weight to the influences of the variables found to be related to participation.

Several policy initiatives and additional research could build on the findings from this study and would contribute to a more complete explanation of the predictive influences on post-secondary participation. For example, three of the variables found to be most influential on participation—academic achievement, advanced mathematics, and academic attainment—are directly manipulable by the K–12 education system. The advanced mathematics variable is more open to policy change than the other two because it is a clearly defined part of the curriculum and is less intricate and nebulous than are achievement or attainment. Greater participation in advanced mathematics is a clear way to begin increasing post-secondary participation among Newfoundland youth.

Advanced mathematics could be studied separately as an indicator of academic achievement rather than participation. The nature of this variable lends itself to an experimental study or to several studies that could be undertaken simultaneously in different geographical regions. The variable is also a natural criterion for a school-based research design where measures would be aggregated to the school level instead of the individual level. In this way, school performance in advanced mathematics as well as individual performance could be demonstrated.

The variables, value of education and barriers, are less within the control of schools but not outside their sphere of influence. Schools experience varying degrees of contact with parents and generally know the family situations of their students, even in urban communities. Professional personnel such as teachers, principals, counsellors, and others have an opportunity to enhance the esteem held for education in families where esteem is known to be low. The value of education variable is in need of much more research. Examples abound of youth from good families who finished high school, did well academically while they were there, were encouraged if not implored by their parents to continue their education, and had brothers or sisters who had gone on to post-secondary education but who opted not to attend after they graduated. Why do such anomalies occur in families where education is demonstrably highly valued? Also, how does esteem for education in the home contribute to the decision of siblings to enrol or not enrol in post-secondary education?

Financial constraints prevented many eligible high-school graduates in the study from enroling in post-secondary education. Despite recent revisions, many students believe that the Canada Student Loan Program is inadequate to meet their financial needs. Yet, little or no research has been undertaken in Newfoundland about access to or the effects of the student loan program on participation in further education. Access to loans will likely become even more of a crucial factor in the decision of future high-school graduates to enter post-secondary education. Post-secondary students currently depend heavily on the student loan program but a trend may be emerging where there may be a reduction in demand due to increasing hesitation by students to accumulate large debts to obtain higher education when there is no assurance they will find subsequent employment to repay these debts. The number of students defaulting on their loans might also increase in the near future, which could result in policy responses by government to curtail access and availability even more than is now perceived to exist.

Other barriers such as lack of access to courses and programs, lack of career direction, and insufficient knowledge of occupations and educational options were also identified as important impediments for many youth. Several of the post-secondary administrators said that general information was known about participation in post-secondary education but that specifics were lacking on many of the pertinent factors believed to affect it. Further research is warranted into the specific nature of the effects of access to programs, career focus, and knowledge of occupational and educational options as barriers to participation. Variables such as guidance, career planning, and career information especially require more research. Contextual research is needed to assess if differences apply in larger schools vs. smaller schools, between males and females, between rural and urban areas, and within a school system. Some of the basic assumptions underlying present career education curricula need to be examined. The focus currently is on providing information on careers and educational options based on the assumption that the more information that students have, the better their decision making about post-secondary participation. This assumption may be only partly valid; the emphasis, for example, may need to be placed on the way students process the information that is already available or on their perceptions of the value of such information to their career decision making.

With a few deviations, the effects of the study variables on participation were in the direction that was expected and were generally similar to the findings of previous research. Many of the variables can be directly manipulated by educational institutions in order to generate changes that could lead to greater participation in post-secondary education. It is important that such changes be made. Severe economic conditions continue to face many parts of Canada and educational attainment of Canadians is viewed as fundamental to the Federal Government's current plans for economic and social readjustments in the country. Higher education in particular is viewed as an important means for revitalizing provincial labour forces and for creating new employment opportunities especially in struggling provincial economies.

References

Ashton, D.N. (1988). Educational institutions, youth and the labour market. In D. Gallie (Ed.), *Employment in Britain* (pp. 406–433). Oxford: Basil Blackwell.

Blau, P.M., & Duncan, O.D. (1967). *The American occupational structure*. New York: John Wiley & Sons, Inc.

Boyd, M., Goyder, J., Jones, F.E., McRoberts, H.A., Pineo, P.C., & Porter, J. (1985). *Ascription and achievement: Studies in mobility and status attainment in Canada*. Ottawa: Carleton University Press.

Breton, R. (1972). *Social and academic factors in the career decisions of Canadian youth*. Ottawa: Department of Manpower and Immigration.

Creese, G.L., Guppy, L.N., & Meissner, M. (1991). *Ups and downs on the ladder of success: Social mobility in Canada* (Statistics Canada, General Social Survey Analysis series). Ottawa: Minister of Industry, Science and Technology.

Curtis, B. (1989). *The barriers project*. Thunder Bay, ON: Confederation College of Applied Arts and Technology.

Empson-Warner, S., & Krahn, H. (1990). *Unemployment and occupational aspirations: A panel study of high-school graduates* (Research discussion paper No. 70). Edmonton, AB: Population Research Laboratory, Department of Sociology, University of Alberta.

Feather, F. (1983). *Future training and retraining: Needs and potential* (Background paper No. 6). Global Management Bureau Inc.

Hayden, M., & Carpenter, P.G. (1990). From school to higher education in Australia. *Higher Education, 20* (2), 175–196.

Krahn, H., & Lowe, G.S. (1989). *Youth workers in the service economy*. Edmonton, AB: Department of Sociology, University of Alberta.

Looker, E.D. (1993). Interconnected transitions and their costs: Gender and urban/rural differences in the transitions to work. In P. Anisef & P. Axelrod (Eds.), *Transitions: Schooling and employment in Canada* (pp. 43–64). Toronto: Thompson Educational Publishing.

Mason, G. (1985). Transitions to work: Survey of recent literature. *Transition Learning, 1* (1), 18–76.

McGrath, S.J. (1993). *Post-secondary Participation in Newfoundland*. Unpublished doctoral thesis, University of Alberta, Edmonton, AB.

Organization for Economic Cooperation and Development (1986). *Measures to assist workers displaced by structural change.* Paris, France: Author.

Picot, G. (1987). *Unemployment and training* (Research paper No. 2). Ottawa: Statistics Canada, Analytical Studies Branch, Social and Economic Studies Division.

O'Neill, G.P. (1981). Post-secondary aspirations of high-school seniors from different social-demographic contexts. *Canadian Journal of Higher Education, 11* (2), 51–66.

Royal Commission on Employment and Unemployment. (1986). *Education for self-reliance: A report on education and training in Newfoundland.* St. John's, NF: Queens Printer.

Samuelson, L. (1988). *The out-of-school experiences of dropouts: Labour market success and criminal behaviour.* Ph.D. dissertation, Dept. of Sociology, University of Alberta, Edmonton, AB.

Sewell, W.H., & Shah, V.P. (1967). Socioeconomic status, intelligence, and the attainment of higher education. *Sociology of Education, 40* (1), 1–23.

Sharpe, D.B., & Spain, W.H. (1991). *The class of '89: Initial survey of level III (grade 12) high-school students.* St. John's, NF: Centre for Educational Research and Development, Memorial University of Newfoundland.

Statistics Canada. (1991). *Education in Canada, A statistical review for 1990–91* (Catalogue 81–229 Annual). Ottawa, ON: Minister of Supply and Service.

Williams, T. (1972). Educational aspirations: Longitudinal evidence on their development in Canadian youth. *Sociology of Education, 45* (2), 107–133.

21

"Having It All" in the Nineties: The Work and Family Aspirations of Women Undergraduates

Lorna Erwin

University-educated women still lag behind men in graduate degrees earned, job outcomes, income, and so forth (cf. Bellamy & Guppy, 1991). Further, the educational and career aspirations of significant numbers of even the most committed and well-prepared female students tend to be lowered or compromised over the course of their undergraduate experience at rates and in ways that distinguish them from their male counterparts (cf. Holland & Eisenhart, 1990). This chapter explores the paradox of continuing gender inequality in educational and career outcomes despite initial high aspirations and women's improved access to university programs. Testimony from in-depth interviews with 180 female undergraduates attending a large commuter university is presented with an eye to the ideologies, belief systems, and cultural expectations that shape their career aspirations. The focus is on how these seventeen- to twenty-year-olds have constructed their occupational aspirations; also on those subjective aspects of their undergraduate experience that tend to undermine their confidence and commitment.

Three assumptions influenced the design of this research. First, women's own understanding of the factors determining their educational and career options must be a central research object. Second, cohorts of relatively well-prepared and highly motivated female students most acutely embody the contradictions of persistent gender inequality in education and work. Third, taking into account the independent impact of race and class on gender differences must be a priority.

One hundred and eighty first-year female undergraduates, divided equally between the Arts and Science faculties, were selected. The process involved a systematic random sample of entering first-year students, all of whom had graduated from high school the preceding spring. The majority of the sample were white and middle-class; 36% were members of visible minorities, and 40% were among the first in their families to attend university. The response rate was 90%. The information reported here reflects some of the major tendencies and themes that emerged out of the interviews.

FINDINGS

The vast majority of these young women have always taken a university education for granted. Very few had struggled with this decision or encountered any obstacles; attending university was assumed to be part of the natural or logical progression of their lives and essential to their future plans. None cited their gender, class, race, or ethnicity as any kind of barrier to their educational goals or felt they had to justify their aspirations. Few gave priority to their social lives over their educational commitments. Many said there was little time for socializing after school work, part-time jobs, and family responsibilities. On average Arts students spend ten hours per week studying, compared with at least eighteen hours per week for those in Science. The majority either didn't care or didn't want to establish a romantic relationship in the near future. Romance, they believed, will come later in their lives (albeit later usually meant a couple of years at most), when they have completed, or are close to completing, their education.

> I don't have a boyfriend, and I don't want one till I finish school. It would just get in the way right now. My focus is my future; work now, play later is my philosophy.

The most striking findings have to do with the high career expectations of the interviewees. All of them planned to work on completing university, and not just in stopgap jobs. An overwhelming majority talk of establishing themselves in professional, managerial, or scientific careers, holding positions marked by both personal autonomy and incomes adequate to the purchase of "a nice home and lots of travel." Yet, while these young women profess themselves determined to pursue lucrative and stimulating careers, they have given little thought to strategies for realizing these aspirations, beyond obtaining a degree. Few anticipated obstacles to their career goals; somehow "things will just work out." Many of the participants had not decided on a specific occupation; among those that had, there was an orientation toward professions that have traditionally been dominated by women. Teaching and social work, for example, were the fields most frequently mentioned by the Arts students. Many of the science majors expressed interest in medicine but were generally thinking of sub-specialities like paediatrics, obstetrics, and family practice. Those aiming at law often spoke of specializing in family law. The few who did aspire to non-traditional female vocations were all in science and were interested in careers as engineers, researchers, or, in one case, as an astronaut.

A common complaint was lack of knowledge about different educational programs and career possibilities—a problem they attributed to poor guidance and career counselling. Fewer than 10%, for example, felt that they had been given adequate, or even reliable, information in high school, and many professed shock on hearing how difficult it was to get into professional or graduate programs. Very few of those aspiring to highly competitive programs like education, law, and medicine (where typically 80% to 90% of applicants are rejected) had alternative plans. They would frequently ask the interviewer about rejection rates; when informed, for example, that, somewhat less than 15% of medical school applicants were successful, they were taken aback.

> Guidance counselling, now that's a joke. If you were depending on the guidance office to help you figure out what to do with your life, you're in big trouble.

They tell you: if you're smart take the advanced program and go to university. If you're a girl and you're good in science, they really push you to take science.That's what happened to me. But the problem is I didn't really enjoy science in high school, and I really hate it in university. I don't want to be a doctor. And from what I hear, I wouldn't get into med school anyway. So what am I suppose to do? I'm now thinking about teaching high school or something. But I hear the faculty of education is also hard to get into. Anyway, I'm not too worried. I guess I'll figure out what to do before I graduate.

Such a blasé outlook was typical of the majority of the participants, who had yet to decide on a specific occupation. They expressed little anxiety, expecting that their choice of career would crystallize during their university education. The confidence of these young women that they will be able to successfully establish careers suggests high parental support for their ambitions. It also suggests an idealistic view of schooling and achievement as a meritocratic process little affected by gender, race, or social class, or by the vagaries of the labour market.

An overwhelming majority of these young women wanted to marry and have children and talked of their futures in dualistic terms. Putting off children until their careers were "established" is acceptable, but they were not willing to wait too long. Twenty-eight was the upper limit for most respondents, with thirty-two as the highest age given for having a first child. Some said that, at this point in their lives, they "can't really imagine" how career and family can be combined. Most, however, had given the matter some thought. Some talked of finding work that is compatible with a primary commitment to childrearing and homemaking; others spoke of marrying someone who will share childcare and domestic responsibilities; employing a nanny and other kinds of household help was also mentioned. Especially remarkable are the conflicts, doubts, and contradictions voiced by the interviewees when discussing their futures. While they talked about being committed to careers, they still assumed that, as women, they will have primary responsibility for childrearing and household management. Their work lives, for instance, were typically seen as cyclical, adjusting to the demands of parental and domestic responsibilities. Children, when they are young, will be the principal focus of their lives, while work commitments will take on greater importance once the kids are in school full-time. By the same token, a good job was often defined as one with flexible demands—one that can accommodate domestic responsibilities.

I'm going to be a psychologist or a dentist. I'll wait until my kids are five or six, and then set up my own practice at home. A job where you can work out of your home. There will be a nanny, but I'll also be around to make sure everything is OK. I can have lunch with my kids, comfort them when they have accidents, see them take their first steps, and still have a great career.

The young women who talked about sharing domestic and childcare responsibilities with husbands or of paying for childcare services were even more ambivalent. While on one level it was expected that their future mates would share equally in family responsibilities, there was actually a lot of concern about finding willing partners. By the same token, those who spoke of hiring nannies or using daycare were frequently apprehensive about having their children cared for by someone outside the family.

> My husband will do almost everything. I don't even know how to cook. I'd
> probably do dishes ... Taking time off when I have kids would really impact on
> my career. The person I'm going out with now, he'd never take time off for kids.
> If I had a different husband, then I'd probably expect him to take time off. Or
> maybe I'll get a babysitter.

The vast majority felt strongly that daycare is "not good for children." While
some of this antipathy reflected exposure to negative accounts of daycare that
had appeared in the media, most of it was more deeply ideological. Good child
rearing, as they saw it, requires a primary caregiver (usually a female family
member) who will be in the home a great deal of the time and will have a
single-minded focus on the children. They frequently cited their own child-
hoods—in which their mothers or a grandmother had been at home all day—as
the ideal. None rejected this model of child rearing as unrealistic. (As one
respondent blithely put it: "I would rather rely on family than on daycare. My
mother is pretty young, so she could look after my kids.") By the same token,
many felt uneasy, even guilty, that they weren't planning to be full-time
mothers.

> Childcare? Now that is a problem, because I don't really like the idea of daycare.
> A lot of the problems that we have with children today, especially in school, is
> because they didn't have a mother there to help them out. I guess I'll have to
> send my kids to daycare, but maybe I'll be lucky and my husband will help out.

What stands out in these accounts is the contrast between the clarity and
conviction with which these women spoke about both their career and family
commitment, and the hesitancy and confusion that characterizes their explanations of how they will successfully combine these aspirations. The strategies
imagined are naive and clearly uninformed by experience. There are few role
models, structural resources, or ideologies for these women to draw on in
envisioning their future roles. Moreover, the majority did not think that there
were any cultural representations of their lives; few had books, TV shows,
magazines, or advertisements with which they identified.

> I don't know of anything that represents my life. I mean I watch lots of TV—"The
> Young and the Restless," "Melrose Place," "Beverly Hills 92011"—and I love those
> shows. It's escapism. It's how I relax when I've finished studying. I know what
> they show isn't real life. That's why I watch it.

Fifteen percent of the sample either did not anticipate having children or
saw them as a low priority. This minority were unequivocal that their primary
commitment was to their future vocations, and their goals tended to be precisely
formulated. Most of them planned to attend graduate school or obtain a
professional degree with a view to entering fields that are still male dominated.
They also tended to see motherhood and careers as highly problematic if not
downright incompatible—a belief rooted partly in personal observation. A
number of them, for example, related how their mothers' careers had been
derailed by children and how they had suffered as a result.

> My mom got married before she had her career on track, so she never did finish
> her schooling. I will definitely have my masters and my career on track before I
> even consider getting married. But I don't think I want to get married ... What I
> really want is to become an astronaut.

The idea that men would participate equally in household and childrearing tasks likewise struck the minority as highly implausible—a myth as one respondent put it—especially in light of what they had observed about their male acquaintances.

> Right now, I don't plan on having any children. Relationships have an impact on schooling and career choice, and I don't want that. I look at the men I know. They say one thing, but they do something else. They might say they'll share childcare; but when push comes to shove, when the kid gets sick or something like that, it's the mother's problem. I don't really know what I want to do, probably a physicist or chemist, something in atmospheric science—the kind of work that doesn't allow time off for children.

Some were also perceptive about the kinds of informal discrimination they are likely to encounter as they seek to enter scientific or engineering fields.

> It's very hard for women to succeed in the sciences. So few females take engineering, and those that do experience trouble in university. There are no examples of women in science as Nobel Prize winners. It's mostly guys in the program, and the professors are all men. As a women, you feel afraid to ask any of them for help. They look down on you. You're just one of the girls who isn't doing well. And they expect that girls won't do as well.

One is heartened by such voices, but unfortunately they are lonely, isolated in their resoluteness. For many, the "trouble" they will encounter during their undergraduate and graduate years will be too much. And as they scale back their ambitions, or abandon them, the cost to society will be very high.

DISCUSSION

The desire of these young women for professional self-realization is likely to be sharply compromised by the cultural imperatives of motherhood. The few who appear to be critically aware of the problems inherent in combining careers with mothering were not planning to have children. The ideas of the majority for overcoming the constraints and barriers they will encounter are vague, capricious, and individualistic. Yet, these latter women are not caught up in romantic fantasies. Nor are they suffering from false consciousness, despite the glibness of their views about "having it all." Indeed, one might conclude that they very tentativeness and the air of unreality that marks their thinking about their lives beyond the university reflect a shrewd understanding of the gender-related costs of high career commitments. What is obvious, in any case, is that their perceptions of male domestic privilege and the culturally defined responsibilities of motherhood often result in a reigning in of their ambitions. Such interpretations and responses are reflective of the contradictory discourses available to these women. That women should pursue careers has become firmly entrenched in the culture of both our corporate and educational institutions, but this has not eradicated traditional understandings of women's responsibility for the domestic sphere. The participants in this study believe that higher education and the career possibilities it opens up are as available to them as they are to men; but they still see raising children and running a home as something for which they are uniquely fitted and responsible. Hence the importance of helping undergraduate women understand and negotiate the contradictions they face. The university may not be able to alter the structural barriers that constrain women's options. It can, however, be a site which challenges hegemonic notions and the cultural processes which legiti-mate them. Policy makers need to expand their mandate beyond the *material outcomes* of schooling (e.g., rates of participation) to the *cultural outcomes*. Joanna Wyn and Bruce Wilson identify cultural outcomes as the consequences of schooling which reflect "power over circumstances," that is, the capacity to participate with others "to change the circumstances that block the aspirations and hopes of identifiable social groups ... " (1993, p. 79). All levels of schooling must implement curriculum, targeted at both male and female students, that facilitates critical thinking about the contradictory forces that women confront and identifies the structural basis of their oppression and blocked mobility.

References

Bellamy, L.A., & Guppy, N. (1991). Opportunities and obstacles for women in Canadian higher education. In J. Gaskell & A. McLaren (eds.) *Women and education* (pp. 163–192). Calgary: Detselig Enterprises Limited.

Holland, D., & Eisenhart, M. (1990). *Educated in romance: Women, achievement, and college culture.* Chicago: University of Chicago Press.

Wyn, J., & Wilson, B. (1993). Improving girls' educational outcomes. In J. Blackmore & J. Kenway (eds.), *Gender matters in educational administration and policy: A feminist introduction* (pp. 71–80). London: Falmer Press.

22

In Transition from High School to University: First-year Perceptions of the Process

E.L. Donaldson

Aprofile of what happens to students in Canadian universities is being established although the picture remains shadowy. More research has been done about the marketplace outcome of an educational credential than upon the quality of learning (Baichman-Anisef, et al., 1993). Student attrition is known to be higher during first-year; less attention has been directed toward attrition within the university disciplines such as the seepage of science students (McKeown, MacDonell, Bowman, 1993; Codding, 1994). Pre-entry background variables are less influential than on-campus experiences with regard to student achievement; therefore university policies presumably have considerable influence on student learning but they are perhaps less influential with respect to student destinations (Gomme, Hall & Murphy, 1993). Social and academic integration influence achievement, but classroom environments are more important to student development at commuter universities than they are at residential institutions (Grayson, 1994). The preferred change agent to develop effective policies is faculty although the perceived influence is administration (Small, 1994; McKeown et al., 1993).

Knowledge of how students perceive the transition to university assists faculty in teaching their respective disciplines. Categories developed for a previous study of secondary student transitions were adapted in a study about chemistry students reported here (Donaldson, 1989). Patterns of behaviour that evolved as students moved through the transition process included:

(1) reentry (transfers who limit contact with the school culture);

(2) ongoing problems (persistent personal and social difficulties);

(3) floundering (seemingly, or appears, lost and aimless, but not drowning);

(4) bottleneck (school system difficulties specific to a particular time period); and

(5) easy passage (appeared to be ensconced in more adult life style).

The first-year chemistry course, the sixth largest at a commuter campus in western Canada, has an equitable gender balance in first-year enrolment. The enrolment in this course was 899 students in 1990 but only 11 students graduated with a bachelor's degree in chemistry, only 7 graduate degrees were awarded, and not all cooperative education positions for undergraduate chemistry students were filled. This high attrition rate was a concern to the Department of Chemistry and was the motivation for this study initiated in 1991. The research had four objectives: (a) to compare student profiles of two cohorts of chemistry students, (b) to identify student understandings of science culture and science literacy, (c) to track undergraduate students as they completed their first two years of university, and (d) to integrate the research results with planned curriculum change within the discipline and with first-year experience initiatives at the university. In this paper, the focus is on (a) and (d). Those who wish a copy of the complete report should contact the author.

METHOD

First-year chemistry students participated in a survey about student intentions and perceptions of the university experience. Student respondents self selected the transition category that best fit them. Baseline data were obtained from an in-class questionnaire administered during phase one (1991) of a two-stage study. Phase two (1993) data were collected, using the same method, after an interim year during which the Department of Chemistry initiated many changes. Sixty percent of students in each group participated—572 from phase one and 607 from phase two. Phase three was a follow-up telephone interview of 65 phase one respondents, approximately two years after the initial survey. This group included 10 science students, 10 chemistry students, 10 education students, 24 students from other disciplines, and 11 students who had withdrawn from university.

Each questionnaire was organized into six sub-sections including pre-entry demographics and personal attributes, science literacy, the Chemistry 201 learning environment, first-year university experiences, intended destinations, part-time work, and withdrawal information when relevant. Questions common to all three data bases include the transition patterns (the dependent variable in this paper) and 57 other questions, plus final first-year chemistry achievement scores and the academic major subsequently selected by students in the follow-up sample.

RESULTS

Most students reported an easy passage from high school to university. Furthermore, gender differences were not significant with regard to transition patterns. In Table 22.1 frequencies of student responses to a question asking that they select the phase which "best describes your transition from high school to university" remained constant for both first-year cohorts. Phase three seniors, who were further from the initial transition phase, differed somewhat. Students experiencing problems comprised more than 30% of the first-year students. Students perceiving that they had floundered increased from approximately 7% to 20% as they became more senior. Among seniors, less than 10% reported personal and social ongoing problems, a drop from more than 25% among first-year students. Further research would clarify whether the shifts resulted from changed perceptions, selection bias in the telephone sample, or from other influences. Students with personal and social problems may withdraw with greater frequency from difficult courses, perhaps from university itself.

Table 22.1: Frequencies of Transition Patterns in Each Phase of the Study

Data Bases	Type of Transition Pattern						
	Easy Passage	Ongoing Problems (personal /social)	Flound-ering (-2 year period)	Re-entry (absent 2 year or more)	Bottle-neck (system delays)	No Answer	Total
Phase One (n = 572)	47.8%	25.8%	6.7%	8.2%	2.6%	8.9%	100%
Phase Two (n = 607)	52.4%	32.4%	7.6%	5.8%	1.0%	0.8%	100%
Phase Three (n = 65)	56.9%	7.7%	21.6%	6.2%	1.5%	6.1%	100%

Although differences between transition patterns and the academic major selected by seniors in the follow-up sample were not statistically significant, 36 percent of the frosh (5 of 14) who had said they were floundering were still in General Studies three years later, 2 had withdrawn from the university, and 2 were in disciplines other than education or science. In addition, 80 percent (total 5) of students reporting ongoing problems had withdrawn from the university; none of the reentry or bottleneck students (total 5) had withdrawn, although 4 of them remained in General Studies. By contrast, of 37 students who had reported an easy passage 73 percent (27) were established in academic majors (11 in science, 7 in education, 3 others in engineering or nursing), 1 had graduated, 5 were no longer at the university, and only 3 remained in General Studies. Thus, it appears that the type of transition students make to the university influences the subsequent passage within the university.

Living arrangements were the most significant difference among students at all three phases. Most first-year students lived at home; greater numbers of reentry students lived alone or in temporary lodgings, but not in residence ($p < .0001$). Higher percentages of students indicating difficulties (on-going problems, floundering, bottleneck) lived off campus with friends or in resi-dence. Eighty percent of the students reporting an easy transition lived in the family home. Most students worried about meeting family expectations, but reentry students were less concerned.

Most students had some concerns about money but the most concerned were reentry students. Students who had worked reported earnings up to $2,000 or between $2,000-$5,000 during the past year. Reentry students more often reported incomes exceeding $10,000. Students having an easy transition were more likely to have earned less than $2,000 because they worked fewer hours. Source of student income was most often family or part-time work; students reporting an easy transition or having ongoing problems were more likely than others to have scholarships.

Table 22.2: Chemistry Achievement Scores

Final Grade	Easy Passage		Ongoing Problems (personal, social)		Floundering (-2 year period)		Re-entry (absent 2 years or more)		Bottleneck (system delays)	
	Percentage of Students in Each Transition Pattern (Phase 1, n = 572; Phase 2, n = 607)									
	P_1	P_2	P_1	P_2	P_1	P_2	P_1	P_2	P_1	P_2
A	23	14	17	9	8	4	17	9	20	11
B	43	51	41	38	47	48	32	43	33	46
C	24	33	30	48	32	48	19	37	40	39
D	5	2	8	3	3	0	15	3	7	2
F/W	4	1	4	4	11	0	17	9	0	2

Note: Withdrawals not calculated separately because of the low number of respondents in Phase 1 (15) and Phase 2 (4).

Most first-year students did not worry about their ability to make friends on-campus but those who did worry most reported ongoing problems. Students with ongoing problems were most likely to skip lunch or to eat off campus. The majority of students reported that their closest on-campus friends were high-school buddies but reentry students more often reported classmates or no one. Reentry students were less positive about social opportunities. Those with ongoing problems were more negative about course content, the learning environment of the university, and more concerned about meeting the academic demands. Flounderers were the least positive about the university as a place where they could develop career paths.

Although most students worried about their ability to succeed academically, those reporting an easy transition were less worried; those with ongoing problems worried most. First-year science students knew they must obtain credit in mathematics if they were to continue in science-related courses. Concern about having sufficient skills to pass that first-year course was greatest among reentry students and those who reported ongoing problems. Final GPA scores for the chemistry course increased from 2.50 to 2.65 (with 4.00 being honours). Table 22.2 indicates where these changes occurred relative to student transitions. In all transition patterns the percentage of students achieving C and B final grades increased between the two cohorts. The numbers of students with ongoing problems who received a B Grade dropped while the numbers of reentry B-level students increased. Class attrition due to failure or withdrawal also declined with the greatest decreases being in the reentry and floundering patterns. However, the number of A-level achievers dropped in all categories; the greatest decline was among those having an easy passage.

Significant differences between phase one and phase two suggested that the pedagogical changes implemented by the Department of Chemistry made a difference to students who preferred learning resources other than the textbook ($p < .01$). More phase one students with ongoing problems reported a diminished interest subsequent to the class ($p < .0007$); this significant difference persisted in the follow-up sample when more students who had had ongoing problems during the transition said they had changed their educational plans as a result of the chemistry course ($p < .007$). On-site observations by the researcher during phase two of the new discovery wet labs (that encourage inductive reasoning) confirmed that students were more actively engaged in learning; the lack of structure challenged them to discuss basic competencies such as how high to turn on the Buntzen burner and how to pronounce difficult nomenclature. Some were uncomfortable although they were undoubtedly learning. In phase two, after an interim year of pedagogical changes, students with ongoing problems still differed significantly from their peers with regard to how well they thought the course was taught ($p < .023$), the extent to which the course increased their interest in chemistry ($p < .0001$), and how much they thought they'd learned in the course ($p < .0297$). They also differed from the other groups in the amount of time each week they had spent studying chemistry; it was less than one hour ($p < .0075$). Pedagogical changes appeared to have assisted mid-range achievers (C-B grades), but the group most difficult to teach remained those who reported ongoing problems in their personal and social lives.

CONCLUSIONS AND IMPLICATIONS

Data about emergent patterns of behaviour when students were in transition to the university indicated significant differences with regard to the university experience. Students reporting an easy passage, the largest group of students, appeared to have a secure family environment, fewer off-campus part-time work distractions, and more on-campus friends. They also did better academically. Students with ongoing personal and social problems, approximately half as many as those who have an easy passage, were less positive about the university academic environment; they worried more about their ability to succeed academically. The smaller number of reentry students were more alone, both at home and on campus, worried both about academic success and money, but showed the most improvement when pedagogical changes were implemented in chemistry. The numbers of students who floundered increased among senior undergraduates. This change could be a reflection of the university experience, combined with maturing personal insight about adult realities. The increase could also be an artifact of the research design with fewer students who had problems with the educational systems persisting.

Students reporting an easy passage to university were more likely to live in the family home and had more high-school friends at university. They had fewer financial problems and worked fewer part-time hours. They had more confidence in their ability to succeed academically and noted more overlap between high school and university chemistry course content. They comprised more of the A and B students in the first-year chemistry course. Fewer earned honours in phase two during the implementation of pedagogical revisions, more achieved Bs and Cs, and fewer failed or withdrew. Students who reported ongoing personal and social problems were more likely to report concerns about course content, the learning environment at the university, and the academic demands of the university. They worried more about their ability to succeed academically and they rated themselves lower in quantitative skills such as mathematics. They had received more scholarships, but they studied less. They also skipped lunch more often or ate off-campus. In phase two, they earned fewer As, Bs, and Ds in chemistry, but more Cs. The same percentage withdrew or failed the course in both cohorts. Reentry students were less likely to be living in the family home. They were less positive about the campus environment and more often ate lunch alone on campus. They were less concerned about meeting family expectations, although they worried about their ability to handle academic demands, including mathematics. During the past year, they had earned more, but they also worried more about money. In phase two, they improved most in academic achievement, more so at the B and C levels than at the A level where the numbers dropped. The profile of the bottleneck students differed only with regard to final grades whereas more of the floundering students received government assistance or worried about how to develop a career path. Otherwise, during first-year university, these two groups of students did not differ substantially from the other types.

The Department of Chemistry has revised many aspects of the course since the initiation of the study. Pedagogical innovations included a new interactive computer laboratory, development of discovery inductive laboratories, faculty guided small-group tutorials, demonstration lectures, and a common final examination that included a written question. Faculty initiatives included the establishment of a first-year steering committee to guide and evaluate curricula changes as well as seminars on pedagogical strategies such as learning styles. General proactive strategies included extra-curricular support for women, promotional posters, and meetings with other university faculty and high schools. Table 22.1 indicates that student final achievement scores improved while student failures and withdrawals declined. In addition, there is a waiting list for the cooperative education program, general participation in senior courses increased with female enrolment exceeding male, and enrolment in the first-year course is now capped (Donaldson & Dixon, 1995). Thus, an analysis of patterns of student behaviour during the transition to university contributed to an understanding of how these patterns affected student perceptions of the campus environment and subsequent university achievement and how the faculty can be effective with regard to assisting students in transition.

Retention policies need to include social support for reentry students and academic support for students with personal and social problems. As well, faculty pedagogical initiatives should be supported. Students who flounder between first and senior undergraduate years also need support, but the effective strategy for such support needs further research. Departments, such as chemistry, interested in attracting students beyond the large first-year prerequisite course, must understand changed student demographics to select appropriate pedagogies. For chemistry, more student interaction in the laboratories and in guided tutorials improved grades among middle-range achievers. More research is required to understand why the overall GPA increased, while the numbers of students earning honours decreased. The classroom dynamic is key to the university experience. Contact between students and professors exemplifies induction into a discipline of knowledge, dissemination of that knowledge, and generation of new insights. As students and professors communicate, the university performs a basic function—maintenance of the intellectual heritage and maturation of youthful talent. The transition of students to, and from the university, should be a priority as administrators implement policies shaped by restructuring plans and smaller budgets.

References

Baichman-Anisef E., Anisef, P., & Axelrod, P. (1993). *The transition from school to work: A bibliography.* Toronto: York University, Institute for Social Research.

Codding, P. (1994). Change in progress: General chemistry at the University of Calgary. *L'Actualitié Chimique Canadienne,* (avril), 10–11.

Donaldson, E. (1989). Links between education and employment: A case study of the transition from school to work. Unpublished doctoral dissertation, University of Toronto, Ontario Institute for Studies in Education, Toronto.

Donaldson, E., & Dixon, E. (1995). Retaining women in science involves more than course selection. *The Canadian Journal of Higher Education, 25 (2)* 29-51.

Gomme, I., Hall, M., & Murphy, T. (1993). In the shadow of the tower: The view of the undergraduate experience. *The Canadian Journal of Higher Education, 23* (3), 18–35.

Grayson, J.P. (1994). First year science in a commuter university: Where to intervene. *The Canadian Journal of Higher Education, 24* (2), 16–42.

McKeown, B., MacDonell, A., & Bowman, C. (1993). The point of view of the student in attrition research. *The Canadian Journal of Higher Education, 23* (2), 65–85.

Small, J. (1994). Reform in Canadian universities. *The Canadian Journal of Higher Education, 24* (2), 1–15.

23

Understanding the Pathway to Employment: The Importance of Going Beyond the Basics in the Career Counselling of Youth

Deborah J. Kennett

The demanding nature of the employment process requires individuals to be highly resourceful (Kennett, Bleasdale, Pitt, & Blom, 1990). Highly resourceful people make use of positive self-statements and problem solving strategies, can delay gratification, and engage in other self-management strategies, whereas low resourceful people are more likely to give up when the going gets tough, produce more negative self-evaluative statements, and fewer task-oriented thoughts (Kennett, 1994a; Rosenbaum & Ben-Ari, 1985). Highly resourceful people are not less affected by threat, pain, emotion, stress, and noxious stimuli, but are better able to handle them (Rosenbaum, 1989a, 1989b). Demands of the employment process also require individuals to have high self-efficacy expectations about work (Kennett, et al., 1990; Betz, 1992; Eden & Aviram, 1993; Lenox & Mezydlo-Subich, 1994). Self-efficacy is the belief in one's abilities to execute a given task or behaviour successfully (Bandura, 1986). Self-efficacy expectations influence thoughts, behaviours, and emotions. Unemployed youth having high self-efficacy expectations about work were more persistent with the job search, used more problem solving and planning strategies, and were more able to deal with rejections by employers than youth having low self-efficacy expectations (Kennett, et al., 1990). Not surprisingly, they were also more successful at attaining and maintaining work than the less efficacious youth. This chapter describes two studies that were conducted in Peterborough, Ontario, between 1990 and 1994. In both studies the importance of self-efficacy expectancies and learned resourcefulness skills on attaining work were examined. The second study also evaluated the utility of providing career and personal counselling on self-efficacy expectancies and learned resourcefulness skills.

PANEL SURVEY OF UNEMPLOYED YOUTH

General Procedures

Participants were unemployed youth who were surveyed at the Canadian Employment Centre and at the Employment Planning Youth Career Centre. Subjects were asked to complete the inventories at time of initial contact (time 1) and then retested with the same inventories 6 months later (time 2). The time–2 contact was attempted by phone, and for those cases in which contact was successful, surveys were sent and returned by mail. The sample of 158 reflects 37% of the youth who were approached at time 1 and, as well, completed the follow-up survey 6 months later. The youth ranged in age from 17 to 25 years (mean = 20.9), had a mean of 10.8 years of education, had left school at a mean age of 17.2 years, and had been out of school for a mean of 2.4 years.

Youth completed Rosenbaum's (1980) Self-Control Schedule (SCS) assessing their general repertoire of learned resourcefulness skills, the Job Seeking Resourcefulness (JSR) inventory assessing the specific self-management strategies they apply when seeking work, and the Job Keeping Resourcefulness (JKR) inventory assessing self-management skills they apply while on the job. These inventories measure the extent to which individuals (1) use positive self-statements to cope with negative situations, (2) apply problem solving strategies, (3) delay gratification, and (4) are capable of self-change in everyday life both when seeking work and while working, respectively. The Job Seeking Efficacy (JSE) and Job Keeping Efficacy (JKE) inventories assesses youth's beliefs regarding their ability to attain work and to maintain work. The SCS, JSE, JKE, JSR and JKR inventories are reliable and valid instruments (Kennett et al., 1990). For all inventories, youth indicated how well each statement or item described them using a 6-point scale (+3 very descriptive of me to –3 very undescriptive of me). Youth also completed a Personal Information inventory. This inventory asked youth about their age, place of residence, education, living arrangement, marital status, dependents, current source of income, work experience, job counselling experience, and current employment.

Results and Discussion

A series of analyses examined the psychological variables differentiating working youth from nonworking youth at follow up. No overall difference was observed between working and nonworking youths at time 1 but a significant difference was found at time 2. At time 2, working youths scored higher in general resourcefulness (SCS), specific resourcefulness (JSR, JKR), and self-efficacy (JSE, JKE) than nonworking youths. In comparison to nonworking youths, working youths showed significantly greater improvements in their job seeking and keeping self-efficacy expectations (JSE, JKE), and job seeking and keeping resourcefulness skills (JSR, JKR). Youth who remained unemployed at the 6-month retest showed either little change or substantial decreases in their beliefs about attaining and maintaining work and in their job seeking and keeping resourcefulness skills. No significant change, however, was observed in the self control (SCS) scores over time reflecting its more stable nature, and no significant differences were observed between the working and nonworking groups.

Moderate to high correlations were observed among the psychological variables (all $ps < .001$) at time 1 and at time 2. Nevertheless, none of the psychological variables at time 1 predicted employment status at follow up. Only at the time 2 testing were significant relationships observed between each of the psychological variables and employment success, ranging from $r = .16$ for the SCS to $r = .37$ for the JKE. In addition, only moderate test-retest correlation coefficients were found between each of the psychological variables at time 1 and time 2. Attaining and maintaining work are novel activities for many youth, thus, these correlations likely reflect the ongoing changes among youth's attitudes, skills and beliefs regarding work. Schlenker and Trudeau note that people's self beliefs and skills are continually changing as new actions erase and replace prior phenomenological knowledge about the self; the degree of change in one's beliefs depend strongly on " ... a) when they are more important to the individual because they lead to satisfaction of personal goals and values, b) when they have been formed through personal experience, as opposed to having been contemplated in the abstract, and c) when they are associated with greater behavioral consistency across situations and audiences" (1990, p. 22).

The socio-demographic factors important to employment success were also examined. A comparison of working and nonworking groups showed no significant differences in gender, educational level attained, marital status, age, number of visits to the Canada Employment Centre, number of occasions that they received vocational counselling, criminal record, or current living arrangement at either time 1 or time 2. The single variable that differed for the working versus the nonworking groups was source of income. Youth on social assistance at time 1 were less likely to gain employment than youth with other sources of income. Eighty percent of those on social assistance at time 1 remained unemployed at time 2, whereas 40% of youth with unemployment insurance and 43% of youth with other means of support at time 1 remained unemployed at time 2 ($X^2 = 10.2$, $p = .006$). Social assistance recipients were more likely to be female, single mothers, less educated, and to have criminal records than youth with unemployment insurance or other sources of income.

Psychological measures were compared for social assistance recipients versus youth with unemployment insurance or other sources of income. Recipients differed from nonrecipients only on time 1 and time 2 beliefs concerning their ability to maintain employment (JKE). For social assistance recipients and nonrecipients respectively, the mean JKE scores were 12.1 and 16.7 at time 1, and 12.5 and 17.7 at time 2. They did not differ significantly on any other psychological variables.

Figure 23.1 provides a schematic representation of the proposed employment attainment model. The model illustrates that specific job seeking and job keeping resourcefulness skills will be used only if individuals are motivated, possess general resourcefulness skills, and hold high self-efficacy expectancies about attaining and maintaining work. Furthermore, the process of looking for and acquiring work strengthens individuals' job resourcefulness skills and beliefs. Looking for work is a novelty for some youth, and requires the use of trial and error strategies. The acquisition of job resourcefulness skills will

Figure 23.1: A Schematic Representation of the Employment Attainment Model

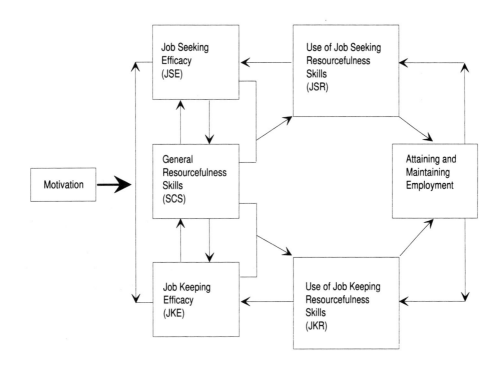

influence job seeking and job keeping self-efficacy expectancies (Bandura, 1986). The findings at time 1 and at the 6-month follow up demonstrated that individuals possessing general resourcefulness skills and high self-efficacy expectancies were more likely to be using specific job seeking and job keeping resourcefulness skills than youth lacking such general skills and beliefs. Personal job-related experiences appeared to influence the acquisition of job resourcefulness skills, which in turn appeared to embellish job seeking and keeping self-efficacy expectancies. Youth who were working at follow up showed significant increases in their job resourcefulness skills and job self-efficacy expectancies. Youth who remained unemployed showed either little change or substantial decreases on the job seeking and keeping measures over the 6-month test-retest interval; it is possible that negative job-related experiences served to diminish these youth's beliefs and skills about attaining and maintaining work.

The employment attainment model also proposes that motivation (having the need and the desire to work) is a pivotal factor triggering the working seeking process. Limited education and job training skills, dependants, or criminal records appear to impede desire to look for work. Harrington (1990) has observed that what a person wants from work also varies according to maturational level and employment status. Adult employed workers placed more value on high achievement and variety, whereas young unemployed youth ranked these attributes lower in importance and, instead, placed more value on high salary and job security. Many uneducated youth foresee themselves as never attaining these values, and, as a result, are less goal directed towards finding work. In addition "many people on welfare make more than they would by working, mostly because minimum wages are so low. Single parents, for example, ... if they stopped drawing welfare and took a minimum-wage job, lost income ranging from $46 in Manitoba to $4,685 in Ontario ... They also usually lose such benefits as free dental and eye care and free prescription drugs when they get a job" (The Canadian Press, 1993, p. A13).

Only source of income, among the demographic variables, discriminated the working from the nonworking. As compared to youth with unemployment insurance or some other means of support, youth on social assistance at time 1 were less likely to achieve employment during the following 6 months. Social assistance recipients were disadvantaged in the job market in as much as they were usually unmarried females with dependants, less educated, and more likely to have criminal records. Analysis of the psychological measures indicated, however, that social assistance recipients were no less resourceful and no less efficacious in their beliefs about their job seeking ability than nonrecipients. Rather, these social assistance recipients differed from nonrecipients only in their self-efficacy expectancies about maintaining work. Social assistance recipients who face particular disadvantages may be motivated to stay on social assistance rather than to risk taking a job for low wages that they believe they will lose anyway (Geroy, 1990). Counselling for these people must not only address their job keeping beliefs but also provide them with practical help to overcome the difficulties fostering these beliefs (Herr, 1992).

Self-efficacy expectations develop through performance accomplishments, emotional arousal, and observational learning, but most importantly through verbal persuasion or encouragement (Betz, 1992; Solberg, Good, & Nord, 1994). Eden and Aviram (1993) emphasize the importance of self-efficacy training to speed reemployment. To boost general self-efficacy on job search activity and reemployment, 66 unemployed persons participated in 8 behavioral-modelling workshop sessions over 2.5 weeks. They found that the workshops boosted self-efficacy as intended, and also increased job-search activity, confirming Bandura's belief that raising self-efficacy intensifies effort. But, perhaps more important, the treatment increased re-employment among participants with low initial self-efficacy scores, but not among those with high initial self-efficacy scores. The authors conclude that "individuals of low self-efficacy on job-search activity and re-employment should be given priority access to scarce behav-ioral-modelling training resources" (Eden & Aviram, 1993, p. 352).

Career counsellors, to be effective, must also teach general learned resource-fulness skills to youth who need it. Learned resourcefulness is acquired over many years (Rosenbaum, 1989a, 1989b). People learn general problem solving, planning and other self-management strategies informally, throughout life, starting in early childhood. People who are already high on these skills may benefit more from job counselling programs because such programs may simply remind these resourceful people to apply these skills to their job-related problems. The results from first evaluation trials of a career readiness training program provide support for the efficacy of general resourcefulness training (Campbell, et al., 1992). The primary goal of the program was to enable behaviourally at-risk adolescents to improve their thinking strategies and their life opportunities. Twenty young offenders between the ages 12 and 16 completed Rosenbaum's SCS before and after the program. Youth's scores on the SCS increased significantly (in fact, threefold), as did positive comments and feedback by teachers, staff and students.

STUDY OF CAREER COUNSELLING

General Procedures

A second study examined the utility of providing career and personal counselling on self-efficacy and learned resourcefulness skills. Youth receiving career counselling (group 1, n = 107) were compared to youth receiving both personal and career counselling (group 2, n = 103) on measures of learned resourcefulness, job skills, job beliefs, and employment status before and immediately after the counselling, and at 3 to 6 month follow up (Kennett, 1994b). The average participant left school at 17 years of age, achieved a high-school grade of 10.6, ranged in age from 15 to 24 years, and was likely to be male (60%). Youths signing up for counselling but failing to attend the workshops, on the average, had a slightly lower education (i.e., Grade 9) and were more likely to be female (64%).

Group 1 participants received a two-day workshop highlighting basic job seeking and keeping skills. Counselling included tips on finding a job, completing applications, tailoring the resume, covering letters, approaching potential employers, preparing for an interview, job safety, budgeting on a limited income, and common concerns employers have with hiring young people. There was some role playing and paper and pencil activities but much of the workshop was lecture-discussion oriented.

Group 2 participants received a four-day workshop that focused on self-statements, planning and problem solving techniques, preventing procrastination, and self-efficacy expectancies relating to work and everyday activities. The first two days of the workshop employed homework, numerous case studies, role playing, and paper and pencil activities. All youth selected a fictitious job ad to which they applied these various exercises. Day two of the workshop ended with the youth planning a job search for day 3. On day 4 these participants met for two hours to discuss their day 3 job search. Day 4 was well attended by participants; 51% attended, but 9% were working, 25% had job interview commitments, and only 15% provided no explanation.

Results and Discussion

The group 2 youth showed significant greater increases on the JSE, JKR, and JKE inventories than group 1 youth immediately following the workshops suggesting that career and personal counselling enhance job skills and beliefs more so than career counselling alone. The extensive role playing and paper and pencil exercises, which were not as predominant for group 1, may also have had some influence on the group differences.

Thirty-six percent (38) of the group 1 youth and 65% (67) of the group 2 youth were able to be contacted at follow up; 50% of group 1 and 66% of group 2 youth were working. Regardless of group, the working youth were more generally resourceful, were more job seeking and keeping resourceful, and possessed higher self-efficacy expectancies about attaining and maintaining work than nonworking youth. For working youths the SCS, JSE and JKE scores increased significantly over time. For nonworking youths, significant decreases on these psychological inventories were observed at follow up. Additionally, the SCS, JSR, JSE, JKR and JKE measures became positively and strongly related to work status over time (r's = .44,.35,.46,.42 and.44, respectively, at follow up), supporting their inclusion in models portraying the employment process.

Group 2 participants also completed a motivation inventory to express their reasons for wanting to work. Youth strongly desired to further their knowledge and skills, gain experience, and get off social assistance. This held true for both youth attaining and not attaining work. Hence, motivation was not a strong predictor of work, beliefs, or skills. Prior to the workshop, group 2 youth were asked about their current job seeking behaviours and about personal aspects they wanted to change. Sixty percent of youth indicated that they typically spent less than 3-hours per day looking for work and that this time was generally used for reading ads in the newspaper or visiting the Employment Centre. Few youth endorsed engaging in active job activities, such as knocking on doors, making phone calls, and writing cover letters. Most thought it was going to be moderately (31%) or very (53%) difficult to find a job, and that finding work was going to take a reasonable amount of effort (93%). The youth had some (46%) or a definite (50%) idea about what work they wanted. However, many youth endorsed needing more education (72%), more training (73%), to improve grooming (10%), and to deal with other problems (34%) such as setting priorities straight, becoming more assertive, improving health, and improving attitudes toward work. Group 2 youth found practising for interviews and phone calls; exercises on writing a cover letter; discussions on self-esteem, attitude, planning and problem solving; inclusion of case studies providing examples of good and bad approaches to dealing with challenges; and other hands-on exercises as invaluable to them. Often, this was their first opportunity to discuss fears, uncertainties, and misfortunes, and to put things into perspective.

CONCLUSIONS

The research findings support the importance of general and specific skills and beliefs to attaining work, and the utility of providing extensive career and personal counselling to youth. Attaining work appeared to enhance youth's beliefs and skills, whereas not attaining work seemed to diminish beliefs and the use of resourcefulness skills and to counteract the effects of counselling. Nonworking youth may benefit from long-term career and personal counselling, whereby they can discuss their personal experiences, including failures or set backs. Counselling must work toward maintaining or building positive self beliefs and use of skills.

References

Bandura, A. (1986). The explanatory and predictive scope of self-efficacy theory. *Journal of Social and Clinical Psychology, 4,* 359–373.

Betz, N.E. (1992). Counselling uses of career self-efficacy theory. *The Career Development Quarterly, 41,* 22–26.

Campbell, D.S., Serff, P., Williams, D., Pharand, G., & Zheng, J. (1992). Thinking in slow motion: Results of first evaluation trials of the breakaway company—A career readiness training program for behaviourally at-risk adolescents. In M. Van Norman (Ed.), *Proceedings of the 18th national consultation on career development* (pp. 56–67). Toronto: University of Toronto Career Centre.

Eden, D., & Aviram, A. (1993). Self-efficacy training to speed reemployment: Helping people to help themselves. *Journal of Applied Psychology, 78,* 352–360.

Geroy, G. (1990). Impact of social economics on early career planning and preparation. In M. Van Norman (Ed.), *Proceedings of the 16th national consultation on vocational counselling* (pp. 18–21). Toronto: University of Toronto Career Centre.

Harrington, T.F. (1990). Are value preferences similar or different when examined cross-culturally? In M. Van Norman (Ed.), *Proceedings of the 16th national consultation on vocational counselling* (pp. 58–69). Toronto: University of Toronto Career Centre.

Herr, E.L. (1992). Emerging trends in career counselling. *International Journal for the Advancement of Counselling, 15,* 255–288.

Kennett, D.J. (1994a). Academic self-management counselling: Preliminary evidence for the importance of learned resourcefulness on program success. *Studies in Higher Education. 19,* 295–307.

Kennett, D.J. (1994b). Employment counselling: Going beyond the basics. In M. Van Norman (Ed.), *Proceedings of the 20th national consultation on career development* (pp. 47–57). Toronto: University of Toronto Career Centre.

Kennett, D.J., Bleasdale, F., Pitt, D., & Blom, C. (1990). Seeking and keeping work: The importance of self-efficacy and self-regulatory skills. In M. Van Norman (Ed.), *Proceedings of the 16th national consultation on vocational counselling* (pp. 88–89). Toronto: University of Toronto Career Centre.

Lenox, R., & Mezydlo-Subich, L. (1994). The relationship between self-efficacy beliefs and inventoried vocational interests. *The Career Development Quarterly, 42,* 302–313.

Rosenbaum, M. (1980). A schedule for assessing self-control behaviours: Preliminary findings. *Behaviour Therapy, 11,* 109–121.

Rosenbaum, M. (1989a). The role of learned resourcefulness in self-control of health behaviour. *Research Reports on Behavioral Medicine, 1,* 4–23.

Rosenbaum, M. (1989b). Self-control under stress: The role of learned resourcefulness. *Advances in Behavioral Research and Therapy, 2,* 249–258.

Rosenbaum, M., & Ben-Ari, K. (1985). Learned helplessness and learned resourcefulness: Effects of noncontingent success and failure on individuals differing in self-control skills. *Journal of Personality & Social Psychology. 51,* 357–364.

Schlenker, B.R., & Trudeau, J.V. (1990). Impact of self-presentations on private self-beliefs: Effects of prior self-beliefs and misattribution. *Journal of Personality and Social Psychology, 58,* 22–32.

Solberg, V.S., Good, G.E., & Nord, D. (1994). Career search self-efficacy: Ripe for applications and intervention programming. *Journal of Career Development, 21,* 63–72.

The Canadian Press, Ottawa. Some make more on welfare. (1993, December 17) *The Peterborough Examiner,* p. A13.

This research was supported by the Counselling Foundation of Canada and the Ontario Ministry of Colleges & Universities, University Research Incentive Fund. I thank Fraser Bleasdale, Donald Pitt, Catherine Blom, Heather Emmett, and EPYC staff for their advice and assistance.

24

Employability Problems for At-Risk Youth: The Need for a Partnership Between School and Industry

Bruno Bourassa and Marc Tardif

The transition from school to work is one of the most important transitions for young people in our technologically advanced society. This transition is a lengthy process that begins before the end of schooling and ends several months after the youth has entered the labour market (Bingham, 1986). Some young people, especially those that have not obtained a secondary school diploma, have a more difficult time than others making this transition. Many of these young people have not acquired skills required by employers and, as a result, have fewer chances of finding and keeping a job. Various transition programs have been implemented in North America and Europe (McMullan & Snyder, 1987; OCDE, 1992) to increase these young people's employability and reduce their rate of unemployment. According to Bingham (1987), increasing a young person's employability makes it easier for him or her to make the transition from school to work. The following definition of employability pertains to at-risk youth:

> The knowledge, skills and attitudes, both general and specific, needed to enter and adapt to the labour market. They can be divided into the following four categories, as they relate to: the individual's *career development* (e.g., decision-making skills, self-knowledge, knowledge of the world of work, the ability to find and keep a job); *the work context* (e.g., punctuality, good interpersonal skills, knowledge of company rules and regulations); *basic education* (e.g., reading, writing and counting skills); *physical, perceptual and motor skills* (e.g., muscular strength and endurance, the ability to perceive shapes, manual dexterity) (Dupont, Bourassa, & Tardif, 1993, p. 99).

A secondary-level Individualized Paths for Learning (IPL) program in life-skills education and work-skills education for young people aged 16 to 18 was introduced in Québec schools in 1989 to more adequately prepare at-risk youth to lead active lives. These young people cannot follow a regular educational path leading to a secondary school diploma because they demonstrate an academic delay of more than two years in their first language and mathematics. This program is divided into two sections. The first section on general education covers basic academic subjects, the teaching of concepts related to life-skills education, and an introduction to the world of work. The second section on work-skills education focuses on a work-study format which ensures that those who will be entering the labour market receive an education that is both concrete and diversified. The program includes three practicums that enable students to develop simple work skills. Candidates receive an attestation of skills for each practicum successfully completed; these certificates are recognized by employers. The two-year program includes 300 practicum hours in the first year and 600 in the second. The relationship between the educational community and the world of work makes the IPL program unique. The Conseil supérieur de l'éducation (1990) was aware that certain modifications and improvements would have to be made to the program when it was implemented. They invited all those involved in the implementation process, as well as researchers, to analyze the program's effectiveness as it evolved, with a view to making any modifications or adjustments that would result in its overall improvement. Bourassa (1993) and Tardif (1993) conducted their research as part of this effort. This chapter will describe the methodologies and present the key findings of these studies.

TWO STUDIES OF THE IPL PROGRAM

Methodology

Tardif (1993) surveyed teachers of the IPL Program to discover the skills needed to increase the employability of at-risk youth. Questionnaires were distributed to the 34 school boards governing the 49 secondary schools that offered the program. Of 174 questionnaires distributed, 124 (71%) were completed and returned. Tardif also distributed the same measurement instrument to 318 employers in the Sherbrooke area who had at least one employee occupying a non-specialized position; 249 questionnaires were returned for a response rate of 78%.

Bourassa's (1993) research was to identify the difficulties encountered by young graduates of the IPL program in integrating into the labour market. Bourassa selected subjects who had obtained at least one attestation of skills, confirming the successful completion of a practicum in the workplace. This study was limited to the territory governed by the Commission scolaire catholique de Sherbrooke, in the Estrie region of Québec. Only 73 of 108 young people who met the selection criteria could be contacted. Six students refused to participate, leaving 67 participants (62% of the original 108); 19 were girls and 48 boys. Fifty-two percent (35) had not completed the two-year program. Bourassa used a semi-structured interview guide to obtain information on the paths chosen by the students for their integration into the labour market. The four categories outlined in the definition of employability were used as a framework to classify difficulties encountered by each of the students.

Results

Bourassa (1993) found that the paths chosen by the 67 young people for integration into the labour market aptly reveal the difficulty that they experienced in making the transition from school to work. A mean of 16.1 months had elapsed from the time they left the IPL program to the time of the first interview. During this time 82% (55) had found at least one job. A total of 102 jobs had been found; 71% (72) were full-time jobs, 29% (30) were part-time jobs. For the most part, these young people were employed as assistants, clerks, and stock handlers. Although a high percentage of these young people succeeded in finding jobs, several were unable to keep them. Of the 55 who found at least one job, only 58% (32) were still employed at the time of the interviews. There were 70 work stoppages. According to the students, 71% (50) were the result of a decision made by the employer (e.g., dissatisfaction, lack of work) and the remaining 29% (20) were for personal reasons given by the employees (e.g., lack of interest, health problems, other employment, other projects). To what degree did the IPL program effectively prepare these young people for their integration into the labour market? A better understanding of their difficulties as well as their teachers' points of view and input by prospective employers may help answer the question.

These young people were sorely lacking from a career development standpoint. Only 62% reported that they knew what type of work they wanted to do while they were students in the IPL program. A number had unrealistic career aspirations, given their level of education (e.g., doctor, optometrist, psychologist, engineer). Furthermore, only 42% were aware of fields in which there was employment potential. These young people barely consulted resource persons or any available written or audiovisual materials, and they rarely participated in activities that might have helped them to decide what type of work they would have liked to pursue once they left school. Teachers and employers place a great deal of importance on career development, but teachers place far greater importance on career exploration and knowledge of the world of work than do employers.

A large number of the young people said that they experienced emotional and interpersonal problems. For example, 50% said they had difficulty controlling their emotions at work (i.e., stress, anger, grumpiness), 48% indicated that they had trouble accepting criticism, 33% had difficulty meeting productivity demands, and 26% found it difficult to respect quality standards. All the elements pertaining to the work context were considered very important by both teachers and employers. Teachers and employers felt that it was important and even essential that young people fully develop skills and attitudes that pertain to the work context in order to be able to successfully enter the labour market.

Difficulty in decoding messages and understanding the meaning of employers' explanations or instructions (48%), an inability to make themselves understood (24%), insufficient mathematical skills (26%), and insufficient writing skills (24%) were among the major difficulties encountered by the young people. In general, teachers and employers agree on the importance of developing good written and oral communication skills as a means of increasing employability. Employers place much greater importance on mathematical ability than do teachers; 72% of employers consider it important to be able to perform six specific mathematical skills, including mental arithmetic, compared to only 61% of teachers.

The types of jobs available to these young people often require physical ability but not all the jobs require physical ability, motor skills, or the use of all the senses. There is a marked difference between the importance accorded to the various sub-categories by teachers and employers. A degree of physical ability is of value for future labourers; 20% of the young people stated that a lack of physical ability and poor physical shape were to blame for their difficulties in adapting to the labour market.

Teachers and employers believe that it was very important for young people to acquire all the types of knowledge, skills, and attitudes that promote their employability. However, young people who participate in the IPL program have a difficult time integrating into the labour market. Can schools and industry better help at-risk youth to successfully make the transition from school to work? By adopting well-structured educational practices, these two partners can help increase young people's employability and ease their transition.

EDUCATIONAL PRACTICES BY SCHOOL AND INDUSTRY FOR IMPROVED WORK-SKILLS EDUCATION

It is important to bridge the existing gap between school and industry if young people without any certification, including a secondary school diploma, are to increase their employability and improve their chances for successful integration into working life (Youth Policy Institute, 1993). Innovation, competitiveness, and the globalization of world markets are bringing about constant change in industry. The labour market is continually evolving and requires a labour force that is both flexible and efficient. Over the past 30 years, schools were entirely responsible for young people's vocational education. Increasingly, the relevance of their teaching is being called into question. Industry denounces the discrepancies that often exist between what is taught in school and what is actually expected of employees. A number of studies conducted here and abroad examine industry's growing desire to help schools better prepare tomorrow's workers (OCDE, 1992).

Faced with a significant failure and drop-out rate, as well as an alarming rate of unemployment, the ministère de l'Éducation du Québec is promoting more and more vocational education programs that favour an increased partnership between secondary schools and industry. Having students alternate between school and the workplace is recommended as a way of bringing the two closer together. Henripin (1994) discusses shared practices adopted by school and industry that have met with success. These practices are also being adopted throughout Canada as a means of increasing the employability of tomorrow's workers (Bloom, 1991; Emploi et immigration Canada, 1994). The proposed partnership between school and industry may initially seem designed purely for socioeconomic reasons; but, it is considered by many to be a very valuable educational approach (Hoyt, 1994; Zay, 1994). Education in the workplace offers industry the opportunity to create a labour force that meets with its approval. It is also an effective means of helping young people find and keep their jobs. This, of course, results in greater social and economic welfare for the entire country. However, shared educational practices are not solely intended to serve the interests of industry or to resolve the current socioeconomic crisis. They are also intended to foster learning among at-risk youth whose past school record has been marred by failure.

The reality of the labour market offers concrete learning situations. Grubb, Davis, Lum, Plihal and Morgaine (1991) believe the educational approach known as teacher talk normally used in schools, is in part responsible for young people's learning difficulties. This approach is based on the principle teachers provide students with an effective way to learn by transmitting knowledge in class. But the content is too often abstract and not understood by students. Material that is taught becomes significant for the learner as he or she can apply it to a particular field. Furthermore, even if a student understands what is being taught, he or she may not be able to apply this knowledge in everyday life. Knowledge must be furthered by means of concrete action; "When learning to swim or skate, it is not sufficient to merely listen to the instructor: one must practise, practise and practise" (ministère de l'Éducation du Québec, 1994, p. 15). Examples from Germany, Japan, Sweden (OCDE, 1992), the United States (Kazis, 1993) and Canada (Emploi et immigration Canada, 1994) illustrate the effectiveness of shared educational practices adopted by schools and industry to prevent students from dropping out, to encourage students that have dropped out to resume their studies, to ensure greater employability for young people, and to enable them to find and keep jobs once they leave school. It is not easy to establish these types of partnerships; certain conditions must be met if such partnerships are to be created and given a chance to develop.

The systemic approach provides a conceptual framework within which a partnership can be analyzed (Zay, 1994) and focuses attention on the interrelations that are at the very core of this cooperative venture. These two systems, school and industry, distinct by virtue of their structure, procedures and objectives, must agree to modify certain principles and practices in order to favour the creation of this new partnership. The players involved must pursue common goals, agree on rules, and outline their respective roles so that this new system can be created and given a chance to develop (OCDE, 1992; Zay, 1994). It is not always easy for teachers and representatives of industry to cooperate effectively (Zay, 1994). Schools fear that industry will interfere with their curricula and they tend to resist proposed changes to their traditional practices, while industry imposes its productivity objectives and preferred teaching approaches. Since the players are quite different, as is the culture and structure of their joint system, creating a partnership means being open to change. Partners working toward the creation of this new entity must be prepared to reconsider some of the ways in which they view reality and to modify or add to existing practices in order to better serve the common cause.

Two key conditions that must be met for a quality partnership to exist. First, partners must believe in the project and place importance on cooperation. Second, they must focus on concrete action that will help sustain and strengthen this joint project. Partners who experience success were often prompted by a small group of people who were highly motivated by the idea of a cooperative venture. Lacey and Kingsley (1988) call these people brokers. Brokers are enthusiastic and work feverishly to promote the idea of a partnership. They establish contacts and gradually form alliances. Often, those who initiate are either representatives from the educational community or industry. As the project evolves, however, players from both sides must get involved. Partnership requires joint participation. Without it, one side or the other might offer assistance but would not necessarily feel like an active participant in the project, as they would be participating in a selective manner that is consistent with their own approach. An effective partnership is the result of close collaboration that makes it possible to plan a program and play an active role in young people's education.

Henripin (1994), Lacey and Kingsley (1988) and the OCDE (1992) recognize the importance of forming a permanent committee composed of representatives from both sides who will constitute the central core of the partnership. Partners should set attainable objectives by first successfully achieving small goals rather than undertaking initiatives that are difficult to effectively organize and manage. This plan involves establishing rules, as well as sharing responsibilities, roles, and tasks to be accomplished. In this way, the partnership begins to take shape, as an entity distinct from either of its two constituents, school and industry. The strength and quality of the partnership and of its educational practices will reside in the central committee's ability to convince and involve not only those from their respective systems, but also representatives from the ministère de l'Éducation, unions, the chamber of commerce, and employment centres, as well as parents. The shared practices will be modified and evaluated on a regular basis in order to ensure the strength and quality of the partnership and better work-skills education.

The IPL program has been subject to very few scientific studies (Bourassa, 1993; Lamothe & Payeur, 1994; Tardif, 1993). Research carried out by Bourassa (1993) reveals that a considerable number of young people in this program did not complete their education, that an alarming number did not find work after leaving school, and that many found themselves unemployed not long after being hired. Their lack of employability was considered to be of the utmost importance by both teachers and employers (Tardif, 1993). The sample was small and the findings may not be generalized to the entire population of young Québecers who took part in the program. Nevertheless, current educational practices may be called into question on the basis of these results. Other research involving IPL teachers from 128 school boards throughout Québec revealed that each school board, and each school for that matter, has its own way of organizing general education for their young people (Lamothe & Payeur, 1994). Very rarely does industry participate in outlining objectives or designing a teaching plan with the school. The lack of shared educational practices adopted by school and industry challenges the very existence of a partnership, within the framework of the IPL program in Québec. The creation and development of a partnership presupposes that the representatives from both sides believe in the project and are committed to it. Schools have taken most of the responsibility for educational planning since the program was implemented in 1989. Schools have called on industry to participate in setting objectives for practical training. Industry seems content to respond to the needs of the school. Chances are that one party's level of enthusiasm and involvement will far outweigh the other's. Objectives regarding educational practices, roles, and responsibilities are unlikely to be clear or agreed upon.

References

Bingham, W.C. (1986). *A cross-cultural analysis of transition from school to work.* Paris: UNESCO, Division of Educational Policy and Planning.

Bingham, W.C. (1987). *Suggestions for policy regarding the integration of young people into working life.* Paris: UNESCO, Division of Educational Policy and Planning.

Bloom, M. (1991). *Profils de partenariats. Partenariats entreprise-établissement d'enseignement qui gardent nos jeunes à l'école* (Rapport No. 70–91-E/F). Ottawa: Conference Board du Canada.

Bourassa, B. (1993). *L'intégration au travail de jeunes en difficulté d'adaptation et d'apprentissage.* Thèse de doctorat non publiée. Montréal: Université de Montréal.

Conseil supérieur de l'éducation. (1990). *Les cheminements particuliers de formation au secondaire: Faire droit à la différence.* Québec: Ministère de l'Éducation, Gouvernement du Québec.

Dupont, P., Bourassa, B., & Tardif, M. (1993). L'employabilité requise des jeunes en difficulté. *Les Actes du CONAT* (pp. 96–107). Toronto: Colloque National Touchant le Développement de Carrière, Career Centre, University of Toronto.

Emploi et immigration Canada. (1994). *Évaluation de l'option alternance travail-études. Rapport Final.* Ottawa: Développement des Ressources Humaines Canada.

Grubb, W.N., Davis, G., Lum, J., Plihal, J., & Morgaine, C. (1991). *The cunning hand, the cultured mind: Models for integrating vocational and academic education.* Berkeley, CA: National Center for Research in Vocational Education (ERIC Document Reproduction Service No. ED 334 421).

Henripin, M. (1994). Les pratiques locales du partenariat éducation-travail au Québec. In C. Landry & F. Serre (Éds.), *École et entreprise: Vers quel partenariat?* (pp. 29–43). Sainte-Foy, QC: Presses de l'Université du Québec.

Hoyt, K.B. (1994). A proposal for making transition from schooling to employment an important component of educational reform. In A.J. Pautler (Ed.), *High school to employment transition: Contemporary issues* (pp. 189–199). Ann Arbor, MI: Prakken Publications Inc.

Kazis, R. (1993). *Improving the transition from school to work in the United States.* Washington, DC: American Youth Policy Forum, Competitiveness Policy Council, and Jobs for the Future (ERIC Document Reproduction Service No. ED 353 454).

Lacey, R.A., & Kingsley, C. (1988). *A guide to working partnerships.* Waltham, MA: Center for Human Resources, Heller School, Brandeis University (ERIC Document Reproduction Service No. ED 295 001).

Lamothe, D., & Payeur, C. (1994). Le partenariat école-entreprise: le cas des cheminements particuliers en insertion sociale et professionnelle. In C. Landry & F. Serre (Éds.), *École et entreprise: Vers quel partenariat?* (pp. 87–100). Sainte-Foy, QC: Presses de l'Université du Québec.

McMullan, B.J., & Snyder, P. (1987). *Allies in education: Schools and business working together for at-risk youth: Findings from the national assessment* (Vol. 1). Philadelphia, PA: Public Private Ventures (ERIC Document Reproduction Service No. ED 291 822).

Ministère de l'Éducation du Québec. (1994). *Préparer les jeunes au 21e siècle.* Québec: Gouvernement du Québec.

Organisation de Coopération et de Développement Économique (OCDE). (1992). *École et entreprises: Un nouveau partenariat.* Paris: Centre pour la Recherche et l'Innovation dans l'Enseignement.

Tardif, M. (1993). L'employabilité des jeunes adultes en difficulté d'adaptation et d'apprentissage, opinions d'enseignants et d'employeurs. Thèse de doctorat non publiée. Montréal: Université de Montréal.

Youth Policy Institute. (1993). Transition from school to employment: One goal three solutions. *Youth Policy, 15* (6&7).

Zay, D. (1994). *La formation des enseignants au partenariat: Une réponse à la demande sociale?* Paris: Presses Universitaires de France/Institut National de Recherche Pédagogique.

This research was made possible with the financial support of the Social Sciences and Humanities Research Council of Canada (SSHRC).

25

Making It: Work and Alternative School in the Transition from Homelessness

Bill McCarthy and John Hagan

Most youths occupy the better part of the day in school or at work, building human and social capital; in contrast, homeless adolescents spend their time on the street—in social assistance offices, food-banks, hostels, and squats, searching for basic necessities such as food, shelter and money. They also hang-out; panhandle, party (i.e., consume drugs or alcohol) and work in the illegal economy. Some enrol in school or find jobs, but most remain out of school and unemployed. McCarthy and Hagan (1991, 1992, 1995) find that since leaving home, 62% of their sample of 390 Toronto street youths had not worked, and although 85% had not completed Grade 12, only 20% attended school. Moreover, 53% had shoplifted goods worth more than $50, 43% had used cocaine, 44% had sold drugs, and 30% had worked in prostitution. These proportions are significantly higher than those reported in other studies of adolescent crime (Hindelang et al., 1981).

Street youths' crime and unemployment experiences likely have several consequences. Studies on crime and work consistently find that offending is highest among the unemployed and escalates with the length of unemployment (Farrington et al., 1986; Thornberry & Christenson, 1984; Good et al., 1986; Hartnagel & Krahn, 1989). However, crime probably precedes offending. According to Hagan (1993), early offending encourages subsequent unemployment by enhancing embeddedness in criminal networks and reducing access to connections that facilitate activities such as finding work. Sampson and Laub (1993) find that early adolescent offending is also linked to several deviant behaviours in adulthood: alcohol abuse, crime and arrests. As well, delinquent youths report weaker occupational commitments as adults, experience more unemployment and more frequently rely on social assistance. Hagan's (1991) analysis of panel data from Toronto area youths provides comparable findings. Research on employment reveals that structural changes and the increasing domination of the service sector further disadvantage youths with minimal human and social capital (Krahn, 1991; Krahn et al., 1993). As Bellamy (1993, p. 138) notes, these youths have "little chance of becoming meaningfully employed."

The above studies suggest that the future for homeless youths looks bleak. Characterized by unemployment, substance use and crime, street life is an unlikely place for youths to experience a successful transition to adulthood. Yet, there are possibilities for change. Although life course studies reveal that individual trajectories are more often consistent in their stability, as well as instability, many are redirected by important transitional experiences or "turning points" (Elder, 1975; 1985). Sampson and Laub (1993) note that the deviant life trajectories of some young delinquents were altered by certain events: joining the armed forces, establishing a secure and supportive relationship, and finding stable employment. Likewise, Hagan (1991) found that many youths who drifted into a delinquent sub-culture in their adolescence exited that sub-culture in their early 20s.

Rosenberg's (1975) theory of dissonance contexts provides one explanation for the changes or discontinuity that characterize some life trajectories. Rosenberg argues that social contexts act as frames of reference. These contexts include the larger social structure and cultural milieu, as well as more specific contexts such as networks and neighbourhoods. Rosenberg notes, however, that people may find themselves in conflicting contexts; situations that are not dissonant in and of themselves, but that are incompatible because of a person's experiences. Rosenberg argues that people resolve this dissonance in several ways: 1) changing their view of themselves; 2) modifying their perceptions of their environments; or 3) exiting a dissonant context and increasing their involvement in non- or less-dissonant situations.

From a distance, homelessness is often defined as a dissonant context. Street youths are outside most of the traditional social institutions that give people status, rewards and security such as family, stable social networks, school and work. Yet, for youths from abusive families or those alienated from school and peers, homelessness may be less dissonant than the living situation they left behind. Youths who establish street networks and revel in the freedom of street life may also experience little conflict. Nonetheless, street youths who enter environments inconsistent with their homeless lifestyle, and participate in these with increasing frequency, may begin to experience dissonance from their simultaneous locations in two opposing worlds. Extended involvement in work or school may introduce several such contradictions: a commitment to scheduling, a continual delay of gratification and a responsiveness to the authority and demands of others.

Work's and school's enhancement of human and social capital may introduce further sources of dissonance. Street youths who study or work for prolonged periods augment their human capital by increasing their skills, knowledge, training and work records. These assets facilitate continued participation in school or the labour force and foster an awareness of the costs of inadequate human capital. Concurrently, these youths may gain access to sources of social capital (Coleman, 1988). Working and studying increase street youths' association with others who may provide important information about job and educational opportunities (Granovetter, 1974). As well, these relationships reinforce the utility of school and work. As these associations solidify and increase, they may emphasize contradictions between work and school and street life, making it harder to reconcile the two worlds. Thus, homeless youth who study or work may find it increasingly difficult to associate with other street youths. This reduction is important because many street activities occur in groups; moreover, street friends are a primary source of learning criminal techniques (McCarthy & Hagan, 1995).

The research reported here investigates the effects of employment and school enrolment on various street (e.g., crime) and social outcomes (e.g., employment) associated with homeless and non-homeless trajectories (Janus et al., 1987). It is important to note, however, that work and school are not likely dramatic events that immediately transform street youths' lives; rather their effects probably unfold over time and accumulate with length of involvement.

DATA, VARIABLES AND METHODS

This investigation uses data from a sample of youths interviewed in Toronto and Vancouver during the summer of 1992. A team of researchers used a variety of data collection instruments including life-calenders, semi-structured interviews, and self-report questionnaires to contact respondents on the street and in agencies that provide services for street youth. Respondents were contacted three times over the summer with approximately a one month interval between each wave of interviews. Seventy-eight percent of the first wave respondents completed a second interview and just over 54% were located for a third interview. This analysis uses data only from the 375 respondents who completed both first and second wave interviews.

As noted above, this study concentrates on two sets of variables: street and social activities. The first group refers to behaviours that characterize a homeless trajectory: hanging-out, searching for food, searching for shelter, panhandling, stealing and using drugs. These measures capture the respondent's general involvement in these activities with other homeless youths during the two weeks preceding the second wave interview (Table 25.1). The second group of items focuses on socially desirable outcomes associated with a non-homeless life-style and a transition out of a street career: continued employment, prolonged attendance at school, and the acquisition of stable shelter (i.e., living in an apartment, a hostel, with family, or with relatives). The items that measure these experiences reflect the respondent's total involvement in the two week period preceding the second interview. For example, second wave employment (Employment T2) refers to the number of days the respondent worked full- or part-time in this two-week period and includes work found through job training programs, as well as through other means. School attendance includes enrolment in regular and alternative educational programs; some street youths remain in, or return to the former, but the majority attend the latter. Alternative education includes street schools funded by social services and public donations, as well as those operated by local boards of education.

The key independent variables in this analysis are first wave employment and school enrolment. These activities were measured with items about work and attending school in the six months prior to the interview and since leaving home. The information collected was used to create additive measures of total work and school involvement for this period. For example, someone who last worked or attended school in June of 1992 (the month data collection began) was coded as six, those who last worked or were enroled in May were classified as five, and so on. For each street and social outcome, an estimated ordinary least-squares (OLS) model explored the effects of employment and school enrolment in the months before the first wave interview on the outcomes measured at the time of the second interview approximately one month later. A number of control variables including age, gender, and previous criminal activity test the robustness of any effects derived from work and school (Table 25.1). Controls for crime were collected in the first interview and refer to total theft and drug use since leaving home. Theft is measured with a four item additive scale consisting of theft of goods worth less than $50, taking objects worth more than $50, stealing from a car, and break, enter and theft. The drug-use scale combines items that measure use of cannabis, acid, and cocaine.

A measure of the respondents' average grade in their last year of school and a scale measure of self-confidence were used to control for the effects of human capital. Self-confidence used two items that asked how strongly the respondents agreed or disagreed with the following statements: "I can do just about anything I set my mind to," and "I am responsible for my own successes." These statements capture elements of what Clausen (1991) calls adolescent competence or self-efficacy—an attribute strongly related to adult employment and stable careers and marriages. The study also controlled for embeddedness in criminal street networks. This variable was measured with an additive scale that combined estimates of the proportion of street friends who had been arrested with the proportion who had committed a theft of an object worth between $5 and $50.

RESULTS

The homeless experiences of the youths surveyed in this study resemble those documented in earlier research (McCarthy & Hagan, 1992). When first interviewed, only 36% of respondents reported employment for any time in 1992 and only 33% indicated that they had attended school in this period. At the time of the second interview, 28% of youths were working and 21% were in school. Since leaving home approximately 60% of respondents had been involved in theft, 90% had used drugs, and over 80% reported that at least half of their street friends had been arrested or had committed a theft. The summary statistics reported in Table 25.1 reveal that the majority of youths had been involved with other homeless youths in the activities categorized as street outcomes. In the two weeks prior to the second interview, respondents and other street friends typically searched for food, panhandled, and committed a theft at least once or twice. Searching for shelter, using drugs, and hanging-out were even more common.

Consistent with our hypothesis, the findings reported in Table 25.2 reveal that first wave employment reduced participation in street activities with other homeless youths in the two weeks before the second wave interview. First wave employment (Employment T1) is negatively and significantly related to respondents' assessments of their involvement in hanging-out, searching for food and shelter, panhandling, stealing, and using drugs. Importantly, the effects of employment remain even after the introduction of some of the most powerful predictors of deviant and criminal activity—age, gender, previous

Table 25.1: Variable Names and Descriptive Statistics (n = 375)

Dependent Variables	x	sd
Street Outcomes:		
Hanging-Out with Street Friends T2[a]	3.67	1.31
Searching for Food with Street Friends T2[a]	1.92	1.21
Searching for Shelter with Street Friends T2[a]	2.22	1.31
Panhandling with Street Friends T2[a]	1.71	1.20
Theft with Street Friends T2[a]	1.36	.85
Using Drugs with Street Friends T2[a]	2.77	1.53
Social Outcomes:		
Employed T2[b]	2.05	3.85
Attending School T2[b]	1.32	2.97
Living in Stable Shelter T2[c]	6.89	5.29

Independent Variables	x	sd
Age[d]	19.90	2.49
Gender[e]	.66	.47
Competence[f]	8.70	1.37
Average Grade[g]	3.84	1.48
Employed T1[h]	1.69	2.65
Attending School T1[h]	1.59	2.56
Theft T1[i]	4.62	1.92
Drug Use T1[i]	8.72	5.11
Criminal Street Friends[j]	13.85	5.59

[a] 1 = Never, 2 = Once or twice, 3 = A Few Times, 4 = Often, 5 = Most of the time
[b] 1 = Employed/in school (full-/part-time) for each day in the two weeks prior to the second interview (maximum = 14), 0 = Unemployed/out of school
[c] 1 = Living in a hostel, with family or relatives, or in their own apartment for each day in the two weeks prior to the second interview (maximum = 14), 0 = Living on the street
[d] In years
[e] 0 = Females, 1 = Males
[f] Sum of 2 items coded individually 1 = Strongly Disagree, 2 = Disagree, 3 = Uncertain, 4 = Agree, 5 = Strongly Agree
[g] 1 = 0 to 40, 2 = 41 to 50, 3 = 51 to 60, 4 = 61 to 70, 5 = 71 to 80, 6 = 81 to 100
[h] 0 = Unemployed/not in school in 1992, 1 = Employed/in school (full-/part-time) in January 1992...6 = Employed/in school (full-/part-time) in June 1992
[i] 0 = Never, 1 = 1, 2 = 2, 3 = 3-4, 4 = 5-9, 5 = 10-19, 6 = 20-29, 7 = 30-59, 8 = 60 or more
[j] 0 = None, 1 = 1 to 10%, 2 = 11 to 20%...10 = 91 to 100%

Table 25.2: Effects of Work and School During the First Wave on Street Activities with Homeless Friends at the Time of the Second Wave (n = 375)

	Hanging Out T2			Searching for Food T2			Searching for Shelter T2		
	b	s.e.	β	b	s.e.	β	b	s.e.	β
Age	-.07	.03	.14*	.02	.03	.05	-.01	.03	-.02
Gender	.14	.15	.05	.17	.14	.07	-.02	.15	-.01
Competence	-.08	.05	-.08	-.09	.04	-.10	-.06	.05	-.07
Average Grade	-.04	.05	-.04	-.08	.04	-.10	-.08	.05	-.09
Employed T1	-.07	.02	-.14*	-.05	.02	-.11*	-.06	.02	-.13*
School T1	.02	.03	.04	.03	.02	.05	.03	.03	.07
Theft T1	.02	.01	.08	.02	.01	.12	.02	.01	.10
Drug Use T1	-.01	.01	-.02	.01	.01	.02	.01	.02	.01
Criminal Street Friends T1	.04	.01	.18*	.01	.01	.04	.02	.01	.07
Constant	5.33			2.15			3.01		
R^2	.10			.07			.06		

	Pan-Handling T2			Stealing T2			Using Drugs T2		
Age	-.05	.03	-.10	-.02	.02	-.07	-.04	.03	-.07
Gender	-.28	.14	-.11*	.25	.09	.14*	.35	.15	.11*
Competence	-.07	.04	-.08	-.09	.03	-.15*	-.06	.05	-.05
Average Grade	-.06	.04	-.07	-.00	.03	-.01	-.13	.05	-.13*
Employed T1	-.05	.02	-.11*	-.04	.02	-.12*	-.06	.02	-.10*
School T1	-.01	.02	-.03	.05	.02	.14*	.07	.03	.12*
Theft T1	.02	.01	.09	.05	.01	.35	.04	.01*	.15*
Drug Use T1	.01	.01	.06	.01	.01	.02	.12	.02*	.40*
Criminal Street Friends T1	.04	.01	.18*	.01	.01	.03	.02	.01	.06
Constant	3.11			2.12			2.86		
R^2	.10			.23			.32		

* $p < .05$ (two-tailed)

criminal involvement, school grades and competence (McCarthy & Hagan, 1992)—as well as measures of adolescent self-confidence.

The effects of enrolment in school contrast sharply with those for work. Only one of the effects is in the expected direction and the only significant effects are opposite that predicted; that is, attendance at school is positively related to involvement in theft and using drugs with street friends. The counter-intuitive effects of school are placed in context in Table 25.3. As expected, first wave employment is positively related to the frequency of working and of having stable shelter during the two weeks prior to the second interview; as well, enrolment in school at the first wave interview is positively associated with attendance at school in the second wave. However, second wave employment also increases with first wave school attendance. This

Table 25.3: Effects of Work and School during the First Wave on Social Activities at the Time of the Second Wave (n = 375)

	Employed T2			School T2			Stable Shelter T2		
	b	s.e.	β	b	s.e.	β	b	s.e.	β
Age	.10	.08	.06	-.03	.06	-.02	.54	.12	.26*
Gender	.40	.41	.05	-.21	.34	-.03	-.55	.60	-.05
Competence	-.20	.13	-.07	-.02	.11	-.01	.21	.19	.06
Average Grade	.19	.13	.07	-.05	.11	-.02	.25	.18	.07
Employed T1	.62	.07	.43*	.04	.06	.03	.30	.10	.15*
School T1	.15	.07	.10*	.38	.06	.33*	-.19	.11	-.09
Theft T1	.01	.04	.01	-.01	.03	-.01	-.01	.05	-.01
Drug Use T1	.01	.04	.01	.05	.03	.08	.06	.06	.06
Criminal Street Friends T1	-.03	.03	.04	-.01	.03	.01	.03	.05	.03
Constant	-.09			1.38			-7.62		
R^2	.23			.11			.13		

* P < .05 (two-tailed)

relationship raises the possibility that any positive effect of attending school may operate indirectly through its affect on employment. Attending school may not directly discourage drug-use, stealing or hanging-out with street friends, but it does facilitate employment which in turn deters these activities.

Our in-depth interviews with street youths support the statistically-based conclusions of this research. These reveal that most homeless youths come to realize the detrimental nature of street life. According to one respondent, homelessness was a continual repetition of the same aggravating experiences: "Between living on the streets, being in jail and trying to find a place again, I just kept going in circles and circles." Many also refereed to the deleterious effects of hanging-out and partying with street friends. As one youth noted:

> I could find a job—once I put my head doin' something I can get it done. It's just, like, that I have a problem with getting thing's done, though. Drugs and alcohol ... I always start partying rather than looking for jobs.

Those who recognized the shortcomings of street life usually referred to school and work as their most likely means for leaving the streets. These youths aspired to conventional careers—shipping, trades, secretarial work, retail, police work, social work, teaching, and health care—and assumed that these traditional adult trajectories would begin with the ending of their street lives. However, many youths recognized that their opportunities are limited by their lack of education and work experience. One youth succinctly described this predicament when relating his problems finding work: "Lack of education, no experience. That's 'bout it." Many youths not only acknowledged these limitations but anticipated the difficulties of surmounting them. One young woman noted,

> like, if I wanted to be a hang-glider instructor, I'd have to pay for a course just to learn how to hang-glide ... And I'd probably have to keep training and keep

training and keep paying 'til I got good to become an instructor. That would costs lots ... And I didn't finish school yet.

Another woman identified her entrapment by the circular logic of a work-world that demands job experience while also denying it:

Uh, I look too weird. I don't have the job experience, I mean I do have some minor experience but I don't have a lot ... And for awhile I was too young. People thought I was just stupid. A stupid kid who didn't really know anything ... But I mean, it's kind of stupid-you can't get experience if you don't have a job. But you can't get a job if you don't have experience, so, that's basically it.

Despite their lack of human capital, the majority of youths were hopeful about their futures. Their optimism is poignantly revealed in one youth's insight about work and the reasons behind his decision to enrol in an alternative school program, "Getting a chance, to um, succeed in life ... to get better jobs and, get yourself educated ... and to know things about, life. About the human being."

A considerable body of research (Elder, 1975, 1985) reveals that, for the most part, consistency and stability characterise life trajectories. This does not fare well for homeless youths who are typically embedded in criminal networks, involved in crime, unemployed, and have minimal education. Yet, for some youths obtaining secure employment or returning to school may act as turning points in a homeless trajectory and increase the likelihood of escaping the street. Thus, government and social policies that create employment opportunities or establish alternative routes for schooling will not only enhance opportunities for leaving the street, they will improve the possibilities that homeless youths will make successful transitions to enriching and rewarding adult lives.

References

Bellamy, L. (1993). Life trajectories, action, and negotiating the transition from high school. In P. Anisef & P. Axelrod (Eds.), *Transitions: Schooling and employment in Canada* (pp. 137–158). Toronto: Thompson Educational Publishing.

Clausen, J. (1991). Adolescent competence and the shaping of the life course. *American Journal of Sociology, 96*, 805–842.

Coleman, J. (1988). Social capital in the creation of human capital. *American Journal of Sociology, 94*, S95-S120.

Elder, G. Jr. (1975). Adolescence in the life cycle: An introduction. In S. Dragastin & G. Elder Jr. (Eds.) *Adolescence in the life cycle: Psychological change and social context* (pp.1–23). New York: John Wiley and Sons.

Elder, G. Jr. (1985). Perspectives on the life course. In G. Elder, Jr. (Ed.) *Life course dynamics-trajectories and transitions, 1968–1980* (pp.23–49). Ithaca: Cornell University Press.

Farrington, D., Gallagher, B., Morley, L., St. Leger, R., & West, D. (1986). Unemployment, school leaving, and crime. *British Journal of Criminology, 26*, 335–356.

Good, D., Pirog-Good, M., & Sickles, D. (1986). An analysis of youth crime and employment patterns. *Journal of Quantitative Criminology, 2*, 219–236.

Granovetter, M. (1974). *Getting a job: A study of contacts and careers.* Cambridge, MA: Harvard University Press.

Hagan, J. (1991). Destiny and drift: Subcultural preferences, status attainments, and the risks and rewards of youth. *American Sociological Review, 56*, 567–582.

Hagan, J. (1993). The social embeddedness of crime and unemployment. *Criminology, 31*, 465–492.

Hartnagel, T., & Krahn, H. (1989). High-school dropouts, labor market success, and criminal behavior. *Youth & Society, 20*, 416–444.

Hindelang, M., Hirschi, T., & Weis, J. (1981). *Measuring delinquency.* Beverly Hills, CA: Sage.

Janus, M., McCormack, A., Burgess A., & Hartman, C. (1987). *Adolescent runaways: Causes and consequences.* Lexington, MA: D.C. Health.

Krahn, H. (1991). The school-to-work transitions in Canada: New risks and uncertainties. In W. Heinz (ed.) *The life course and social change: Comparative perspectives* (pp.43–69). Weinheim, Germany: Deutscher Studien Verlag.

Krahn, H., Mosher, C., & Johnson, L. (1993). Panel studies of the transition from school to work: Some methodological considerations. In P. Anisef & P. Axelrod (Eds.) *Transitions: Schooling and employment in Canada* (pp. 137–158). Toronto: Thompson Educational Publishing.

McCarthy, B., & Hagan, J. (1991). Homelessness: A criminogenic situation? *British Journal of Criminology, 31*, 393–410.

McCarthy, B., & Hagan, J. (1992). Mean streets: The theoretical significance of situational delinquency among homeless youth. *American Journal of Sociology, 98*, 597–627.

McCarthy, B., & Hagan, J. (1995). Getting into street crime: The structure and process of criminal embeddedness. *Social Science Research, 24*, 63–95.

Rosenberg, M. (1975). The dissonant context and the adolescent self-concept. In S. Dragastin & G. Elder Jr. (Eds.) *Adolescence in the life cycle: Psychological change and social context.* New York: John Wiley and Sons.

Sampson, R., & Laub, J. (1993). *Crime in the making: Pathways and turning points through life.* Cambridge, MA: Harvard University Press.

Thornberry, T., & Christenson, R.L. (1984). Unemployment and criminal involvement: An investigation of reciprocal causal structures. *American Sociological Review, 49*, 98–411.

This work was made possible by a grant from the Social Sciences and Humanities Research Council of Canada's Strategic Areas Division.

PART IV

Preparation for Intimacy and Family Life

26

Research on Preparation for Intimacy and Family Life: Research and Policy Implications

Yvonne Unrau and Judy Krysik

SUMMARY OF THE RESEARCH

Intimacy refers to close personal relationships that individuals seek to establish throughout the life span. Individuals are expected to engage in a range of intimate relationships over the life course. These include attachments to caretakers, close personal friends, and intimate partners. The process of acquiring and maintaining significant attachments with others is an important part of psychosocial development and has consequences for individual well-being and family life. Individuals who fail to develop secure emotional attachments in childhood, and who subsequently have problems making the transition from attachment to parents to attachment with peers in adolescence, are more likely to experience relationship problems in later life. In contrast, individuals with well-developed emotional attachments show lower incidents of negative responses to stress, have a greater sense of meaning to their lives, experience a stronger sense of well-being, and are more resistant to depression (Marshall, 1989). It is often assumed that learning how to live within a family and establish intimate relationships will occur naturally. Most youth transition from adolescence to adulthood without detrimental emotional consequences; for some it is a period that has long-lasting negative consequences for establishing and maintaining intimate relationships. Research examining the development of intimate relationships focuses mainly on social and family influences.

Significant social and economic forces have changed life in ways that urge new forms of adaptation in the context of everyday living. The increase of women in the work force, for example, and the increase in divorce and non-marital births have impacted the organization of family life and the structure of the family (Amato, 1994). Although the median age of marriage for women and men has remained in the low-to-mid 20s over the past century, the variance has spread considerably. This implies greater diversity in the ways that adolescents in the 1990s establish and experience intimacy (Arnett & Taber, 1994).

Male and female experiences of developing intimate relationships are different. Generally, males have greater difficulty forming intimate relationships than females. A comparison of men and women in their college years showed that women had higher overall psychosocial development scores, implying that women adapt better to the cognitive, emotional, and social demands of college life (Zuschlag & Whitbourne, 1994). Marshall (1989) found that males seem more likely than females to avoid dealing with problems that arise in relationships or to even admit that a problem exists. Males in the study frequently withdrew from their partners and sought satisfaction by other means. Such behaviour was associated with both immediate and long-term negative effects in current relationships and also on the male's capacity for intimacy with subsequent partners.

Failure to develop the capacity for intimacy in males has also been linked to sexual offending behaviour. Marshall (1989) notes that males constitute the bulk of known sexual offenders. Research efforts have generally attempted to explain this gender difference in offending behaviour as a biological predisposition for aggression in males and have neglected to consider how uniquely women and men develop intimacy. The problem can also be explained by the frequent failure to attain intimacy on the part of males. Research has found, for example, that loneliness significantly predicted reported incidents of past sexual aggression (Check, Perlman, & Malamuth, 1985).

The topic of intimacy achieves heightened relevance at the time when adolescents struggle with sexual relationships and sexual orientation. The ability to attain an integrated sense of self is developed during adolescence. For the most part, however, gay adolescents have not had supportive and affirmative opportunities to explore their gay identity during adolescence (Fischer & Narus, 1981). Positive role models that could counter social stigmatization and isolation are lacking to gay adolescents. Sex-role stereotyping has particularly negative consequences for gay individuals with respect to views about intimacy (Fischer & Narus, 1981).

Much of the research on intimacy has focused on examining the parent-child relationship and how early family experiences may impact the development of intimacy in later life. All three papers included in this section focus on the role of family in developing healthy relationships later in life. Jocelyne Thériault explores the relationship between mother-adolescent relationships and adolescents' capacity for intimacy in sexual relationships. Deborah Hay investigates how experiences of child sexual abuse impact upon the development of intimacy. Gerald Adams focuses on the role of family and faculty in influencing young adult's development of close relationships in first year university.

Parent-child relations appear to have a great influence on the types of relationships children establish as they transition from adolescence to young adulthood. Normative developmental transitions are likely to occur when affective experiences of parents and their children are moderate and stable (Tubman & Lerner, 1994). Research supports that parents can play an active role in facilitating the formation of friendships for young adolescents. Parents who more frequently talk to their children, encourage peer socialization, and connect with other parents influence an adolescent's ability to establish companionship with friends (Vernberg, Beery, Ewell, & Abwender, 1993). Young adolescents have stronger feelings of warmth and intimacy toward parents when time is spent together talking and problem-solving (Herman & McHale, 1993). The process of normative development in adolescence, however, can also be disrupted by parental behaviours. When parents themselves feel lonely they may form dysfunctional attachments to their children and may discourage their children from forming bonds outside of the family (Marshall, 1989). Further, exposure to family violence in childhood has been associated with problems in developing healthy relationships in adulthood (Bernard & Bernard, 1983).

Many youth seek support and direction for personal issues during the adolescent years. The mother is the preferred parent to turn to in times of stress and need (Benson, Arditti, Reguero de Atiles, & Smith, 1994; Papini, Farmer, Clark, Micka, & Barnett, 1990; Paterson, Field, & Pryor, 1994). Contact with friends is sought for social support while adult communication is favoured when making more consequential decisions (Hunter & Youniss, 1982). A study from New Zealand found that adolescents rated the quality of affect for friends lower than for parents (Paterson et al., 1994). The role of the father in parent-child relations also has been an area of investigation. Amato (1994) found that fathers are important figures in the lives of young adults. Closeness to fathers positively influenced both son's and daughter's happiness, life satisfaction, and ability to deal with psychological distress, regardless of the relationships with their mothers (Amato, 1994).

The relationship between adolescents and their parents is an important area of research, particularly since there has been an increase in the number of lone-parent families over the past two decades. In 1991, lone-parent families, of which 82% were headed by a woman, were up 12% from 1986 and double that of 1971 (La Novara, 1994). This increase is a product of rising divorce rates and the growing number of births to women who have never married. Several studies, however, support that divorce may produce delayed effects that reveal themselves in early adulthood (Furstenberg & Teitler, 1994; Aquilino, 1994). Gabardi and Rosen (1992) surveyed 300 college students from divorced and intact families and found that attitudes toward intimacy and marriage differed. Individuals from divorced families reported having more sexual partners and a greater desire for sexual involvement in dating relationships than individuals raised in non-divorced families. For both groups, parent marital conflict was positively related to negative views of marriage and a greater number of sexual partners. Divorce also has consequences for the quality of relationships between each parent with their child. Aquilino (1994) reported the results of a study examining the impact of divorce on parent and adult-child relations for 4,516 young adults. The results revealed that by the time children reached early adulthood, relationship quality with non-custodial fathers was, on average, no better than that of children who never lived with their fathers. Becoming the non-custodial parent after divorce had negative consequences for long-term, father-child relations, but not necessarily for mother-child relations. The findings indicate that the development of close intimate relationships between adult children and their fathers is maintained or enhanced only when the divorcing father becomes the custodial parent. Mothers, in contrast, are able to maintain close intimate ties with their children whether or not they remain the primary caregiver with the exception being if the custodial father remarries. Generally, the long-term impact of parental divorce on children's ability to develop intimate relationships has received less attention than its short-term impact.

POLICY IMPLICATIONS

The preceding review of the research leads to five recommendations for Canadian public policy. First, the value of strong emotional attachments and intimate ties should be given greater importance in the vision of a good society. Often healthy relationships are considered in terms of their contribution to the domains of employment and education as opposed to viewing the institutions of employment and education as potential contributors to the development of healthy relationships. Considering the development of healthy relationships as a legitimate social pursuit means that public support be given to women and men for their dual roles as employees and family members. Flexible work schedules, quality and affordable child care, family leave, and the promotion of a more equal sharing of domestic responsibilities among women and men are examples of policies that support the development of a society that values quality relationships. Government has the opportunity to be an exemplary employer to promote this vision.

Second, males tend to have more difficulties dealing with conflict and expression of feelings than females, whereas females tend to have difficulty with too much emotional connectedness. Yet, girls tend to be the primary recipients of family life programs within secondary schools. Research and programming needs to be more integrated so that services are targeted to those who would benefit most. This implies the need for increased partnering among health, welfare, and education professionals who could work together to promote a more holistic view of health to adolescents that includes the development of healthy relationships.

Third, there are many gaps in research for particular subgroups of children who are at risk for relationship difficulties. These groups include gay and lesbian youth, children living in public care, and teenage mothers. Targeting scarce resources to vulnerable groups is especially important in this period of fiscal restraint. Given the lack of research on what works for these vulnerable groups, service and programs should be designed with an evaluative component. Monitoring client service delivery and client outcomes through program evaluations has the potential to create a system of ongoing feedback that could be used to make informed decisions about program development and expenditures.

Fourth, although early family life experiences are known to be critical, developing healthy relationships is not only a private family matter. Societal influences are operating in education, media, and sport and recreational systems that are counter productive to the development of healthy relationships. Policy needs to consider the effects of these influences on family life and development of healthy relationships.

Finally, on a more general level, stronger alliances need to be established between social service delivery agents, policy makers, and researchers so that research information is more timely and useful. Findings from evaluative studies on programs that are remedial in nature are needed to help divert resources from programs that are not effective or efficient to the development of community-based services that reinforce abilities in persons and families to develop healthy relationships. These programs can be as diverse as are needed in a given area. For instance, adult literacy programs have been instrumental in facilitating intimate experiences between parents and their children. The development of healthy relationships is not only a private family matter, but is a collective responsibility in which society needs to work to support the family to fulfil its role.

RESEARCH AGENDA

Five research gaps have been identified through the preceding review. First, the research lacks attention to cultural factors. Culture, although acknowledged as an important variable in many studies, has been used primarily as a control variable. The transition from adolescence to young adulthood should be considered within a cultural context. Socialization of adolescents is broadly or narrowly defined, depending on one's culture (Arnett & Taber, 1994). Broad socialization encourages individual differences and self-expression, while narrow socialization favours conformity to prescribed family rules.

Second, researchers must be willing to accept a broader definition of intimacy and healthy relationships among adolescents. If conventional definitions of family life are used to define successful outcome, then researchers may inadvertently support the notion of family as a structure at the expense of quality relationships or risk neglecting nontraditional family structures such as foster families, extended families, gay and lesbian unions, and peer groups.

Third, research is needed to determine what factors constitute healthy relationships. Most people transition through adolescence and successfully maintain relationships with their family of origin, as well as, establish new relationships outside the family. What individual and social factors are needed for adolescents to develop healthy relationships? How is it that some children living in adverse family environments go on to develop positive relationships, while others do not? Knowing what is involved in developing healthy relationships is important for developing accurate assessment tools and effective interventions.

Fourth, more research is needed to specifically address groups of adolescents who experience particular difficulty with intimacy (e.g., gay and lesbian adolescents, pregnant and parenting youth, youth with disabilities, and youth in out-of-home care). Gay and lesbian youth need special attention as they face the task of making their gay identity known to their families and others and as they encounter fears of rejection that are beyond the norm for most adolescents. Children who live in foster or group care deal with the special issue of emancipation from a system instead of a family. These children also face special identity issues that can interfere with the development of healthy relationships. Teenage mothers are at risk for low education, poverty, and relationship problems. Lack of access to the necessities of life strain parent-child relationships, threaten secure attachments, and place subsequent generations of children at risk for relationship problems. Youths who have experienced physical, sexual and emotional abuse, and youths that have lived with family violence are at risk for developing relationship difficulties in the transition from adolescence to adulthood. It is important that research target these special groups so that their difficulties can be more effectively addressed.

Finally, there are three strategies for research that deserve particular attention. First, it is timely that existing programs and policies be directly evaluated for both outcome and cost effectiveness. Knowing what works and what does not is essential for informed decisions about continued services. Second, when examining program success, healthy relationships ought to be considered as an outcome measure in conjunction with the more usual measures of educational attainment and employability. Finally, because the development of healthy relationships is a life course process, longitudinal studies are particularly important. Research that includes both qualitative and quantitative information are particularly informative because they offer normative findings and a meaningful context of those studied.

References

Amato, P. (1994). Father-child relations, mother-child relations, and offspring psychological well-being in early adulthood. *Journal of Marriage and the Family, 56,* 1031–1042.

Aquilino, W. (1994). Impact of childhood family disruption on young adults' relationships with parents. *Journal of Marriage and the Family, 56,* 295–313.

Arnett, J.J., & Taber, S. (1994). Adolescence terminable and interminable: When does adolescence end? *Journal of Youth and Adolescence, 23,* 517–537.

Benson, M.J., Arditti, J., Reguero de Atiles, J.T., & Smith, S. (1994). Intergenerational transmission: Attributions in relationships with parents and intimate others. *Journal of Family Issues, 13,* 450–464.

Bernard, M.L., & Bernard, J.L. (1983). Violent intimacy: The family as a model for love relationships. *Family Relations, 32,* 283–286.

Check, J.V.P., Perlman, D., & Malamuth, N.M. (1985). Loneliness and aggressive behaviour. *Journal of Social and Personal Relations, 2,* 243–252.

Fischer, J.L., & Narus, L.R. (1981). Sex roles and intimacy in same sex and other sex relationships. *Psychology of Women Quarterly, 5,* 444–455.

Furstenberg, F.F., Jr., & Teitler, J.O. (1994). Reconsidering the effects of marital disruption: What happens to children of divorce in early adulthood? *Journal of Family Issues, 15,* 173–190.

Gabardi, L., & Rosen, L.A. (1992). Intimate relationships: College students from divorced and intact families. *Journal of Divorce and Remarriage, 18,* 25–56.

Herman, M.A., & McHale, S.M. (1993). Coping with parental negativity: Links with parental warmth and child adjustment. *Journal of Applied Developmental Psychology, 14,* 121–136.

Hunter, F.T., & Youniss, J. (1982). Changes in functions of three relations during adolescence. *Developmental Psychology, 18,* 806–811.

La Novara, P. (1994). Changes in family living. In *Canadian Social Trends* (Vol. 2, pp. 171–174). Toronto: Thompson Educational Publishing.

Marshall, W.L. (1989). Intimacy, loneliness, and sexual offenders. *Behaviour Research and Therapy, 27,* 491–503.

Papini, D.R., Farmer, F.F., Clark, S.M., Micka, J.C., & Barnett, J.K. (1990). Early adolescent age and gender differences in patterns of emotional disclosure to parents and friends. *Adolescence, 15,* 959–1001.

Paterson, J.E., Field, J., & Pryor, J. (1994). Adolescents' perceptions of their attachment relationships with their mothers, fathers, and friends. *Journal of Youth and Adolescence, 23,* 579–600.

Tubman, J.G., & Lerner, R.M. (1994). Affective experiences of parents and their children from adolescence to young adulthood: Stability of affective experiences. *Journal of Adolescence, 17,* 81–98.

Vernberg, E.M., Beery, S.H., Ewell, K.K., & Abwender, D.A. (1993). Parents' use of friendship facilitation strategies and the formation of friendships in early adolescence: A prospective study. *Journal of Family Psychology, 7,* 356–369.

Zuschlag, M.K., & Whitbourne, S.K. (1994). Psychosocial development in three generations of college students. *Journal of Youth and Adolescence, 23,* 567–577.

27

The Role of Mother-Adolescent Competence in the Timing of Sexual Initiation and in the Development of a Mature Intimacy Capacity Towards the Loving Partner

Jocelyne Thériault

Studies concerning education towards a responsible sexuality during adolescence have focused, for the most part, on the prevention of pregnancy, STDs, and AIDS. These studies have generated useful information, but have not identified the fundamental determinants of responsible adolescent sexual behaviour. Responsible sexual behaviour during adolescence refers to notions of social competence (the capacity for intimacy with loving partner) and sexual competence (the capacity for on time sexual initiation). What factors relate to the incapacity to establish mature, intimate relationships with one loving partner? What factors relate to precocious sexualization? Family relations were examined as significant factors.

Theories on adolescent development provide accounts of the role of the family in social and sexual development. In this chapter, two of them are briefly outlined. They are built on an attachment perspective and address the pressures toward continuity and changes in the development of dyadic relationships. Both contribute to process models needed to understand the impact of adolescent bonds on adolescent behaviour (Noller, 1994). The evolutionary theory of socialization (Belsky et al., 1991) claims that the timing of puberty, the onset of sexual activity during adolescence, and the prior organization of interpersonal relations are inferred from childhood developmental experiences and from behavioral patterns derived from these experiences. In this context, precocious sexual activity will have psycho-socio-economic antecedents of "dysfunction" operating from childhood. The family differentiation model (Allison & Sabatelli, 1988) sheds light on the antecedents of precocious sexual activity without specifically focusing on the sexual aspects of adolescent development. This model is formed from the two key variables of family differentiation and personal individuation. The constant demands for change brought forth by adolescence demands a reorganization of family relations. This reorganization must permit a balance between connectedness and separateness to the parents. A troubled family differentiation provokes adolescent individuation at an inappropriate age, can be expressed by a pseudo-intimate rapport with ones peers, and the symbiotic nature of this rapport takes place at the expense of the development of a personal identity.

A number of empirical studies support propositions relating family development to adolescent social and sexual development. Studies have demonstrated that a secure attachment to parents is a good predictor of social competence during pre-adolescence and adolescence (Sroufe et al., 1993). Difficulties in gaining autonomy towards parents, as well as difficulties in remaining connected to ones parents during adolescence, are both related to problems of internalizing and externalizing behaviours during adolescence (Allen et al., 1994; Powers et al., 1994; Allison & Sabatelli, 1988). The family is a significant factor in the development of internalizing and externalizing behaviour problems during adolescence and is in turn influenced by the community and the social environment (Mason et al., 1994; Lerner et al., 1994; Huffman & Hauser, 1994). The negative emotional states created by a weak parent-child relationship are specifically related to precocious sexual behaviour and the use of drugs (Whitbeck et al., 1992). Small and Kerns (1993) state that adolescents who are more vulnerable to unwanted sexual contacts have experienced sexual abuse, the use of drugs and alcohol, and demonstrate an important conformity to their parents and peers. Family conflicts and the father's absence during adolescence are predictors of an early onset of menarche during adolescence (Moffit et al., 1992) and therefore precocious sexual behaviour. Di Blasio and Banda (1992) find that a weak proximity to ones parents has an impact on adolescent sexual behaviour. Peer selection mediates this relationship. Adolescents weakly related to their parents find peer groups particularly attractive because these seem to offer alternative sources of proximity and, in this context, sexual behaviour reflects more a need for dependency than a need for autonomy (Giovacchini, 1986) and can be used to satisfy needs other than sexual ones (Hajcak & Garwood, 1988). In these conditions, sexual behaviour becomes hazardous. The adolescent would be more inclined to repeat the same behaviour of promiscuity again and again in the hope of finally satisfying his or her otherwise unsatisfied emotional needs.

The significant variables of Allison and Sabatelli's model (1988) have been integrated to those of Belsky and colleagues (1991) to conceptualize the process of responsible sexualization and the impact of family determinants (mother-adolescent competence) and social determinants (intimacy with partner). This research was used to develop a causal sequence leading to precocious sexualization and irresponsible sexual behaviour. By unifying significant variables of theories presented here to research results having empirically supported these theories, there seems to be sufficient support to assume that: a weak level of competence in the mother-adolescent relationship provokes a need for investing massively in a loving partner in order to compensate for the lack of connection met in the family. This compensatory and defensive investment takes place at an inappropriate age and prematurely leads to sexual behaviour. Sexual needs, newly felt since puberty, along with the need to compensate by investing in a boyfriend or girlfriend pushes the adolescent into precocious sexual behaviour. The more sexual behaviour is used in a defensive manner, which seems to be the case in precocious sexual behaviour, the more it will have a tendency to repeat itself. Failing to find true satisfaction in the sexual act, primary needs for dependency (needs of proximity to the mother) will manifest themselves repetitively in a passive intimacy type of rapport to the partner, this promoting promiscuity, unstable sexual conduct, and many sex partners. The developmental sequence leads to risk-taking in irresponsible sexual behaviour; these risks affect the individual, his or her family, and society by HIV infection, early pregnancy, early parenthood, and so forth.

METHOD

The present study is a preliminary step in a research program aimed at establishing a model of prediction for irresponsible sexual behaviour among early adolescents. The model is composed of family, social, and contextual variables. The present research explores the role of mother-adolescent competence in the timing of sexual initiation and in the development of a mature intimacy capacity with a loving partner. Two questions guide this research. First, does the type of family competence developed towards the mother distinguish sexually precocious adolescents from the others? If so, what dimensions of family competence distinguish the most sexually precocious adolescents from the others? Second, is the relationship between family competence and social competence developed towards the loving partner empirically verifiable? If so, what dimensions of family and social competencies are interrelated? Family competence is operationalized in terms of the adolescent's perceived capacity in maintaining satisfying relations of connectedness and separateness with his or her mother. The concept of social competence is operationalized in terms of the adolescent's perceived capacity for engaging in intimate exchanges with a loving partner. The expression sexually precocious refers to having had one or many experiences of sexual intercourse at the age of 14 years or less.

The research subjects were 656 students, enroled in a regular curriculum, in grades 10, 11 and 12, from a francophone high-school in the Montréal area. Each student completed the ICQ(M), PAIR(M) and QSD questionnaires. The ICQ(M), a translated, modified and adapted version of the original ICQ questionnaire (Burhmester et al., 1988) was used to measure self-perceived family competence. The ICQ(M) is intended for adolescents and measures self-perception of interpersonal competence in relationship to one's mother. Factorial analysis of the ICQ(M) (Thériault, 1994) reveals a four factor structure of emotional support (alpha = 0.88), self disclosure (alpha = 0.84), conflict management (alpha = 0.78) and negative assertion (alpha = 0.78). The PAIR(M), a translated, modified and adapted version of the original PAIR questionnaire (Shaefer & Olson, 1981), was used to measure self-perceived social competence. PAIR(M) measures self-perception of one's capacity in establishing intimate rapport with a loving partner. Factorial analysis of the PAIR(M) (Thériault, 1994) reveals four factors: passive intimacy (alpha = 0.74), active intimacy (alpha = 0.68), sexual intimacy (alpha = 0.619) and social intimacy (alpha = 0.0605). The Socio-Demographic questionnaire (SDQ) was created for this study and measures variables deemed as significant in determining precocious sexual behaviour during adolescence. In addition to the sexual status (precocious/non-precocious), it gathers information on variables such as educational status (grades 10, 11, 12), socioeconomic status, family structure, family conflicts, sexual history, and timing of puberty. The three instruments were combined in a questionnaire and were distributed to class-groups of 30 individuals. Each class-group was allowed 50 minutes to answer. Youth who claimed to have been sexually abused and those whose questionnaires were not complete were excluded from the study; 411 (236 girls, 175 boys) were available for analyses of the ICQ(M), 232 subjects (119 girls, 133 boys) were available for analyses of the PAIR(M) (i.e., those who claimed to have a girlfriend or boyfriend), and 533 (237 girls, 296 boys) were available for analyses of the QSD.

RESULTS

The variance analyses of the ICQ(M) demonstrate that only negative assertion toward mother tends to distinguish sexually precocious subjects from the others. The sexually precocious had higher scores of negative assertion to their mothers than the others. However, a p value of .06 merely indicates a tendency to discriminate the groups of subjects rather than effective discrimination. The dimensions of competence to the mother such as self-disclosure, emotional support, and conflict management did not distinguish the sexually initiated at 14 years or less from the initiated at 15 years and more and the non-initiated. The dimension of emotional support in relationship to the mother tends to distinguish the sexually precocious subjects from the others when it is analyzed in interaction with the perceived measure of proximity to the father (QSD). The variance analysis of the score for emotional support ICQ(M) tends to show an interaction effect (non-parallel) between the variables sexual precocity and proximity to the father ($F(4.298) = 2.13$, $p = 0.0767$). Among the sexually precocious, the average score of those who are not close to their father is smaller than the score of those who are very close to their father ($t(298) = 2.17$, $p = 0.0306$). In the same manner, among those who claimed to be not close to their father, the average score of the sexually non-initiated is higher than the average score of the precocious subjects ($t(298) = 2.08$, $p = 0.0383$).

These results suggest that the relationship to the father could mediate the relationship to the mother among precocious subjects. The sexually initiated at 14 years of less would need to feel close to their father in order to give emotional support to their mother. Such a mediation would not be necessary among the initiated at 15 years and more and the non-initiated in order for them to give emotional support to the mother. Table 27.1 provides the average score of emotional support according to the precocity and proximity to the father categories; Table 27.2 provides the variance analysis of the emotional support score according to the sexual precocity (Preco) and proximity to the father (Prox.father) categories.

Pearson correlation coefficients were conducted between the scores of the ICQ(M) and those of the PAIR(M) to answer the second research question, is the relationship between family competence and social competence empirically founded? Two of the four dimensions of the ICQ(M) are significantly correlated to two of the four dimensions of the PAIR(M), but the correlations are weak.

Table 27.1: Average Value (Number of Subjects) of the Emotional Support Score (ICQ(M)) according to the Sexual Precocity and Proximity to the Father Variables

	Sexual Precocity			
Prox. father	**Yes, < 14**	**Yes, > 14**	**No**	**Total**
Very	20.39(18)	17.71(7)	18.63(51)	18.91
Somewhat	18.92(25)	19.59(27)	18.66(111)	19.06
Not	16.07(15)	18.23(13)	18.60(40)	17.63
Total	18.46	18.51	18.63	

Table 27.2: Variance Analysis of the Emotional Support Score (ICQ(M)) According to the Sexual Precocity and Proximity to the Father Variables

Source	dl.	Sum of Squares	F	p
Sexually precocious	2	1.37	0.04	0.9586
Prox. father	2	75.37	2.33	0.0990
Preco* Prox	4	137.94	2.13	0.0767
Error	298	5006.35		

Emotional support from the ICQ(M) and passive intimacy from the PAIR(M) presented a significant positive correlation coefficient (r = 0.17305, p < .02). Emotional support from the ICQ(M) and active intimacy from the PAIR(M) presented a significant negative correlation coefficient (r = 0.15703, p < .03). Conflict management from the ICQ(M) and active intimacy from the PAIR(M) also presented a significant negative correlation coefficient (r = 0.17891, p < .01). The results tend to suggest that (1) the more adolescents are able to emotionally support their mother, the less they are capable of showing supportive intimacy towards their boyfriend/girlfriend and to feel efficient in fulfilling his or her expectations; (2) the more they are capable of emotionally supporting their mother, the more they are inclined to demonstrating a passive-distant intimacy towards their boyfriend or girlfriend and to feel inefficient in fulfilling his or her expectations; and (3) the more they are capable of managing their conflicts with their mother, the less they are capable of demonstrating supportive intimacy towards their boyfriend or girlfriend.

Simple variance analyses were conducted on the ICQ(M) scores to determine if the competence in the relationship to the mother varies according to the sexes and the average ages of the subjects. The ANOVA on each of the four scores of the ICQ(M), according to the sexes, show that negative assertion distinguishes the girls from the boys. The girls had significantly higher scores than the boys (p < .04). Competence in the relationship to the mother was independent of the average age of the adolescents. The variance analyses of each of the 4 scores of the ICQ(M) according to the ages 13–14, 15, 16, and 17–18 showed no significant differences.

DISCUSSION

This study suggests that the type of family competence, particularly the mother-adolescent competence, distinguishes sexually precocious adolescents from the others. Two facets of competence are involved; both are related to the management of emotions. Negative assertion seems related to experiences of separateness to the mother while emotional support seems related to experiences of connectedness to the mother. Sexually precocious adolescents distinguish themselves from the others on both dimensions of competence. Sexually precocious adolescents have more of a tendency to assert their negative emotions than others. Moreover, emotional support towards the mother is weaker among them than that the non-precocious in situations where the adolescent claims not to be close to his or her father. These results are consistent with views that problems of externalizing behaviour during adolescence, such as precocious sexual behaviour (Jessor & Jessor, 1977), are related to problems in maintaining experiences of connectedness to the parents (Allen et al., 1994). This data reinforces other findings that family relations during childhood are not the only ones that influence later adaptation (Mason et al., 1994). Even during adolescence, strategies of managing emotions are learned and reinforced in the family context (Huffman & Hauser, 1994).

The results suggest that family and social competencies are interrelated. The type of family interaction developed in regards to the mother may be related to the type of social competence developed in regards to the loving partner. The emotional dimension of the competence towards the mother (emotional support) allows the connection between family competencies and social competencies. The more adolescents display experiences of connectedness, emotional support towards the mother, the less they tend to feel competent in fulfilling their loving partner's expectations. Moreover, the more they display experiences of separation towards the mother, conflict management, the less they tend to feel competent in fulfilling their loving partner's expectations. In short, these results show that the dimensions of separateness and connectedness to the mother are both related to self-perceived social non-competence. How can these surprising results be interpreted when the traditional documentation claims that parental autonomy (that is separation) during adolescence is the best guarantor for future social adaptation (Blos, 1967)? Or, conversely, that experiences of connectedness to the family are the best guarantor for future social adaptation (Gilligan, 1987)? These results make sense if they are placed in the context of Allison and Sabatelli's model (1988) that stresses the importance of a balanced rapport between experiences of connectedness and separateness that link the adolescent to his or her family. This balanced rapport between experiences of separateness and connectedness to the mother was not attained by some adolescents. Too much experience of connectedness to the mother and too much experience of separation to the mother would lead them to the same result—a troubled intimacy towards the loving partner, that is a troubled social competence, which in turn leads to a probable precocious sexual behaviour. Therefore, this exploratory study offers clues to the effect that responsible adolescent sexual conduct is determined partially by the development of family competencies. Further, it seems logical to think that the responsible adolescent's sexual conduct will have an impact on the later development of his or her parental competencies.

These indicators of a relationship between family and sexual competencies must be considered with caution because the study's limitations. The weak correlations may be partially attributable to the instruments (PAIR-M; ICQ-M). These instruments are at an exploratory stage of utilization and their parameters are not yet perfectly determined. The use of a seven point Likert type scale, the elimination of certain items that were deemed to be not significant in the factorial analyses, and reformulating a few items may have contributed in increasing the discriminatory potential of these instruments. This was an exploratory and preliminary study. The study of the relationship between family and sexual competencies must be done in a context in which coexisting contextual social variables are considered. The research program ultimately aims at establishing, during future studies, a prediction model for the irresponsible adolescent sexual behaviour.

When the probable importance of family relations on the development of sexual and social competencies has been recognized, the next priority is to situate the family in the larger context of the social environment. The community and the social environment of the family have an effect on children and adolescents behaviour and that parental behaviour mediates this link (Mason et al., 1994). An increase of the youth's empowerment is necessarily attributable to an increase in parental competence, which seems dependent on the structural characteristics of the environment especially on the state of the economy. All interventions on the matter of prevention of risk-taking behaviour in the sexual, emotional and social spheres must be conceptualized in a context of multidisciplinary research. The ecological perspective seems to be the model which can guide this conceptualization. Priority is placed on the improvement of fundamental knowledge concerning healthy or normal process of development during adolescence (Hauser & Huffman, 1994; Huffman & Hauser, 1994). Better understanding the healthy emotional, social, and sexual process of development during adolescence will permit a better understanding of how some adolescents manage to emerge from difficult contextual conditions while demonstrating a level of mental health relatively high while others develop problem behaviour.

Social policies need to be aimed at identifying and changing society's structural characteristics that seriously affect the family and its parental competencies. Further, social policies need to be centered on promoting a better understanding of normal sexual, emotional, and social process of development of the adolescent in the different contexts in which he or she lives. These could promote the empowerment of adolescents in their own lives. Increased empowerment in the lives of the adolescent would enforce positive interactions on personal, family, academic, and community levels. In this way a youth who feels productive and responsible can give meaning to his or her life. And society will have access to the immense resource potential that the youth have at their disposal.

References

Allen, J., Hauser, S., Eichkholt, C., Bell, K., & O'Connor, T. (1994). Autonomy and relatedness in family interactions as predictors of expression of negative adolescent affect. *Journal of Research on Adolescence, 4* (4), 535–552.

Allison, M., & Sabatelli, R. (1988). Differentiation and individuation as mediators of identity and intimacy in adolescence. *Journal of Adolescent Research, 3* (1), 1–16.

Belsky, J., Steinberg, L., & Draper, P. (1991). Childhood experience, interpersonal development, and reproductive strategy: An evolutionary theory of socialization. *Child Development, 62,* 647–670.

Buhrmester, D., Furman, W., Wittenberg, M.T., & Reis, H.T. (1988). Five domains of interpersonal competence in peer relationships. *Journal of Personality and Social Psychology, 55,* 6, 991–1008.

Blos, P. (1967). The second individuation process of adolescence. *Psychoanalytic Study of the Child, 22,* 162–168.

Di Blasio, F., & Benda, B. (1992). Gender differences in theories of adolescent sexual activity. *Sex Roles, 27* (5–6), 221–239.

Gilligan, C. (1987). Adolescent development reconsidered. In C.E. Irwin, Jr. (Ed.), *Adolescent social behaviour and health: New direction for child development* (pp. 63–92). San Francisco: Jossey-Bass Inc.

Giovacchini, P. (1986). Promiscuity in adolescents and young adults. *Medical Aspects of Human Sexuality, 20* (5), 24–31.

Hajcak, F., & Garwood, P. (1988). What parents can do to prevent pseudo-hypersexuality in adolescents? *Family Therapy, 5* (2), 99–105.

Hauser, A., & Huffman, L. (1994). Introduction: Affective process in adolescence. *Journal of Research on Adolescence, 4* (4), 465–467.

Huffman, L., & Hauser, S. (1994). Afterword: Reflexions and future direction. *Journal of Research on Adolescence, 4* (4), 657–662.

Jessor, R., & Jessor, S. (1977). *Problem behaviour and psychosocial development.* New York: Academic Press.

Lerner, R., Entwisle, D., & Hauser, T. (1994). The crisis among contemporary American adolescents: A call for the integration of research, policies & programs. *Journal of Research on Adolescence, 4* (1), 1–4.

Mason, C., Cauce, A., Gonzales, N., Hiraga, Y., Huffman, L., & Hauser, S. (1994). An ecological model of externalizing behaviour in African-American adolescents: No family is an island. *Journal of Research on Adolescence, 4* (4), 639–655.

Moffit, T., Belsky, J., & Siliva, P. (1992). Childhood experience and the onset of menarche: A test of a sociobiological model. *Child Development, 63,* 47–58.

Noller, P. (1994). Relationships with parents in adolescence: Process and outcome. In R. Montemayor, G. Adams & T. Gulotta (Eds.), *Personal relationships during adolescence* (Advances in Adolescent Development, vol. 6). Newbury Park, CA: Sage Publications.

Powers, S., Welsh, D., & Wright, V. (1994). Adolescent's affective experience of family behaviour: The role of subjective understanding. *Journal of Research on Adolescence, 4* (4), 585–600.

Shaefer, M.T., & Olson, D.H. (1981). Assessing intimacy: The Pair Inventory. *Journal of Marital and Family Therapy, 7,* 47–60.

Small, S., & Kerns, D. (1993). Unwanted sexual activity among peers during early and middle adolescence: Incidence and risk factors. *Journal of Marriage and the Family, 55,* 941–952.

Sroufe, L., Bennett, C., Englund, M., & Urban, J. (1993). The significance of gender boudaries in preadolescence: Contemporary correlates and antecedents of boundary violation and maintenance. *Child Development, 64,* 455–466.

Thériault, J. (1994). Dimensions de la différenciation familiale et de la socialisation aux pairs à l'adolescence. *Annales du 62e Congrès de l'ACFAS, 62,* 379.

Whitbeck, L., Hoyt, D., Miller, M., & Kao, M-Y. (1992). Parental support, depressed affect, and sexual experience among adolescent. *Youth and Society, 24* (2), 166–177.

28

Childhood Sexual Abuse: Implications for the Development of Intimate Relationships in Adolescence and Adulthood

Deborah Hay

Child sexual abuse is associated with a range of immediate and long-term effects (Kendall-Tackett et al., 1993; Beitchman et al., 1992). Some of the most persistent, and least understood, involve difficulties with intimate relating. Adult survivors often describe feelings of social isolation, distrust of others, a history of unstable (often abusive) relationships, marital and sexual difficulties, and difficulties parenting their own children (Cole & Putnam, 1992; Cole & Woolger, 1989; Harter et al., 1988). A large body of literature has demonstrated the importance of close relationships for physical and mental health (Hartup, 1989; Reisman, 1985), but little research has examined the nature of the interpersonal difficulties survivors experience, how they develop, or their implications for later adaption.

Child sexual abuse usually occurs in the context of a trusting relationship between a child and an adult (Badgley, 1984; Rogers, 1990). For most children, it is a significant interpersonal event. Children develop knowledge about self, others, and relationships via interactions with others (Bowlby, 1982; Hartup, 1989). From these experiences, children construct mental representations that guide their expectations and attitudes about current and future relationships (Bretherton & Waters, 1985). Children who are manipulated, coerced, or threatened into participating in sexual activities by adults who they admire and trust may develop expectations and knowledge that differ significantly from children who have not been abused (Cole & Putnam, 1992; Janoff-Bulman, 1992). Finkelhor and Browne (1988) suggest that "when children attempt to cope with the world through these distortions, it may result in many of the problems commonly noted in victims of sexual abuse" (p. 62). Little empirical work has sought to test these hypotheses. The research presented in this chapter offers some preliminary insights into the types of expectations and attitudes that survivors may develop and how these may impede the development of close relationships throughout the life span.

INTERPERSONAL RELATIONSHIPS OF ADULTS SEXUALLY ABUSED AS CHILDREN

Understanding how child sexual abuse impacts the development of intimate relating requires longitudinal research conceptualized within a developmental model of stress and coping (Friedrich, 1988). Unfortunately, these studies do not yet exist. Retrospective studies with adults have limitations; nevertheless, adult survivors can often reflect on and talk about their experiences in ways that children and adolescents cannot. Corbett (1995) interviewed seven adult female survivors ages 22 to 55 and Miller (in progress) interviewed seven adult male survivors ages 36 to 53 years. Corbett (1995) specifically asked participants how their views of themselves, others, and relationships were impacted by the abuse. Miller (in progress) asked the more general question, "How do you feel the sexual abuse you experienced as a child affected you?" Only data central to the development of intimacy are presented.

All participants identified significant difficulties in developing and maintaining close relationships. Many described themselves as friendless through childhood and adolescence. All reported marital difficulties or difficulties establishing satisfying romantic relationships. Many men described the difficulties they experience relating to their own children.

> I never used to have any relationships. Well, I wasn't aware that I did. I was in my own little world and they were all out there. So I just kind of interacted with people. I didn't really have relationships with them (Corbett, 1995).

> I probably wouldn't have even addressed the issue of sexual abuse if it wasn't for the relationships I'm in, because there's something wrong. There isn't a relationship. We're two ships in the night. Sometimes I think my wife and I are two single parents living in the same house (Miller, in progress).

Participants identified a variety of factors that impeded their ability to develop satisfying, intimate relationships. All but one of the participants reported that as children and adolescents they developed negative expectations and beliefs about other people. They used words such as dangerous, cruel, unpredictable, hurtful, untrustworthy, conniving, controlling, and manipulative to describe others. These views of others impaired their ability to trust, and led to defensive reactions like withdrawal, aggression, and the presentation of a false self.

> I was so worried about getting hurt … I was so busy hurting everyone else so that they couldn't get to me first (Corbett, 1995).

> I was extremely defensive. I saw myself as a porcupine. I kept well guarded and was very sarcastic if anybody tried to get to close (Corbett, 1995).

The consequence was peer rejection, social and psychological isolation, and limited opportunities to acquire contradictory information about other people and relationships. Self development was also affected as many participants came to view themselves as hostile and aggressive. Negative expectations of others often continued into adulthood and resulted in a history of abusive relationships. Some participants described how they seemed drawn to people who treated them badly.

> I didn't expect people to treat me good. I was a very lonely little girl. I felt very isolated. I had very few friends. I guess there [were so many] things that happened

that I just expected to be treated badly and I think that message went through into my marriage (Corbett, 1995).

I am afraid of letting them get too close to me and me being vulnerable because it would be a whole lot harder to be hurt by a nice guy who I would expect not to hurt me than by someone who I expect to hurt me. It doesn't hurt because I expect it" (Corbett, 1995).

One woman reported more hopeful, but equally maladaptive perceptions of others.

For some reason, despite all the sexual abuse I was still very, very trusting of people. I was almost naive. I could be used and abused. I trust too easily (Corbett, 1995).

Participants indicated that distorted self-perceptions also contributed to interpersonal difficulties. They used words like dirty, ugly, unworthy, stupid, mutilated, damaged, unlovable, and marked to describe how they felt as children. Low self-confidence, concerns that others would discover what bad people they were, and feelings that they did not deserve positive regard further isolated participants from peers.

I could have really good relationships with people on a very casual basis, but any deeper … I was always afraid that if I let people get too close they would find out what a monster I was. That was my real fear—let them get too close and they're going to find out what a horrible person you are (Corbett, 1995).

It was difficult for me to feel loved or good enough to get close to people. I don't believe that someone really good could love me and want me in their life so I try to sabotage it (Corbett, 1995).

Participants also reported feeling different from other children. Many experienced this sense of not belonging, even as adults.

I was different from anybody that I knew. It [the abuse] made me grow up in some ways faster than others and yet my world was different. I didn't know how to relate. I was holding secrets and I didn't know how things worked. Guilt and different things I couldn't relate to anybody. I didn't go out to try to make friends. I was hard to reach, too. I wouldn't talk very much unless I really had to (Miller, in progress).

I felt almost like an alien or something. I have been different all my life. I think that's because I was abused. That does make a person different (Corbett, 1995).

Several participants coped with their feelings of low self-worth and not belonging by moulding themselves to meet the expectations and wishes of others. The abuse taught them, "you must conform—be what others want you to be—otherwise there will be no relationship." This often led to revictimization, a lack of self-knowledge and identity, difficulties participating in mature relationships based on reciprocity and mutuality, and, still, a profound sense of not belonging.

I was very afraid of not pleasing people. I was manipulated by a lot of people because I was too eager to please and it seemed that no matter what I did I was never, never accepted or never felt comfortable (Miller, in progress).

I had to know what the other person wanted because I had to fit in otherwise I would be, I don't know, rejected. I literally didn't have an identity (Miller, in progress).

One of the most interesting observations participants made was related to the establishment of same-sex peer relations in childhood and adolescence. Gender is a significant determinant in friendship formation (Hartup, 1983). Same-sex friendships predominate through childhood and adolescence. Same-sex friendships increase the probability of similarities between friends and reduce potential conflict. They enhance closeness and identification and are critical to the development of intimacy (Sullivan, 1953). Both women and men who were abused by males reported that they avoided same-sex friendships in childhood and adolescence. For women, this was because they viewed females as weak and vulnerable. They identified with males to counteract their feelings of vulnerability. The men coped with feelings of vulnerability by avoiding contact with other males. The consequences of avoiding same-sex relationships in childhood and adolescence are unclear. However, it may increase feelings of isolation and impair identity development.

Participants described relationships as risky and costly. A focus on risks and costs made participants reluctant to establish relationships, and may have discouraged others from initiating relationships with them (East, 1989).

> Intimacy means that people know my weak spots and they can take advantage of that (Corbett, 1995).

> If I ask them then they're doing me a favour and I'm beholden to them and I'm going to have to come across. With my mother, what did I have to do? I had to come across sexually. I had to pay a big price. I'm just convinced that I will always have to pay the full price, whatever that happens to be (Miller, in progress).

All participants reported disrupted sexual development. A tendency to over-sexualize relationships, difficulties with touching, equating sex with intimacy and love, sexual dysfunction, and using sex to meet nonsexual needs interfered with the development of both platonic and romantic relationships. Several noted the loss of normal sexual experiences and activities during adolescence. This contributed to feeling out of sync with peers.

> My dad was never available [emotionally or physically] because he was an alcoholic. So when he did start abusing me sexually, I associated love and sex. I was finally getting some attention from this man. One thing that I learned during the sexual abuse was that I have to be a sexual person to be loved (Corbett, 1995).

Several participants noted that their beliefs and perceptions had changed in the process of healing. While still cautious, they were more willing to take risks. But, they felt ill-equipped and lacked pre-requisite skills and knowledge for intimate relating.

> I've really missed out on something here and I don't even know what I've all missed out on. I know parts of it because I have watched movies. I have read books. I have occasionally seen two people who I thought loved each other and cared for each other and so I've got a bit of a dim view of what this is all suppose to be about. But I really don't have a good idea (Miller, in progress).

Affective distortions and deficits in emotional development were one of the major impediments to intimacy. Many participants numbed their feelings or dissociated in order to cope with the abuse and the negative feelings about themselves. They had difficulty understanding their own and other people's emotional needs and reactions, and expressing emotions appropriately.

> Like in conflicts with my wife, if we get into an argument, I'll [click out]. It's disastrous because I'm not there any more, I'm not understanding what she's upset about. I'm not sensing her upsetness. We get no resolution. If anyone begins to display their displeasure or dissatisfaction ... I click out (Miller, in progress).

Participants talked about how these difficulties affected current relationships. They may have also impacted earlier relationships. Empathy is a major component of intimacy (Paul & White, 1990), and reading emotional cues is critical for successful social interaction (Malatesta, 1988).

In summary, participants identified a variety of ways in which the effects associated with sexual abuse and their childhood environments impeded their ability to develop satisfying, intimate relationships. They described beliefs and expectations about others, themselves, and relationships that led to emotional and physical distancing from others and the development of maladaptive social behaviours. They described how a childhood of unhealthy relationships resulted in limited social skills and knowledge, and a profound sense of not knowing how to relate to others. Distorted sexual development impaired intimate relating in both platonic and romantic sexual relationships. A number of questions remain. To what extent are these types of distortions related specifically to child sexual abuse? Are there cohort effects? Only one participant received treatment as a child, and most disclosed their abuse during a time of limited acceptance or public awareness. Participants described how the lack of response by adults reinforced their negative beliefs.

SOCIAL DEVELOPMENT OF ADOLESCENTS SEXUALLY ABUSED AS CHILDREN

Hay, Berg, and Safnuk (1995) addressed some of these questions in a study that examined social development in 11 adolescents aged 13 to 18 years who were sexually abused as children. Adolescence involves the construction of new strategies for coping with changes in interpersonal relationships and for redefining the self in response to new biological, emotional, and social realities (Brion-Meisels & Selman, 1984). Intense friendships, romance, and sexual experimentation are critical components of adolescence. Data from the adults suggest that the meaning of these experiences may be different for survivors as compared to their non-abused peers, and the strategies that they construct to cope with them may also be different.

Hay, Berg, and Safnuk (1995) assessed a range of social skills, knowledge, and reasoning using self and parent report measures and semi-structured interviews. Nonabused clinical and nonabused nonclinical control groups were included. There were no statistically significant group differences in terms of social skills, knowledge, or reasoning. Youth in the sexually abused group, however, perceived themselves to be significantly less popular and well-liked than did youth in the control groups. Their self-perceptions were supported by parent ratings. It is not clear from this data whether they actually experience more peer rejection or simply perceive themselves to be less well-liked. A qualitative analysis of the interviews revealed differences in the youths' ability to reason about hypothetical situations and their lived experiences. The youth knew what they should do, but were unable to do it. The youth eloquently described the difficulties they have had overcoming their beliefs and expectations that others are untrustworthy and that intimacy is dangerous, and how these beliefs affected their ability to develop close friendships.

> If people ask me a question I usually ask them a question back, I don't really talk. And that's really a barrier for me in forming friendships because most of the time I really want to. I just want to know them (and) have them know me. If there is a problem that I can help them with I'll help them, but they don't step in on my territory (Female, 18 years).

> [Why is trust important in close friendships?] There has to be a sense of knowing, or at least believing that you are not going to be trampled and squished and torn to pieces (Male, 18 years).

There was evidence that, like the adults, the adolescents associated intimacy with risk.

> [What does being a friend for a long time do?] When it [time] strengths it [the friendship] sometimes that can be damaging as well. If you get to be good enough friends with someone, I would think you want to trust someone, you want to let them know more about you and often you tell them things that are really, really important to you, and they are not to the other person and the other person may start thinking "What a drip!" Alternatively you could tell them something that shocks them out of their shells like you were sexually abused ... maybe the other person can't handle that ... so strengthening can be damaging as well (Male, 18 years).

Like the adults, some of youth in the sexually abused group had difficulty recognizing close relationships.

> Like the very best friend I had in the world used to be my roommate, so I don't know if I would classify her as a friend or not. We were talking about this the other day and it never occurred to me that I could actually call her a friend. I'm not sure ... like I spent last night with her and we were just chatting a lot about everything and it was really comfortable, like I feel really comfortable around (her) so I guess I'd call her a friend but I don't know if I really would. I'm not sure to me what a friend would be (Female, 18 years).

In summary, these findings provide further support that survivors of child sexual abuse may develop perceptions of others and relationships that negatively impact upon their ability to form close, satisfying relationships. Fear and distrust may stop them even when they have the knowledge and skills to effectively engage in intimate interactions. The youth described extreme difficulty relating to peers. The success with which these young people will be able to accomplish the developmental tasks related to intimacy may depend on the extent to which they can change their perceptions and expectations and use their newly gained knowledge to engage with others. Negative perceptions of others and relationships were not unique to survivors of child sexual abuse. Youth, in the clinical control group, who had experienced physical and emotional abuse, held similar beliefs. The specific distortions related to sexuality that the adults described may be specific to sexual abuse. This question could not be addressed as the youth in the sexually abused group were not willing to discuss these issues.

IMPLICATIONS FOR RESEARCH AND SOCIAL POLICY DEVELOPMENT

The results of these studies suggest that distorted views of self, other, and relationships may negatively impact upon the development of intimate relationships through the life span. The studies are limited by small sample sizes, and retrospective and cross-sectional designs. Further research employing longitudinal designs, and both self and other report (parents/guardians, acquaintances, friends) as well as observational measures is needed. Not all survivors will be affected and not all in the same way. Studies examining factors related to resiliency will be critical in designing effective prevention and treatment programs.

The research available suggests that sexual abuse poses a significant risk to social-emotional development and the establishment and maintenance of healthy relationships in childhood, adolescence, and adulthood. The consequences reach far beyond the individual survivor. Poor peer relations in childhood are associated with increased risk for dropping out of school, delinquency, adult criminality, mental health problems in later life, and marital and occupational difficulties (Parker & Asher, 1987). A comprehensive national policy on child sexual abuse is needed. Combating child sexual abuse requires a coordinated effort by the various departments and levels of government responsible for children and families, and a policy that recognizes the multidimensional nature and effects of abuse.

Prevention, in terms of stopping the occurrence of child sexual abuse, must be given high priority in policy development. However, there is a need for tertiary prevention directed at assisting victims in coping with the potential adverse effects of abuse. The development of an integrated policy for the assessment of survivors and provision of treatment and follow-up services is needed. Services should be available to survivors and families not only at disclosure and immediately after, but at all subsequent critical developmental junctures. Supporting survivors in negotiating the developmental tasks of each period will promote continued success and adaption. This is does not necessarily mean continuous, long-term treatment, but rather developmentally sequenced treatment programs, where level of intervention is determined by need at each period (James, 1989). Little research has assessed the effectiveness of therapeutic interventions for survivors. Exactly what services should be provided when is unclear. Funding for the development and evaluation of intervention programs is needed. Studies that design and target interventions to address the sequelae associated with specific developmental issues will be particularly useful (Cicchetti et al., 1988). Research should be grounded in developmental theory and employ developmentally appropriate assessment and evaluation tools.

Victims' perceptions of self, others, and relationships and the effects of these perceptions on the development of close relationships at each developmental period are critical areas for assessment and intervention. Particular challenges confront survivors during adolescence. The developmental push during adolescence for increased trust, self-disclosure, reciprocity, autonomy, and physical intimacy creates a powerful dilemma for adolescent survivors who struggle to be accepted by peers and yet associate intimacy with risk and danger. Adolescence may be a critical time for increased support.

The difficulties the adult male survivors experienced in loving and nurturing their own children were particularly poignant. Research examining the impact of child sexual abuse on boys has lagged behind that of girls, partly because it was thought uncommon, and partly because it was doubted that it had a significant effect (Watkins & Bentovim, 1992). Recent research indicates that the rate of sexual abuse in boys is much higher than previously thought; surveys of men in the general population suggest that 3 to 9% of men are sexually victimized as children (Finkelhor, 1984) and research belies the idea that boys are not affected by abuse (Watkins & Bentovim, 1992). Social policy needs to recognize that boys and men are also victims of abuse. It can work to counteract social attitudes that affect under-reporting by males (homophobia, the perception of that males enjoy all forms of sexual contact). Of particular concern is the divergence in referrals for boys and girls in adolescence, with the referral of boys dropping significantly (Cupoli & Sewell, 1988). By increasing awareness of the sexual victimization of males, and by providing therapeutic services specifically designed to meet the needs of male survivors, social policy can make a significant contribution to enhancing the lives of male survivors and their families.

More research on gender differences in terms of impact and therapeutic needs is required. Such research needs to be grounded in theory and an understanding of gender-specific socialization practices, and cultural attitudes and stereotypes. How do socialization practices and social constructions of gender influence the impact of sexual abuse for male and female survivors? How do the different social environments of males and females enhance or impede healing?

Increased programming to support survivors in their roles as parents is needed. Variables such as maternal unavailability, marital conflict and violence, and a child's poor relationship with parents increase the likelihood that a child will be sexually abused (Finkelhor & Baron, 1986; Paveza, 1988). These findings suggest that intergenerational transmission of child sexual abuse may not be direct (victims do not necessarily become victimizers), but indirect (Alexander, 1992). Survivors' sexual abuse may affect their ability to nurture and relate to their children. This may place the children at-risk for attachment disorders and lead to a host adaptational challenges, including sexual abuse. Assisting survivors when they are establishing their own families reduces the likelihood that effects of their sexual abuse will be passed to the next generation.

Increases in treatment funding for survivors should not occur at the expense of funding for prevention programs or services for offenders. The elimination of child sexual abuse requires a multi-faceted approach that includes primary, secondary, and tertiary prevention. A well-conceived social policy on child sexual abuse is particularly important during times of fiscal restraint. Clearly defining goals and priorities is imperative to thoughtful fiscal decision-making.

References

Alexander, P. (1992). Application of attachment theory to the study of sexual abuse. *Journal of Consulting and Clinical Psychology, 60,* 185–195.

Badgley, R. (1984). *Sexual offenses against children* (Report of the Committee on Sexual Offenses Against Children and Youths). Ottawa: Canadian Government Publishing Centre.

Beitchman, J., Zucker, J., DaCosta, G., Akman, D., & Cassavia, E. (1992). A review of the long-term effects of child sexual abuse. *Journal of Child Abuse and Neglect, 16,* 101–118.

Bowlby, J. (1982). *Attachment and loss* (Vol. 1). New York: Basic Books. (Original published in 1969).

Bretherton, I., & Waters, E. (1985). *Growing points in attachment theory and research: Monographs of the Society for Child Development, 50,* (Serial No. 209), 66–104.

Brion-Meisels, S., & Selman, R. (1984). Early adolescent development of new interpersonal strategies: Understanding and intervention. *Social Psychology Review, 13,* 278–291.

Cicchetti, D., Troth, S., & Bush, M. (1988). Developmental psychopathology and incompetence in childhood: Suggestions for intervention. In B. Leahy & A. Kazdin (Eds.), *Advances in clinical child psychology* (Vol. 11, pp. 1–71). New York: Plenum.

Cole, P., & Putnam, F. (1992). Effect of incest on self and social functioning: A developmental psychopathology perspective. *Journal of Consulting and Clinical Psychology, 60* (2), 174–184.

Cole, P., & Woolger, C. (1989). Incest survivors: The relationship of their perceptions of their parents and their own parenting attitudes. *Child Abuse and Neglect, 13,* 409–416.

Corbett, L. (1995). Self and other representations in women who have been sexually abused as children: A qualitative approach. Unpublished doctoral dissertation. University of Saskatchewan.

Cupoli, J., & Sewell, P. (1988). 1059 children with a chief complaint of sexual abuse. *Child Abuse and Neglect, 12,* 151–162.

East, P. (1989). Early adolescents' perceived interpersonal risks and benefits: Relations to social support and psychological functioning. *Journal of Early Adolescence, 9,* 374- 395.

Finkelhor, D. (1984). *Child sexual abuse: New theory and research.* New York: Free Press.

Finkelhor, D., & Baron, L. (1986). Risk factors of child sexual abuse. *Journal of Interpersonal Violence, 1,* 43–71.

Finkelhor, D., & Browne, A. (1988). Assessing the long-term impact of child sexual abuse: A review and conceptualization. In L. Walker (Ed.), *Handbook on sexual abuse of children* (pp. 55–71). New York: Springer.

Friedrich, W. (1988). Behavioral problems in sexually abused children: An adaptational perspective. In G. Wyatt & G. Johnson Powell (Eds.), *Lasting effects of child sexual abuse* (pp. 171–192). Newbury Park, CA: Sage.

Harter, S., Alexander, P., & Neimeyer, R.A. (1988). Long-term effects of incestuous child abuse in college women: Social adjustment, social cognition, and family characteristics. *Journal of Consulting and Clinical Psychology, 56,* 5–8.

Hartup, W. (1983). Peer relations. In P.H. Mussen (Ed.), *Handbook of child psychology* (Vol. 4, pp. 103–196). New York: Wiley.

Hartup, W. (1989). Social relations and their developmental significance. *American Psychologist, 44,* 120–126.

Hay, D., Berg, L., & Safnuk, T. (1995, March). Social development of adolescents sexually abused as children. Poster session presented at the Biennial Meeting of the Society for Research in Child Development, Indianapolis, IN.

James, B. (1989). *Treating traumatized children: New insights and creative interventions.* Lexington, MA: Lexington Books.

Janoff-Bulman, R. (1992). *Shattered assumptions: Towards a new psychology of trauma.* New York: The Free Press.

Kendall-Tackett, K., Meyer Williams, L., & Finkelhor, D. (1993). Impact of sexual abuse on children: A review and synthesis of recent empirical studies. *Psychological Bulletin, 113,* 164–180.

Malatesta, C. (1988). The role of emotions in the development and organization of personality. In R. Thompson (Ed.), *Nebraska symposium of motivation: Socioemotional development* (pp. 1–55). Lincoln, NE: University of Nebraska Press.

Miller, C. (in progress). The long-term affects of child sexual abuse on male survivors. Doctoral dissertation in progress. University of Saskatchewan.

Paul, E., & White, K. (1990). The development of intimate relationships in late adolescence. *Adolescence, 25,* 375–400.

Parker, J., & Asher, S. (1987). Peer relations and later personal adjustment: Are low-accepted children at-risk? *Psychological Bulletin, 102,* 357–389.

Paveza, G. (1988). Risk factors in father-daughter child sexual abuse. *Journal of Interpersonal Violence, 3,* 290–306.

Reisman, J. (1985). Friendship and its implications for mental health or social competence. *Journal of Early Adolescence, 5,* 383–391.

Rogers, R. (1990). *Reaching for solutions. The summary report of the special advisor to the Minister of National Health and Welfare on child sexual abuse in Canada.* Ottawa: National Clearinghouse on Family Violence, Health and Welfare Canada.

Sullivan, H. (1953). *The interpersonal theory of psychiatry.* New York: Norton.

Watkins, B., & Bentovim, A. (1992). The sexual abuse of male children and adolescents: A review of current research. *Journal of Child Psychology and Psychiatry, 33,* 197–248.

This research was supported by Saskatchewan Health Services Utilization and Research Commission, The University of Saskatchewan President's SSHRC Fund, and The University of Saskatchewan Women's Studies Research Unit.

29

Family, Academic, Peer and Individual Influences on the Formation of Intimacy during the First Year of University

Gerald R. Adams, Bruce A. Ryan, Leo J. Keating,
Sheila Marshall and Maria Ketsetzis

The transition from adolescence to young adulthood highlights the important role of the social context in understanding individual development (Silbereisen & Todt, 1994). The potential interplay of family, school, and peer relations on individual differences and development are apparent as the adolescent leaves the parental household, develops (or is expected to develop) new peer and romantic relationships, and enters the work force and/or the post-secondary education system. No single institution or set of social relationships is responsible for assisting and guiding a youth in the move toward financial and social independence. Reviews of research (Pascarella & Terenzini, 1991) recognize the important influences of faculty and student relations, diversity of experience, individual motivations and commitments, independence in thinking or emotional well-being, and intellectual ability in predicting psychosocial development during the transition from adolescence to adulthood. Unfortunately, the role of family has mostly been ignored as young people enter university. However, recent social changes, such as living at home for longer periods of time to attain more education to secure employment, stimulates increased concern about prolonged family influences on older adolescents and young adults. Therefore, the family as well as, faculty, and student-peer relational systems may influence psychosocial development. Further, aspects of decision-making strategies, selection of goals and commitments, and development of emotional autonomy, as individual characteristics, are influenced by socialization experiences within these relational systems. These individual characteristics are part of the person-in-context that comes to either form or not form intimate relationships with others.

Close relationships were identified in this study as the target behaviours of intimacy and social relations; they are encircled with varying layers of influences that are arranged along a proximal-distal dimension. Individual characteristics, such as decision-making styles, the making of goals and commitments, and degree of emotional autonomy, are a set of variables adjacent to the target behaviours which have a close association with the psychosocial process of creating intimate and social relations. The next level (or distal) set of variables involve the university relational system and includes relations with faculty members, advisors, students, and peers. It is mostly within this context that young adults interact and experience the social contacts that allow for the discovery of friends, lovers, and new peer acquaintances outside of the family. Finally, the family relational system comprises the most distant set of variables. Like the university relational system, the family provides a context for expression, debate, conflict and compromise, but is less central than the university environment for meeting new age-mates during the transition from adolescence to young adulthood. An analogue to the Family/Schools Relationships Model (Ryan & Adams, 1995) was proposed and tested to determine the complexity and range of influences on young adult interpersonal development. The model was tested using correlational and linear structural equation modelling techniques. Pertinent findings are presented in this chapter.

METHOD

Data were taken from an ongoing longitudinal study of the role of family and peer processes on academic performance and psychosocial development (Adams & Ryan, 1994). First year data were solicited from a randomly drawn list of 800 students who were recently admitted into one of four degree programs at the University of Guelph. Returned surveys were obtained from 351 first year entry students. Complete data, appropriate for these analyses, were available from 212 (70 males and 142 females) first-year students. Subjects with no experience in having an intimate close relationship were excluded from the analyses. Ninety-six percent of the sample was between 18 and 20 years old.

Close relationships. Items from the Student Developmental Task and Lifestyle Inventory (Winston & Miller, 1987) were adapted for use in this study. Responses were obtained using a true or false format.

Intimacy in relations with a partner was measured by items such as: My partner and I regularly discuss or make plans on how we will spend our time together; Within the past twelve months I have successfully resolved a major disagreement with my partner. Importance of social relations was measured by items such as: I find relationships with my close friends not as important to me as they were a year ago; Within the past year there have been a number of occasions when I was mistaken about the closeness of a relationship. Items measuring intimacy and the importance of social relations were assessed using a true or false response format.

Individual characteristics. Emotional autonomy (Winston & Miller, 1987) included items such as: I seldom express my opinion in groups if I think they will be controversial or different from what others believe; I seldom bounce ideas off other people in order to obtain their views of my thinking. The true and false format was employed. Measures of diffuse-avoidant decision-making style were drawn from the Identity Styles Inventory (Berzonsky, 1989). These items measure a cognitive strategy of avoiding decision-making or remaining highly diffused in responses. Example items were: I'm not really sure what I'm doing in school; I guess things will work themselves out; Many times by not concerning myself with personal problems, they work themselves out. The Identity Styles Inventory also includes several items measuring the establishment of commitments. Sample items included in this study were: Regarding religious beliefs, I know basically what I believe and don't believe; I know what I want to do with my future; I have some consistent political views; I have a definite stand on where the government and country should be headed. The items measuring decision-making and commitment were responded to on a five point scale from not at all like me through very much like me.

University relational system. Single items were used to measure relationships within the program of the student's major. Respondents were asked to respond to statements using five point scales to characterize each of the following relationships: Relationship with other students in the program in which you are enroled; Relationships with faculty members in your program; Relationships with advisors and other officials in your program. End points of the scales included reserved, competitive, uninvolved, sense of alienation versus supportive, friendly, sense of belonging for other students; remote, difficult, impersonal, discouraging versus approachable, helpful, understanding, encouraging for faculty members; and remote, discouraging, unsympathetic versus approachable, helpful, open-minded for advisors and other officials. Degree of involvement with scholastic peers was measured by several true or false items from a questionnaire by Pace (1966). Example items were: Student government is more concerned with academic than with social affairs; A lecture by an outstanding scientist would be poorly attended.

Family relational system. Characteristics of the family system were measured by two subscales of the Family Environment Scale (Moos & Moos, 1976). Family expressiveness was measured by such items as: Family members often keep their feelings to themselves; We say anything we want to around home. Family conflict was measured by items such as: We fight a lot in our family; Family members hardly ever lose their tempers; Family members often criticize each other. Items were responded to on a five point scale from (1) never to (5) always.

RESULTS

Means, standard deviations, estimates of internal consistency, and the simple correlation matrix are available upon request. Standardized coefficients for each predictive relationship between the variables specified from the Family/University Relational Systems Model were determined using LISREL. Values of less than .10 in the initial just-identified model were set to zero in the over-identified model reported here. This last step produced a nonsignificant chi-square goodness of fit (X^2 (26) = 15.24, $p < .95$) and a goodness of fit index of .987. The significant (but modest) standardized coefficients are included in Figure 29.1.

The over-identified model presented in Figure 29.1 has 18 significant pathways with all levels (or classes of variables) making some contribution to the predictive outcomes. Only one individual characteristic predicts intimacy in relationships. That is, having the ability to establish a commitment is predictive of intimacy in relations (beta = .16). Two other direct effects are observed on intimacy. Having a conflictual family (gamma = -.10) and being

Figure 29.1: Over-Identified Model

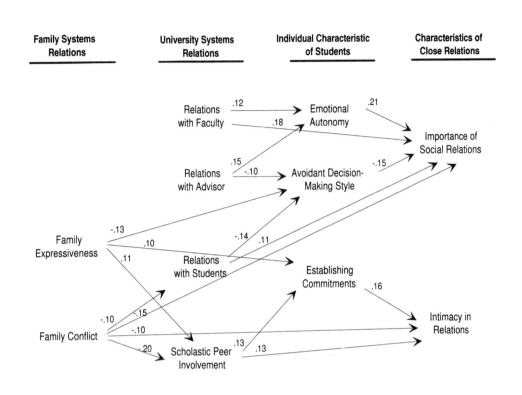

involved with scholastic-oriented peers (beta = .13) have negative and positive influences, respectively, on intimacy formation. Indirect effects are also observed. Family expressiveness positively influences the establishment of commitments (gamma = .10) and involvement with scholastic peers (gamma = .10). In turn, peer involvement not only has a direct effect (beta = .13) on intimacy formation, but an indirect effect on intimacy through the connection between peer involvement and establishment of commitments (beta = .13). Finally, family conflict is a negative influence on involvement with scholastic peers (gamma = -.20) and in turn, effects on intimacy formation through peer involvement and the establishment of commitments. The general pattern for intimacy formation is that family expressiveness enhances the establishment of commitments and scholastic peer involvement. In turn, commitments and peer involvement enhance intimacy in relations. In contrast, family conflict has a negative direct effect on intimacy and indirect effects through its negative association with peer involvement and the additional associations of peer involvement with commitments and intimacy.

The importance of social relations to young adults is directly influenced by each remaining class of variables. Avoidant decision-making style (beta = -.15) has a negative influence on social relations and the formation of emotional autonomy has a positive influence (beta = .21). Other direct effects include positive relations with faculty (beta = .18) and students (beta = .11) and negative influences through family conflict (gamma = -.15). A number of indirect effects are also observed. These effects are mediated through either an avoidant decision-making style or the level of emotional autonomy of the student. Avoidant decision-making style, which has a negative influence on the importance of social relations, is predicted by family expressiveness (gamma = -.13), relationships with advisor (beta = -.10) and with students (beta = -.14). Further, family conflict is a negative influence on relations with students (gamma = -.10) while student relations hold a negative association with avoidant decision-making. Again, family expressiveness has productive influences on the importance of social relations by young adults, while family conflict has negative direct and indirect influences. Family, faculty, advisors, and classmates all influence the establishment of young adults' views of the importance of social relations. Family expressiveness and conflict had no direct or indirect effect on the development of emotional autonomy; however, relations with faculty and advisors did predict emotional autonomy, and indirectly through emotional autonomy the development of a positive attitude about the importance of social relations.

DISCUSSION

The findings indicate that expressive and open families facilitate their young adult children's ability to establish commitments while discouraging the use of an avoidant style of decision-making. Further, expressive families appear to encourage involvement with scholastic peers while in college, perhaps due to the expressive and open nature of intellectually-oriented students. All of the indirect effects of family expressiveness are enhancing of other influences on intimacy formation. Family expressiveness, however, has no direct effect on the target outcomes in this study. In contrast, family conflict has a broad negative direct and indirect effect on close relationship formation.

Family and faculty influences are unassociated in their influences on the characteristics of close relationships among young adults. This is consistent with the notion that families and schools are worlds apart (Epstein & Lee, 1995). Families do have influences on peer relations in this investigation. For example, family conflict has a negative influence on establishing positive relationships with other students and becoming involved with scholastic-oriented peers. The university relational system mainly has indirect effects through decision-making style, commitments, and emotional autonomy. Different aspects of the university relational system have different indirect effects on close relationships. Positive relations with advisors and students, which are likely to be filled with intimate personal discussion, decrease the likelihood of using a diffused and avoidant decision-making style. Within the university context only involvement with scholastic-oriented student-peers facilitates the establishment of commitments. Making important commitments to goals and establishing a purpose or meaning to life may be one primary influence that comes from involvement with scholastic peers.

Building a sense of emotional autonomy during the college years is not influenced by family effects, but by relationships that emerge with faculty and advisors. Perhaps conversations, discussions, debates, and decision-making with these university officials promote a sense of standing on one's own and defending a self-perspective that enhances emotional autonomy. Finally, individuals that use an avoidant decision-making style are unlikely to come to view the importance of social relations as central to their well-being. However, developing a strong sense of emotional autonomy, which is likely to be an expression of emotional independence and self-worth, enhances the importance of belonging. Intimacy, in contrast, is only likely to come within close relationships after one is ready to establish commitments. This investigation offers one illustration of what can be gained by using a relational systems context in understanding human behaviour. The importance of many social roles (family, teachers, advisors, student-peers) to the ultimate social well-being of an individual has been illustrated here. Yet little is know about the complex relational systems that influence adolescents on their way to young adulthood. This study indicates that families provide a foundation of development. Teachers, advisors and peers hold their own influence and mediate parental or family influences on social development. Social policy needs to recognize the extensive implications of intergenerational, direct and indirect effects, that can occur from the treatment of one generation and the influences that might occur through a given policy on the next generation.

Educational environments that provide and encourage a strong scholastic and healthy competitive focus will influence stronger intellectual development as well as have a secondary influence on psychosocial development. Educational systems are influencing the social well-being of students as well as employability through educational preparation. While academic training provides the intellectual skills for employment, individual characteristics determine success. For example, employability is determined not only by training but also the ability to relate with and cooperatively work for others. These findings are re-assuring in that the family and school contexts can be supported and facilitated to enhance a sense of belonging and the need for social relationships. Belonging reduces a sense of social alienation and social relationships provide support and assistance in coping that, in turn, reduces or minimizes stress. Thus, families, schools, and peers can promote positive social development during the transition from adolescence to adulthood.

References

Adams, G.R., & Ryan, B.A. (1994). Family and school influences on identity development in adolescence. A research grant funded by the Social Sciences and Humanities Research Council, Ottawa, Canada.

Berzonsky, M.D. (1989). Identity style: Conceptualization and measurement. *Journal of Adolescent Research, 4*, 268–282.

Epstein, J.L., & Lee, S. (1995). National patterns of school and family connections in the middle grades. In B.A. Ryan, G.R. Adams, T.P. Gullotta, R.P. Weissberg & R.L. Hampton (Eds.), *The family-school connection: theory, research and practice* (pp. 108–154). Newbury Park, CA: Sage Publications.

Moos, R., & Moos, B.S. (1976). Typology of family social environments. *Family Process, 15,* 357–371.

Pace, R. (1966). *College and university environment scales technical manual.* Princeton, NJ: Educational Testing Service.

Pascarella, E.T., & Terenzini, P.T. (1991). *How college affects students.* San Francisco, CA: Jossey-Bass Publishers.

Ryan, B.A., & Adams, G.R. (1995). The family-school relationship model. In B.A. Ryan & G.R. Adams (Eds.), *The family-school connection: Theory, research, and practice.* Newbury Park, CA: Sage Publication, Inc.

Silbereisen, R.K., & Todt, E. (Eds.). (1994). *Adolescence in context: The interplay of family, school, peers, and work in adjustment.* New York: Springer-Verlag.

Winston, R., Jr., & Miller, T. (1987). *Student developmental task and lifestyle inventory manual.* Athens, GA: Student Development Associates.

This research was supported by a grant from the Social Science and Humanities Research Council of Canada.

PART V
Preparation for Responsible Community Living

30

Preparation for Responsible Community Living

Brenda Copeland, Andrew Armitage and Deborah Rutman

This group of chapters is distinguished by attention to the non–economic aspects of transition from youth to adulthood. Young people are facing this transition in a demographic and economic context of limited and changing employment opportunities and increased attention to economic rationalism. Economic rationalism concentrates attention on the labour market (Wyn, 1996). However labour market entry is only one aspect of preparation for responsible community living. Economic rationalism provides a limited view of employment and has potential to distract attention from human concerns such as life style, community living, identity and sense of belonging, interpersonal and family relationships, culture and creativity. These concerns are common themes that link these chapters together, as do the continuing struggles against inequalities based on gender, class, race, ethnic origin, ability and sexual orientation.

What is meant by preparation for responsible community living? Preparation indicates getting ready for some purpose. Responsible (the Latin origin is "a promise in return") implies an obligation and a reciprocal relationship, yet it is also used to indicate that youth are conditional members of the adult community. This conditional membership is indicated both by attention to youth obligations within responsible living and by the implicit message that youth are not already responsible community members because they need preparation. Community indicates a common set of ties and interests and is used both in the sense of a network or networks of social relations and in the macro sense of a collective whole that is able to follow agreed courses of action outside the market economy. Responsible community living includes us all.

SUMMARY OF THE RESEARCH

The existing research can be classified into five categories based on the interests that appear to direct the research enterprise. The categories are social indicator related research, social science studies of issues of social concern, youth directed studies, government contracted research, and synoptic secondary source reviews. Social indicator related research is exemplified by the attempts to establish social indicators on the state of the child (Barnhorst & Johnson, 1991) and report cards on the health and well being of youth (Center for the Study of Social Policy, 1991; National Collaboration for Youth, 1990). The focus is on an overall assessment of how a particular jurisdiction is doing, often in comparison with other regions, ethnic groups, and time. Rutman (1994) provides a critical review of this work; there are no examples of this work in this group of chapters.

Application of social science to issues of social concern is characterized by attempts to derive guidance for social intervention. An example of such is McDonald, Allen, Westerfelt and Pialvin's (1993) comprehensive review of the impact that foster care has had on the adult lives of former children in care. Adult functioning was divided into four critical outcomes: adult self sufficiency, behavioral adjustment, family and support systems, and sense of well being. Most of the papers in this section have a similar social intervention interest (Butcher, 1996; McAlpine et al., 1996; DeKeseredy, 1996; McKay et al., 1996; Kerr, 1996). The general message is that if the community understood how youth are prepared for responsible community living then policy makers and professionals would have both the support of the community and the knowledge to better assist youth.

Youth directed studies are the products of a commitment to the voice of youth. Examples are provided by participatory models of research whereby young people and adults together construct a design and conduct the research (Canadian Mental Health Association, 1992a; 1992b; Raychaba, 1993; Zammit et al., 1995). Adults and youth co–participate in varying degrees; the emphasis of the conclusions is on statements and needs of youth for values such as respect, caring, opportunities for participation, choices, responsibility, and security (Canadian Mental Health Association, 1992a; 1992b). Often there is an action orientation with an explicit message that institutional barriers must be removed for young people's participation (Beaton et al., 1994; Zammit et al., 1995). There are no examples of youth directed studies in this group of chapters but the methodologies used by Erickson, McKay and colleagues, Wood, and Kerr look for, and represent some of the voices of youth.

Two of the chapters in this section (McKay et al., 1996; Wood & Griffiths, 1996) were the results of government contracted research; government sponsors a substantial body of research with a primary management or political purpose. Government contracted studies are not published in any consistent manner; thus knowledge of how this body of literature is being used in relation to youth in transition is limited. Synoptic secondary source reviews such as Santrock's (1992) deserve mention due to the influence this literature plays in the development of knowledge, values, and assumptions regarding young people and hence on the development of policy, professional practice, and research. Santrock (1992) utilized sociological and psychological literature to describe adolescent development, often in relation to problematic behaviours. There are no examples of this type in this group of chapters.

Three principal themes emerge from chapters in this section. First is research on lifestyle or the collaborative development of leisure, sport, and physical activity and their significance for youth in transition to adulthood (Butcher, 1996; McKay et al., 1996; Kerr, 1996). Second is research on the effect of childhood experience on attitudes and coping capacity during the transition to adulthood (McAlpine et al., 1996; DeKeseredy, 1996), and the third is participant observation studies of the behaviour and social relations of youth in transition within their community (Erickson, 1996; Wood & Griffiths, 1996). Together, these principal themes illustrate the dimensions of the development of self, of the sense of belonging, and of the different social relations, and draw attention to the holistic nature of young people and communities.

IMPLICATIONS FOR CANADIAN PUBLIC POLICY

Important common themes from these chapters have implications for Canadian public policy. The first is to maintain a balance in social policies between economic rationalism and social justice. One part of that balance comes by recognizing that employment is only one of the transition points from youth to adulthood. Youth in the 1990s face life transitions in a world where many of the secure jobs have been filled by the preceding baby boom generation and similar opportunities are no longer available. Further, governments in the 1990s are faced with fiscal and political/ideological limits on the role that they can play in responding to youth. Nevertheless many of the voices of youth reveal that they are not pessimistic and wish to participate in our communities. Youth can bring initiative, generosity, and critical perspectives to communities. Policies need to be focused on youth strengths and provisions made for access to full participation. Demographic and market structural forces have created a major gap in living standards among generations. Social justice requires that the existence of this gap be recognized and collective actions organized towards reducing it.

The lifespan perspective is important for policies based on an understanding of the values and social structures that society requires to provide connections among the transitions from childhood to adolescence, and to adulthood. DeKeseredy's (1996) study of dating behaviour traces the origins of abusive behaviour to childhood patterns within boy–girl relationships; McAlpine and colleagues' (1996) study of the coping capacity of adolescent mothers traces the origins of that capacity to the behaviour of these women's parents towards them when children; and Wood and Griffiths' (1996) stark study of Inuit youth shows the severe problems that a community encounters when there is little continuity in the way of life between generations. A long-term perspective is required for social policy and its effects. Such policies and their implementation are an investment in the social infrastructure, perhaps justifiable as a means of avoiding other forms of social cost which will be incurred if these investments are not made (Coles, 1996; National Youth in Care Network, 1995).

Supportive policies are needed for youth to provide for a balanced and healthy lifestyle during the transition process to adulthood. The works of Butcher, McKay and colleagues, and Kerr indicate the importance of physical activity, satisfying leisure, and healthy lifestyle during and beyond this transition. These works point to ways in which existing use of sports related resources in communities and in schools should be revised to emphasize connections between lifestyle and health. Policy connections are needed between physical activity and health costs to support investment of social resources that contribute in a positive way to health rather than investing in medical interventions to ameliorate the loss of good health. A conclusion from McKay and colleagues (1996) is the necessity to respond to the interest and needs of youth. This suggests that programs for youth need to be designed by youth, staffed by youth, and be available where youth are. Both Erickson's (1996) study of street drug markets and youth and Wood and Griffiths' (1996) study on Inuit youth question the extent to which behaviour born of necessity or boredom is being criminalised. The criminal label has long-term consequences for youth in their access to social opportunities and has long-term costs for society by expanding a criminalized sub–culture. Both criminal policies and enforcement practices should be re-examined.

Policy cannot be devised for youth as if youth was some useful single social category. Differences in social experience determined by gender, class, race, ethnic origin, ability, sexual orientation, and rural/urban origins pervade the experiences of youth just as they do adults. These differences also provide important continuities of experience between youth and adults and are the social pathways (Wyn, 1996) through which transition from youth to adulthood occurs. Public policy and social practice need to be attentive to these pathways. The principle of equity needs to be imbedded in all social policies through continued attention to the ways in which discrimination has been perpetuated. Progress has been made in some fields but there is concern that a backlash is occurring and that gains made in the past decade may not yet be secure. Aggregate social policy conducted by governments at the federal, provincial or municipal levels will always have a tendency to categorize and homogenize social experience. Thus, it is important to provide for community development and professional practice processes which can attend to the voices of youth and to their experience. A final conclusion, principally from Wood and Griffiths' paper, is that some parts of Canadian society may need to move beyond equity of treatment and establish a separate political identity and separate political structures. The problems that have resulted from the intersection of Canadian society and Inuit society may lie beyond the ability to prevent or cure. Attempts to intervene are often more damaging than helpful. The challenge for social policy is to devise ways whereby intrusion and imposition can be reduced.

RESEARCH AGENDA

Research must be congruent with the values inherent in responsible community living, i.e., reciprocity, obligation, communities, and participation, to provide knowledge that is useful for public policy and for citizens of all ages. A commitment to congruence with these values raises several methodological issues. Research and public policy are political and value laden endeavours. Inherent in responsible community living and in research with communities are the challenges of voicing, hearing, understanding, and acting across differences. Youth voices compete with power and political forces within research and public policy arenas. Partnerships with young people require opening doors and removing barriers for collaboration and understanding. Some researchers and communities have begun to act on the assumption that young people have unique knowledge gained through their own experience and that only through direct partnership relations can young people's voices be heard. The experiences and voices of youth must be involved and visible in the research for researchers, practitioners, and policy makers to fully understand the needs of youth. Research models that have been primarily qualitative in nature, such as participatory action models of research (Beaton et al., 1995; Canadian Mental Health Association, 1992a; 1992b; Zammit et al., 1995), phenomenological models (Burke, 1994; Jones, 1994) and ethnographic inquiries (Artz, 1994), have resulted in the most successful youth-adult partnership ventures in which youth voices are visible in the processes and products of the research.

Furthermore, thoughtful considerations must be given to dissemination of research and policy documents in accessible forms to bring about research and policy connections. Commitment needs to be shown by researchers to continue to research with young people, communities, government, and others as a cooperative enterprise that is driven by the values of reciprocity and obligation. Commitment to research as a cooperative enterprise is not without challenges and barriers. Collaborative, participative research endeavours require time and resources and are contrary to pressures for short-term results. Data collection and analysis require an evaluation, from the different perspectives of those involved, of the type and use of methods employed. Clarity in the mandate and ownership of the research is required to address the challenges in fulfilling the obligations of collaboration created by differences in the relations among research institutions, government, community, and young people.

Five content areas require further research. First, attention is required to the definition of responsible community living. Inquiries examining the transition to adulthood require attention to the concerns of individuals, family, and community rather than solely a focus on labour market entry. Examination of the development of self, of the sense of belonging, and of the different social relations within communities contribute to a holistic appreciation of the transition processes and pathways. Second, how do younger children's experiences and learning opportunities prepare them for life transitions? Awareness programs in relation to healthy lifestyle and abusive relationships are not enough (Butcher, 1996; DeKeseredy, 1996). Useful knowledge would be derived from chronicling the development, implementation, and evaluation of programs designed to help children develop skills and attitudes for respectful and safe relationships across genders and to develop a satisfying lifestyle. Third, descriptions and evaluation of current youth-related programs are needed to highlight community work that often goes unnoticed. Examining current successes, lessons learned, and participant/program provider experiences is necessary to inform the development of new programs. Four, acknowledgment and better understanding of the diversity of youth is required. This includes examining the advantages and disadvantages that are present lifelong as well as understanding those normally not given attention, such as gay and lesbian youth or young people with differing abilities. And fifth, accessing and utilizing today's communication technologies such as the Internet or the SCREAM Youth Rights Network (Canadian Youth Foundation, 1994) is required to increase understanding of the current and future communities that we will be sharing with upcoming generations.

References

Artz, S. (1994). Violence in our schools and the violent school girl. In H. Coward, (Ed.), *Anger in our city: Youth seeking meaning* (pp. 1–66). Victoria, BC: University of Victoria, Centre for Studies in Religion and Society.

Barnhorst, R., & Johnson, L. (Eds.). (1991). *The state of the child in Ontario.* Toronto: Oxford University Press.

Beaton, C., Lapointe, J., McGinty,R., Meier, M., Miegon, S., Keller, D., & McAdam, J. (1994). *Phase 1: Child and youth advocacy initiative*. Victoria, BC: Community Social Planning Council of Greater Victoria.

Burke, S.J. (1994). *Is there someone there? Support in the lives of adolescent sexual offenders*. Unpublished master's thesis, University of Victoria, Victoria, British Columbia.

Butcher, J. (1996). Facilitating physical activity participation among young adults. In B. Galaway & J. Hudson (Eds.), *Youth in transition: Perspectives on research and policy*. Toronto: Thompson Educational Publishing.

Canadian Mental Health Association (1992a). *Bridging the gap: Goals for the development of youth policy*. Ottawa, ON: Author.

Canadian Mental Health Association (1992b). *Changing the way things work: Young people's guide to social action*. Ottawa, ON: Author.

Canadian Youth Foundation (1994). *Scream: Youth rights network*. Ottawa, ON: Author.

Center for the Study of Social Policy (1991). *Kids count data book*. Washington, DC: Author.

Coles, B. (1996). Youth transitions in the United Kingdom: A review of recent research. In B. Galaway & J. Hudson (Eds.), *Youth in transition: Perspectives on research and policy*. Toronto: Thompson Educational Publishing.

DeKeseredy, W. (1996). Woman abuse in Canadian university and college dating relationships: The contribution of physical, sexual, and psychological victimization in elementary and high-school courtship. In B. Galaway & J. Hudson (Eds.), *Youth in transition: Perspectives on research and policy*. Toronto: Thompson Educational Publishing.

Erickson, P. (1996). Youthful involvement in illicit street drug markets: Avenues for prosperity or roads to crime? In B. Galaway & J. Hudson (Eds.), *Youth in transition: Perspectives on research and policy*. Toronto: Thompson Educational Publishing.

Jones, D. (1994). *The voice of the child: The experience of former youth-in-care in having their views heard*. Unpublished master's thesis, University of Victoria, Victoria, British Columbia.

Kerr, G. (1996). The role of sport in preparing youth for adulthood. In B. Galaway & J. Hudson (Eds.), *Youth in transition: Perspectives on research and policy*. Toronto: Thompson Educational Publishing.

McAlpine, D., Grindstaff, C., & Sorenson, A. (1996). Competence and control in the transition from adolescence to adulthood: A longitudinal study of teenage mothers. In B. Galaway & J. Hudson (Eds.), *Youth in transition: Perspectives on research and policy*. Toronto: Thompson Educational Publishing.

McDonald, T.P., Allen, R.I., Westerfelt, A., & Piliavin, I. (1993). *Assessing the long-term effects of foster care: A research synthesis* (Special Report Series No. 57). Madison, WI: Institute for Research on Poverty, University of Wisconsin.

McKay, S., Reid, I., Tremblay, M., & Pelletier, R. (1996). The impact of recreation on youth in transition to adulthood: A focus on youth-at-risk. In B. Galaway & J. Hudson (Eds.), *Youth in transition: Perspectives on research and policy*. Toronto: Thompson Educational Publishing.

National Collaboration for Youth (1990). *Making the grade: A report card on American youth*. Washington, DC: Author.

National Youth in Care Network (1995). *Gambling with our lives*. Ottawa, ON: Author.

Raychaba, B. (1993). *Pain ... lots of pain*. Ottawa, ON: National Youth in Care Network.

Rutman, D. (1994). *Child and youth status report cards: Do they make the grade?* unpublished paper. Victoria, BC: University of Victoria.

Santrock, J. (1992). *Life-span development* (4th ed.). Dubuque, Iowa: Wm. C. Brown.

Wood, D., & Griffiths, C. (1996). The lost generation: Inuit youth in transition to adulthood. In B. Galaway & J. Hudson (Eds.), *Youth in transition: Perspectives on research and policy*. Toronto: Thompson Educational Publishing.

Wyn, J. (1996). Youth in transition to adulthood in Australia: Review of research and policy issues. In B. Galaway & J. Hudson (Eds.), *Youth in transition: Perspectives on research and policy*. Toronto: Thompson Educational Publishing.

Zammit, S., Goldberg, M., & Rutman, D. (1995). *Profiles of the "youth well-being" project*. Victoria, BC: University of Victoria.

31

Facilitating Physical Activity Participation Among Young Adults

Janice Butcher

An important aspect of responsible community living is responsibility for one's own health and well-being. Physical activity can make important contributions to physical and mental health and is a valuable strategy for assisting youth in becoming responsible adults.

The time of transition to adulthood, however, is a time of decreased participation in physical activity. This chapter is a review of the research on physical activity and describes a prospective study in progress. It outlines the benefits of physical activity, prevalence of physical activity for this age group, research on determinants of physical activity, and effectiveness of interventions that have been used to increase activity. It concludes with strategies for facilitating physical activity during this important transitional period.

BENEFITS OF PHYSICAL ACTIVITY

Governments and institutions are looking for preventative measures to lower health expenditures. Physical activity has potential for improving the health of the general population and has been advocated as a public health strategy (Sallis & McKenzie, 1991; McGinnis, 1992). The 1992 International Consensus Symposium on Physical Activity, Fitness, and Health provided a comprehensive analysis of the effects of physical activity on 21 body systems and tissues, and 24 diseases and conditions (Bouchard et al., 1994). The 1993 International Consensus Conference on Physical Activity for Adolescents concluded that "physical activity has important effects on the health of adolescents, and the promotion of regular physical activity should be a priority for physicians and other health professionals" (Sallis & Patrick, 1994, p. 302). A summary of the beneficial effects of physical activity on adult physical health, all-cause mortality, and longevity is provided by Blair, Wells, Weathers and Paffenbarger (1994). Specific benefits include reduced incidence of coronary heart disease, cerebrovascular disease (stroke), non-insulin-dependent diabetes, and osteoporosis. Research supports that "regular exercise provides protection against the development of some cancers, particularly colon cancer in men and women, and breast cancer in women" (p. 47). Past thought was that these physical benefits could only be obtained from vigorous physical activity. However, there is a growing consensus that health benefits (as opposed to fitness benefits) can be derived from less intense exercise than the usual exercise prescription (Pate et al., 1995). This new lifestyle approach of cumulative moderate activity may be more appealing to inactive adults and may be easier to promote. The greatest health benefits can be derived for those who are totally inactive and this group should be targeted for physical activity.

Physical activity also has positive mental health and psychological contributions (Craig et al., 1994; Leith, 1994). Martinsen and Stephens' (1994) review concluded that various psychological benefits are associated with exercise, with the beneficial effects being best documented for depressive disorders. In addition, there is ample research and anecdotal evidence for the effects of physical activity on stress reduction and "feeling good." Positive self-esteem is an important component of psychological well-being and has been suggested as the single best variable defining emotional or life adjustment (Craig et al., 1994). Wankel and colleagues (1994) reviewed the relationship between self esteem and physical activity, and, in spite of a number of methodological weaknesses, concluded that "appropriate physical activity can lead to improvements in body-image and self-esteem" (p. 162). An increased sense of mastery and control is one of the hypothesized mechanisms for the positive effects of physical activity on self esteem. Adolescents making the transition to adulthood may have few opportunities for this sense of mastery and control and thus physical activity can have important immediate effects.

PHYSICAL ACTIVITY AMONG YOUNG ADULTS

What is the present status of physical activity participation among young adults? Most research has focused either on children's and youths' physical activity or on adult physical activity, but not on the transition. For example, Sallis' (1993) review of physical activity from 6–16 years reported a consistent decline in physical activity with age, with males decreasing about 2.7% per year and females decreasing about 7.4% per year. The 1988 Canada Fitness Survey (Stephens & Craig, 1990) provides cross-sectional data on the Canadian population from 10 to 65+ years. A general decline was found in physical activity participation from childhood to old age, based on energy expenditure. For females, the pattern of declining activity began in adolescence, while for males there was a pronounced decline only after leaving high school. The decline was steepest during the transition to young adulthood, between the 15–19 year-old group and the 20–24 year-old group (39% to 26% of females classified as "active," males 69% to 47%). Kemper's (1994) longitudinal study in Holland found a rapid decline in physical activity from ages 13–17 for both boys and girls, and only a further small decline to age 21. However, in aerobic fitness, there was a gradual decline for females from ages 13—21, while for males aerobic fitness was steady from 13—17 and then declined to age 21. Kemper (1994) suggested that switching from walking and bicycling to driving vehicles and reduced opportunities for participation in competitive sport may account for the decline in physical activity.

The International Consensus Conference on Physical Activity for Adolescents recommended two guidelines for the amount of physical activity:

> First, all adolescents should be physically active daily or nearly every day as part of their lifestyles. Second, adolescents should engage in three or more sessions per week of activities that last 20 minutes or more and that require moderate to vigorous levels of exertion. Available data suggest that the vast majority of U.S.

adolescents meet the first guideline, but only about two thirds of boys and one half of girls meet the second guideline (Sallis & Patrick, 1994, p. 302).

Are active adolescents also active adults? Studies on the relationship have had conflicting findings. An American study by Scott and Willetts (1989) compared 1300 subjects on leisure activities, including sports activities, during their high-school years and again when they were in their early fifties. The relationship was significant for women only—the greater the involvement in sports activities during adolescence, the more frequent the participation at mid-life. Dishman and Sallis (1994) concluded that participation in high-school sports and past free-living activity during childhood were not positive determinants of adult physical activity. Sallis and McKenzie's (1991) explanation for the conflict is that many studies examined team sports during youth, rather than health-related fitness behaviours; a relationship should not be expected since most adult physical activity does not involve competitive team sports.

The matter of tracking physical activity from adolescence to adulthood is currently being addressed by a prospective study. The study is designed to examine physical activity participation during the transition from late adolescence to young adulthood. The objectives are to generate a detailed profile of physical activity participation patterns during the last year of high school and then two years later, and to examine the determinants of physical activity participation of young adults. A total of 1680 students from 16 high schools in eight suburban school divisions of Winnipeg were surveyed during Fall 1994. These respondents will be resurveyed by mail two years later. Three types of physical activity were measured: a) competitive sports including intramural, inter-school, community club, private club sports, and sports played recreationally with friends; b) lessons and classes; and c) individual exercise and sports. Several social learning and demographic variables were measured to determine which are the best predictors of participation after leaving high school. This study will provide important data on the relationship between adolescent and adult physical activity and will assist in devising strategies and programs to facilitate participation.

DETERMINANTS OF PHYSICAL ACTIVITY

A number of recent reviews have summarized the literature on determinants of physical activity for adults (Sallis & Hovell, 1990; King et al., 1992; Dishman & Sallis, 1994), and for children (Sallis et al., 1992). Dishman and Sallis' (1994) recent synopsis of the adult determinants literature included 33 studies conducted between 1988 and 1992 in both supervised exercise settings and free-living settings. They identify six categories of determinants:

(1) *Demographic variables.* Education, income, male gender, and age are consistent and powerful correlates of physical activity habits.

(2) *Cognitive variables.* Self-efficacy (a belief that one can successfully perform a desired behaviour) receives the most support as a cognitive determinant, but this might reflect a selection bias with active individuals reporting high self-efficacy due to past success. Expectations of benefits, intention to exercise, and self-motivation receive generally consistent support. Perceived barriers to exercise, including lack of time, are

negatively associated, but attitudes and knowledge are not found to be related to activity.

(3) *Behaviours.* Other health behaviours such as alcohol use, smoking, and diet are not related. Past free-living activity during adulthood and past program participation are positively related for free-living and supervised activity respectively, but this information is not that useful without knowledge of why adults got involved in the first place.

(4) *Social influences.* Social support from family and friends is consistently related to physical activity in cross-sectional and prospective studies.

(5) *Physical environment.* Such factors as season, cost, access to facilities, and home equipment have been included in studies but none of these variables have produced strong support although there is a methodological problem with assessing these variables only through self-report.

(6) *Characteristics of physical activity.* Intensity and perceived effort have been included in studies and are negatively associated with participation.

Much of the research has used social cognitive theory (Bandura, 1986); studies with adolescents have found support for these variables. A study using social learning variables with a sample of Grade 9 and 11 students found that self-efficacy, perceived barriers, and family support were most related to exercise for females, while self-efficacy, friend support, and perceived benefits were related to exercise for boys (Zakarian et al., 1994). Anderssen and Wold (1992) examined parental and peer influences on leisure-time physical activity in young adolescents (grade 7), and found that direct help from parents in exercising hard and perceived physical activity of best friend correlated most highly. Tappe and colleagues (1989) investigated perceived barriers to exercise among adolescents and found that the major barriers were time constraints, unsuitable weather, school and schoolwork, and lack of interest or desire. Reynolds and colleagues (1990) found that self-efficacy, intention to exercise, and social influences of family and friends were most related to physical activity. No studies have specifically examined determinants of young adult participation.

INTERVENTIONS

Numerous interventions have been used, or suggested, to increase participation in physical activity. King (1994) provided a comprehensive description of four types of interventions:

(1) Personal approaches using variables associated with individual adherence, including psychological, cognitive, and environmental strategies. These interventions can be delivered through face-to-face counseling, through broadcast or print media, or by telephone.

(2) Interpersonal approaches using group or class formats for exercise. This is the most popular type of exercise program with both advantages and disadvantages. However, if all sedentary people came to such programs, the present structure could not handle everyone.

(3) Organizational or environmental approaches focusing on changing aspects of a setting or environment (e.g., organizational rules or policies, community norms, or availability of facilities) and removing or minimizing barriers.

(4) Institutional or societal approaches involving public policy and legislation. Much has been done, for example, with smoking cessation but little with facilitating physical activity.

Most of the research evaluating interventions has been conducted on the personal approach. Dishman and Sallis (1994) reviewed the effectiveness of individual intervention programs including behaviour modification, cognitive behaviour modification, and health education approaches. All three types of programs increased frequency or time spent in activity for limited periods of time (4 to 20 weeks). However, total activity was not increased enough to reliably increase physical fitness or reduce risk for future morbidity or mortality. Leith and Taylor (1992) conducted a review on behaviour modification and exercise and reported "the potential efficacy of behaviour modification in improving exercise adherence" (p. 68). The real issue is encouraging maintenance of physical activity for a lifetime.

STRATEGIES FOR FACILITATING PHYSICAL ACTIVITY

The determinants research suggests both general strategies for increasing physical activity and specific strategies for various organizations that have potential for delivering programs to young adults. First, demographic characteristics cannot be changed but should be considered in planning programs. Groups with typically low physical activity, such as low income individuals and females, should be targeted. Cognitive strategies for enhancing self-efficacy and self-motivation, and for overcoming barriers should be considered. Prospective exercisers must understand the benefits of activity but less time needs to be spent on knowledge of fitness, since knowledge and attitudes have not been found to be related to activity. Social influences are important and individuals should be assisted in identifying people who can offer social support. Second, the characteristics of physical activity are important for adherence. Moderate intensity programs lead to better adherence. The lifestyle approach should be promoted rather than traditional vigorous intensity exercise. Third, theoretical models of health behaviour should also be applied in planning strategies. One of the most promising theories is the stages of change theory (Prochaska & Marcus, 1994). Donovan and Owen (1994) suggested different strategies for people in different stages. People in the precontemplation stage may best be influenced by an emphasis on the health and quality-of-life benefits of exercising. Those at the contemplation stage may be more influenced by the enhancement of their confidence to exercise, and those at the action stage may benefit from a focus on social support for continuing to exercise. Fourth, strategies should be targeted for specific age groups. King (1994) outlined age-group features and examples of physical activity programs for several developmental milestones. The features she notes for individuals leaving high school and entering the work force are increased time and scheduling constraints, short-term perspective, and employer demands. She recommends a choice of activities that are convenient and enjoyable, a focus on immediate outcomes, and co-educational non-competitive activities.

Schools provide the best opportunity for preparing young adults for a lifetime of participation in physical activity because they touch the vast majority of the population. Thus, they offer the greatest public health potential (Sallis

& McKenzie, 1991). What can schools do? They should prepare students for the transition to adulthood when programs and facilities will not be as accessible, and give them the skills and knowledge necessary to participate in physical activity independently. A lifestyle education program should include at least seven elements:

(1) Understanding the benefits of physical activity and the importance of physical activity in maintaining physical and mental health.

(2) Identifying programs and facilities in the community for physical activity.

(3) Offering a variety of activities, particularly activities that do not require a great deal of athletic skill.

(4) Concentrating on skill development in lifetime activities so that students feel enough self-efficacy to participate in a variety of activities on their own.

(5) Training in behavioral skills and self-management techniques including goal setting, self-monitoring of activity, self-reinforcement strategies, problem solving skills to overcome barriers to exercise, and time management strategies to assist in finding time to exercise.

(6) Understanding the importance of social support and actively identifying people in students' lives who can provide social support.

(7) Developing strategies for relapse prevention.

Such a program would arm school leavers and graduates with the tools necessary to pursue an active adult lifestyle.

The opportunities for physical activity are less structured and less accessible once students leave high school. Community groups must take over the role formerly played by schools. One of the primary vehicles for physical activity participation during the school years is competitive sport programs provided by schools and community clubs. However, participation in competitive sports tends to decline even during high school (Lindner et al., 1994) and many students who were quite active in school do not continue on with competitive sports after graduating. Local, provincial, and national sport governing organizations must make an effort to inform and recruit students into their adult leagues and programs. In Manitoba there are over 90 provincial sport organizations offering programs that could potentially assist students in bridging the gap from high school to adult programs. Universities and colleges must provide both sport and individual exercise programs that appeal to young adults. They are in a good position to offer comparable programs to those previously offered in schools. Programs must be made available to all young adults, especially those who are not attending post-secondary institutions. The YM/YWCA and fitness clubs are just two examples of agencies that could provide these programs.

Many high school leavers go directly into the work force. These worksites could provide physical activity opportunities for their employees. Shephard (1986) outlined the benefits of these programs including employee morale and productivity as well as reduced health insurance costs and absenteeism. National policies should promote employee physical activity programs and assist worksites in establishing such programs. The health care system has the potential to reach the majority of the young adult population and to encourage physical activity as a public health strategy. Pender and colleagues (1994) and

Sallis and Patrick (1994) recommend the active involvement of physicians and other health care professionals in promoting physical activity. One example is the PACE (Physician-based Assessment and Counseling for Exercise) program to assist primary-care physicians in counseling adults about the adoption and maintenance of regular physical activity (Pender et al., 1994). National promotional campaigns are another strategy to promote physical activity. Programs like Participaction and Active Living have produced some effective promotions although some of their material should be targeted to specific age groups, including young adults. Donovan and Owen (1994) provide an overview of social marketing and make suggestions for tailoring promotions to segments of the population.

NATIONAL POLICY RECOMMENDATIONS

Young adults should be encouraged to take responsibility for their own health behaviours, including physical activity. The long-term benefits would be a healthier adult population and a transmission of these values to the next generation. Six specific recommendations are offered for Canadian policy makers:

(1) Physical activity should be promoted as a public health strategy to reduce health care costs and to improve the physical and mental health of young adults.

(2) Research on the determinants of physical activity and the effectiveness of interventions during the transition from late adolescence to young adulthood should be funded. Little is known about this age period although several authors have suggested that it is particularly useful for interventions to target transitional periods (Sallis et al., 1992; King, 1994).

(3) Preparation, piloting, and dissemination of a lifestyle education program for senior high school students should be funded.

(4) Programs and facilities for physical activity such as bicycle paths and jogging trails should be funded and promoted.

(5) A physician counseling package to assist physicians in assessing and promoting physical activity should be prepared and distributed.

(6) Physical activity should be promoted in conjunction with other health behaviours such as smoking cessation, weight control, and stress management.

References

Anderssen, N., & Wold, B. (1992). Parental and peer influences on leisure-time physical activity in young adolescents. *Research Quarterly for Exercise and Sport, 63,* 341–348.

Bandura, A. (1986). *Social foundations of thought and action: A social cognitive theory.* Englewood Cliffs, NJ: Prentice Hall.

Blair, S., Wells, C., Weathers, R., & Paffenbarger, R. (1994). Chronic disease: The physical activity dose-response controversy. In R. Dishman (Ed.), *Advances in exercise adherence* (pp. 31–55). Champaign, IL: Human Kinetics.

Bouchard, C., Shephard, R., & Stephens, T. (1994). (Eds.), *Physical activity, fitness and health: International proceedings and consensus statements.* Champaign, IL: Human Kinetics.

Craig, C., Russell, S., & Cameron, C. (1994). *Benefits and impact of physical activity for Ontario.* Ottawa: Canadian Fitness and Lifestyle Research Institute.

Dishman, R., & Sallis, J. (1994). Determinants and interventions for physical activity and exercise. In C. Bouchard, R. Shephard & T. Stephens (Eds.), *Physical activity, fitness and health: International proceedings and consensus statements* (pp. 214–238). Champaign, IL: Human Kinetics.

Donovan, R., & Owen, N. (1994). Social marketing and population interventions. In R. Dishman (Ed.), *Advances in exercise adherence* (pp. 249–290). Champaign, IL: Human Kinetics.

Kemper, H. (1994). The natural history of physical activity and aerobic fitness in teenagers. In R. Dishman (Ed.), *Advances in exercise adherence* (pp. 293–318). Champaign, IL: Human Kinetics.

King, A. (1994). Clinical and community interventions to promote and support physical activity participation. In R. Dishman (Ed.), *Advances in exercise adherence* (pp 183–212). Champaign, IL: Human Kinetics.

King, A., Blair, S., Bild, D., Dishman, R., Dubbert, P., Marcus, B., Oldridge, N., Paffenbarger, R., Powell, K., & Yeager, K. (1992). Determinants of physical activity and interventions in adults. *Medicine and Science in Sports and Exercise, 24* (Suppl.), s221-s236.

Leith, L. (1994). *Foundations of exercise and mental health.* Morgantown, WV: Fitness Information Technology.

Leith, L., & Taylor, A. (1992). Behaviour modification and exercise adherence: A literature review. *Journal of Sport Behaviour, 15,* 60–74.

Lindner, K., Butcher, J., & Johns, D. (1994). Recall of competitive sport participation by urban Grade 10 students. *CAHPER Journal Research Supplement, 1,* 1–9.

Martinsen, E., & Stephens, T. (1994). Exercise and mental health in clinical and free-living populations. In R. Dishman (Ed.), *Advances in exercise adherence* (pp. 55–72). Champaign, IL: Human Kinetics.

McGinnis, J. (1992). The public burden of a sedentary lifestyle. *Medicine and Science in Sports and Exercise, 24* (Suppl.), s196-s200.

Pate, R.R., Pratt, M., Blair, S.N., Haskell, W.L., Macera, C.A., Bouchard, C., Buchner, D., Ettinger, W., Heath, G.W., King, A.C., Kriska, A., Leon, A.S., Marcus, B.H., Morris, J., Paffenbarger, R.S., Patrick, K., Pollock, M.L., Rippe, J.M., Sallis, J., & Wilmore, J.H. (1995). Physical activity and public health. A recommendation from the Centers for Disease Control and the American College of Sports Medicine. *Journal of American Medical Association, 273,* 402–407.

Pender, N., Sallis, J., Long, B., & Calfas, K. (1994). Health care provider counseling to promote physical activity. In R. Dishman (Ed.), *Advances in exercise adherence* (pp. 213–236). Champaign, IL: Human Kinetics.

Prochaska, J., & Marcus, B. (1994). The transtheoretical model: Applications to exercise. In R. Dishman (Ed.), *Advances in exercise adherence* (pp. 161–180). Champaign, IL: Human Kinetics.

Reynolds, K., Killen, J., Bryson, S., Maron, D., Taylor, C., Maccoby, N., & Farquhar, J. (1990). Psychosocial predictors of physical activity in adolescents. *Preventive Medicine, 19,* 541–551.

Sallis, J., & Patrick, K. (1994). Physical activity guidelines for adolescents: Consensus statement. *Pediatric Exercise Science, 6,* 302–314.

Sallis, J. (1993). Epidemiology of physical activity and fitness in children and adolescents. *Critical Reviews in Food Science and Nutrition, 33,* 403–408.

Sallis, J., Simons-Morton, B., Stone, E., Corbin, C., Epstein, L., Faucette, N., Iannotti, R., Killen, J., Klesges, R., Petray, C., Rowland, T., & Taylor, W. (1992). Determinants of physical activity and interventions in youth. *Medicine and Science in Sports and Exercise, 24* (Suppl.), s248-s257.

Sallis, J., & McKenzie, T. (1991). Physical education's role in public health. *Research Quarterly for Exercise and Sport, 62,* 124–137.

Sallis, J., & Hovell, M. (1990). Determinants of exercise behaviour. *Exercise and Sport Sciences Review, 18,* 307–330.

Scott, D., & Willets, F. (1989). Adolescent and adult leisure patterns: A 37-year follow-up study. *Leisure Sciences, 11,* 323–335.

Shephard, R. (1986). *Fitness and health in industry.* Basel, Switzerland: Karger.

Stephens, T., & Craig, C. (1990). *The well-being of Canadians: Highlights of the 1988 Campbell's Survey.* Ottawa: Canadian Fitness and Lifestyle Research Institute.

Tappe, M., Duda, J., & Ehrnwald, P. (1989). Perceived barriers to exercise among adolescents. *Journal of School Health, 59,* 153–155.

Wankel, L., Hills, C., Hudec, J., Mummery, W., Sefton, J., Stevenson, J., & Whitmarsh, B. (1994). *Self-esteem and body image: Structure, formation and relationship to health-related behaviours.* Ottawa: Canadian Fitness and Lifestyle Research Institute.

Zakarian, J., Hovell, M., Hofstetter, C., Sallis, J., & Keating, K. (1994). Correlates of vigorous exercise in a predominantly low SES and minority high-school population. *Preventive Medicine, 23,* 314–321.

The Canadian Fitness and Lifestyle Research Institute has funded the research described in this chapter.

32

The Impact of Recreation on Youth in Transition to Adulthood: A Focus on Youth-at-Risk

Stacey L. McKay, Ian S. Reid, Mark S. Tremblay and René Pelletier

The transition from childhood to adulthood is a difficult one even in the best of times. For a significant number of youth, however, this could be considered the worst of times. The National Commission on Youth (1980) noted that many of the traditional institutions that assist youth in the transition to adulthood are changing, crumbling, and even collapsing. The decline of the family is well documented, the school systems are attacked by students, parents, and employers for their failure to teach marketable skills, and governmental bodies at all levels have been largely unresponsive to the plight of youth. Alternative measures, such as recreation, are being sought to fill the gap and aid youth, especially those considered to be at additional risk, in their transition to responsible, contributing, adult members of the community. The role of recreation in reducing lifestyle and behavioural risks for youth is a growing area of interest in academic, government, and community sectors. More work is needed to elucidate the extent of the relationship between recreation and the behaviours that place youth at risk. A literature review, focus group analysis, and a summary of initiatives taking place across the country was undertaken to examine the impact and benefits of recreation on Canadian youth-at-risk. The results of this work are reported in this chapter.

REVIEW OF THE LITERATURE

Youth-at-risk are on a continuum ranging from low risk to chronic deviance. This continuum can be viewed as a funnel with all youth being at risk, albeit very low risk. Youth drop further and further into the funnel towards chronic deviant behaviour as they demonstrate more risk factors. Fortunately, as these youth move down the funnel their numbers decrease (McKay, 1994). Recreation is defined as being all those socially acceptable activities that a person chooses to do in order to make their leisure time more interesting, more enjoyable, and more personally satisfying (Fitness Canada, 1987). Recreation services are a valuable tool in preventing youth problems, reducing substance abuse and other antisocial behaviours (Ryan, 1991), and in encouraging socially productive attitudes, values, and habits (Violas, 1978). The underlying assumption is that social outcomes are influenced by recreation and that activity can be utilized as a control mechanism for adolescent behaviour. Recreation has an impact on the psychological, physiological, and social development of youth.

Recreation can have a positive effect on boredom, mood, self-esteem, and character development. Boredom is viewed as an important factor in adolescents' lives because of its link to affective states such as depression, hopelessness, loneliness, and distractibility (McGiboney & Carter, 1988). Boredom has also been linked to alcohol use among college (Orcutt, 1984) and high-school students (Sides, 1992), smoking among high-school students (Smith & Caldwell, 1989), deviant behaviour at school (Wasson, 1981) and over-eating (Mehradian & Riccioni, 1986). Youth who participate in appropriate recreation activities have a decrease in leisure boredom, and subsequently a decrease in deviant behaviour (Iso-Ahola & Weissinger, 1990). Participation in recreation and regular physical activity is also related to improved self-concept and self-esteem, reduced depressive symptoms, decreased stress and anxiety, improved self-acceptance, and enhanced psychological well-being (Hull, 1990; Calfas & Taylor, 1994). Weyerer (1992) reported that subjects who were inactive had three times the risk of depression compared to those who were active. Exercise and physical activity also improve self-efficacy and sense of competence (McAuley, 1994). These psychological variables represent many of the traditional predictor variables that identify youth-at-risk (McKay, 1994). The ability of recreation to positively impact these predictor variables presents a strong case for the use of these activities as prevention and/or intervention strategies to reduce behavioural risk factors for youth, and to ease the transition of youth to adulthood.

Numerous health and physiological improvements resulting from recreation participation have also been demonstrated (Bouchard et al., 1994). For instance, there is a significant negative correlation between physical activity and smoking (Wankel & Sefton, 1994). More than 80% of Canadians between the ages of 10 and 24 who are active have never smoked (Stephens & Craig, 1990). The results of the International Consensus Conference on Physical Activity Guidelines for Adolescents detailed the health benefits related to habitual physical activity (Sallis, 1994). Specifically, regular physical activity can improve aerobic fitness (Morrow & Freedson, 1994), skeletal health (Bailey & Martin, 1994), reduce obesity (Bar-Or & Baranowski, 1994), and lower blood pressure (Alpert & Wilmore, 1994). There are also short-term responses to exercise that occur which may be beneficial in reducing risk factors for some youth. For example, exercise can reduce anxiety (Landers & Petruzzello, 1994), post-exercise blood pressure (Rowland, 1990), muscle tension (Sime, 1990), and can serve as an effective tranquillizer, particularly in mildly hypertensive adolescents (Rowland, 1990).

Recreation activities provide an excellent medium for social development to occur (Malina, 1994). Recreation has a positive impact on family-related, peer-related, and school-related issues and these impacts can significantly influence a youth's social development and transition to adulthood. Recreation behaviour appears to be both affected by, and have an effect on, marriage and family factors (Holman & Epperson, 1984). Some parent-adolescent problems may stem from the lack of congruence between what teenagers do with their parents and what they would like to do. Orthner and Mancini (1990) reported that husbands and wives who share leisure time in joint activities report a higher level of satisfaction within the marriage than those who do not. This in turn contributed to a healthy home environment for the children, good marital communication, and family stability.

Research examining peer-related issues has centred around socialization. Stokowski and Lee (1991) noted that small recreation groups provide significant socializing experiences for group members. This includes social bonding of intimate family and friends, individuals developing identities, learning social roles, establishing and reinforcing norms of behaviour, enhancing group solidarity, and creating social meanings (Stokowski & Lee, 1991). These observations are significant in that peer association has been shown to be a strong predictor of deviance (Warr, 1993). Participation in constructive recreation programming helps to ensure that desirable peer socialization occurs. Recreation is also believed to have a positive impact on academic achievement. Roggenbuck, Loomis, and Dagostino (1990) indicated that there were considerable gains in factual knowledge, recognition memory, and skill development as a result of recreation. Pursuits such as reading, writing poetry, or writing short stories as recreation is strongly related to school achievement (Heyns, 1978). In addition, kids who were regularly active performed as well or better academically, exhibited positive attitudes about school and themselves, were less aggressive and played better with other children (CAHPER, 1992).

Research has examined specific types of recreation programs and their impact on youth development. The research examining the impact of wilderness challenge programs such as Outward Bound, has shown that, although no significant long-term reduction in recidivism rates were realized, a reduction in the seriousness of subsequent criminal behaviour did result (Castellano & Soderstrom, 1992). Wright (1983) stated that a clear positive difference was experienced by the experimental group in the areas of self-concept, locus of control, personal efficacy, self-empowerment, and cardiovascular fitness after taking part in a wilderness program. In addition, McDonald and Howe (1989) and O'Brien (1992) found that there were significant effects on self-destructive behaviour, sociability, academic achievement, social consciousness, hopelessness, social pessimism, self-confidence, sense of excitement, sense of acceptance, and racial integration as a result of participating in wilderness challenge programs.

Community-based intervention programs offer a number of services aimed at positively impacting youth-at-risk. These include after-school tutoring, scouting activities, cultural events, recreational and art activities, drug education, ethnic identity programs, and individual/group counselling (Roundtree et al., 1993). Barton & Butts (1990) have reported positive impacts in school achievement and interest, communication with parents, hopefulness about the future, recidivism rates, antisocial behaviours, and self-esteem as a result of participation in recreation activity.

Research conducted on the general effects of sport participation has demonstrated psychological and social benefits for youth-at-risk. Athletes tended to be less deviant than non-athletes, regardless of gender and socio-economic status (Hastad et al., 1984). Wankel and Berger (1990) concluded that sport participation had a positive impact on enjoyment, physical health, psychological well-being, socialization, intergroup relations, community integration, educational attainment, social status and social mobility. Improved self-esteem and self-mastery were also benefits of sport participation (Iso-Ahola et al., 1988). One notable exception to the positive effects of sport participation is the increased use of anabolic steroids associated with certain types of activities (Williams, 1994).

Playing video games has become a popular recreational pursuit for youth whether it be in an arcade or at home. Ellis (1984) discovered that video arcades instigate or facilitate deviant behaviour among relatively few youth; these few are more likely to be at the arcade late at night and experience weak parental social control. Those youth who visited the arcade before 10:00 pm had better academic achievement than those who did not visit the arcade at all or those who visited after 10:00 pm (Ellis, 1984). The literature is clear. Recreation can have a positive effect on a youth's transition to adulthood by playing a significant role in youth's psychological, physiological, and sociological development.

IDENTIFICATION OF IMPACTS AND BENEFITS

To better understand the impact and benefits of recreation on youth-at-risk 64 focus group sessions were held in 16 Canadian communities. At least one focus group was from each province and territory (Reid et al., 1994). Four focus group sessions were held at each location targetting administrators/policy makers, frontline workers, youth (14-18 years of age), and parents. Participants in the administrator and frontline worker groups represented a wide variety of education, social services, criminal justice, and other community organizations. Recreation personnel were always the minority. The youth and parent groups were subdivided to represent youth at varying stages on the youth-at-risk continuum—low risk to chronic deviance. This stratification of parents and youth was randomized across the provinces. Focus groups were also randomly assigned to equally represent urban and rural settings. A total of 465 persons participated.

Interest in, and expressed concern about, youth-at-risk and recreation was high in every focus group and community. Participants in each of the four target groups thought that there was incredible potential for recreation to positively impact youth-at-risk and assist in their development to adulthood. The focus group participants stated repeatedly that recreation can help youth-at-risk by improving self-esteem, providing positive role models, teaching teamwork and social skills, promoting self-confidence, providing a sense of belonging, reducing risk factors for disease, giving youth something constructive to do, providing a means of releasing stress, promoting positive morals and values, teaching cognitive, leadership and life skills, providing an opportunity for racial integration, enhancing cultural awareness, providing a sense of community, fostering family support, and promoting the wellness of youth. One social services administrator stated, "Recreation is critical."

There was a general consensus that efforts to provide recreation services impacting on youth-at-risk need to be better coordinated and advertised. A number of organizational constraints that inhibited the provision of services for youth-at-risk were identified. These included the narrow mission of the organization that may only focus on younger children, or on adults, leaving youth with little to no services; union agreements and budget limitations that restricted access hours and the types of available services; and the fear of liability action and the cost of liability insurance that frequently prevented an organization from offering activities such as adventure based programs and skateboarding areas. The rules and regulations of many agencies and/or facilities regarding personal behaviour was recognized as an internal constraint. Many of the youth indicated that they had been kicked out for their behaviour. The administrators noted that this practice often resulted in denying youth who could really benefit from recreation. Other constraints included the lack of interorganization cooperation; the lack of a holistic approach; the lack of understanding of the role and benefits of recreation by political decisions makers; the short-term political view of governmental bodies; the lack of trained leaders; and the lack of understanding and appreciation of youth-at-risk and their respective values, needs, and interests.

Focus group participants indicated that successful programs need to have youth spearheading the initiative. Programs also need to be flexible, accommodating, inexpensive (or free), with good leadership and community support. Programs directed towards youth-at-risk should be nonthreatening and emphasize participation rather than competition. Many felt that fiscal, logistical, and societal barriers and constraints discourage youth-at-risk from taking part in traditional recreation programs and services. The constraints most frequently cited were youth being unable to pay for equipment, travel, and registration; not having access to transportation; not knowing about programs and services; programs and services being over-structured; an overemphasis on competitive sports and adult focused programs; a lack of youth services in the community; time pressures; class discrimination; racial discrimination; gender bias; lack of family and parental support; interpersonal constraints; and lack of skill.

The need to empower youth, provide good leadership, establish parental and family support, provide increased government support, develop partnerships, create youth centres, reform current programming initiatives to reflect the needs of youth-at-risk, and continue research were repeatedly mentioned as the primary issues. The need to approach youth-at-risk issues holistically was also a pervasive attitude. Recreation can provide both prevention and intervention functions, and be a vital tool in preparing youth for responsible community living.

CURRENT INITIATIVES

A survey examining specific information on recreation initiatives designed to address the needs of youth-at-risk was distributed nationally (Reid et al., 1994). Respondents were also asked to forward any reports or materials that described and evaluated the programs. The survey was initially distributed to an exhaustive listing of provincial and national organizations that offered recreation services and services for youth. Initially only 32 responses were received from the original 315 questionnaires; however, an additional 64 responses were received through a pyramid distribution effect. Most of the 96 responses described successful programs and provided some details surrounding the initiative. These model programs highlighted many of the recommendations, success variables, and issues that were raised through the literature review and focus groups including development of youth drop-in centres, community-based programming, partnerships, funding, evaluation, outreach programming, cultural programming, youth directed activities, alternative measures, and media campaigns.

The majority of programs and initiatives were local initiatives, preventative in nature, and targeted at those aged 6 to 24 years. Of these, most of the programs were offered to youth 12 to 18 years of age. The clientele represented the entire youth-at-risk continuum. A number of programs were specifically designed to meet the needs of female youth and those of different ethnic and cultural origins. Programming for female youth-at-risk was fitness oriented and concentrated on body-image and self-esteem. Most of the 12 responses that indicated culturally specific programs were targeted at native youth, with a few addressing the needs of Afro-Canadian youth. Some multicultural programming was reported in accordance to the ethnic makeup of the community. Success of a program was usually based on the number of participants. Several respondents claimed, however, that their program resulted in a reduction in vandalism, violence and drug use, tension between ethnic groups, and smoking. Others stated an increase in school attendance.

RESEARCH, POLICY AND PROGRAMMING IMPLICATIONS

This exploratory study was designed to provide a foundation for investigating the impact and benefits of recreation on Canadian youth-at-risk, and in turn provide insight into the transition from childhood to adulthood. It examined the present state of research in the area of youth-at-risk and recreation; the views, knowledge, and perceptions of key stakeholders concerned with the development of youth; and, the status of programming addressing the needs of this population. The potential impact of recreation on youth development is significant, but there are gaps in knowledge that must be addressed. The most prevalent gap is the lack of direct empirical evidence of recreation's impact on the transition from youth to adulthood. There is considerable evidence of recreation's impact on youth and on adults, but not on the transition from youth to adulthood. The majority of research addressing the role of recreation has concentrated on youth participation patterns, level of participation, and whether these are predictors of adult participation in recreation and physical activity. Offord, Hanna, and Hoult (1992) have indicated that the correlation between childhood and adult levels of participation are weak or non-existent. Longitudinal and/or cross sectional studies with direct comparisons between youth and adult behaviours need to be conducted to better address this gap.

A number of policy implications emerged from this work. Participants from all four focus groups in every site across Canada called for a community-based interorganizational strategy for youth be developed by each local community. The strategy should specify the role of various services, including recreation, in the development and implementation of the strategy. At the federal, provincial and local government levels, a strategy should be created to increase awareness and appreciation of the benefits and roles that recreation plays with youth, facilitate a broad range of program and service opportunities for youth and their families, initiate strategic alliances, and identify the needs of youth, the necessary resources, and participation constraints. Federal and provincial governments should initiate coordinated amendments to current legislation governing civil action for liability claims in order to encourage additional recreation programs for all youth, including those at-risk.

Local recreation organizations must become active partners, if not leaders, in community development, community health, and in its renewal. New community development approaches must be established as well as new partnerships and new personnel resources and practices. Municipal organizations responsible for the provision of local recreation services should re-examine their mission, policies, and procedures to facilitate this community development role and offer recreation services that target youth-at-risk. An information centre with one central number for all youth-related services should be established in each community to coordinate, orchestrate, and integrate existing programs.

Provincial and territorial governments should establish a Youth Secretariat where they do not exist. Specific responsibilities of the Secretariat would include support for the development and implementation of provincial and territorial youth strategies and pilot projects to test integrated approaches to service delivery, the development of local and regional youth committees in strategic planning and community development, government policy coordination and policy identification, and program and service coordination issues and problems. Initiatives and policies must be developed to include, not exclude, youth-at-risk. The Federal Government of Canada should initiate and facilitate the development of a national youth development strategy. Youth-at-risk must be a priority of such a strategy. In addition, the strategy should identify the creation of a National Youth Secretariat as a priority. Each federal department and agency having a primary, secondary, or tertiary youth mandate should be represented within the Secretariat.

Programming implications were also identified. Programs need to be organized and operated by youth, for youth. Strategies and related programs should be developed that actively integrate all youth, particularly youth-at-risk, into the decision making process for the delivery of all youth oriented services, but especially recreation and physical activity. The youth participants suggested, and administrators and frontline workers concurred, that communities establish a network of youth drop-in centres with a focus on recreation services. A change from competition-based to participation-based programming is needed to entice less skilled youth to participate. Agencies must go beyond traditional programming if youth-at-risk are to be involved. More attention has to be devoted to cultural activities and the diverse needs of a multi-cultural community. Agencies responsible for recreation should develop equal opportunity policies and strategies for their services and staff. More female only activities need to be offered to encourage female youth to participate, and to provide more equitable gender recreational opportunities in the community. Discrimination against females participating in male activities needs to be addressed. Appropriate communication strategies must be instituted in homes, schools, and recreation organizations to increase awareness of programs. Financial support programs should be developed that facilitate the direct involvement of youth and their families in recreation services.

A specific youth-at-risk leadership training program for recreation professionals should be developed as part of an employment and leadership development strategy. Leaders need to be well trained and properly educated in the area of youth issues, behaviour modification, community development, and recreation. The leaders must also have a good understanding and appreciation of youth and their issues.

Societal changes have had adverse effects on youth development, creating a sub-population of youth who are at-risk. Lack of co-operation among school, police, home, counselling, and social service organizations has lead to outcomes contradictory to professed goals. In addition, recreation is often left out of the equation, even though it plays a significant role in a youth's development (Kelly, 1990). Recreation has tremendous potential to work in partnership with other youth-related services to encourage and facilitate the responsible transition to adulthood.

References

Alpert, B.S., & Wilmore, J.H. (1994). Physical activity and blood pressure in adolescents. *Pediatric Exercise Science, 6* (4), 361–380.

Bailey, D., & Martin, A. (1994). Physical activity and skeletal health in adolescents. *Pediatric Exercise Science, 6* (4), 330–347.

Bar-Or, O., & Baranowski, T. (1994). Physical activity, adiposity, and obesity among adolescents. *Pediatric Exercise Science, 6* (4), 348–360.

Barton, W., & Butts, J. (1990). Viable options: Intensive supervision programs for juvenile delinquents. *Crime and Delinquency, 36* (2), 238–256.

Bouchard, C., Shephard, R., & Stephens, T. (Eds.). (1994). *Physical activity, fitness, and health: International proceedings and consensus statement.* Champaign, IL: Human Kinetics Publishers, Inc.

Calfas, K., & Taylor, W. (1994). Effects of physical activity on psychological variables in adolescents. *Pediatric Exercise Science, 6* (4), 406–423.

CAHPER (Canadian Association for Health, Physical Education, and Recreation) (1992). *More than sport campaign (Sport Yukon).* Whitehorse, YK: Yukon Community and Transportation Services.

Castellano, T., & Soderstrom, I. (1992). Therapeutic wilderness programs and juvenile recidivism: A program evaluation. *Journal of Offender Rehabilitation, 17,* 19–46.

Ellis, D. (1984). Video arcades, youth, and trouble. *Youth & Society, 16* (1), 47–65.

Fitness Canada (1987). *National recreation statement.* Ottawa, ON: Health Canada.

Hastad, D., Segrave, J., Pangrazi, R., & Petersen, G. (1984). Youth sport participation and deviant behaviour. *Sociology of Sport Journal, 1,* 366–373.

Heyns, B. (1978). *Summer learning and the effects of schooling.* New York: Academic Press.

Holman, T., & Epperson, A. (1984). Family and leisure: A review of the literature with research recommendations. *Journal of Leisure Research, 16* (4), 277–294.

Hull, R. (1990). Mood as a product of leisure: Causes and consequences. *Journal of Leisure Research, 22* (2), 99–111.

Iso-Ahola, S., LaVerde, D., & Graefe, A. (1988). Perceived competence as a mediator of the relationship between high risk sports participation and self-esteem. *Journal of Leisure Research, 21* (1), 32–39.

Iso-Ahola, S., & Weissinger, E. (1990). Perceptions of boredom in leisure: Conceptualization, reliability and validity of the leisure boredom scale. *Journal of Leisure Research, 22* (1), 1–17.

Kelly, J. (1990). *Leisure.* Englewood Cliffs, NJ: Prentice Hall.

Landers, D., & Petruzzello, S. (1994). Physical activity, fitness and anxiety. In C. Bouchard, R.J. Shephard, & T. Stephens (Eds.), *Physical activity, fitness and health: International proceedings and consensus statement* (pp. 868–882). Champaign, IL: Human Kinetics Publishers, Inc.

Malina, R. (1994). Benefits of physical activity from a lifetime perspective. In H.A. Quinney, L. Gauvin, & A.E.T. Wall (Eds.), *Toward active living* (pp.47–53). Champaign, IL: Human Kinetics Publishers.

McAuley, E. (1994). Physical activity and psychosocial outcomes. In C. Bouchard, R.J. Shephard, & T. Stephens (Eds.), *Physical Activity, Fitness and Health: International Proceedings and Consensus Statement* (pp. 551–568). Champaign, IL: Human Kinetics Publishers, Inc.

McDonald R., & Howe, C. (1989). Challenge/initiative recreation programs as a treatment for low self-concept children. *Journal of Leisure Research, 2,* 242–253.

McGiboney, G., & Carter, C. (1988). Boredom proneness and adolescents' personalities. *Psychological Reports, 63*, 741–742.

McKay, S. (1994). A review of the effectiveness of recreation prevention and intervention efforts with at-risk and juvenile delinquent populations. Unpublished master's thesis, Texas A&M University, College Station, TX.

Mehradian, A., & Riccioni, M. (1986). Measures of eating-related characteristics for the general population: Relationships with temperament. *Journal of Personality Assessment, 50* (4), 610–629.

Morrow, J., & Freedson, J. (1994). Relationship between habitual physical activity and aerobic fitness in adolescents. *Pediatric Exercise Science, 6* (4), 315–347.

National Commission on Youth (1980). *The transition of youth to adulthood: A bridge too long.* Boulder, CO: Westview Press, Inc.

O'Brien, K. (1992). Effective programming for youth at-risk. *The Voice,* (Summer), 16–17, 47–48.

Offord, D., Hanna, E., & Hoult, L. (1992). Recreation and the development of children and youth: A discussion paper. Unpublished manuscript, McMaster University, Hamilton, Ontario.

Orcutt, J. (1984). Contrasting effects of two kinds of boredom on alcohol use. *Journal of Drug Issues, 14* (Winter), 161–173.

Orthner, D., & Mancini, J. (1990). Leisure impacts on family interaction and cohesion. *Journal of Leisure Research, 22* (2), 125–137.

Reid, I., Tremblay, M., McKay, S., & Pelletier, R. (1994). Canadian youth: Does activity reduce risk? An analysis of the impact and benefits of physical activity/recreation on Canadian youth-at-risk. Unpublished manuscript, University of New Brunswick, Fredericton.

Roggenbuck, J., Loomis, R., & Dagostino, J. (1990). The learning benefits of leisure. *Journal of Leisure Research, 22* (2), 112–124.

Roundtree, G., Grenier, C., & Hoffman, V. (1993). Parental assessment of behavioral change after children's participation in a delinquency prevention program. *Journal of Offender Rehabilitation, 19*(/2), 113–130.

Rowland, T. (1990). *Exercise and children's health.* Champaign, IL: Human Kinetics Publishers, Inc.

Ryan, J. (1991). Breaking the circle of destruction. *Parks and Recreation, 26* (3), 46–48, 74.

Sallis, J. (Ed.). (1994). *Pediatric exercise science.* Champaign, IL: Human Kinetics Publishers, Inc.

Sides, E. (1992). Boredom, anxiety, and alcohol consumption among high risk adolescents. Unpublished Master's Thesis: University of North Carolina, Greensboro.

Sime, W. (1990). Discussion: Exercise, fitness, and mental health. In C. Bouchard (Ed.), *Exercise fitness, and health* (pp.627–633). Champaign, IL: Human Kinetics Publishers, Inc.

Smith, E., & Caldwell, L. (1989). The perceived quality of leisure experiences among smoking and non-smoking adolescents. *Journal of Early Adolescence, 9*(1/2), 153–162.

Stephens, T., & Craig, C. (1990). *The well-being of Canadians.* Ottawa, ON: Canadian Fitness and Lifestyle Research Institute.

Stokowski, P., & Lee, R. (1991). The influence of social network ties on recreation and leisure: An exploratory study. *Journal of Leisure Research, 23* (2), 95–113.

Violas, P. (1978). The play movement. *The training of the urban working class* (pp. 67–92). Chicago, IL: Rand McNally.

Wankel, L., & Berger, B. (1990). The psychological and social benefits of sport and physical activity. *Journal of Leisure Research, 22* (2), 167–182.

Wankel, L., & Sefton, J. (1994). Physical activity and other lifestyle behaviors. In C. Bouchard, R.J. Shephard, & T. Stephens (Eds.), *Physical activity, fitness and health: International proceedings and consensus statement* (pp. 530–554). Champaign, IL: Human Kinetics Publishers, Inc.

Warr, M. (1993). Age, peers, and delinquency. *Criminology, 31* (1), 17–40.

Wasson, A. (1981). Susceptibility to boredom and deviant behaviour at school. *Psychological Reports, 48*, 267–274.

Weyerer, S. (1992). Physical inactivity and depression in the community. *International Journal of Sports Medicine, 13*, 492–496.

Williams, M. (1994). Physical activity, fitness, and substance misuse and abuse. In C. Bouchard, R.J. Shephard, & T. Stephens (Eds.), *Physical activity, fitness and health: International proceedings and consensus statement* (pp. 918–930). Champaign, IL: Human Kinetics Publishers, Inc.

Wright, A. (1983). Therapeutic potential of the outward bound process: An evaluation of a treatment program for juvenile delinquents. *Therapeutic Recreation Journal, 15* (2), 33–42.

33

The Role of Sport in Preparing Youth for Adulthood

Gretchen A. Kerr

Sport is often cited as a means for preparing youth for adulthood. Sport is said to contribute to psychosocial development by building self-esteem and character, and teaching the skills of problem-solving, decision-making, and coping with stress. Sport provides a miniature life situation in which to practise life skills. Conversely, injuries, burnout, eating disorders, and high stress levels are also commonly associated with the athletic experience (Kerr & Goss, 1995). The dumb jock image pervades the world of sport. There are too many unfortunate stories of athletes abusing their bodies with steroids, or being denied normal life experiences, all in the pursuit of excellence. As Huxley writes, "like every other instrument man has invented, sport can be used for good or evil purposes" (1969, p. 186).

One needs to consider the social context in which the activity takes place to reconcile these diverse views of sport. Sport takes many forms, including street hockey played by a group of neighbourhood kids, school programs, structured after-school activities, and elite or highly competitive pursuits. The degree of involvement in sport and the level of competition are important mediators in the relationship between athletic participation and developmental variables. Recreational activities, school sports, and moderate competition are generally more conducive to psychosocial development than elite sport. Virtually all adolescents come into contact with athletics within the school system. This chapter will examine the influence of sport participation within the secondary school setting on psychosocial variables.

ATHLETIC PARTICIPATION AND PERSONAL QUALITIES

Conventional wisdom claims that athletic participation is conducive to the overall development of adolescence and subsequent adulthood. Socialization through sport purports to build character, discipline, self-esteem, the ability to delay gratification, and the acceptance of authority (Spreitzer, 1994). Sport has been viewed as a means of socializing youth into basic values of competition, honesty, cooperation, courage, fair play and achievement (Fejgin, 1994). Fejgin (1994) controlled for background variables such as sex, race, family income, parental education, and Grade 8 data, and found that athletic participation contributed directly to increased self-concept, an internal locus of control, and fewer discipline problems in Grade 10. Furthermore, the influence of athletic participation was greater than that of family income, parental education, sex and race, on all outcome variables except for educational aspirations. Athletic participation, in comparison with academic clubs, had slightly less influence on educational aspirations but a greater effect on self-concept. Athletics and participation in music or drama had similar influences on reducing discipline problems.

Female athletes have been found to be more achievement-motivated, independent, poised, tough-minded, and internally-controlled than non-athletes (Henschen et al., 1982; Kleiber & Hemmer, 1981). Athletic participation is perceived by female athletes as contributing to confidence, positive body image, higher energy levels, better health, and general sense of well-being (Snyder et al., 1975; Snyder & Spreitzer, 1976). Melnick, Vanfossen, and Sabo (1988) tested 5,669 female students in their sophomore and senior years on the variables of perceived popularity, self-esteem, and sense of mastery. Athletic participation was associated with higher self-esteem and a greater sense of mastery. Athletic participation was found to contribute directly to perceived popularity and extracurricular involvement when the effects of socioeconomic status and sophomore results were controlled. Socioeconomic status influences both psychosocial characteristics and patterns of athletic participation. It is characteristic of middle-class girls to have higher self-esteem scores and higher rates of participation in athletics. So it is possible that socioeconomic differences rather than athletic socialization account for the findings.

Holland and Andre (1994) reported that male high-school students who were involved in sport had significantly higher levels of self-esteem than male non-athletes. This was true regardless of whether the males were in sex-appropriate sports such as football or sex-inappropriate sports such as gymnastics. Conversely, the self-esteem levels of the female athletes depended upon whether they participated in sex-appropriate or sex-inappropriate sports. Females in sex-appropriate sports such as gymnastics had significantly higher self-esteem than female non-athletes. However, there were no significant differences between the self-esteem levels of females in sex-inappropriate sports such as basketball and female non-athletes. Melnick, Sabo & Vanfossen (1992a) found that African-American and Hispanic students who participated in sports were significantly higher in self-reported popularity than their non-athletic peers. Furthermore, those students who were involved in athletics were also more involved in other extracurricular and community activities than were their non-participant peers. These associations were reported in both urban and rural settings. Spreitzer (1994) found that athletes were significantly more likely than non-athletes to take on additional extracurricular activities apart from sport. These findings debunk the popular belief that sport drains young people's time and energy or narrows their range of involvements in and out of school.

ATHLETIC PARTICIPATION, ACADEMIC ATTAINMENT AND ASPIRATIONS

Whether school sport programs support or interfere with the educational mission of high schools continues to be a point of serious debate. No area of sport sociology has provoked more attention and research than the influence of sport participation on academic achievement. An annotated bibliography (SIRLS Database, 1986) included 30 citations of articles on sport and academic achievement. Most of the research indicated that the academic performance of athletes is equal to or greater than that of non-athletes, although a few cited non-significant relationships (Houser & Lueptow, 1978; McElroy, 1980; Snyder, 1985). The research has been criticized for methodological flaws in design, misinterpretation of correlational findings for causal relationships, and the inherent weaknesses of cross-sectional research (Greendorfer, 1987); nevertheless, most of the empirical evidence supports the view that athletic involvement enhances the academic role.

Much of the research on athletic participation has addressed the development of educational aspirations. The results have generally indicated sport participation is positively associated with increased educational aspirations. An early study by Rehberg and Schafer (1968) revealed that high-school boys who were involved in athletics were more likely to plan on attending college than their non-athletic peers. The relationship was strongest for boys who are not as predisposed toward college (low SES, low academic standing, low parental encouragement). These findings have since been replicated by others (Spady, 1970; Spreitzer & Pugh, 1973). Spady (1971) proposed that participation in sport led youth to have a high self-perceived peer status which tended to increase educational aspirations. Otto and Alwin (1977) used multiple regression and path analytic procedures to follow a cohort of 17-year-old males over a 15-year interval. They found that sport participation of male students in high school was positively related to educational and occupational aspirations, after controlling for socioeconomic status, I.Q., and grades. A one-year follow-up of a national sample of high-school seniors indicated that athletic participation in high school had a significant impact on students' educational orientation and college-oriented behaviour. Sport participation in high school positively affected educational attainment, occupational status, and income 15 years later (Otto, 1982). Similarly, Howell, Miracle and Rees (1984) found that sports participation in high school was related to educational attainment five years later.

There has been much less research on girls, but the results are consistent. Wells and Picou (1980), in a Louisiana study of high-school seniors, found that female athletes held higher educational goals and stronger plans to attend college than their non-athletic peers. Moreover, female athletes from lower socioeconomic origins held significantly higher educational aspirations than their non-athletic peers. Melnick, Vanfossen and Sabo (1988) also found that athletic participation was positively related to school grades, standardized achievement scores, educational aspirations, and college attendance for women. The work of Marsh (1993) indicated that sport participation during the last two years of high school positively affected academic self-concept, educational aspirations, homework, and subsequent college attendance (after controlling for background variables and outcomes collected during the sophomore year). The positive effects of sports participation generalized across sex, race, socioeconomic status, and ability level.

A study of black, Hispanic, and white males (Snyder & Spreitzer, 1990) indicated that a greater percentage of students who participated in high-school sports went to college as compared to non-athletes. White male athletes from higher social status families with good parental relations and higher cognitive development were seven percentage points more likely to attend college than their non-athletic peers under the same circumstances. Black athletes from higher social status families with good parental relations and higher cognitive development were 17 percentage points more likely to attend college than their non-athletic counterparts. At the other end of the continuum, white athletes from low socioeconomic families with poor parental relations but good cognitive development were 17 percentage points more likely to attend college than their non-athletic counterparts. Black athletes, under the same circumstances, were 20 percentage points more likely to attend college than their non-athletic peers. Hanks (1979) found that participation in athletics has a much greater influence when social class status and academic aptitude are low. Snyder and Spreitzer (1990) also concluded that the positive influence of athletic involvement on educational attainment is even more evident among students who, for social reasons, are less predisposed to pursue their education. Melnick, Sabo and Vanfossen (1992a) found that sports participation had no influence on self-reported grade point averages or educational expectations among African-American and Hispanic youth. Although athletics did not seem to enhance academic performance, there were no minority subgroups in which athletes did not at least equal the academic record of their non-athletic counterparts.

Fejgin (1994) studied the same 22,696 students in Grade 8 and again in Grade 10 to examine the effects of sports participation on personal and academic outcomes. After controlling for background variables (gender, race, family income, parent education, and Grade 8 data), athletic participation appeared to contribute to higher grades and educational aspirations. The longitudinal nature of this study enables one to cautiously conclude that participation seems to positively affect these outcomes regardless of whether students with higher grades and educational aspirations choose to participate in sports in high school. In a longitudinal analysis of an 18–24 age cohort, Spreitzer (1994) found that athletes in high school were more likely to continue their education after high school and more likely to complete a baccalaureate degree than their non-athletic counterparts. Howell and Picou (1983) examined the effects of participation in high-school athletics on earnings eleven years after graduation. They controlled for socioeconomic background, educational-occupational plans, and schooling, and found that the payoff for participation in high-school sports was approximately $212 per month for white males and $120 per month for black males. Howell, Miracle and Rees (1984) did not find an economic payoff as a result of athletic involvement but suggested that high-school athletic participation may interact with educational attainment to affect adult earnings.

In general, the relationship between athletic participation and academic achievement is positive at the high-school level. Athletes tend to perform better academically than their non-athletic peers. No studies have found that sports participation negatively affects academic outcomes. The notion of the dumb jock is clearly a misconception. In addition, a consistent positive relationship has been found for athletic participation and educational aspirations. The relationship of athletics to aspirations such as attending college are even stronger for students from disadvantaged groups.

ATHLETIC PARTICIPATION, DROPPING-OUT OF SCHOOL, AND DELINQUENCY

Dropping out of high school is associated with lower occupational and economic prospects, poorer mental and physical health, decreased intergenerational mobility, and subsequent criminal behaviour (McNeal, 1995). It is of tremendous practical significance to identify the antecedents or correlates of dropping out of high school. Early work in this area suggested that students who were engaged in athletics had substantially lower dropout rates than did nonparticipants (Coleman, 1965; Vaugn, 1968). More recently, Melnick, Sabo and Vanfossen (1992b) reported that athletic participation decreased the dropout rate from American high schools for rural black males, suburban Hispanic males, and rural Hispanic females. McNeal (1995) investigated the effects of a variety of extracurricular activities on the high-school dropout rate. Athletics was found to be the most prestigious extracurricular activity compared to fine arts, academic, and vocational activities. Athletes were in greater positions of status, power and influence than any other group of students. On average, students in athletics were 1.7 times less likely to drop out of high school than were non-athletes. Black students in athletics were 1.9 times less likely to drop out than black students who were not involved in school athletic programs when socioeconomic status and academic abilities were controlled. In contrast, those in fine arts activities were 1.2 times less likely to drop out. McNeal concluded that athletic participation reduces the probability of dropping out by approximately 40% and is especially important for black students and students from low socioeconomic levels. In comparison with the influence of the other extracurricular activities on drop-out rates, " ... participation in athletics has the largest impact, both directly and as an intervening variable" (McNeal, 1995, p. 76).

How does participation in school athletics keep students in school? It may be that students stay in school because they enjoy sports and the friendships and popularity that sports foster. Sport participants are more apt than their nonparticipant peers to see themselves as being popular, an outcome that is magnified for minority youth. Melnick, Sabo and Vanfossen (1992a) have suggested that athletics promotes an allegiance, or identification with the school. As Marsh writes, " ... participation in sport leads to an increased commitment to, and involvement with, or identification with school and school values" (1993, p. 35).

Does participation in athletics deter delinquent behaviour? Research has consistently supported the hypothesis that male students involved with athletics partake in significantly fewer deviant behaviours and have significantly fewer encounters with the police (Landers & Landers, 1978; Schafer, 1969; Segrave & Hastad, 1984). Spreitzer (1994) reported a significant negative relationship between athletic participation in high school and the use of alcohol six years later. Furthermore, the greatest deterrence effects of athletic participation seem to be with low-status youth (Segrave & Chu, 1978; Segrave & Hastad, 1982). Schafer (1969) also reported that delinquency rates were significantly lower for male athletes who were low achievers academically or were from blue-collar families. Landers and Landers (1978) propose that athletes are less delinquent than many non-athletes because they learn, through sport, about the importance of accepting control by authority and abiding by conventional norms and values. Less research has addressed the deterrence theory with respect to girls and young women but the few studies conducted found that female athletes get into trouble with the police significantly less often than female non-athletes (Buhrmann, 1977; Buhrmann & Bratton, 1978; Segrave & Hastad, 1982). Buhrmann and Bratton concluded that "the profiles of deviants and athletes are almost diametrically opposed" (1978, p. 33). Diegmueller writes, " ... girls who participate in sports are far more likely to stay in school and avoid destructive behaviour (e.g., use drugs, have an unwanted pregnancy) than those who do not" (1994, p. 8). Hastad, Segrave, Pangrazi and Petersen (1984) extended the research on sport and delinquency to include preadolescents. The results of their work supported the deterrence theory for sixth-grade male and female students. The negative association between youth sport participation and deviant behaviour is particularly apparent for boys. Male participants reported 17.7% less composite deviance (drug-related, school-related, and nonschool-related) than male nonparticipants. The data also indicated that youth sport participation is positively related to peer status whereas deviance has a significant negative association with peer status.

SOCIAL AND POLICY IMPLICATIONS

Participation in sport has consistently been found to keep youth in school and reduce delinquent behaviour. Furthermore, most research has reported that athletic participation enhances academic standing. No studies have provided empirical support for the dumb jock concept or the notion that sport detracts students from academic performance. There have been numerous hypotheses proposed to explain the positive influence of sport on psychosocial development. The work on deterrence theory indicates that athletic participants are more likely to be popular and to associate with others who maintain prosocial standards. In contrast, deviants tend to associate with other deviants who are more likely to view deviant behaviour as legitimate. Thus, the peer networks and peer status afforded athletes may serve to further enhance their psychosocial development. A common form of discipline used in adolescence is to deny or withdraw their participation in sport. This method of discipline may be counterproductive and have unintended consequences of separating adolescents from conventional society.

Otto and Alwin (1977) refer to the healthy interpersonal skills that are learned in athletics and are readily transferable and marketable outside of sport. They also speculate that athletics may raise the visibility of participants and provide them with an early label or definition of being successful. Sport may expose participants to interpersonal networks, contacts, and information channels that are beneficial in establishing later careers. Athletic participants may develop social networks that reinforce or enhance their feelings of confidence, values of achievement, and prosocial behaviour. Rehberg and Schafer (1968) found that athletes tended to have friends who had more positive educational attitudes, aspirations and behaviour than did the friends of nonathletes. Segrave and Hastad (1984) reported that athletes were more likely to associate with significant others who tended towards conformity and emphasized adherence to social norms.

Athletes may have greater feelings of interest, identification, and commitment to their schools and teachers than do many nonathletes (Marsh, 1993; Snyder & Spreitzer, 1990). This enhanced attachment may socialize athletes to conformity behaviour (Finn, 1989; Marsh, 1993). Being on a school team means being recognized by the system as a good citizen which may in turn create a deeper commitment to the school, its values and main mission of academic work (Fejgin, 1994). Schafer has suggested that for athletes, "school is a source of success-experience and a positive public and private evaluation of self" (1969, p. 42). Buhrmann found that the athlete "enjoys high positive status among her peers as well as her teachers" (1977, p. 29).

"Athletic programs may well provide important opportunities for adolescents to be drawn into the legitimate system of conformity and achievement" (Segrave & Hastad, 1984, p. 134). Participation in sport requires an adjustment to rigid rules, regulations and coach's authority (Whitson, 1986) and teaches the importance of compliance, possibly making it easier to accept other school rules and formal authority (Fejgin, 1994). Fejgin (1994) postulates that athletic involvement may affect educational aspirations through its positive effects on self-concept, locus of control, and discipline. Sport involves experiences of success and failure that are highly visible to the individual and to peers. The direct, observable link between an athlete's performance and outcome helps to establish an internal locus of control. Athletic participation may lead to a heightened sense of popularity and self-worth that spills over to academic achievement (Snyder & Spreitzer, 1990). Athletic participation may lead adolescents to acquire skills, such as the abilities to organize and manage one's time, to strengthen attitudes such as self-discipline and delay of gratification, or to receive social rewards (Holland & Andre, 1987).

Adolescents who participate in school sports have higher academic standings and aspirations, higher self-esteem and sense of mastery over their lives, lower dropout rates from school, and less delinquency. A socially inclusive model of physical activity should be incorporated as a regular part of the school curriculum. The traditional sport paradigm should be abandoned in favour of a multicultural physical activity curriculum. A variety of programs need to be offered to allow all students, regardless of sex, age, race, socioeconomic status and ability level, the opportunity to experience the benefits of athletic participation. The focus should be on activities that are suitable throughout the life span, and that do not require facilities or athletic giftedness. In this way, athletic participation may be a mechanism by which to enhance the psychosocial development of our youth.

References

Buhrmann, H. (1977). Athletics and deviance: An examination of the relationship between athletic participation and deviant behaviour of high-school girls. *Review of Sport and Leisure, 2,* 17–35.

Buhrmann, H., & Bratton, R. (1978). Athletic participation and deviant behaviour of high-school girls in Alberta. *Review of Sport and Leisure, 3,* 25–41.

Coleman, J. (1965). *Adolescents and the schools.* New York: Basic Books.

Diegmueller, K. (1994, May 25). Efforts to boost girls' participation in sports urged. *Education Week,* p.8.

Fejgin, N. (1994). Participation in high-school competitive sports: A subversion of school mission or contribution to academic goals? *Sociology of Sport Journal, 11*, 211–230.

Finn, J. (1989). Withdrawing from school. *Review of Educational Research, 59*, 117–142.

Greendorfer, S. (1987). Psycho-social correlates of organized physical activity. *Journal of Physical Education, Recreation and Dance, 58*, 59–64.

Hanks, M. (1979). Race, sexual status and athletics in the process of educational achievement. *Social Science Quarterly, 60*, 482–496.

Hastad, D., Segrave, J., Pangrazi, R., & Petersen, G. (1984). Youth sport participation and deviant behaviour. *Sociology of Sport Journal, 1*, 366–373.

Henschen, K., Edwards, S., & Mathinos, L. (1982). Achievement motivation and sex-role orientation of high-school female track and field athletes versus nonathletes. *Perceptual and Motor Skills, 55*, 183–187.

Holland, A., & Andre, T. (1987). Participation in extracurricular activities in secondary school: What is known, what needs to be known? *Review of Educational Research, 57*, 437–466.

Holland, A., & Andre, T. (1994). Athletic participation and the social status of adolescent males and females. *Youth & Society, 25*, 388–407.

Houser, W., & Lueptow, L. (1978). Participation in athletics and academic achievement: A replication and extension. *Sociology of Education, 49*, 304–309.

Howell, F., Miracle, A., & Rees, C. (1984). Do high-school athletics pay? The effects of varsity participation on socioeconomic attainment. *Sociology of Sport Journal, 1*, 15–25.

Howell, F., & Picou, J. (1983). Athletics and income achievements. Paper presented at the annual meeting of the Southwestern Sociological Association, Houston, Texas.

Huxley, A. (1969). *Ends and means: An enquiry into the nature of ideals and into the methods of their realisation.* London: Chatto & Windus.

Kerr, G., & Goss, J. (1995). Personal control in elite, female gymnasts: The relationships among locus of control, self-esteem and trait anxiety. *The Journal of Sport Behaviour,* in press.

Kleiber, D., & Hemmer, J. (1981). Sex differences in the relationship of locus of control and recreational sport participation. *Sex Roles, 7*, 801–810.

Landers, D., & Landers, D. (1978). Socialization via interscholastic athletics: Its effects on delinquency. *Sociology of Education, 51*, 299–303.

Marsh, H. (1993). The effects of participation in sport during the last two years of high school. *Sociology of Sport Journal, 10*, 18–43.

McElroy, M. (1980). School sport socialization: A test of differential effects for disadvantaged youth. *Journal of Sport Psychology, 2*, 115–123.

McNeal, R. (1995). Extracurricular activities and high-school dropouts. *Sociology of Education, 68*, 62–81.

Melnick, M., Sabo, D., & Vanfossen, B. (1992a). Educational effects of interscholastic athletic participation on African-American and Hispanic youth. *Adolescence, 27*, 295–308.

Melnick, M., Sabo, D., & Vanfossen, B. (1992b). Effects of interscholastic athletic participation on the social, educational and career mobility of Hispanic girls and boys. *International Review for the Sociology of Sport, 27*, 57–75.

Melnick, M., Vanfossen, B., & Sabo, D. (1988). Developmental effects of athletic participation among high-school girls. *Sociology of Sport Journal, 5*, 22–36.

Otto, L. (1982). Extracurricular activities. In H. Walberg (Ed.), *Improving educational standards and productivity* (pp. 217–233). Berkeley, CA: McCuthan.

Otto, L., & Alwin, D. (1977). Athletics, aspirations and attainments. *Sociology of Education, 42*, 102–113.

Rehberg, R., & Schafer, W. (1968). Participation in interscholastic athletics and college expectations. *American Journal of Sociology, 73*, 732–740.

Schafer, W. (1969). Some sources and consequences of interscholastic athletics: The case of participation and delinquency. *International Review of Sport Sociology, 4*, 63–79.

Segrave, J., & Chu, D. (1978). Athletics and juvenile delinquency. *Review of Sport and Leisure, 3*, 1–24.

Segrave, J., & Hastad, D. (1982). Delinquent behaviour and interscholastic athletic participation. *Journal of Sport Behaviour, 5*, 96–111.

Segrave, J., & Hastad, D. (1984). Interscholastic athletic participation and delinquent behaviour: An empirical assessment of relevant variables. *Sociology of Sport Journal, 1,* 117–137.

SIRLS Database. (1986). Sport and academic achievement [annotated bibliography]. *Sociology of Sport Journal, 3,* 87–94.

Snyder, E. (1985). A theoretical analysis of academic and athletic roles. *Sociology of Sport Journal, 3,* 210–217.

Snyder, E., Kivlin, J., & Spreitzer, E. (1975). The female athlete: An analysis of objective and subjective role conflict. In D. Landers (Ed.), *Psychology of sport and motor behaviour* (Vol. II, pp. 165–180). University Park, PA: Pennsylvania State University.

Snyder, E., & Spreitzer, E. (1976). Correlates of sport participation among adolescent girls. *Research Quarterly, 47,* 804–809.

Snyder, E., & Spreitzer, E. (1990). High-school athletic participation as related to college attendance among black, Hispanic and white males. *Youth & Society, 21,* 390–398.

Spady, W. (1970). Lament for the letterman: Effects of peer status and extracurricular activities on goals and achievements. *American Journal of Sociology, 75,* 680–702.

Spady, W. (1971). Status, achievement, and motivation in the American high school. *School Review, 79,* 379–403.

Spreitzer, E. (1994). Does participation in interscholastic athletics affect adult development? A longitudinal analysis of an 18–24 age cohort. *Youth & Society, 25,* 368–387.

Spreitzer, E., & Pugh, M. (1973). Interscholastic athletics and educational expectations. *Sociology of Education, 46,* 171–182.

Vaugn, R. (1968). Involvement in extracurricular activities and dropout. *Journal of College Student Personnel, 9,* 60–61.

Wells, R., & Picou, J. (1980). Interscholastic athletes and socialization for educational achievement. *Journal of Sport Behaviour, 3,* 119–128.

Whitson, D. (1986). Structure, agency and the sociology of sport debates. *Theory, Culture and Society, 1,* 64–78.

Competence and Control in the Transition from Adolescence to Adulthood: A Longitudinal Study of Teenage Mothers

*Donna D. McAlpine, Carl F. Grindstaff and
Ann Marie Sorenson*

Women who have their first child during adolescence face an accelerated transition into adulthood often characterized by economic and social disadvantage. Women who give birth during adolescence are likely to have lower levels of education, less participation in the labour force, higher subsequent fertility, less marital stability, and less income than women who delay childbirth (Grindstaff, 1988; Chilman, 1980). Some research examines the characteristics of the family of origin that increase the probability of young women becoming teenage mothers (McLanahan & Bumpass, 1989); little attention has been given to how characteristics of the family of origin shape variations in outcomes among young mothers. There is wide variation in the experiences of young mothers as they enter adulthood; some women are able to manage the transition more easily than others (Furstenberg et al., 1987). This chapter examines variation in the experience of young mothers by focusing on the factors that shape their self-perceived competence in adulthood. What characteristics of the families of origin facilitate the development of self-esteem and perceived-control (mastery) in these women when they reach adulthood? What are the pathways through which family characteristics influence these women's feelings of competence? The interest is on differences within the group of young mothers and not on comparisons between young mothers and other women.

CONCEPT OF COMPETENCE

The meaning of competence remains somewhat elusive. Some theorists and researchers advance definitions of competence based on accomplishments; a variety of dimensions of competence have been examined including scholastic achievement, occupational prestige, economic affluence, and relational stability (Clausen, 1991; Harter, 1985; Digman & Digman, 1980). This research has helped document the precursors and consequences of achievement. Such a view of competence, however, neglects the reality of power differences reflected in gender, ethnicity, and social class as they relate to defining normative standards of achievement and in affording access to resources that facilitate the attainment of these standards. Quite a different concept of competence is rooted in the idea that competence represents a primary human motivation to actively interact with the environment, as agents responsible for consequences and outcomes (White, 1959; Smith, 1968). This definition moves from one based on behaviour or achievement to one based on perceptions; competence is reflected in perceptions that one has the capacity to negotiate the demands and challenges of the environment.

Smith (1968) argues for such a view of competence. One key component is self-esteem, or the degree to which an individual believes she or he is a person of worth and value. Individuals who believe they matter are more likely to have the self-confidence to attempt to actively shape their own lives. A second central component proposed by Smith is perceived efficacy, or the degree to which individuals' feel they have some control over the forces that influence their lives. Individuals who perceive that they have some control over their present circumstances, or future pathways, are motivated towards effective interaction with the environment. This component of the self-concept will be referred to as mastery but has been variously referred to as internal locus of control, self-efficacy, and perceived-control (Bandura, 1977; Rotter, 1966). Feelings of esteem and mastery are two central personal attributes that reflect perceived competence. Conceptions of one's self as important, worthwhile, and efficacious reflect a capacity to try to manage daily challenges and create new opportunities even in circumstances marked by serious disadvantage.

Self-perceived competence is influenced both by the opinions of others, and by the consequences of one's own behaviour (Gecas & Schwalbe, 1983). The metaphor of the looking glass (Cooley, 1902) has been evoked to describe the influence of opinions of others on the formation of sense of self. Simply put, Cooley argued that individuals' self-concepts are shaped by their perceptions of how others' view them. Children's perceptions of self may be primarily shaped through the reflected appraisals of their parents, given that parents are the most important agents of socialization. Gecas (Gecas, 1982; Gecas & Schwalbe, 1983) emphasizes the efficacious component of the self-concept and argues that self-esteem derives not only on the appraisals of others, but from personal experiences of success or failure. An individual's sense of self is a product of his or her experience. Individuals who have found that their own efforts have been demonstrably effective are more likely to develop feelings of self-efficacy.

Parents shape their children's perceived competence both through their reflected appraisals and through their influence on the child's experience of success and failure. Parenting styles characterized as supportive, caring, and affectionate are likely to encourage the development of positive feelings about self in children (Gecas & Seff, 1990). In contrast, authoritarian parenting styles represented by the use of coercion or force negatively impact a child's self-image (Gecas & Seff, 1990). Moreover, children's perceptions of parental attitudes and behaviours more strongly impact the development of self-concept than do actual parenting behaviour (Gecas & Schwalbe, 1986; Gecas & Seff, 1990). Parents may also facilitate their children's effective interaction with the environment, especially relating to education and family development. The family represents the earliest social context where children may gain the experience of efficacy. Parents may encourage activities that promote feelings of mastery such as education, and their judgements of these efforts will effect their children's perceived competence in these activities. Parenting styles characterized by overprotectiveness inhibit the development of feelings of autonomy in children and constrain their willingness to try new challenges that are crucial to the development of feelings of esteem and mastery (Gecas & Seff, 1982).

Family relations are conditioned by structural arrangements. Of central importance in this context is social class. Children of parents who lack access to resources face more limited opportunities than their affluent counterparts. Homes headed by single-parent mothers are disproportionately economically disadvantaged. Children from intact homes or who are financially privileged may be at an advantage in their access to activities, such as educational achievement, that encourage positive self-concepts. The focus on family is not intended to deny the importance of direct experience of success or failure. Families may directly affect their children's access to opportunities for achievement.

RESEARCH METHODS

The data presented in this chapter came from two waves of a three-wave prospective study of pregnant adolescents conducted in Middlesex County in southwestern Ontario. The initial wave of data collection occurred between 1983 to 1986 when young pregnant women who intended to carry their baby to term were recruited for the study primarily through family physicians, obstetricians, and gynaecologists practising in the area. Interviews were completed with 284 women in this first wave of data collection. Respondents were asked to participate in a second survey approximately four to eight weeks after their delivery; 261 women were successfully re-interviewed. In 1992 the women who were interviewed shortly after delivery were re-contacted and asked to participate in a third wave of data collection. Of the 261 women who participated in data collection shortly after birth, 213 were successfully re-interviewed approximately 6 years later for a response rate of 82%. Data collected at base-line (when these women were pregnant) and at approximately six years following the birth of the child are used. The base-line data point is Wave 1, and the six-year follow-up data is Wave 2. The final sample consists of the 213 women who were interviewed at both points in time.

One dimension of competence, mastery, is measured with the seven item mastery scale developed by Pearlin and Schooler (1978). Respondents were asked to indicate how strongly they agreed or disagreed with seven statements describing feelings of control. Example items include "My future depends mostly on me" and "I have little control over what happens." Possible responses ranged from strongly agree to strongly disagree. Items were recoded where necessary and summed to arrive at a scale where high scores reflect high levels of perceived competence. The scale had adequate reliability in both waves (Chronbach's alpha is .73 at wave 1 and .70 at wave 2). Respondents completed a six item version of Rosenberg's (1979) self-esteem scale at both waves. Respondents were asked to indicate how strongly they agreed or disagreed with statements reflecting perceived self-worth. Example items include "I have a number of good qualities" and "I am a person of worth." Items were coded so that high scores indicate high self-esteem. This scale also demonstrated excellent reliability (in both waves Cronbach's coefficient alpha exceeds.85).

Respondents were asked about their parents' occupations but little useable information was available about income. Father's occupation was used as the measure of social class, where available, otherwise mother's occupation was used. Responses were coded using the Hollingshead occupational prestige scale (Hollingshead & Redlich, 1958). Scores range from 1 to 7 with higher scores representing less prestigious occupations. Respondents were also asked about their living arrangements up until the age of sixteen. A dummy variable was computed that distinguished between those who lived with two parents and those who had other living arrangements (i.e., single parent, other adult).

Four separate measures of family environment were utilized: over-protection, support, abuse, and parental psychopathology. To measure overprotection, respondents completed a version of the parental bonding instrument (Parker et al., 1979) during the first wave of data collection. Women were asked to think back over their relationship with their mother and father while growing up when responding to thirteen questions about parental overprotection. Possible responses ranged on a four point scale from never to very often. Responses were summed for both mother and father so that high scores on the protection scale indicate perceived overprotectiveness, and lower scores indicate that respondents perceived their parents as encouraging autonomy and independence. Both the maternal and paternal overprotection scales had reliability coefficients above.85. The mean of the scales for respondents' mother and father was computed for a single measure of parental overprotection. Respondents also completed the family sub-scale of the provisions of social relations scale (PSR) (Turner et al., 1983) during the first wave of data collection. These six items tap the degree to which respondents believe themselves to be supported by their families. Cronbach's coefficient alpha for this scale was.90. High scores on the PSR indicate greater perceived support.

During the second wave of data collection, respondents were asked whether their parents had ever been physically abusive using questions developed from the work of Straus and his associates (Straus & Kantor, 1994). They were asked about whether they had ever been "hit with something," "kicked, punched or bit," and "beaten enough to cause bruises." They were also asked about the frequency of these specific abusive behaviours on a scale ranging from rarely to very often. A summary scale ranging from zero to three was computed based on responses to these questions. The three score indicates that the respondent reported that at least one type of abuse occurred frequently, and zero indicates that the respondent did not experience any of these forms of physical abuse. Respondents were asked a series of questions about parental depression and alcohol or substance use to measure parental psychopathology. Two variables were created: the first indicating whether either parent ever had a significant period of depression and the second whether either parent had a problem with substance/alcohol abuse.

During both interviews, respondents were asked to report how many years of schooling they had completed, their employment status and their marital status. Moreover, during the second interview, these women were also asked

Table 34.1: Descriptive Statistics: Measures of Competence and Characteristics of Respondents and Their Families[1]

Measures of Competence

		Wave 1		Wave2	
Mastery	$\overline{X}$	26.0 (5.5)	*	27.9 (3.9)	
Self-Esteem	$\overline{X}$	25.7 (4.5)		26.6 (4.8)	

Demographic Characteristics

		Wave 1		Wave 2	Census Data[2] (London)
Age	$\overline{X}$	18.1 (1.4)	*	25.8 (1.6)	25.0
Education:					
Years Completed	$\overline{X}$	10.3 (1.4)	*	11.2 (1.7)	14.2
High School Graduate	%	21.1	*	48.4	87.8
Marital Status:					
Married/Commonlaw	%	34.3	*	63.4	31.4
Divorced/Separated	%	0		22.5	.5
Never-Married	%	65.7		14.1	68.1
Employed Full-/Part-time	%	23.5	*	37.6	86.4
Personal Income	$\overline{X}$	NR		12429	19132
Household Income	$\overline{X}$	NR		29049	58884

Characteristics of Family of Origin

Structural Factors:		
Social Class	$\overline{X}$	4.8 (1.5)
Two-Parent	%	74.6
Parent-Child Relationship:		
Abuse	$\overline{X}$	.9 (.96)
% Ever abused		52.6
% Frequently abused		7.0
Overportection	$\overline{X}$	14.3 (7.8)
Support	$\overline{X}$	23.7 (6.0)
Parental Psychopathology:		
Substance Use	%	33.8
Depression	%	28.2

[1] Numbers in parentheses are standard deviations
[2] These data are derived from the 1991 Census Public Use Microdata file on Individuals and consist of the sample of women ages 24-26 who have not had children.
* Significant change p ≤ .05
NR = not reported

about their personal and household income and about the number of times they had been pregnant since the first interview.

RESULTS

Table 34.1 summarizes the demographic characteristics of this sample. In the first wave, during pregnancy, the women ranged in age from 13 to 20, with the mean age being 18.1 years. Approximately seven years later the women ranged in age from 20 to 29, with the mean age being 25.8 years. Table 34.1 also provides descriptive information about self-esteem and mastery, and characteristics of respondents and their families. Perceptions of mastery and self-esteem increase over time; the average score for both measures of competence is significantly higher during wave 2 when the women were adults.

The transition into adulthood was accompanied by significant changes in the social and economic status of these women. During the first wave, 66% of the women were single, defined as not married or living in common-law relationships. By the second wave, 23% had been divorced or separated and 14% were never-married. There were also significant changes in employment status and education levels. The average years of school completed was 10.3 years at wave 1 and 11.2 years at wave 2. More women were employed by the second interview (38% versus 24%). The first wave of data collection did not include information on income, however at the second wave the mean personal income for these women was approximately $12,500, while the mean household income was significantly higher at approximately $29,000.

Table 34.1 presents comparison information derived from census data about the demographic characteristics of women who had not had a child but were in the same age group, and from the same geographic region as the women included in the study. Women who had not had children had substantially higher levels of education, income, and participation in the labour force; young women who had not had children were less likely to have been married or to have been divorced or separated. The women who had their first child during adolescence appear to be significantly disadvantaged in adulthood when compared to their counterparts who had not had children.

The average social class score for respondents' families was 4.8, but the most important statistic relating to occupation is the distribution. The most frequent occupational category reported was semi-skilled (28%), while 22% of the sample reported that their father's were either small business owners or professionals. The majority of the sample were raised in two-parent households. Mean scores are provided for each of the measures of abuse, support, and overprotection. The majority of the sample indicated that they had been physically abused by at least one parent. Approximately 7% of these women reported frequent abuse by at least one parent. Approximately one-third of respondents indicated that one of their parents had a substance abuse problem, while over one-quarter indicated that one of their parents had a significant episode of depression.

Did these characteristics of respondents and their families influence levels of perceived competence when controlling for other relevant factors? Of primary interest is whether family factors exerted an influence independent of demographic factors. Table 34.2 presents results of examining the contribution

Table 34.2: Regressions of Wave 1 Competence Measures on Characteristics of Respondent and Family Variables[1]

Independent Variables	SELF-ESTEEM						MASTERY					
	Model I		Model II		Model III		Model I		Model II		Model III	
	b	B	b	B	b	B	b	B	b	B	b	B
Structural												
Social Class	-.13	-.04	-.15	-.05	-.10	-.03	-.48+	-.13	-.42+	-.12	-.31	-.09
Two Parents	-.73	-.07	-.69	-.07	-.82	-.08	-.96	-.07	-.34	-.03	-.59	-.05
Parental Psychopathology:												
Parental Substance Use			-1.46*	-.15	-1.47*	-.16			-.81	-.07	-.76	-.06
Parental Depression			1.16	.12	1.23	.12			-2.23*	-.18	-2.15*	-.18
Parent-Child Relationship												
Abuse			-.89*	-.19	-.82*	-.18			-.60	-.11	-.50	-.09
Over-protectivenes			.01	.01	-.00	-.01			-.15*	-.21	-.15*	-.22
Support			.14	.18	.13*	.17			.17*	.19	.17*	.19
Characteristics of Responent												
Education					.52+	.17					.71*	.19
Employment					-.36	-.03					.76	.06
Marital Status					1.02	.11					.86	.07
R^2	.00		.13		.15		.01		.25		.28	

[1] All regressions control for respondent's age at time 1.
b = unstandardized beta; B = standardized beta
*p ≤ .05; + p ≤ .10

of these factors for explaining levels of self-esteem and mastery during pregnancy (wave 1). Table 34.2 presents the regressions of self-esteem on all independent variables. Model I includes only the structural characteristics of family of origin—social class and family structure. Neither variable exerts an influence on self-esteem. The remaining characteristics of family are included in the regression shown in Model II. Parental abuse, substance use, and support exerted significant independent effects on levels of self-esteem. Specifically, higher levels of abuse and lower levels of parental support were associated with lower self-esteem. In addition, parental substance use was associated with lower levels of self-esteem among these women.

Model III controls for education, employment, and marital status of respondents to assess whether these factors influence the association of family structure and self-esteem. Higher levels of education were associated with higher self-esteem but controlling for education did not significantly reduce the effects of the previously significant family characteristics.

Table 34.2 also presents parallel regressions with mastery as the dependent variable. Neither structural factor is significant but social class approaches statistical significance (p = .06), and its effect is in the expected direction. Model II includes the other family characteristics and indicates that parental depression, over-protectiveness, and support are all associated with mastery. Adolescents who reported that one of their parents had a significant period of depression also report lower levels of mastery. Overprotectiveness is inversely related to feelings of control, and support is positively related to perceived mastery. Controls were also introduced for the demographic characteristics of the respondents; education was also significantly associated with mastery. Higher levels of education were associated with higher perceived control. Together these factors explain more of the variance in mastery (28%) than they do in self-esteem (15%).

The predictors of self-esteem and mastery during adulthood (wave 2) are examined for long-term effects of characteristics of family of origin. Including self-esteem or mastery as measured at wave 1 in this regression allows for an examination of predictors of change in levels of competence over the transition period. Including measures of education, marital status, and employment gathered at the second wave permits an assessment of how changes in these characteristics are associated with changes in perceived competence. Table 34.3 presents the information. Abuse during childhood exerts a direct effect on self-esteem during adulthood, controlling for prior levels of self-esteem. Support from family exerts a direct effect on feelings of mastery during adulthood. Taken together these findings indicate that abuse from parents was the most important predictor of changes in self-esteem, while parental support predicts changes in mastery over this seven year period. Thus, family characteristics continued to influence perceived competence, net of their impact on demographic characteristics of the respondents or their impact on earlier levels of competence.

Family life is associated with self-esteem and mastery, both in adolescents and adulthood. In adolescence, these women's self-esteem was most significantly influenced by parental substance use and emotional support and abuse, while mastery was influenced by parental depression, overprotection, and emotional support. The findings concerning the importance of family suggest that relationships with parents were central to the development of positive self-concepts among children (Gecas & Seff, 1990). The most important findings concerned experiences during adulthood. For young adolescent mothers experiences in their family of origin were critical for perceptions of their competence as adults. Moreover, these feelings of mastery and esteem are shaped more directly by family background than by the level of education, or marital and economic status of these women. The findings also show that variations in level of self-esteem and mastery during adulthood were linked to family background. Views of self as competent were critically important both to internal well-being and to how one manages the challenges of life.

The focus on individuals' perceptions of self does not preclude consideration of social structures. These women became mothers during a period of their lives that societal norms dictate was too early and stereotypes suggest was

Table 34.3: Regressions of Wave 2 Competence Measures on Characteristics of Respondent, Wave 1 Competence and Family Variables[1]

	WAVE 2 SELF-ESTEEM						WAVE 2 MASTERY					
	Model I		Model II		Model III		Model I		Model II		Model III	
	b	B	b	B	b	B	b	B	b	B	b	B
Wave 1 Measures												
Education	.65*	.25	.51*	.19	.21	.08	.51+	.15	.39	.11	.37	.11
Employment	-.64	-.07	-.54	-.06	-.67	-.08	.66	.06	.52	.05	.55	.05
Marital Status	.86	.11	.57	.07	.69	.09	1.14	.11	.99	.10	1.06	.10
Family Characteristics												
Social Class	.11	.04	.13	.05	.20	.08	-.41+	-.13	-.35+	-.11	-.35	-.11
Two Parents	.53	.06	.75	.09	.67	.07	.17	.02	.28	.02	.21	.02
Parental Substance Use	-.95	-.12	-.54	-.07	-.66	-.08	-.27	-.03	-.14	-.01	-.15	-.01
Parental Depression	.06	.01	-.28	-.03	-.35	-.04	-.20	-.02	.18+	.02	.20	.02
Abuse	-.90*	-.23	-.67*	-.17	-.60*	-.15	-.76*	-.15	-.67+	-.13	-.60	-.12
Over-Protectiveness	-.04	-.08	-.04	-.08	-.04	-.09	-.02	-.03	.01	.01	.01	.01
Support	.09*	.15	.06	.09	.03	.04	.18*	.22	.15*	.19	.13*	.16
Wave 1 Competence			.28*	.33	.29*	.34			.18*	.20	.17*	.20
Wave 2 Measures:												
# Pregnancies					-.19	-.06					-.37	-.09
Marital Status					-.89	-.11					-.83	-.08
Education					.24	.10					-.09	-.02
Employment					.26	.03					-.30	-.03
Income					.14	.12					.23+	.16
R^2	.22		.31		.34		.17		.20		.23	

[1] All regressions control for respondent's age (Time 1).
b = unstandardized beta; B = standardized beta
*p ≤ .05; + p ≤ .10

---

inevitably problematic for mother and child. They grew up during a historical time where becoming a women presaged limited opportunity, unequal economic rewards, and other types of gender discrimination. These larger gender systems have shaped how these women see themselves, the avenues for achievement they have available, and the ways they have been treated by their families. These nonquantitative predictors of women's perceptions of esteem and mastery are important to the interpretation of these empirical findings. Focus on the specific characteristics of family life that may encourage or hinder feelings of competence is not inconsistent with an awareness of the pervasive significance of broader social structures.

POLICY IMPLICATIONS

The emotional quality of family life influences the sense of competence for these mothers while they are adolescents and when they become adults. The structure of the family of origin, whether it is headed by one or two parents, does not appear to matter, but the quality of attachments to family is important. Thus, policy makers should actively resist the current discourse centred around family values, with its implied suggestion that a return to the traditional patriarchal family is desirable. This is not to suggest that families should not be valued by policy makers. Indeed, they should. However, families should be re-defined as healthy relationships, whatever structural form they may take. Policies focused on strengthening and supporting healthy relationships would prove valuable.

The results also indicate the importance of early intervention. Emotional support from family during childhood and adolescence increases perceived competence in adulthood, independent of characteristics of the respondent such as economic and educational achievement. Similarly, the experience of abuse in childhood continues to influence perceived competence, particularly feelings of self-esteem, in adulthood. Specific interventions focused on teaching parents the skills to be supportive, rather than coercive or abusive, and to encourage autonomy instead of being overprotective appear to be most important. These types of interventions are particularly valuable to prevent intergenerational transmission of problems in families. For example, Jeffery (1994) reports that mothers who have high self-esteem and mastery are likely to transmit feelings of competence to their children. Moreover, she finds that parenting styles is one possible pathway from maternal self-esteem and mastery to children's perceived competence. The development of positive parenting skills is likely to have an impact over generations. The family of origin may be central to the transition into adulthood, particularly for adolescents at risk. It may be necessary to examine prior experiences within families of young adults experiencing difficulties instead of solely concentrating on present circumstances. This is particularly important given that achievement, such as education, does not fully compensate for difficulties in one's family of origin.

References

Bandura, A. (1977). Self-efficacy: Toward a unifying theory of behavioral change. *Psychological Review*, *84*, 191–215.

Chilman, C.S. (1980). Social and psychological research concerning adolescent childbearing: 1970–1980. *Journal of Marriage and the Family, 42*, 793–805.

Clausen, J.S. (1991). Adolescent competence and the shaping of the life course. *American Journal of Sociology, 96*, 805–842.

Cooley, C.H. (1902). *Human nature and the social order.* New York: Schocken Books.

Digman, J.M., & Digman, K.C. (1980). Stress and competence in longitudinal perspective. In S.B. Sells, R. Crandall, M. Roff, J.S. Strauss & W. Pollin (Eds.), *Human functioning in longitudinal perspective: Studies of normal and psychopathic populations* (pp.219–231). Baltimore: Williams and Wilkins.

Furstenberg, F.F. Jr., Brooks-Gunn, J., & Morgan, P.S. (1987). *Adolescent mothers in later life.* Cambridge: Cambridge University Press.

Gecas, V., & Seff, M.A. (1990). Families and adolescents: A review of the 1980s. *Journal of Marriage and the Family, 52,* 941–958.

Gecas, V., & Schwalbe, M.L. (1983). Beyond the looking-glass self: Social structure and efficacy-based self-esteem. *Social Psychology Quarterly, 46,* 77–88.

Gecas, V. (1982). The self-concept. *Annual Review of Sociology, 8,* 1–33.

Grindstaff, C.F. (1988). Adolescent marriage and childbearing: The long-term economic outcome. *Adolescence, 23,* 45–58.

Harter, S. (1985). The perceived competence scale for children. *Child Development, 53,* 87–97.

Hollingshead, A.B., & Redlich, F.C. (1958). *Social class and mental illness: A community study.* New York: Wiley.

Jeffery, S.K. (1994). The relationship between maternal and child competence. Unpublished thesis, The University of Western Ontario.

McLanahan, S., & Bumpass, L. (1989). Intergenerational consequences of family disruption. *American Journal of Sociology, 94,* 130–152.

Parker, G., Tupling, H., & Brown, L.B. (1979). A parental bonding instrument. *British Journal of Medical Psychology, 52,* 1–10.

Pearlin, L.I., & Schooler, C. (1978). The structure of coping. *Journal of Health and Social Behavior, 22,* 337–356.

Rosenberg, M. (1979). *Conceiving the Self.* New York: Basic Books.

Rotter, J.B. (1966). Generalized expectancies for internal versus external control of reinforcement. *Psychological Monographs, 80* (Whole No. 609).

Smith, B.M. (1968). *Social psychology and human values.* Chicago: Aldine Publishing Company.

Straus, M.A., & Kantor, G.K. (1994). Corporal punishment of adolescents by parents: A risk factor in the epidemiology of depression, suicide, alcohol abuse, child abuse, and wife beating. *Adolescence, 29,* 543–561.

Turner, R.J., Frankel, G., & Levin, D.M. (1983). Social support: Conceptualization, measurement, and implications for mental health. *Research in Community and Mental Health, 3,* 67–111.

White, R.W. (1959). Motivation reconsidered: The concept of competence. *Psychological Review, 66,* 297–333.

This research was supported by a research grant funded by the National Health Research and Development Program, Health and Welfare Canada to principal investigator R. Jay Turner.

Woman Abuse in Canadian University and College Dating Relationships: The Contribution of Physical, Sexual, and Psychological Victimization in Elementary and High-School Courtship

Walter S. DeKeseredy

anadian researchers devoted little attention to the "multidimensional nature of woman abuse" in Canadian university and college dating relationships prior to the late 1980s (DeKeseredy & Hinch, 1991). Those interested in woman abuse in intimate, heterosexual relationships have concentrated primarily on the incidence, prevalence, distribution, and sources of non-lethal physical assaults on married, cohabiting, separated or divorced women. Several recent quantitative and qualitative data sets show that sexual and psychological victimization of heterosexual women is common in Canadian post-secondary school courtship (DeKeseredy & Kelly, 1993a; Schwartz & DeKeseredy, in press). Data generated by a national representative sample survey of female undergraduates show that 22% were physically assaulted, 28% were sexually abused, and 79% were psychologically abused in the year before the survey (DeKeseredy & Kelly, 1993a). These findings are similar to those obtained in comparable surveys conducted in the United States (Koss et al., 1987; White & Koss, 1991).

The abuse of intimate female partners does not start in post-secondary school courtship. The handful of North American non-representative sample surveys show that many female high-school students are at great risk of being victimized by their dating partners (DeKeseredy & Schwartz, 1994). Patterns usually associated with wife or cohabiting abuse and female victimization in university or college dating appear in high-school relationships, and often for similar reasons. These studies, however, cannot establish the extent of such behaviour in the high-school population at large; only large-scale random sample surveys can achieve this goal. The same can be said about reliable estimates of the extent of woman abuse in North American elementary school dating relationships (grades 1 to 8). No survey has been conducted on this problem. Since many elementary school girls date heterosexual boys (Holmes & Silverman, 1992), it is fair to hypothesize that some of them are likely to be abused. Young boys are heavily influenced by a key determinant of woman abuse in university or college dating relationships—the ideology of familial patriarchy (DeKeseredy & Kelly, 1993b; Mercer, 1988).

Sudermann and Jaffe reviewed research on male-to-female victimization in adolescent dating relationships and concluded that "[v]iolence in adolescent dating relationships ... may be viewed as a precursor of violence in adult relationships" (1993, p. 3). Interpretations such as this, however, are based on comparisons of completely different college and high-school samples; the data are not directly relevant to their arguments (DeKeseredy & Schwartz, 1994). Several major research gaps need to be filled. The main objectives of this chapter are (1) to provide estimates of the prevalence of woman abuse in elementary and high-school courtship which are derived from a Canadian national representative sample of male and female undergraduate students, (2) to show that female victimization in post-secondary school dating relationships has some roots in earlier types of courtship, and (3) to propose several primary prevention strategies that may reduce the likelihood of young males becoming adult perpetrators.

METHOD

The information reported here came from a Canadian national representative sample survey of community college and university students conducted in the autumn of 1992 (DeKeseredy, 1995; DeKeseredy & Kelly, 1993a, 1993b; Pollard, 1993). Two questionnaires, one for men and another for women, were administered to 95 undergraduate classes across the country. Both French and English language versions were administered. Response rates were very high with less than one percent of the participants refusing to answer. The sample consisted of 3,142 people, including 1,835 women and 1,307 men. The median age of female respondents was 20 and the median age of males was 21. Most of the participants identified themselves as either English or French Canadian; 82% of the men and 78% of the women were never married. All respondents were carefully and repeatedly instructed that all questions in the survey referred only to events that took place in dating (non-marital) relationships. The sample was composed mainly of first and second year students; 42% of the women and 27% of the men were enroled in Arts programs. Approximately 3% of the women were members of sororities and 6% of the men belonged to fraternities.

Woman abuse was defined as any intentional physical, sexual, or psychological assault on a female by a male dating partner (DeKeseredy & Kelly, 1993a, 1993b). Four questions were used to measure the prevalence of this problem in elementary school courtship (grades 1 to 8); men were asked to report their abusive behaviour, while women were asked to disclose victimization. Each female was asked to circle "yes" or "no" in response to these questions:

In elementary (high) school, did a male dating partner and/or boyfriend ever ...

- threaten to use physical force to make you engage in sexual activities?

- use physical force in an attempt to make you engage in sexual activities, whether this attempt was successful or not?
- intentionally emotionally hurt you (i.e., insult, say someting to spite you)?
- intentionally physically hurt you?

The methodology for the college/university portion of this study are described elsewhere (DeKeseredy, 1995; DeKeseredy & Kelly, 1993a, 1993b; Kelly & DeKeseredy, 1994). Generally, sexual abuse was measured through the use of relevant questions from a slightly modified version of the Sexual Experiences Survey (Koss et al., 1987), while physical and psychological abuse were measured through relevant questions from a slightly modified version of the Conflict Tactics Scale (Straus & Gelles, 1986).

RESULTS

Of the men who answered the elementary school questions:

- 1.7% (12) stated they threatened to physically force their dating partners to engage in sexual activities.
- 1.5% (11) reported having physically forced women to engage in sexual activities.
- 18.6% (133) reported having been emotionally abusive.
- 3.6% (26) admitted to having been physically abusive.

Women reported markedly higher rates of victimization:

- 3% (25) stated that their partners threatened to physically force them to engage in sexual activities.
- 4.3% (36) revealed that they were physically forced to engage in sexual acts.
- 23.7% (198) said that their partners emotionally hurt them.
- 7.2% (60) disclosed having been physically hurt.

High-school students spend more time dating than those in elementary school and thus, spend greater time-at-risk of abuse (Ellis & DeKeseredy, 1996). For the women, 89% stated that they dated in high school, while 38% stated that they dated in elementary school. The equivalent figures for the men are 87% in high school and 48% in elementary school. This higher rate is evident in reporting emotional abuse by men, but only slight differences are evident in the other male self-report measures. For example:

- 1% (11) stated that they threatened to use physical force to make their partners engage in sexual activities.
- 2.3% (25) reported having used physical force to make women engage in sexual activities.
- 33.4% (362) disclosed having emotionally hurt their dates.
- 1.4% (15) admitted to having physically hurt theirdates.

All the female data support the hypothesis that the more time at risk, the more likely women are to be abused in high-school courtship.

- 8.3% (131) stated that their partners threatened to physically force them to engage in sexual activities.
- 14.5% (228) revealed that their dates physically forced them to engage in sex acts.
- 49.7% (780) reported having been emotionally hurt.
- 9.1% (143) stated that their partners physically hurt them.

Three previous Canadian surveys on high-school abuse have been conducted (Mercer, 1988; Jaffe et al., 1992; Sudermann & Jaffe, 1993). It is difficult to compare the findings presented here with any of these studies. The other surveys asked questions directly of high-school students where as this national survey asked university and community college students about their high-school experiences; thus, students who did not pursue a post-secondary school education were eliminated from the sampling frame. The results of the present study can only be compared to Mercer's (1988) because Jaffe and colleagues (1992) and Sudermann and Jaffe (1993) did not directly ask respondents to report whether they were victims or perpetrators of abusive behaviour. Instead, they asked high-school students to indicate whether they experienced abuse, leaving open the possibility for each individual respondent to state that they were either an offender or a victim. It is unclear how Mercer (1988) measured abuse because she does not report her questions. Nevertheless, a review of her findings reveal the following differences:

- A higher percentage of her high-school male respondents admitted to having been sexually abusive (12%), while 16% of the university/college respondents reported being sexually abused in high school, somewhat lower than Mercer's (20%).
- Mercer's male and female physical abuse figures are very similar to those generated by the present study.
- This study's male (33%) and female (50%) psychological abuse statistics are markedly higher than Mercer's (17% male; 13% female). This could be because she seems to have limited psychological abuse to something called verbal abuse, although the question is not reported or discussed by Mercer (DeKeseredy & Schwartz, 1994).

Do men who abuse their college or university dating partners establish these patterns at a younger age? Do men begin patterns of victimization in elementary and high school and bring them to post-secondary school? Such patterns existed in each of the three areas of physical, sexual, and emotional abuse. Although most physical abuse obviously takes place after high school, 55% (17) of the 31 men who claimed that they were intentionally physically abusive in elementary and high-school courtship also admitted to similar acts after high school. Two-thirds of these men were in the autumn term of their first year (39%) or second year (28%) at the time of the survey. Thus, the time-at-risk for college and university students was short. A similar pattern was seen with the small number of men who admitted using force to make a dating partner engage in sexual activities. Eight (32%) of the 25 elementary and/or high-school admitters also disclosed similar forced behaviour in college or university. From a retrospective look, 8 (35%) of the 23 men who admitted to using force in college or university also admitted to having used it in elementary and/or high-school dating relationships. Forty-eight percent of the men admitted to abusing women emotionally. Virtually all (96%) of the men who admitted such abuse in elementary and high school, also admitted to using similar forms of abuse after high school. Eighty-five percent of the men who had dated since elementary school admitted to having been emotional abusers since high school.

Women reported more victimization than men but the patterns were the same. Retrospectively, 38% of the women who reported being physically or sexually assaulted since high school had had a similar experience earlier. Moreover, of those women who were physically harmed in college or university, 25% reported similar episodes in high school. The pattern of emotional abuse matched that for male offenders. Sixty-five percent reported being emotionally abused in some way since high school. Virtually all (96%) of the women who reported abuse in high school or elementary school reported that it happened again after high school.

POLICY IMPLICATIONS

The research reported here adds to the information on woman abuse in North American high-school dating relationships and marks the start of the development of a data base on the physical, sexual, and psychological victimization of females in elementary school. This exploratory study attempted to determine whether abuse in these two educational contexts persists into university or college dating relationships. The information suggests that many men come to college or university with the full armoury of ideology and behaviours necessary to abuse women (DeKeseredy & Schwartz, 1994). How can we prevent young boys from becoming abusive in adolescent and adult heterosexual, intimate relationships? Elementary and high-school-based educational and awareness programs, such as videos, workshops, presentations, plays, and classroom discussions are relevant prevention programs. These programs help show young people what love should be (Fitzpatrick & Halliday, 1992), may reduce the incidence and prevalence of woman abuse in courtship (Bohmer & Parrot, 1993), help provide an atmosphere in which students show more respect for each other (Bohmer & Parrot, 1993), reach a large audience (Jaffe et al., 1992), and can change attitudes, increase knowledge and change behavioral intention (Jaffe et al., 1992; Sudermann & Jaffe, 1993). Many abused female teenagers want school educational programs and strongly believe that these initiatives would have helped prevent them from entering violent relationships (Fitzpatrick & Halliday, 1992). Furthermore, if these programs are not provided, students will typically receive a biased education from either gossip or the uninformed and sensational media (Bohmer & Parrot, 1993).

There is growing community support for school-based interventions and several school boards have developed prevention strategies. Even so, teachers and administrators should not take a "haphazard, one-classroom-at-a-time approach" because it does not offer "system-wide sponsorship and coverage" (Jaffe et al., 1992, p. 131). Instead, every student, teacher, and administrator should participate. School-based prevention programs throughout Canada should attempt to increase knowledge about woman abuse, address the patriarchal forces that perpetuate and legitimate woman abuse, promote knowledge about early warning signs of abusive patterns in intimate relationships, expand definitions of abuse to include verbal, emotional, physical, and sexual victimization, provide information on community-based social support services, and develop an ongoing, system-wide commitment to preventing woman abuse and all violence in relationships (Jaffe et al., 1992).

References

Bohmer, C., & Parrot, A. (1993). *Sexual assault on campus: The problem and the solution*. Toronto: Macmillan.

DeKeseredy, W. (1995). Enhancing the quality of survey data on woman abuse: Examples from a national Canadian study. *Violence Against Women, 1*, 158–173.

DeKeseredy, W., & Hinch, R. (1991). *Woman abuse: Sociological perspectives*. Toronto: Thompson Educational Publishing, Inc.

DeKeseredy, W., & Kelly, K. (1993a). The incidence and prevalence of woman abuse in Canadian university and college dating relationships. *The Canadian Journal of Sociology, 18*, 157–159.

DeKeseredy, W., & Kelly, K. (1993b). Woman abuse in university and college dating relationships: The contribution of the ideology of familial patriarchy. *The Journal of Human Justice, 4*, 25–52.

DeKeseredy, W., & Schwartz, M. (1994). Locating a history of some Canadian woman abuse in elementary and high-school dating relationships. *Humanity & Society, 18*, 49–63.

Ellis, D., & DeKeseredy, W. (1996). *The wrong stuff: An introduction to the sociological study of deviance* (2nd ed.). Toronto: Allyn and Bacon.

Fitzpatrick, D., & Halliday, C. (1992). *Not the way to love: Violence against young women in dating relationships*. Amherst, NS: Cumberland County Transition House Association.

Holmes, J., & Silverman, E. (1992). *We're here, listen to us!* Ottawa: Canadian Advisory Council on the Status of Women.

Jaffe, P., Sudermann, M., Reitzel, D., & Killip, S. (1992). An evaluation of a secondary school primary prevention program on violence in intimate relationships. *Violence and Victims, 7*, 129–146.

Koss, M., Gidycz, C., & Wisniewski, N. (1987). The scope of rape: Incidence and prevalence in a national sample of higher education students. *Journal of Consulting and Clinical Psychology, 55*, 162–170.

Mercer, S. (1988). Not a pretty picture: An exploratory study of violence against women in high-school dating relationships. *Resources for Feminist Research, 17*, 15–23.

Pollard, J. (1993). *Male-female dating relationships in Canadian universities and colleges: Sample design, arrangements for data collection and data reduction*. Toronto: Institute for Social Research, York University.

Schwartz, M., & DeKeseredy, W. (in press). *Sexual assault on the college campus: The role of male peer pressure*. Thousand Oaks, CA: Sage.

Straus, M., & Gelles, R. (1986). Societal changes and change in family violence from 1975 to 1985 as revealed by two national surveys. *Journal of Marriage and the Family, 48*, 465–479.

Sudermann, M., & Jaffe, P. (1993). Violence in teen dating relationships: Evaluation of a large scale primary prevention program. Paper presented at the annual meeting of the American Psychological Association, Toronto.

White, J., & Koss, M. (1991). Courtship violence: Incidence in a national sample of higher education students. *Violence and Victims, 6*, 247–256.

This research was supported by a grant from Health Canada's Family Violence Prevention Division. Thanks is extended to Martin D. Schwartz, Betsy Stanko, Dragan Milovanovic, John Pollard, Brian MacLean, and the Ottawa Regional Coordinating Committee to End Violence Against Women for helpful comments and criticisms.

Youthful Involvement in Illicit Street Drug Markets: Avenues for Prosperity or Roads to Crime?

Patricia G. Erickson

A career involving the exchange of illegal goods or services has much in common with more conventional occupational pursuits. The would-be incumbent considers incentives and discentives, educational or other skill requirements, and short and long-term plans. It is useful to distinguish work from career. Work may refer to any number of activities for which an individual receives payment in some form. Career refers to a series of related activities, whether legal or illegal, which form a focal point for the organization of the individual's life (Faupel, 1991). The appeal of delinquent and drug use activities to youth and the subsequent trajectory of criminal careers has received considerable study and commentary (Adlaf et al., 1994; Agnew, 1994; Nagin et al., 1995). The more specific attraction of drug market involvement has attracted less attention (Smart et al., 1992). In particular, the rise and expansion of cocaine markets as a magnet for youthful entrepreneurs has been largely ignored in Canada, though a small but growing literature attests to this phenomenon in the United States (Williams, 1989; Reuter et al., 1990; Reuter & MacCoun, 1992). Much of the US research has focused on patterns of violence and adult criminality in the crack trade (Fagan & Chin, 1991a; Inciardi & Pottieger, 1994; Johnson et al., 1994), but some studies of adolescents have been conducted (Altshuler & Brounstein, 1991; Inciardi & Pottieger, 1991; Dembo et al., 1993; Dembo et al., 1994). The illicit drug market is organized in a pyramid, with a very few large-scale importers at the top, a multitude of street level sellers and their customers at the bottom, and a hierarchy of wholesale and retail distributors inbetween. The research is limited, but available studies have suggested that the activities carried out by sellers vary widely according to the social groups involved, the types of drugs, and pressures from control agencies (Fagan & Chin, 1991b). Some of the more vivid accounts are found in the pages of fiction, such as Seth Morgan's *Homeboy* and Richard Price's *Clockers*, two realistic novels about the dealing culture in American cities.

This chapter will review the relevant literature and consider its applicability to youth in transition in Canada. Preliminary findings from a community-based Toronto study of illicit drug markets that appear to have a youthful component will be presented. The evidence from this research in progress shows that it would be a mistake to assume that US-style drug markets and the concomitant violence cannot take root in areas of urban deprivation and high unemployment in this country. This chapter will concentrate on the particular evolution and features of the crack cocaine market. Street drug markets provide the most visible and accessible opportunities for youth. While many drug transactions do occur on the street (or in adjacent parks, bars and donut shops), this relatively public activity is matched by a considerable and very discreet traffic among middle-class users and dealers (Waldorf et al., 1994). Many of the anti drug and anti trafficking images that fill the popular media reflect only a part of the whole picture of the delivery of illegal substances to consumers across the spectrum of class, occupational, educational, and racial groups.

THE AMERICAN RESEARCH

Cocaine was first introduced in the smokable form of crack in the mid–1980s in the USA; a number of properties have fostered the rapid growth of the trade (Fagan & Chin, 1991a; 1991b). The intense, reinforcing properties of the "high" guaranteed demand. The preceding popularity of powder cocaine, taken by nasal inhalation, had created a receptive consumer base. Crack could be sold in small amounts, or hits, at a low unit cost. This meant low entry costs for sellers. Since it was new (though preceded by the more expensive and dangerous freebase form extracted with volatile solvents) no organized competition existed. The lack of economic opportunities in inner city neighbourhoods made the profitability of crack sales attractive both to experienced sellers and to newcomers.

The highly lucrative crack trade became exceptionally violent as well. The predominant location of the market in socially disorganized neighbourhoods, with large numbers of otherwise unemployed young men, and gang alignments, led to aggressive escalation of local drug wars over the control of territory (Klein et al., 1991). Women, too, became involved in the cocaine economy (Fagan, 1994). Violently predisposed individuals may self select into crack use and sale; the multiple transactions involved on the street and the need for protection of one's person and drugs from others also ensure violent interactions (Fagin & Chin, 1991a). The inherently violent nature of unregulated, illegal markets was brought into bold relief in the crack scene (Goldstein, 1985; Goldstein et al., 1989). Reuter and colleagues (1990), in their landmark study of drug selling in Washington, D.C., expressed a growing concern that:

> The rapid growth of street drug markets, particularly for crack cocaine, has apparently provided a new set of highly paid, albeit risky, illegal earnings opportunities for young persons with poor prospects in the legitimate job market. This phenomenon has been particularly striking in urban areas characterized by a high incidence of poverty and social disorder. Some observers fear that increasing involvement in drug selling will lead to fewer young males from poor urban communities completing high school and to lower work force attachment (p. v).

To test this perception with systematic research, Reuter and others began to conduct investigations aimed at revealing the nature and extent of youthful involvement in street drug markets and their appeal as an alternative career path.

Inciardi & Pottieger (1991) interviewed 254 serious delinquents in Miami of whom 80% were involved in the crack business. All were under 18 years of age, over 90% were dropouts or were attending Grade 10 or less, a similar high proportion had been expelled or suspended from school at some time, and only 7% were legally employed. The sample was mixed by sex (85% male, 15 % female) and race (43% white, 40% black, 17% hispanic). Most had been committing other types of crime prior to starting to sell drugs, but intensification of criminal activities, especially violent crime, was associated with greater involvement in the crack business. All those involved in selling crack also used it, with three quarters being daily or near daily users; the heaviest users were also the most frequent sellers. The attractions of dealing went beyond the profits to be made, particularly since most of the more involved dealers spent large amounts of money on crack in addition to being paid with crack. There is an appeal to the drug dealing lifestyle—the thrills and excitement, the frenzied activity that may produce profits, recognition, and upward mobility for youths with few other prospects. Even the real risks of violence, arrest, overdose, and death are translated into challenges to be outwitted and overcome. "Participation in the crack trade ... provides its own kind of intoxication for the youths entangled in it" (Inciardi & Potteiger, 1991, p. 269).

This pattern was repeated in a longitudinal study of juvenile detainees in Tampa, Florida (Dembo et al., 1994). The followup sample of 229 male youths, of whom 46% were white, 45% black and 6% hispanic, was examined for their cocaine (crack was not specifically identified or separated from powder cocaine) selling behaviour. These youths were not well equipped to compete on the basis of formal education and job skills, and regarded the drug business as a risky but profitable way to meet their material and status needs. Early involvement in drug dealing was associated with a greater likelihood of subsequent cocaine use for both whites and non-whites. Selling cocaine was a popular activity among these youths; most who got involved tended to continue it over time. Dembo and associates also identified important black-white differences in drug use, selling and other criminal activities. Black youth were more involved in cocaine sales; white youth had greater involvement in general theft crimes and alcohol and marijuana use. White youths who were cocaine sellers were relatively more deviant from the norms of their social and cultural setting than were black cocaine sellers. Among black youth, selling cocaine is "rational, motivated, adaptive, and environmentally embedded" behaviour that is valued in their milieu (Dembo et al., 1994, p. 1829).

Reuter, MacCoun & Murphy designed a study "to illuminate the role of drug selling in the economic life of persons at risk of long-term poverty" (1990, p. iii). Their main sources of data pertained to adults aged 18 or over living in the Washington DC area in 1985 to 1988, and were obtained from official records and interviews with probationers. Those charged with, or self-report-ing, the commission of a drug selling offence were predominantly young, male, and black. These researchers estimated that a substantial fraction of the District's young black males participated in drug selling and approximately one in six aged 18 to 20 was charged with a trafficking offence. Details of drug selling activities revealed that many sold drugs on a part-time basis, and also held legitimate jobs, but drug selling income far outstripped their legal earnings. To make, on the average, $40,000 tax free dollars annually was not a risk-free enterprise; for one year of regular dealing, the chance of incarceration was estimated to be one in 4.5, that of a serious injury one in 14, and fatality one in 50 (Reuter et al., 1990, p. 104). Their findings confirmed the importance of drug selling for young, poorly educated black males in that city.

The dearth of research on the attractions of drug dealing for adolescents led Reuter and colleagues (1990) to a secondary data analysis of a 1988 survey of 9th and 10th graders conducted by the Urban Institute in inner city public schools in Washington DC. This survey of 387 adolescents examined their involvement in, and attitudes towards, drug dealing. One in six of these young people reported selling drugs, and over half of those had done so more than five times; 70% of sellers had not used drugs themselves. Even among those who neither sold nor used drugs, about two thirds thought that other students were selling drugs. The adolescents saw drug selling as an intrinsic part of their world. The young respondents were also asked about their perceptions of the risks and returns of drug selling. Both profits and risks were viewed as high in general, but sellers saw the activity as more financially rewarding and less dangerous than did the nonsellers. Fifty percent of the frequent dealers (more than 5 times in previous year) thought serious injury or death was a very likely outcome in a year of dealing drugs, 38% that arrest was similarly possible, and 25% that a prison sentence would be the result. Fifty-nine percent of the frequent dealers estimated that their drug-selling friends earned more than $1,000 a week. These results paint a picture of a young cohort of drug sellers likely to accept serious risks for the sake of profits, but it is important to note that these estimates were for a general "dealer year" rather than their own estimate of personal risk. The latter perception may be of a considerably lower risk, given the feelings of invincibility that tend to characterize this age group. About 10% of the adolescents saw drug selling as a possibility after they left school, and 63% of the frequent sellers saw it as continuing, but most did not think drug selling would be their main occupation. When asked about how much they admired persons in a variety of occupations, 82% "did not at all admire" someone who sold drugs; the only lower rated occupation was pimp. Professional athletes and doctors got the highest ratings (77% and 73% respectively). These youngsters were not totally severed from more conventional career aspirations; however, the reality may be that the pathway to economic survival, or even success, may be found more on the pathway of the crack trade than a college education.

Another study has examined the perceptions of youths about the reasons and risks of the crack trade (Dembo et al., 1993). In depth interviews were conducted with 34 black youths who were involved in crack dealing. Respondents were age 22 or younger and lived in two housing projects in a Florida urban community. Most had left school and had no other legitimate employment. Economic gain seemed to be the principal reason for their dealing; most said they were not currently using crack, and they sold it "to earn lots of money" and "because legal jobs pay too little." Their average income in the past week from crack sales was $672. About one quarter of the respondents reported that dealer-buyer and dealer-dealer violence was a risk to them, and half cited death as a possibility. Two-thirds of these dealers indicated that they had hurt or killed someone through their association with the cocaine trade. The findings described a group of young blacks who "... felt hopeless about the prospects of attractive, well paid work ... and were more concerned about these drawbacks of their lifestyle [lack of education and an obsession with acquiring personal luxury items] than they were about being arrested, going to prison, or experiencing violence or death on the streets" (Dembo et al., 1993, p. 95).

In summary, research on adolescents and young adults involved in the crack trade has demonstrated that selling this drug can be highly profitable compared to legitimate employment. Younger persons may start dealing without using, but crack selling increases the likelihood of crack use as time goes by. Since the most involved sellers tend also to be the heaviest users, actual profit from crack sales can be largely absorbed by their own habit. Many crack sellers had prior involvement in delinquent activities; crack selling appears to intensify other criminal behaviours, particularly violent crime. Crack markets are rooted in deprived and socially disorganized neighbourhoods in the inner cities. The dealer image may provide an ambivalent role model for youth, but the potential profits from crack selling outweigh the many serious risks for many minority black males with limited options in the mainstream economy. The generalizability of these conclusions is limited by the nature of the samples studied thus far, mainly of already delinquent or criminal youth, located in Washington, DC or Florida. This phenomenon has been little studied outside the USA.

THE CANADIAN RESEARCH

The question remains as to the relevance of this career option for young Canadians, and whether Canadian areas of urban deprivation are fostering an environment that could make the USA reality part of Canada. Research has been conducted in Canada on cocaine and crack users, but none has been carried out specifically on involvement in crack selling or the structure of the illicit market in Canadian locales (Cheung et al., 1991; Erickson & Weber, 1994; Erickson et al., 1994). Smart and associates (1992) have described the characteristics of high-school students who sell drugs, mainly cannabis. The involvement of minorities in recorded drug trafficking offenses cannot be assessed in a comprehensive way since official criminal justice statistics on arrests and sentencing are not recorded by race or ethnicity (except for Aboriginals). This is in contrast to the USA, where official data clearly show that nonwhite minorities have been disproportionately criminalized for drug crimes, particularly crack cocaine (Blumstein, 1993; Chambliss, 1994).

Smart, Adlaf and Walsh (1994) examined the relationship between the experience of drug problems and the socioeconomic status of neighbourhoods in a sample of high-school students. The highest rates of alcohol and other drug use and problems occurred in 6 of the 79 geographical areas with the lowest SES characteristics; five of the areas contained substantial amounts of downtown, low cost, sub-standard housing, and government subsidized housing. The sixth area was a more suburban locale where a high rate of alcohol use predominated over other drug use and problems. Other aspects of poverty in these high problem areas should be examined in relation to specific types of drug problems such as dealing (Smart et al., 1992).

Henry (1994), drawing extensively on interviews and participant observation in the Caribbean community in Toronto, reported that the predominant criminal activities involved drug dealing, rather than other forms of crime, and were primarily motivated by economic reasons. Motives, besides profit, included rebellion against family and a feeling of belonging in another group. Drug selling "may serve the function of providing a baseline for the marginalized youth who do not feel that they can fit into Canadian society. They lack the education, training and social skills to make them adaptable" (Henry, 1994, p. 199). This account, while anecdotal, is reminiscent of the American studies of inner city black youth.

TORONTO EAST DOWNTOWN STUDY

A new study was initiated in a community referred to as Toronto East Downtown (TED) to further highlight the Canadian situation. The total population of TED is about 34,000. TED is a highly diverse area of Toronto with a mix of expensive old mansions, renovated homes, new highrise condominiums, public housing projects, and a variety of hostels for the homeless. Historically TED was noted for a large skid row population, prominent street prostitution, and a high concentration of injection drug users; more recently it has been identified as the locale for a fairly public trade in crack.

Interviews began in early 1995 with individuals in a variety of key informant groups. Residents—both the well and the under housed—social service workers, police officers, and users and sellers involved in the crack business were interviewed. Sources all independently confirmed that, while crack had been around for several years, use and selling had intensified in TED since 1993, and were widespread and visible. The study is still ongoing. This chapter will concentrate on the material gained from interviews with 20 people who were involved in crack distribution in TED. Working through trusted intermediaries, individuals were contacted and brought into a local agency office on a no-names basis. They took part in about a 3/4 hour interview and were paid $10.00. Three women and 17 men took part, ages ranged from 20 years to late 50's, and race as observed was white (13 respondents), black (4 respondents) or Aboriginal (3 respondents). Nearly all were Canadian born and raised, and had been in the neighbourhood for several years.

Most respondents were intermediaries or flexers, i.e., users who bought crack and sold it to other users in order to provide their own supply rather than to profit financially. Their transactions were at the street level; they took risks that the overseeing dealers do not. Nevertheless, they could describe the organization of the trade in the area and the roles played by other participants. Also a couple of those interviewed had occupied niches somewhat higher up on the ladder at some time, working more directly for a larger scale dealer as driver or enforcer. One person had been a non-using seller "on the corner, 24/7" (24 hours a day, 7 days a week) before a reversal of fortunes led to his heavy use of crack. On the whole, respondents divulged incriminating information about their own drug use, selling, and other criminal activities. Their openness and reliability as insiders was considered to be high. Independent confirmation is, of course, not available. But the respondents, having agreed to an anonymous interview, had little to lose by being honest, and seemed to welcome the opportunity to tell their story to a non-judgmental witness.

According to the respondents, crack was brought in from the northern suburbs by taxi, often carried by youths. Crack was readily available in the area; the price has gone down over the past year, from over $200 to $180 for an "8-ball" or 3 1/2 grams. The market was open rather than gang or group controlled at least at the street level; no one knew, or wanted to know, who was Mr. Big. There were hundreds of users in the area, from 50 to 100 flexers on the street, from five to ten dealers at any one time on the corner and several more dealers in the nearby public housing complex. This amounts to something on the order of thousands of individual transactions daily.

The potential profits, at least for those who resist the use of crack, were considerable. The respondent who had been a non-using dealer at one time reported an income of $5,000 a week, selling in the day and operating a crack house at night. Another respondent, a woman who dealt mostly to other prostitutes, and who worked in cycles of two or three days selling then a binge of use, said it was easy to make "$600 in four hours or even $800 on a good day." Violence was viewed as an omnipresent possibility, though more likely to involve beatings and slashings than lethal force. Many respondents bore scars and expressed some anxiety about being hurt, but others felt that if you did not cheat people and were careful you could avoid injury. The risk of arrest was a likely prospect at some point (most already had a criminal record) but not particularly worrisome, unless a long federal sentence was possible.

No youths under 20 were interviewed, but the respondents had some interesting observations on the youth role in crack distribution. Adolescents were known to act as couriers bringing the drugs in from elsewhere. Kids were said to take the initiative to offer crack outside of the video games and other stores in the area, and were described as very adept with the necessary concealment techniques. Groups of youths from the projects also sold in the park, and had a reputation for being dangerous if crossed. The projects themselves, an easy place to buy crack, were also viewed as risky because "you could be robbed of your money when you showed it (and not given any drugs)." A racial element, when mentioned, was to the effect that "most of the users down here are white, but the guys on the corners are all black." The youths from the projects involved in selling were also usually identified as nonwhite. This does provide some preliminary evidence that the attractions of crack selling have not gone unnoticed among minority youth who may have limited employment prospects in this area of downtown Toronto. Interviews conducted with residents, police and social service workers were not at odds with this observation.

CONCLUSION

One purpose of this paper was to identify the prospects for a successful transition of youth to the world of legitimate work when lucrative illegitimate opportunities were available in their immediate social environment. The lessons from the USA are that the crack market provides an easy entry, highly profitable alternative, and is exploited by a substantial proportion of inner city youth. The unanswered question from these studies is whether the appeal of crack selling is primarily to those youths with certain stable individual characteristics which predispose them to engage in serious delinquency and later crime, or whether the social circumstances—poverty and limited opportunities—provide a potent lure for almost any youth in this environment (Nagin & Paternoster, 1994).

The US researchers have drawn implications for both prevention and later stage interventions. Dembo and associates (1993; 1994) urge the adoption of various strategies such as remedial education and job training that will enhance the stake of minority groups in mainstream society. Those already in contact with the justice system would benefit more from early intervention that involves a coordinated response on the part of families, therapeutic, and educational services than from court ordered punishment. This echoes the more forceful recommendation of Inciardi and Pottieger (1991) to seize the opportunity for compulsory intervention and treatment referral when young crack offenders are arrested. Reuter and colleagues (1990) recognized that long range solutions (such as improved schooling, greater economic opportunities, and drug use prevention programs) are needed to reduce demand, but will not likely change the current behaviour of those involved in drug market exchanges. Reuter and associates recommend that the relation between risks and rewards be communicated effectively to discourage entry for those most immediately attracted to this career. This might be done by stressing both the real dangers of drug selling and the limits of short-term financial gain relative to that from more long term, modest wage, but steady employment. Clearly there are no simple answers to this complex problem.

Canada needs research to identify the parameters of this issue in large urban centres. The extent of youthful involvement in drug selling can be assessed through a variety of methods, including official record data of arrests and sentences, interviews with identified offenders, surveys of those still in school, and community based studies that focus on high risk environmental factors. To gain entry and trust among youth in a high risk area like the housing projects will require a sustained ethnographic study by committed field workers. It is important to act sooner rather than later to provide improved opportunities for young people living in poverty, in areas of urban deprivation, with limited access to job training, higher education or employment. Canada's greater provision of health and social services, compared to the USA, may help to limit the demand for crack, and thus the profitability of the trade, among the most vulnerable individuals and communities. This preliminary study has indicated that it would be unwise to be complacent about the potential of an already existing crack market to offer a tempting avenue for prosperity to some youth in transition. The need goes beyond economic opportunities. Canada must reinforce the sense of belonging to a viable community where youth feel they have a stake in their own and their country's future.

References

Adlaf, E., Smart, R., Walsh, G., & Ivis, F. (1994). Is the association between drug use and delinquency weakening? *Addiction, 89,* 1675–1681.

Agnew, R. (1994). The techniques of neutralization and violence. *Criminology, 32* (4), 555–580.

Altshuler, D., & Brounstein, P. (1991). Patterns of drug use, drug trafficking and other delinquency among inner city adolescent males in Washington, DC. *Criminology, 29* (4), 589–622.

Blumstein, A. (1993). Making rationality relevant—The American Society of Criminology 1992 Presidential address. *Criminology, 31* (1), 1–16.

Chambliss, W. (1994). Policing the ghetto underclass: The politics of law and law enforcement. *Social Problems, 41* (2), 177–194.

Cheung, Y., Erickson, P., & Landau, T. (1991). Experience of crack use: Findings from a community-based sample in Toronto. *Journal of Drug Issues, 21* (1), 121–140.

Dembo, R., Williams, L., & Schmeidler, J. (1994). Cocaine selling among urban black and white adolescent males. *The International Journal of the Addictions, 29*(14), 1813–1834.

Dembo, R., Hughes, P., Jackson, L., & Mieczkowski, T. (1993). Crack cocaine dealing by adolescents in two public housing projects: A pilot study. *Human Organization, 52* (1), 89–96.

Erickson, P., & Weber, T. (1994). Cocaine careers, control and consequences: Results from a Canadian study. *Addiction Research, 2* (1): 37–50.

Erickson, P., Adlaf, E., Smart, R., & Murray, G. (1994). *The steel drug: Cocaine and crack in perspective* (2nd ed.). New York: Lexington Books.

Fagan, J. (1994). Women and drugs revisited: Female participation in the cocaine economy. *Journal of Drug Issues, 24* (1), 179–225.

Fagan, J., & Chin, K. (1991a). Violence as regulation and social control in the distribution of crack. In M. De La Rosa, E. Lambert, & B. Gropper (eds.), *Drugs and violence* (pp. 8–43). Rockville, MD: National Institute on Drug Abuse.

Fagan, J., & Chin, K. (1991b). Social processes of initiation into crack. *Journal of Drug Issues, 21* (2), 313–343.

Faupel, C. (1991). *Shooting dope: Career patterns of hard-core heroin users.* Gainesville, FL: University Press of Florida.

Goldstein, P. (1985). The drugs/violence nexus: A tripartite conceptual framework. *Journal of Drug Issues, 15* (4), 493–506.

Goldstein, P., Brownstein, H., Ryan, P., & Bellucci, P. (1989). Crack and homicide in New York City, 1988: A conceptually based event analysis. *Contemporary Drug Problems. 16* (4), 651–687.

Henry, F. (1994). *The Caribbean diaspora in Toronto: Learning to live with racism.* Toronto: University of Toronto Press.

Inciardi, J., & Pottieger, A. (1991). Kids, crack and crime. *Journal of Drug Issues, 21* (2), 257–270.

Inciardi, J., & Pottieger, A. (1994). Crack-cocaine use and street crime. *Journal of Drug Issues, 24* (2), 273–292.

Johnson, B., Natarajan, M., Dunlap, E., & Elmoghazy, E. (1994). Crack abusers and noncrack abusers: Profiles of drug use, drug sales and nondrug criminality. *Journal of Drug Issues. 24* (1), 117–141.

Klein, M., Maxson, C., & Cunningham, L. (1991). "Crack," street gangs, and violence. *Criminology, 29* (4), 623–650.

Nagin, D., & Paternoster, R. (1994). Personal capital and social control: The deterrence implications of a theory of individual differences in criminal offending. *Criminology, 32* (4), 581–606.

Nagin, D., Farrington, D., & Moffitt, T. (1995). Life-course trajectories of different types of offenders. *Criminology, 33* (1), 111–139.

Reuter, P., & MacCoun, R. (1992). Street drug markets in inner-city neighbor-hoods: Matching policy to reality. In J.B. Steinberg, D.W. Lyon, & M.E. Vaiana (Eds.), *Urban America: Policy choices for Los Angeles and the nation* (pp. 227–251). Santa Monica, CA: RAND.

Reuter, P., MacCoun, R., & Murphy, P. (1990). *Money from crime: A study of the economics of drug dealing in Washington, D.C.* Santa Monica, CA: RAND.

Smart, R., Adlaf, E., & Walsh, G. (1994). Neighbourhood socio-economic factors in relation to student drug use and problems. *Journal of Child and Adolescent Substance Abuse, 3* (1), 37–46.

Smart. R., Adlaf, E., & Walsh, G. (1992). Adolescent drug sellers: Trends, characteristics and profiles. *British Journal of Addiction, 87*, 1561–1570.

Waldorf, D., Murphy, S., & Lauderback, D. (1994). Middle-class cocaine sellers: Self-reported reasons for stopping sales. *Addiction Research, 2* (1), 109–126.

Williams, T. (1989). *The cocaine kids.* Reading, MA: Addison-Wesley.

The research was supported by the Drugs-Violence Task Force of the U.S. Sentencing Commission. The author is grateful to Beric German of Street Health, Toronto, for facilitating access to respondents in the area, and to the anonymous participants for their participation in the interviews.

37

The Lost Generation: Inuit Youth in Transition to Adulthood

Darryl Wood and Curt Taylor Griffiths

The impact of social change and cultural transformation is most severely felt by youth. This has been the experience of Inuit youth and young adults in the Canadian north who are often referred to as the lost generation. This chapter examines the issues surrounding the transition of Inuit in the Canadian north from youth to adulthood. The difficulties which Inuit youth experience in the transition to adulthood are due to a multiplicity of historical and contemporary factors. Chief among these are the replacement of the traditional, land-based society of Inuit with one centered on permanent settlements, the displacement of the socialization role of the family, extended family and elders by southern, non-Inuit systems of education, and restraints imposed on youth and young adults by geography, economy, and the dynamics of settlement life.

The materials presented in this chapter have been gathered from published ethnographic accounts of changes in Inuit child rearing and socialization practices and from findings from the Baffin Region Crime and Justice study (Griffiths et al., 1995). Ethnographic accounts by Chance (1990), Balikci (1970), Condon (1987), and Rasing (1989; 1994) show that the experiences of Inuit in Alaska, in the central Canadian Arctic, and in the eastern Canadian Arctic are similar in terms of the socialization of youth. The Baffin Region Crime and Justice Study was a multi-year (1990–1994) study which examined all facets of crime, the delivery of justice services, and the potential for the development of community-based justice services and programs. The project team conducted interviews with a large number of Inuit and non-Inuit, including community residents, justice and social service personnel, and other resource persons such as nurses, school teachers, and store managers. The study also generated information about Inuit youth. This study also examined the experience of Inuit in one region of the Canadian north but the issues that are present are applicable to other regions as well.

The impetus for the study was provided by the increasing concern being voiced by Inuit communities and organizations about the high rates of violent and property-related offenses in the Baffin Region, the perception that alcohol and drug abuse are increasing, and that many youth are at risk of suicide. These issues assume even greater importance because Inuit are the fastest growing population of any racial or ethnic group in Canada. Forty-seven percent of Inuit are under the age of 19, as compared to 27% of the population for Canada as a whole (Irwin, 1988). Population growth, which is predicted to double by the year 2025 (Irwin, 1988), will continue to put pressures on housing, community services, the economy, and upon Inuit social relationships, including child socialization and preparation for adulthood.

SOCIALIZATION IN NOMADIC AND SETTLEMENT TIMES

In presettlement times, Inuit lived as "a small-scale society whose members, living together in camps that changed in location and size in accordance with the rhythm of the seasons, strongly depended on each other for their survival and well-being" (Rasing, 1994, p. 25). Almost every aspect of social life among Inuit was geared toward survival. All individuals had tasks to perform which ensured the survival of the larger social group and its individual members. Tasks were allocated by age and gender. The socialization of Inuit youth was marked by its permissive nature and by its emphasis on teaching subsistence skills which were necessary for the survival of the family and for the group (Balikci, 1970). "In nomadic times, the permissive and rather passive practices of child rearing were very effective" (Rasing, 1989, p. 85). In the present day, Inuit child rearing practices remain rather permissive (Briggs, 1985, p. 40) but there is no longer an emphasis upon subsistence skills as those skills are no longer relevant in a sedentary setting. This one aspect of the change from nomadic to settlement times has had tremendous repercussions for preparing youth for the transition to adulthood and for responsible community living.

By contemporary standards, the transition from childhood to adulthood in nomadic times was very rapid. The ethnographic record indicates that there was no period of adolescence in land-based, subsistence culture. Rather, the latter part of childhood was spent learning the subsistence skills of the same-sex parent. Adulthood was attained once the child had learned those skills well enough to marry and form his or her own family (Balikci, 1970). Condon describes the patterns of interaction between adults and youths in presettlement times:

> Youngsters maintained regular and close interactions with parents and other adults. Presettlement camp life was more demanding and harsh, requiring close cooperation and contact among household members. While young people had a certain degree of freedom and autonomy, the need to learn from and work closely with parents, combined with the lack of alternate behaviour settings and peers, ensured the rapid maturation of Inuit youngsters (1987, p. 190).

Balikci (1970, p. 105) notes that learning took place exclusively through the process of observation, rather than through formal teaching. Briggs (1985, p. 42) points out that, in traditional Inuit society, children were discouraged from asking questions so that they would learn to use their minds; learning through observation was encouraged. Life was precarious and it was necessary for Inuit youth to learn subsistence skills. Balikci points out that "the upbringing of small children was characterized by consistent permissiveness" (1970, p. 108), although children were rarely separated from their parents for any length of time. Those children "grew up in close association with the adult world, free to observe and imitate their parents. They became conscious of the respective roles of each parent early, as adult activities were easily visible and there was nothing hidden in the igloo" (Balikci, 1970, p. 108). Inuit youth grew up within a close knit family group that provided safety, security, and a clear route to adulthood. There was little time or opportunity for Inuit youth to become involved in trouble or to become alienated from the group.

Perhaps no one development has had more impact on the Inuit of the Eastern Arctic as their transformation from a subsistence society, based on the land, to permanent settlements. Many Inuit lived a nomadic hunting and gathering existence on the land until the late 1950s. Life revolved around the seasons, the land, and the animals. The change from a society and culture focused on a nomadic existence to the sedentary life in permanent settlements has had consequences for the culture and the people. Life on the land had been harsh and unforgiving; life in the permanent settlements has been devastating and the aftershocks are still being felt by communities and their residents.

In many ways, Canada's Inuit have adjusted to the technological and lifestyle changes thrust upon them. New methods of travelling by motorized snowmobiles, hunting with high-powered rifles, and caching food in refrigerated storage lockers have all been incorporated into the lifestyle of Inuit. The Inuit communities of the Arctic are now linked by telephone, fax, and video conference. Community cable companies send in the latest news, sports, and entertainment from the urban centres of Toronto, Vancouver, and Detroit. The Inuit have moved from a subsistence lifestyle dictated by a harsh environment to life in permanent settlements that provides them with a measure of control over their environment. There are remnants of nomadic culture. Hunting and fishing are still a source of sustenance for Inuit families. Time spent on the land with family and friends, away from the settlements, is now cherished. *Inuktitut*, the Inuit language, is the primary language of the community schools in grades 1 through 3 and is spoken among community residents with pride.

Westernization provided the Inuit with both an increased material standard of living and increased the dependency of the Inuit on the government. Government agencies have replaced communities and families as providers of services and Inuit communities have become dependent on outside government for education, medical care, criminal justice, and social services. Shamanism has been largely eradicated, the extended family groupings have been replaced by nuclear families, modern schools have replaced the oral tradition of teaching the young, and the elders in many communities no longer play a role in community life. Inuit culture has been displaced by that of the *Qallunaat* (white Europeans). Inuit have had considerable difficulty in adapting to this new culture. In the words of one Inuit resident, "The people have come from a very self-reliant existence into one that is a welfare state run by the government. A lot of people have lost their sense of purpose and sense of values and that has taken a drastic toll on families and on the community."

Inuit today are confronted with social, political and economic changes that have significant implications for youth and for their transition to adulthood. One development that had a significant impact upon child-rearing practices and the socialization of children was the arrival of the *Qallunaat*. Churches and schools soon followed and this undermined the traditional role of the elders, removed from parents much of the teaching function for children, and created distances between the generations. Even though the Inuit have been able to retain elements of traditional culture, while at the same time accommodating and integrating modern technology into settlement life, they have been less successful in adapting their child-rearing practices and the ways in which they prepared youth for the transition to adulthood and the realities of settlement life.

SOCIAL AND CULTURAL CHANGE AND INUIT YOUTH

Social change has had a significant impact on the communities generally and on the youth in particular. One high-school teacher offered the following observation:

> The young people here don't know where they belong. This community has been in a traumatic stage of transition for 30 years. Thirty years ago there was no television. There really wasn't radio. There was no postal service. People were still living in skin tents in the summer and igloos in the winter. To a large extent this community has gone from the Stone Age to the 20th century in 30 years. Young people between the ages of 17 and 30 have never known anything settled in their lives.

This view was echoed by an elder who stated, "Today we're living a life where we're walking where there is no trail. We're living in a stage where there is no vision." The settlements that youth are being socialized in and where they will live as adults are often unstable environments, characterized by a lack of economic opportunities, high levels of crime (particularly violent crime) and trouble, and dependency on outside government agencies and organizations. These factors, combined with the geographic isolation of Inuit communities, create an environment in which the transition to adulthood holds few incentives for youth. There is a conflict in the goals and desires of today's Inuit youth. On the one hand, they want to remain and settle in their home communities while, on the other, they desire all that is seen on television and in the movies. Condon found that, of the 35 Inuit youth whom he interviewed, only 6 expressed a desire to live elsewhere when grown up (1987, p. 174).

Early childhood is still marked by its rather permissive nature (Rasing, 1989, p. 85), but Inuit youth now go through a transitory period of adolescence when moving from childhood to adulthood. Inuit youth live a life that is largely unencumbered by parental direction or instruction and other persons of authority in the community until the age of 18 for females and 25 for males. Inuit adolescents spend a great deal of time out of the home away from parents and with their own peer group. These youth have considerable autonomy and there are few controls over the range and types of activities in which they engage. As Condon has noted:

> Adult regulation of adolescent activities is minimal, and young people are, by and large, free to schedule their own lives. While parents exert some control over the activities of kids and younger teenagers, older teenagers, especially boys, are allowed to conduct their lives unfettered by constraints established by parents and other adults. The adolescent peer group, a social entity virtually nonexistent in the presettlement era, has become fully entrenched as the primary sphere of adolescent social activities and interactions (Condon, 1987, p. 189).

This high degree of adolescent autonomy, in conjunction with the extensive amount of time spent with the peer group, has deleterious effects on the social and emotional development of Inuit youth.

The contrast between the role and position of youth in traditional Inuit culture and the autonomy that youth have in contemporary settlement life causes difficulties for communities and for youth who are in transition to adulthood. First, the high level of adolescent autonomy provides the opportunity for youth to become involved in trouble in the community. Many of the respondents who were interviewed during the Baffin crime and justice study identified the permissive attitude of Inuit parents as a source of difficulty. A second problem is that the time spent in their peer group often results in youth not respecting those persons who are outside the group. According to an Inuit employee of the Northwest Territories government, Inuit youth "have very little respect for authority figures, especially for the RCMP or white people who come into the community to work." A final problem is that the adolescent autonomy among Inuit youth is partially responsible for a communication gap between generations. The communication gap has led, according to a non-Inuit social worker, to a situation where the traditional ethic of looking out for one another in hard times has been diluted. This social worker described the communication gap among the Inuit of the Baffin Region:

> No one talks. People live in the same house for years and years. Fathers don't talk to sons. Mothers don't talk to daughters. You have ten people living in a house. You'd think they'd be gabbing and know everything about everybody. They don't say two words.

The lack of communication between family members creates situations in which the problems being experienced by Inuit youth are not discussed.

THE EDUCATION OF INUIT YOUTH

The transition to adulthood has been hindered, rather than facilitated, by the imposition of western style education systems on the Inuit. In nomadic times, Inuit youth moved from childhood to adulthood when they had mastered the hunting or housekeeping skills taught to them by their parents. An Inuit elder recalled how the education of Inuit youth changed with the move to permanent settlements and the introduction of formal schooling:

> When the government moved in providing houses, schools, welfare and everything, and our people started moving in, this is where the big change was. Nobody can undo that. What's done is done already. When we were living in the camps, the children would do anything we wanted them to do, day in, day out. They were with us all the time. But when school starts at six, the parents have got nothing to do with it. That's when the big disturbance started from. Not only do they get out of their parents, they are in a different world altogether. I learned by watching my parents during the waking hours. I learned by watching. They didn't even teach me. After the children started going to school, they had to be taught everything. Now the only thing the children listen to is loud music and the only thing they watch is the television, not the parents.

The failure of "southern style" education, which is often unconnected with traditional Inuit culture, has created a situation where Inuit youth are unprepared to compete in an information-based, technological world. An Inuit community administrator in the Baffin Region noted, "They [the youth] are caught in the middle because they didn't finish school; they can't do this job and they haven't been out on the land so they really can't be hunters either. They're caught in the middle and they don't have any kind of outlet."

Concerns were expressed by many Inuit and non-Inuit interviewed during the Baffin project that Inuit parents did not evidence an interest in the education of their children. A primary reason for this was that parents themselves had little experience with or understanding of the formal school system. The permissiveness of Inuit parents is also an impediment to the formal educational process. Ironically, the formal education system contributes to the lack of direction and confusion which Inuit youth feel as they move toward adulthood. One educator noted:

> Inuit youths are taught in Inuktitut the first four years of school. That's fine. But the kids are not literate in either language by the time they hit high school. They can't comfortably read and write in Inuktitut and they cannot read and write properly in English. So they've been left stranded between the two worlds and they're not getting enough of either one.

One result of the hybrid education system is that Inuit youth are often unable to communicate their needs and desires to older generations of Inuit or to the non-Inuit service providers. There is widespread concern among Inuit that youth will not be prepared to assume positions of leadership as adults. An elder in one Baffin community stated,

> there are going to be more problems to deal with and the community has to be prepared. There are going to be land claims and self-government. Right now, we don't have the people who are educated. We have a lot of young people with no education. Twenty years from now, who is going to be running the community? Who do we expect to run the community in ten years? The young people who are the drop-outs? Are these the people that are going to be running our community?

Formal schooling, premised on non-Inuit models of instruction and learning, remains a foreign entity for many Inuit whose traditional learning was premised on observation and skill development.

The difficulties which Inuit experience with education are compounded by the lack of a viable economic base in a large number of the communities. Irwin provides a particularly pessimistic assessment of the economic environment in which Inuit youth will grow into adulthood:

> The present economic prospects for the Inuit may well be one of the worst in Canada marked as it is by poor levels of education and high unemployment. If current trends continue most of the Inuit living in the Arctic in the year 2025 will be second generation wards of the State whose society, economy and culture may have more in common with an urban slum than with life their grandparents knew (1988, p. 40).

Many Inuit communities are afflicted by high rates of unemployment and lack a viable economic base that would provide incentives for youth to pursue and complete their education. According to a non-Inuit high-school teacher, "We've created a society here of people dependent on dollars from the outside in return for nothing because there's no real economic base here for any kind of a society other than a hunting/gathering society." The rates of social assistance approach 80% in several of the communities of the Baffin Region and many of the employment positions which do exist are government-related. The capacity of these communities to provide realistic employment possibilities for Inuit youth are limited. A critical component of the transition from youth to adulthood is the presence of adult role models. For Inuit, the failures of the formal system of education and the difficulties they have experienced in adapting traditional practices to life in permanent settlements have contributed to the absence of adult role models for Inuit youth. The diminishing importance of traditional role models, such as hunters and trappers, and the absence of adults who are successful in the western world has created a situation in which Inuit youth are uncertain what their aspirations should be. This, in turn, is a primary contributor to the lack of direction among Inuit youth. Adult status remains ill-defined within the context of settlement life.

POLICY IMPLICATIONS

The Inuit are faced with many challenges, including the fastest growing population of any group in the country, the lack of a viable, self-sustaining economic base in many of the communities, and the dilemma of how to hold onto their culture and traditions while adjusting to the social, political and economic changes that are occurring around them. The creation of the new Inuit territory of Nunavut provides a political framework within which these issues might be addressed. It is uncertain, however, what specific policy and programmatic initiatives will be forthcoming from the federal government, the government of the NWT, and the new government of Nunavut that might successfully address the difficulties that Inuit youth experience in the transition to adulthood.

Strategies will be required to mobilize community residents, develop a positive settlement culture, and create viable economies. Approaches are required to solicit and sustain the interest of community residents in initiatives that will assist youth in the transition from youth to adulthood. These approaches must transfer ownership of problems from outside government to the community and work to reduce the dependency of Inuit communities. Strategies are required which will inspire community residents to begin the process of developing a settlement culture that would provide a positive context for the transition of Inuit youth to adulthood. When the life on the land was replaced by life in permanent settlements, the Inuit had little time to adapt before they became nearly totally dependent on outside agencies for all facets of community and family life, including the education and socialization of children. This dependency continues and is a major impediment to communities beginning a process of establishing a positive settlement culture. Strategies are also required to create viable economic foundations in Baffin Region communities to provide opportunities and incentives for youth. Currently, many rely heavily on various forms of social assistance. The lack of a viable economic foundation in Inuit communities is a key structural impediment to Inuit youth and adults.

There may be distinct limits, however, in the extent to which externally imposed policies, regardless of their origins, can significantly alter the conflicts that Inuit youth experience. Many of these are deeply entrenched in Inuit culture and in the individual communities, as well as being impacted by such macro-level factors as geography and economics. This will require that Inuit communities assume the lead in identifying and addressing the issues that surround settlement life generally, and the difficulties that afflict the transition of Inuit youth to adulthood specifically.

References

Balikci, A. (1970). *The Netsilik Eskimo*. Garden City, NY: Natural History Press.

Briggs, J.L. (1985). Socialization, family conflicts and responses to culture change among Canadian Inuit. *Arctic Medical Research Journal, 40,* 40–52.

Chance, N.A. (1990). *The Iñupiat and Arctic Alaska: An ethnography of development*. Fort Worth, TX: Holt, Rinehart and Winston.

Condon, R.G. (1987). *Inuit Youth: Growth and change in the Canadian Arctic*. New Brunswick, NJ: Rutgers University Press.

Griffiths, C.T., E. Zellerer, D. Wood, and G. Saville (1995). *Crime, Law, and Justice among Inuit in the Baffin Bay Region, Northwest Territories, Canada*. Burnaby, B.C.: Criminology Research Centre, Simon Fraser University.

Irwin, C. (1988). *Lords of the Arctic: Wards of the state*. Ottawa, ON: Health and Welfare Canada.

Rasing, W.C.E. (1989). *Crime, socio-legal control and problems of change: A legal anthropological study of Igloolik, NWT*. Ottawa, ON: Department of Indian Affairs and Northern Development, Canada.

Rasing, W.C.E. (1994). *"Too many people:" Order and nonconformity in Iglulingmuit social process*. Nijmegen, Netherlands: Recht & Samenleving.

PART VI

Research Agenda

38

Direction for Future Research

Joe Hudson and Burt Galaway

The summary Chapters 6, 15, 26, and 30 make a number of recommendations for Canadian research on youth in transition. These include recommendations for research approaches and methods, as well as for focusing future research efforts.

RESEARCH APPROACHES AND METHODS

Youth and their move into independence is a series of processes involving interplays between individual biographies, their multiple relationships, and social institutions. There are many paths to adulthood and research is needed on the variety of roles young people carry out and the causes and consequences of carrying out these roles. Research needs to give attention to understanding the various settings in which young people develop, including families, schools, neighbourhoods, and community organizations. The multi-dimensional nature of youth transitioning to adulthood means that research efforts need to address questions about relationships between and among different dimensions of transitioning, including housing transitions, domestic, and school to work.

Transitioning to adulthood is not a set of experiences that can be easily located in universal age categories. Social arrangements and economic circumstances have eroded linkages between chronological age and adult status. Restricting attention to a limited age group, such as sixteen- to nineteen-year-olds, can give a misleading view of the processes involved in youth transitioning to adulthood. Many of the problems faced during late adolescence have been set in motion long before and, for many, transitions to adulthood are not accomplished until well into the third decade. Longer time horizons are needed for studying youth transitions. Attention also needs to be given to research on the effects of different cultural arrangements. Cross-cultural research, both within and between countries, is necessary. In this way, comparisons can be made using both survey and case study methods.

Research efforts must be coordinated across different policy sectors to better fit with policy agendas. A collaborative approach to research on youth in transition is needed. Policy makers need to be involved at the outset in shaping the research agenda and deciding what topics should be given research priority. Program and policy decision makers should identify the pressing questions, researchers should design appropriate methodologies for answering those questions, and together they should identify policy implications. Informal collaborative arrangements are not likely to be sufficient and more formal efforts are needed, such as research and policy forums that bring together researchers and the policy community. For their part, researchers must take seriously the information and time demands of policy makers. Grabbing the money and running to carry out one's own research priorities in one's own time is not likely to endear researchers to policy makers, nor produce useful information that is used in setting policies and implementing programs.

A variety of research methods are useful in studying youth transition experiences and events. Both quantitative and qualitative methods are called for, including use of self-report methods, such as questionnaires, interviews, client logs, and checklists, along with observational methods and records. The questions to be answered along with the resources available should dictate the methods used, not the methodological biases of investigators.

Three types of research efforts are needed: a life course approach, usually involving a longitudinal design; a biographical approach; and, using both approaches, evaluation research to answer questions about transition policies and programs. The life course perspective requires longitudinal designs that follow the same group of persons over time in order to describe their life transitions. In this approach, attention needs to be given to illuminating processes of individual development, as well as processes underlying change in communities and institutions. Research needs to move beyond the isolated assessment of single settings to examine the effects of a variety of influences on young people. This will require researchers from different disciplines using a variety of data collection methods. A biographical approach is also recommended. This can complement a life course approach to studying life transitions. The focus is on the individual's experiences and decisions related to transitions. A variety of qualitative methods should be used to better understand unique experiences of individuals in making transitions and the way these influence other concurrent and subsequent transitions. Program evaluation is the third general type of research called for in these chapters. The focus of this research should be on evaluating transition policies and programs, using multiple methods and giving full recognition to the limitations of an exclusive reliance on single discipline inquiries.

Some of the chapters specifically recommend effectiveness types of evaluation studies. This call for effectiveness evaluations is likely to be premature, given the state of transition programming. Many intervention programs, especially newly implemented programs, may not meet the necessary preconditions for an effectiveness evaluation. The preconditions for testing program effectiveness are a clearly described set of program interventions, specification of the results, goals, or objectives that are expected to be achieved, and a plausible rationale linking interventions with expected results, goals, or objectives. Other purposes for evaluating transition programs may be more appropriate than testing effectiveness. For example, given the program's stage of development, it may be much more important to document the need for the transition program or describe program implementation and monitor operations. Evaluation is needed to get inside programs and to document implementation experiences. Information on program processes can lead to better understanding of the way program activities interact with participants. The challenge for evaluators and program decision makers is to tailor evaluation designs to the stage of program development, while providing information that is used to improve program operations.

FOCUS OF FUTURE RESEARCH EFFORTS

Recommendations are made in respect to the specific focus or subject matter of future research on youth transitions. One recommendation is for research to aim at answering questions about positive transition experiences and those factors contributing to responsible community living, resiliency, and active participation in political, social, and cultural groups. Another recommendation is for research to focus on vulnerable groups and those young people most at risk for not making a successful transition to adulthood. In particular, attention needs to be given to the effects of gender, race, and ethnicity on transitioning experiences and effects. Young people in care, young people with disabilities and special needs, young people excluded from school, and young people who become involved in crime are particularly vulnerable to transition problems. Aboriginal youth in Canada are overly represented in all of these categories and therefore future research needs to give attention to this growing group of young persons, along with other groups such as immigrants and other minorities. The social and psychological consequences of transition difficulties experienced by these vulnerable youth need research attention, particularly in respect to the way educational and training policies and programs serve them.

Research is needed on the neighbourhood and family settings in which young people grow and develop. The physical and social conditions of these settings need to be systematically examined in relation to their impact on the young people. What are the elements of neighbourhoods that lead to responsible community living? What are the formal and informal supports available to young persons in different communities? Research is also recommended on the role of the family and its effects on youth transitions. A number of questions are posed in the chapters, including the influence of changes in family structure on family relationships and understanding how families deal with adversity.

Research is needed about school-to-work transitions. A number of questions are identified including the consequences of different pathways to employment, the effects on transitions of such factors as family support and esteem for education, financial constraints, education and training curricula, and employment equity. What is the relationship between training programs and job placement, between the cost of vocational training and increase in earnings, and the relative benefits of cooperative education in which students earn academic credit for working with employers? What are the processes that sustain interest in and attachment to school and those that compromise it?

How can research results be more effectively disseminated and used? It is simply not enough for a researcher to write a report with recommendations and expect that decision makers will read the report, choose a course of action, and implement it. It is naïve to expect that research findings are a normal part of policy makers' reading material. Research findings must be persuasively and engagingly communicated to the policy community; dissemination should be an ongoing process rather than stopping with the production of a technical report or publication. Researchers must write their reports to influence policies by producing readable publications and taking seriously the responsibility to make the practical implications of their findings clear. In short, researchers need to help practitioners understand and apply the research findings and take seriously their responsibility for providing direct and practical help to adapt policies and programs to fit with research findings. Research should be used to inform policy, fully appreciating that research cannot be an unambiguous guide to policy.